MW00989030

In a time when US culture is incredibly fragmented, and the way forward seems to revolve around social media power dynamics, *Cultural Engagement* is a welcome and needed resource. By itself, part 1 offers a concise review of the literature on culture, its importance, and how it is formed. In part 2, Josh and Karen curate the best thinking on timely and critical contemporary issues—race, gender, work, arts, and challenges to life itself. It is this respectful pairing of differing viewpoints that is rare today, in both secular and Christian circles. Excellently done!

—**Katherine Leary Alsdorf,** founder and director
of Redeemer's Center for Faith and Work

The Christian God never changes. But our culture constantly changes. Every year, every decade, and every century, Christians are faced with new challenges. *Cultural Engagement* gets us back onto the front foot. Instead of fight, fright, or flight, this book shows us how to face contemporary issues in our culture. It also equips us for the future challenges that are just around the corner. This book is a must-read for anyone who no longer wants to run from culture but to see each and every issue as an opportunity to engage culture with a Christian redemptive dialogue.

—**Sam Chan,** City Bible Forum, Australia

Josh Chatraw and Karen Swallow Prior, along with a host of friends, model for all of us what it means to think Christianly about the intersection of the gospel and culture, doing so with courage and conviction while encouraging careful listening, Christlike kindness, and civility. *Cultural Engagement* will form, inform, and motivate readers not only to engage thoughtfully but to live and serve faithfully. This compelling and comprehensive volume should become an essential resource for students, pastors, and thought leaders alike. Highly recommended!

—**David S. Dockery,** president, Trinity International
University and Trinity Evangelical Divinity School

Cultural Engagement: A Crash Course in Contemporary Issues centers important conflicts, worldviews, and etiologies present in the contemporary church in America. As an instructor in intergroup dialogue and cultural diversity, I find this text to be a helpful resource for both Christian higher education professionals and a much broader audience who would benefit from its concise examination of diverse Christian thought manifested in social-political ideologies and practices. This book reminds us that even within the subset known as the American church there are various competing and impactful perspectives that call for deep understanding and not simple caricatures.

—**Christina Edmondson,** dean of intercultural
student development, Calvin College

This book will be extremely useful to any Christian seeking to answer cultural questions from a biblical point of view. I highly recommend it to every believer looking for a resource on cultural engagement that's also faithful to the Scriptures.

—**Phillip Holmes,** vice president of institutional communications, Reformed Theological Seminary

Christians talk a lot about cultural engagement, but our dismal record in recent decades suggests that our engagement strategies need a lot of work. In this provocative and timely book, Joshua Chatraw and Karen Swallow Prior have convened a wide-ranging cast of authors to debate the most pressing issues facing the church today.

—**Thomas S. Kidd,** James Vardaman Distinguished Professor of History, Baylor University

Not only do we Christians lack ready-made answers to some of the pressing issues in our present day cultural life, but most of us are still trying to get clear about the questions. For this we need biblical discernment informed by cultural savvy. Thank the Lord, Karen Swallow Prior and Josh Chatraw have all of that in abundance!

—**Richard J. Mouw,** president emeritus and professor of faith and public life, Fuller Theological Seminary

This book is incredibly needed for "such a time as this." In this day and age, when rhetoric and worldviews are so divisive, and intelligence with grace and integrity is in short supply, Prior and Chatraw manage to bring together authors who nuance ancient biblical ideas with a wisdom that speaks to the ethical issues of our modern age. Pulling no punches in tackling all the toughest issues, this remarkable one-volume compendium is practically encyclopedic in its perspectives that exemplify goodness, truth, and beauty, while showing that Christians can also thoughtfully disagree on nonessential issues without losing unity in the essentials of the faith.

—**Allen Yeh,** associate professor of intercultural studies and missiology, Biola University

CULTURAL ENGAGEMENT

CULTURAL ENGAGEMENT

A Crash Course in Contemporary Issues

Joshua D. Chatraw and
Karen Swallow Prior

ZONDERVAN ACADEMIC

Cultural Engagement
Copyright © 2019 by Joshua D. Chatraw and Karen Swallow Prior

ISBN 978-0-310-53457-0 (hardcover)

ISBN 978-0-310-53458-7 (ebook)

Requests for information should be addressed to:
Zondervan, *3900 Sparks Dr. SE, Grand Rapids, Michigan 49546*

Scripture quotations are taken from the Holy Bible, New International Version®, NIV®. Copyright © 1973, 1978, 1984, 2011 by Biblica, Inc.® Used by permission of Zondervan. All rights reserved worldwide. www.Zondervan.com. The "NIV" and "New International Version" are trademarks registered in the United States Patent and Trademark Office by Biblica, Inc.®

Scripture quotations marked NKJV are taken from the New King James Version®. Copyright © 1982 by Thomas Nelson. Used by permission. All rights reserved.

Scripture quotations marked NASB are taken from the New American Standard Bible®. Copyright © 1960, 1962, 1963, 1968, 1971, 1972, 1973, 1975, 1977, 1995 by The Lockman Foundation. Used by permission. (www.Lockman.org).

Scripture quotations marked ESV are taken from the ESV® Bible (The Holy Bible, English Standard Version®). Copyright © 2001 by Crossway, a publishing ministry of Good News Publishers. Used by permission. All rights reserved.

Scripture quotations marked KJV are taken from the King James Version. Public domain.

Scripture quotations marked CSB® are taken from the Christian Standard Bible®, Copyright © 2017 by Holman Bible Publishers. Used by permission. Christian Standard Bible®, and CSB®, are federally registered trademarks of Holman Bible Publishers.

Any internet addresses (websites, blogs, etc.) and telephone numbers in this book are offered as a resource. They are not intended in any way to be or imply an endorsement by Zondervan, nor does Zondervan vouch for the content of these sites and numbers for the life of this book.

No part of this publication may be reproduced, stored in a retrieval system, or transmitted in any form or by any means—electronic, mechanical, photocopy, recording, or any other—except for brief quotations in printed reviews, without the prior permission of the publisher.

Published in association with the Steve Laube Agency and MacGregor Literary Inc.

Cover design: Brian Bobel Design
Cover art: Brian Bobel; flaticon.com; 10EPS icon / Shutterstock; justinroque / iStockphoto.com
Interior design: Kait Lamphere

Printed in the United States of America

19 20 21 22 23 24 25 26 27 28 29 /LSC/ 15 14 13 12 11 10 9 8 7 6 5 4 3 2 1

For our past and present students at Liberty University and the staff at the Center for Apologetics and Cultural Engagement

CONTENTS

ACKNOWLEDGMENTS

This book was an adventure. It was born out of an unlikely friendship. As an English professor and a theologian, we have different skill sets and academic training. We typically spend our days lecturing, writing, and thinking about different topics. Our personalities are different as well. But we quickly came to see we had a common cause in helping others interact on cultural issues with gospel lenses. Through the years, we have both slowly grown in wisdom and understanding through our engagement with a variety of people who have different perspectives and theological traditions. Through interactions with students on our campus, both in and out of the classroom, we realized how valuable a book like this one could be, introducing a variety of subjects from people representing different backgrounds and vocations. The question that spurred on the project was: could we encourage the maturation process for others by bringing together various voices of professing Christians addressing a range of cultural issues in a single book in a way that would allow readers to engage critically and biblically with different perspectives? As the idea developed, we set out to secure what has turned out to be almost fifty different essays from our very different circles. This made the process and, we think, the final product all the more interesting.

On the way to finishing, Josh changed jobs and moved to a new city. And Karen got hit by a bus (no, we don't mean metaphorically!). She had to undergo major surgery, and we were left scrambling to meet our deadlines. There is no way we could have pulled this ambitious project together without a team helping us at various stages.

One of our essayists, Kayla Snow, contributed significantly to researching and drafting the introductions to each section. Maria Kometer and Allison Kasch helped draft questions for each section, while Maria also kept communications organized with the contributors. Research assistants Rebecca Olsen, Emily Thompson, and Joshua Erb helped track down resources and background on a wide variety of topics. Jack Carson skillfully led the day-to-day operations at the Center for Apologetics and Cultural Engagement, which freed Josh up for projects like this one.

We are especially thankful for Madison Trammel, who caught the vision for the project in the early stages, guided it significantly through the process, and was patient, helpful, and encouraging to the end.

introduction

THE BIG PICTURE

The seemingly endless number of books by "experts" and the detailed analyses offered by academics on the different cultural issues of the day are important. But how does someone even start to understand which books and articles are the ones worth reading? The sheer volume of books on the topics can be intimidating. The painstaking details can be downright confusing for most Christians seeking to be faithful as the cultural scenery continues to change around them. Which books should be read? Who has time to read all this? Where should one begin in wading through the issues?

Without dismissing the importance of detailed pictures of the trees of cultural engagement, this book sets out to provide a panoramic view of the forest of Christian responses to the most pressing issues. Or as we put it in our subtitle, this is a "crash course" on many contemporary issues that face the church today.

Part 1 provides a foundation into understanding culture (chapter 1) and surveys how different Christian traditions' reading of the biblical story has impacted how they understand the church's relationship to the culture (chapter 2). Though many Christian thought leaders disagree about several key issues—as the second part of this book will demonstrate—an increasing number agree that the impact of the church's witness directly relates to the way our character has been formed by the gospel. Our consciences and goals in life are shaped, in large measure, by the cultures we are surrounded by—the media, our family, the place we work, our school, or the church we attend. So before turning to the particular issues, in this opening section we will offer some initial reflections on the importance of virtue and wisdom in engaging with the cultural challenges we face as believers (chapter 3). However, if the church is to offer a foretaste of the coming kingdom, reflecting our King's commitment to holiness, justice, love, peace, and mercy in tangible ways, then we can't simply speak in generalities; we must wrestle with the actual issues.

Part 2 sets out to expose different angles and approaches that confessing Christians have adopted on contemporary cultural issues. Not all the articles in these sections compete with one another. Some overlap and offer different angles on the same topic that are not mutually exclusive. In order to avoid the monotony of reading articles that have been forced in the same format, we allowed room for creativity. And in hopes of avoiding reactionary pieces, the contributors did not view the other articles in their section.[1] The authors themselves are diverse, representing not only different disciplines, but different vocations, sexes, social classes, and races. While some of the authors are academics, many of the contributors are on the "ground level," so to speak, of various causes and issues.

By placing these different pieces side by side, we are not implying they are all equally true or valid. Some are clearly at odds with each other. We each have our own opinions about these issues. And while the myth of neutrality is just that, a myth, we should seek to be *fair* observers and *charitable* readers. We have not put these views together as a way for readers to participate, as with those old choose-your-own adventure books, in a "make your own morality book." The proverb reminds us, "There is a way that seems right to a man, but its end is the way to death" (Prov. 14:12). There is only one comprehensive God's eye vantage point and only one human has this view. We confess to be mere mortals who see only in part, but we also confess that the one human who has this complete view is our Lord and our God. This confession not only affects our view, but it also affects our posture. Bending our knee to the lordship of Christ impacts not only the way we come to his Word but also our posture as we listen and speak.

The competing views in this book are important to be observed together for the simple reason that they are part of the panoramic landscape of the church's engagement with today's world. And learning to become good listeners (and readers!) is one of the first steps in engaging culture with grace and truth. As John Stott has eloquently written: "Dialogue becomes a token of Christian humility and love, because it indicates our resolve to rid our minds of the prejudices and caricatures we may entertain about the other man; to struggle to listen through his ears and see through his eyes so as to grasp what prevents him from hearing the Gospel and seeing Christ; to sympathize with him in all his doubts and fears."[2]

While providing articles representative of various contemporary approaches to these topics, this book does not go into a detailed exegetical analysis of the respective cases. These pieces are meant for nonspecialists and designed to allow readers to see the contours of the big picture, before diving into more detail through independent or collaborative studies. The questions at the end of each

---

1. With the exception of Kenneth Magnuson's article "On Whether Abortion Is Murder: The Questions of Rhetoric and Reality," which was originally written in response to Karen Swallow Prior's article published in this volume as "Pro-Life in Word and Deed."

2. John Stott, "The Biblical Basis for Evangelism," in *Let the Earth Hear His Voice*, ed. J. D. Douglas (Minneapolis: World Wide, 1975), 72.

chapter in part 2 direct readers to further study and discussion of the key biblical texts, the coherence of the arguments, and the rhetorical strategies used.

Part 3 offers a concluding chapter by us and an essay by noted author and speaker Andy Crouch. This closing section is rooted in the conviction that cultural engagement goes wrong if it's not grounded in the truth that creation is simultaneously and intrinsically good, deeply corrupted, and in need of redemption. Both the creation story and the gospel not only remind us of these truths, but they summon us to care for the culture around us. This section offers prescriptive postures and theological guide rails that serve to apply the doctrine of creation and the gospel to our calling as Christians to engage the world around us.

part one

GETTING STARTED

chapter one

CHRISTIANITY AND CULTURE

Should Christians even speak of "engaging culture"?

Some question this terminology, suggesting that the phrase is inadequate or misleading. Andy Crouch, the former editor of *Christianity Today*, expresses this discomfort by comparing the phrase "engaging culture" to the generic social media promotional e-mails used by brands to draw people to their platform without the benefit of actually knowing the individuals they are targeting. "Talking about 'the culture' in this way causes us to stab blindly in the dark, much like Twitter's e-mail. It also causes us to miss our actual cultural responsibility and opportunity."[1] Crouch's worry is that too many people generalize about *the* culture, painting the world with broad brush statements, skipping over actually engaging the diverse people who live within the particular culture*s* that make up our communities.

We're sympathetic to Crouch's concern. We often get into discussions with people who are excited about "cultural engagement," but who are not interacting with people in their local community, the people who comprise the various *cultures* in our world. Engaging "the culture" begins by interacting with our neighbors face-to-face and treating them as individuals rather than simply offering sweeping declarations about a specific generation or a post-Christian society. "Engaging culture" language can also make it seem that "culture" is something *out there*, as if we are not within culture. As we will see in this chapter, we are all swimming in this thing called "culture"—there is no way not to be immersed in it, even for Christians. You might decide to opt out of *a* culture, but no one can opt out of culture.

These possible problems of the phrase notwithstanding, we suggest that the terminology can still be useful. Understanding cultural trends, general assumptions within communities, and the practical reasoning that repeatedly emerges in public discourse are important precisely because they help us engage with

---

1. Andy Crouch, "Stop Engaging 'the Culture,' Because It Doesn't Exist," *Christianity Today*, June 23, 2016, http://www.christianitytoday.com/ct/2016/julaug/theculture-doesnt-exist.html.

individuals. Engaging culture, rightly conceived, includes studying the world around us—to understand its aspirations, longings, institutions, artifacts, ideas, and issues—in order to better engage the *people* within cultures. Missiologists have long utilized cultural studies as they interact in foreign mission fields. The increase in the number of Christian books, conferences, and centers which emphasize the importance of culture is likely because Christians in the West have begun to feel their own communities are foreign to them in certain significant ways.[2] Addressing critical issues and responding to the challenges posed by the changes in culture require cultural competence.

Avoiding Cultural Captivity

Before we start interacting with particular cultural issues, we need to reflect on the definition of culture. Often when we discuss culture with other Christians, we find they are eager to interact with "it," but they haven't stopped to reflect deeply on what "it" is. Mark Noll has memorably characterized the hereditary tendency of evangelical Christians to prioritize activism and pragmatism that is "dominated by the urgencies of the moment" over the "broader or deeper intellectual efforts."[3] This activistic impulse is deeply imbedded in the DNA of many of us with evangelical roots, and it partly explains why we tend to rush in to "engage culture" and then ask questions later. Yet as Ken Myers has pointed out, the recent increased attention paid to culture has not necessarily led to increased aptitude.

> I fear that many well-meaning believers—eager to share the gospel with their neighbors and contemporaries—run the risk of becoming as wise as doves and as harmless as serpents. Shaped more than they realize by the disorders of their culture—especially by the media-inflected impatience with careful and systematic thought, and by a suspicion of formality and

2. Since a full list would make this footnote too long, a few samples will have to suffice. Organizations include ChristianUnion.org, the Colson Center, Jude 3 Project, The Witness: A Black Christian Collective, Trinity Forum, and Christian Cultural Center (though they use the term social engagement synonymously with cultural engagement). Recent books include James Davison Hunter, *To Change the World: The Irony, Tragedy, and Possibility of Christianity in the Late Modern World* (New York: Oxford University Press, 2010); William Edgar, *Created and Creating: A Biblical Theology of Culture* (Downers Grove, IL: InterVarsity Press, 2016); Bruce Riley Ashford, *Every Square Inch: An Introduction to Cultural Engagement for Christians* (Bellingham, WA: Lexham, 2015); Eric O. Jacobsen, *The Space Between: A Christian Engagement with the Built Environment* (Grand Rapids: Baker Academic, 2012); T. M. Moore, *Culture Matters: A Call for Consensus on Christian Cultural Engagement* (Grand Rapids: Brazos, 2007); Kevin J. Vanhoozer, Charles A. Anderson, and Michael J. Sleasman, eds. *Everyday Theology: How to Read Cultural Texts and Interpret Trends* (Grand Rapids: Baker Academic, 2007); and Russell D. Moore, *Onward: Engaging the Culture without Losing the Gospel* (Nashville, B&H, 2015). There is also an increasing emphasis on cultural engagement in Christian universities, such as in the biblical studies department at Judson University in Illinois, the Francis Schaeffer Institute at Covenant Theological Seminary, and the L. Russ Bush Center for Faith and Culture at Southeastern Baptist Theological Seminary.
3. Mark Noll, *The Scandal of the Evangelical Mind* (Grand Rapids: Eerdmans, 1994), 12.

tradition—they admirably want to be more like Jesus, but they're not really sure they want to be more like Paul, Augustine, Aquinas, Calvin, or Jonathan Edwards. What they are missing, I believe, is an awareness that the Church can only engage the culture by *being* a culture.[4]

Myers later adds to this the maxim: "Cultural engagement without cultural wisdom leads to cultural captivity."[5] In other words, engaging culture with right motives but without proper reflection and formation often leads to disappointing and even dangerous results. In order to gain cultural wisdom and avoid cultural captivity, we need first to grasp a multidimensional understanding of the term "culture."

Three Dimensions of Culture

Culture includes (1) formal ideas and worldviews that are directly articulated and passed on to others. While at a popular level this is sometimes the focus of what one means by "culture," the concept is much broader than just beliefs. In addition to formal theories or beliefs, culture also includes (2) precognitive assumptions which are passed on and inherited through (3) the social and physical dimensions of life—the institutions, symbols, customs, and practices of a group of people. These three dimensions of culture are interconnected, but in order to understand the concept, we'll consider each one.

Definitions of Culture

Culture is notoriously difficult to define. Below are some definitions that we are both drawn to and that significantly overlap.

- "A culture is an ecosystem of institutions, practices, artifacts, and beliefs, all interacting and mutually reinforcing. Cultures are rarely entirely homogenous or consistent, but generalizations about specific cultures are nonetheless possible. Despite their complexity, cultures can have an overriding ethos." Ken Myers, *All God's Children and Blue Suede Shoes* (Wheaton, IL: Crossway, 1989), xi.

---

4. Ken Myers, *All God's Children and Blue Suede Shoes: Christians and Popular Culture* (1989; repr., Wheaton, IL: Crossway, 2012), xviii.
5. Ibid.

- Culture is "the complex of values, customs, beliefs, and practices which constitute the way of life of a specific group." Terry Eagleton, *The Idea of Culture* (Oxford: Oxford University Press, 2000), 34.
- Culture is a "historically transmitted pattern of meanings embodied in symbols, a system of inherited conceptions expressed in symbolic forms by means of which men communicate, perpetuate, and develop their knowledge about and attitudes toward life." Clifford Geertz, *The Interpretation of Culture* (New York: Basic Books, 1973), 89.
- Culture is "made up of 'works' and 'worlds' of meaning. Culture is a work because it is the result of what humans do freely, not a result of what they do by nature. Culture is what we get when humans work the raw material of nature to produce something significant. . . . Culture is a world in the sense that cultural texts create a meaningful environment in which humans dwell both physically and imaginatively . . . the lens through which a vision of life and the social order is expressed, experienced, and explored; it is a *lived* worldview." Kevin J. Vanhoozer, *Everyday Theology*, 26.

Note the commonalities within these definitions.

1. Culture is comprised of more than simply beliefs or worldviews.
2. Culture is complex.
3. Culture is communal.

First, culture is made up of articulated and formally processed beliefs. Cultures are filled with ideas and beliefs that are sometimes labeled as "worldviews." When a culture is described as "Christian" or "secular," the adjective often refers to the affirmation of articulated beliefs generally held to by a dominant group within that culture.[6] A Christian worldview includes beliefs such as a God who has existed eternally in three persons and entered into human history in the

---

6. However, a culture that can be described by some religious or ideological belief is also characterized by certain features that cannot be limited to explicit beliefs. For most of human history, the broader features of culture could not be neatly separated from religion; they were deeply intertwined. As Alister McGrath has pointed out, we need to be careful to not draw too much of a distinction between "culture" and "religion": "We must therefore be intensely suspicious of the naïve assumption that *religion* is a well-defined category that can be sharply and surgically distinguished from *culture* as a whole." ("A Particularist View: A Post-Enlightenment Approach" in *Four Views on Salvation in a Pluralistic Age*, ed. Dennis L. Okholm and Timothy R. Phillips [Grand Rapids: Zondervan, 1996], 155). For example, to say someone belongs to a "Hindu culture" is to say something about the practices and norms that go beyond formal religious beliefs.

person of Jesus of Nazareth, who died, rose again, and then ascended to heaven. A secular worldview denies the supernatural and affirms that all things can be explained through natural and material processes. Worldview—an articulated set of beliefs and ideas—is certainly part of culture. Yet while some have almost exclusively stressed this aspect, it is only one dimension of culture.[7]

Second, culture provides precognitive and unarticulated assumptions by which the world around us and by which life itself is interpreted. When I (Josh) was growing up, my best friend left some clothes at my house. My mom found them, washed them, and then sent me to school with them to give them back. When I handed them to him, he said, "Hey, man, these smell like your house!" I didn't know what he was talking about. After all, it was the smell of *my* house. It just seemed normal. This serves as an analogy for how "culture" operates at a precognitive level. Culture has an atmospheric quality. It resembles an odor that can be attached to clothes and fill an entire house but cannot be detected by the person inhabiting them.

The assumptions and attitudes of the culture fill the daily "air" in such a way that people usually don't give much thought to them. Without us normally being aware of it, culture provides a seemingly "default" grid by which we live and interact with the world around us. Philosopher Charles Taylor describes how culture provides frameworks that are "not usually, or even mainly a set of beliefs which we entertain" but rather "the sensed context in which we develop our beliefs."[8] In other words, these interpretive grids have "usually sunk to the level of such an unchallenged framework, something we have trouble often thinking ourselves outside of, even as an imaginative exercise."[9] Taylor refers to these precognitive frameworks as social imaginaries, which—in contrast to the first dimension of culture mentioned above—are not primarily expressed as formally articulated theories that we have reasoned our way to.

For example, ask someone living in a modern Western culture what you should do to cure your recurring visions of ghostly creatures, and you will likely be told to lay off the drugs or go see a medical professional. Ask someone in a traditional culture, and you will likely be sent to the village shaman or priest. The different responses will often seem intuitive, almost automatic reflexes, or common sense due to the given social imaginary. Yet, as our third dimension emphasizes, these social imaginaries are not free-floating. They are expressed in

---

7. For more on the problem of reducing "culture" to articulated beliefs, see James Davidson Hunter, *To Change the World: The Irony, Tragedy, and Possibility of Christianity in the Late Modern World* (New York: Oxford University Press, 2008), 18–31.

8. Charles Taylor, *A Secular Age* (Cambridge, MA: Harvard University Press, 2007), 549.

9. Ibid.

"images, stories, and legends" that are embedded in the institutions, symbols, customs, and practices of a group of people.[10]

Third, culture consists of the social and physical dimensions of life, such as the institutions, symbols, customs, and practices that function as carriers of both the (1) formal ideas and (2) precognitive assumptions about life. Though atmosphere has functioned as a helpful analogy that communicates the unconscious ways culture often works, this should not imply that ideas and assumptions are simply floating in the air, unattached to other aspects of life. Ideas are grounded in the social world around us. As sociologist James Hunter explains, culture takes form in concrete institutions, in which ideas are attached. This means to understand culture, we must understand "the nature, workings, and power of the institutions in which . . . ideas are generated and managed." This is why Hunter suggests it might be more appropriate to "think of culture as a thing" which is made by "institutions and the elites who lead them."[11]

Institutions, the economy, government, education, religions, entertainment, publishing, media, and many more social factors and institutions contribute to and pass on culture. From this we see that culture is the product of complex historical events and instances, which means we should be careful with grand proclamations about how "culture will change if we just do this."

As we begin to understand these dimensions, we realize that culture appears to be dynamic rather than static. Culture is not just an inanimate object that can be repainted—culture is doing things. If we are to understand how to engage culture, we need to better grasp what it is doing and how it is doing it.

Three Actions of Culture

1. Culture Communicates Meaning

The messages communicated by culture express various concerns that together communicate a vision of the meaning of life. Meaning is communicated by form and content. As an example, theologian Kevin Vanhoozer asks us to consider what perfumes communicate. Can a fragrance communicate elegance? I asked a student this question recently, and she quickly responded, "Of course! Chanel No. 5." Fragrance can communicate wealth and refined tastes, such as the smell of luxury leather in a new car. It is important to keep in mind that the smell can't *by itself* communicate wealth or elegance. Perfume companies spend millions of dollars on marketing campaigns that train our senses to smell elegance. In other words, culture—and in this example we see the impact of economic

---

10. Charles Taylor, *Modern Social Imaginaries* (Durham, NC: Duke University Press, 2004), 23–30.
11. Hunter, *Change the World*, 26.

concerns—communicates how to read the world around us. "Cultural statements are vision statements, and cultural texts have the ability to seize our imaginations. The power of cultural communication resides not in the information it conveys but in its role as an information processor. Culture tacitly communicates a program for making sense of life: a hermeneutic or interpretative framework through which we understand the world and read our own lives."[12]

Culture communicates not only by providing the "logic" that gives "order to the world" but also by shaping our "affective and evaluative dimensions, influencing our likes and dislikes as well as our sense of right and wrong."[13] The impact of culture and its ability to tacitly provide the lens by which we read the world around us and make everyday decisions should not be underestimated. For example, in *The Social Animal*, David Brooks creatively weaves various sociological and neurological studies into a fictional narrative of two central characters. Brooks causes readers to reflect more deeply on how deciding actually works. In the past, some have understood decisions to be, rather simply, points in time in which people gather the data and then make a choice.[14] This is naive. Different disciplines are independently pointing us to the conclusion that rather than individuals theorizing our way to decisions, we are "pilgrims in a social landscape." As Brooks explains, "We wander across an environment of people and possibilities. As we wander, the mind makes a near-infinite number of value judgments, which accumulate to formulate goals, ambitions, dreams, desires, and way of doing things."[15] In other words, our culture communicates and orients how we think, live, and decide. We don't just read culture; we "read *through*" the lens culture provides.[16] Without normally providing explicit thesis statements, culture most powerfully communicates by providing prereflective frameworks for meaning and values.

2. Culture Shapes Sensibilities

Ken Myers explains sensibilities as "the orientation of the affections, the posture of the soul, the desires of the heart, the characteristic hungers and expectations."[17] Put in more direct religious terms, culture calls us to worship and cultivates us to be certain kinds of worshipers.

---

12. Vanhoozer, Anderson, and Sleasman, *Everyday Theology*, 29. This section draws upon and modifies Vanhoozer's four categories. See pp. 28–32.

13. Ibid, 29.

14. To see a critique of this view related to politics and religion, see Jonathan Haidt, *The Righteous Mind: Why Good People Are Divided by Politics and Religion* (New York: Vintage, 2012).

15. David Brooks, *The Social Animal: The Hidden Sources of Love, Character, and Achievement* (New York: Random House, 2012), 22.

16. Vanhoozer, Anderson, and Sleasman, *Everyday Theology*, 36.

17. Myers, *God's Children*, vi.

Consider, again, what we can learn from the marketing industry.[18] Marketers make their living by persuading. Their business is to understand what drives human decisions, but rarely do we see marketing campaigns explicitly providing an explicit thesis statement, such as: "You should buy a BMW because it will raise your self-esteem." Nor is it typical to see commercials that provide five reasons to buy a shampoo or a logical progression of statements that lead to the conclusion as to why one should buy a particular kind of automobile. Instead, marketers sell an image of who they think you would want to be, an identity that would seemingly provide fulfillment, or a vision of what life could be like . . . *if* you purchase their product.[19]

Douglas Atkin of Merkley and Partners Advertising explains that instead of the traditional functions of marketing managers, now brand managers are called upon to "create and maintain a whole meaning system for people, through which they get identity and understanding of the world. Their job now is to be a community leader."[20] His description harkens back to the role of religious leaders in traditional societies. Through his research, conducting interviews with devout followers of a religious group or a product, Atkin concludes: "People, whether they are joining a cult or a brand, they do so for exactly the same reasons: they want to belong and they want to make meaning. *We need to figure out what the world is all about and we want the company of others.*"[21] In other words, advertisers now set out to appeal to people's aspirations—their deepest desires as humans.

Marketing campaigns are part of what James K. A. Smith refers to as "cultural liturgies." By liturgy, Smith means communal "formative practices."[22] In the spirit of St. Augustine, Smith stresses the religious nature of humanity. We will give ourselves to something. We will set our hearts on something beyond ourselves. We will worship. The liturgies—practices and habits—that we adopt form us into certain kinds of worshipers. Culture gives us what we assume are default settings that we live and "breathe in" each day, pointing us to certain aims, cultivating us into certain kinds of people—for good or for bad. Cultural practices function as "formative pedagogies of desires."[23] Of course, marketing is

18. James K. A. Smith, *Desiring the Kingdom: Worship, Worldview, and Cultural Formation* (Grand Rapids: Baker Academic, 2009), 76.
19. Ibid. Smith powerfully makes the point we are stressing in this section, and his work has prompted us to reflect on examples of "cultural liturgy" from our own experiences. To make this point in class, I use excerpts from a fascinating series produced by PBS entitled *The Persuaders*.
20. *The Persuaders*, directed by Barak Goodman and Rachel Dretzin, *Frontline*, aired November 9, 2004, on PBS.
21. Ibid. Emphasis ours.
22. Smith, *Desiring the Kingdom*, 24.
23. Ibid.

only one example of the power of culture to cultivate our sensibilities and form us as worshipers. The national calendars (including what holidays we celebrate and how we celebrate them),[24] our smartphones,[25] and entertainment (movies, sporting events, and music)[26] are all parts of culture that are shaping us in powerful ways. And part of their power is that their impact is covert. We rarely think about how these routine parts of life, inherited from within our culture as "normal," affect our discipleship to Christ, often cultivating our hearts to a competing kingdom.

3. Culture Replicates Itself

Culture has been rightly described as "a system of inheritance."[27] In other words, we pass down culture to the next generation through family and institutions. Our practices, ideas, and assumed frameworks are always part of a history that we have received and then pass on—albeit with various modifications. Consider American football as an example. The sport has evolved from intramural and unorganized games being played on college campuses in the early part of the nineteenth century to organized games between colleges in the second half of the nineteenth, to the use of helmets with masks in the first half of the twentieth century and the formation of the American Professional Football Association in 1920, to eventually the complex multi-billion-dollar industry of college and professional football we know today. Football has been in America in some form for about 150 years, and the culture has been passed down to each subsequent generation. During this time, however, the culture (rules, traditions, and practices) has been modified along the way. And not just football. Fashions, business practices, sexual norms, and various other aspects of culture could be traced out chronologically, revealing that culture is both inherited and adapted through time.

However, culture not only reproduces "vertically" by inheritance, but it also reproduces "horizontally" as cultures interact across geographic regions and demographic groups. Globalization, spurred on by modern technology—a world more "connected" than ever before—means the rapid transmission of culture. For one of the most wide-reaching examples of this transmission, the other more universally popular form of football is a case in point. On weekends from August

---

24. Daniel J. Brendsel, "A Tale of Two Calendars: Calendars, Compassion, Liturgical Formation, and the Presence of the Holy Spirit," *Bulletin for Ecclesial Theology* 3, no. 1 (June 2016).

25. Smith, *Imagining the Kingdom*, 142–43.

26. For these and many more examples, see Smith, *Desiring the Kingdom*; Myers, *All God's Children and Blue Suede Shoes*; Neil Postman, *Amusing Ourselves to Death: Public Discourse in the Age of Show Business*, 20th Anniversary ed. (New York: Penguin Books, 2005); Vanhoozer, Anderson, and Sleasman, *Everyday Theology*.

27. Vanhoozer, 30.

through May, English Premier League soccer is transmitted into homes across the planet—from small villages in the Majority World to bustling cities in the most advanced nations in the world. The British soccer culture—which itself is impacted by other cultures due to the influx of foreign players to the league—is being transported around the world. The jerseys, cheers, vernacular, and league rules (e.g., relegation and promotion) are celebrated and embraced internationally.[28] Again, sports are just one example—we could identity the same kind of "horizontal" expansion of culture in just about every domain of life.

And yet cultural reproduction is not uniform. While culture has the ability to spread, some cultures are stagnant or even barren. Studying the cause for such varying growth of culture, or lack thereof, is a complex and debated topic. However, it does seem, as James Hunter has emphasized, that culture most regularly changes from the top down. Hunter points out that while beliefs and values of ordinary people and the creation of new inventions and technologies do play a role in the story of cultural change, the decisive factor regularly comes from the top. After concisely summarizing the rise of Christianity, the Carolingian Renaissance, the Reformation, the Great Awakening, the Anti-Slavery Reforms, the Enlightenment, and European socialism, he concludes that in each case

> we find a rich source of patronage that provided resources for intellectuals and educators who, in the context of dense networks, imagine, theorize, and propagate an alternative culture. Often enough, alongside these elite are artists, poets, musicians, and the like who symbolize, narrate, and popularize this vision. New institutions are created that give form to that culture, enact it, and, in so doing, give tangible expression to it.[29]

In sum, cultures reproduce, but not equally. Some cultures have more longevity and influence over other cultures, usually transforming from the top down.

---

28. See William Edgar, *Created and Creating: A Biblical Theology of Culture* (Downers Grove, IL: InterVarsity Press, 2016), 1–4.

29. Hunter, *To Change the World*, 78. See the entire chapter, "Evidence in History," 48–78. Peter Berger echoes Hunter's point in describing the modern cultural situation: "There exists an international subculture composed of people with Western-type higher class education, especially in the humanities and social sciences, that is indeed secularized. This subculture is the principal 'carrier' of progressive, Enlightened beliefs and values. While its members are relatively thin on the ground, they are very influential, as they control the institutions that provide the 'official' definitions of reality, notably the educational system, the media of mass communication, and the higher reaches of the legal system. I can only point out that what we have here is a globalized elite culture." Peter L. Berger, "The Desecularization of the World: A Global Overview," in *The Desecularization of the World: Resurgent Religion and World Politics,* ed. Peter L. Berger (Grand Rapids: Eerdmans, 1999), 10.

◯◯ Conclusion

While the instinct as Christians to "engage," "transform," or "change" culture often stems from right motives, when done poorly, it can lead to disastrous results. Part of the problem is a failure to grasp the basics of culture. If we don't understand that with which we are engaging—or perhaps better, engaging within—we will often limit our ability to effectively interact with people. In the next chapter we will see how different Christian traditions have understood the biblical story line and how these interpretations have practical implications for how believers interact in culture.

chapter two

BIBLICAL STORY LINES AND CULTURAL ENGAGEMENT

A few years ago a student approached me (Josh) after class. "Dr. Chatraw, I have a question I was hoping you could help me with." His worrisome expression and the hesitancy in his voice led me to expect him to confide in me about some kind of existential doubt or personal apologetic struggle. I reassured him I was glad to try to help. He proceeded to explain, "I have been thinking about Starbucks quite a bit recently." Needless to say, this is not quite what I was expecting. He continued by saying something along the following lines, "Many Christians support this business and yet their stances on many issues go against my Christian convictions. I don't see how we can be justified in frequenting their stores. What do you think about this?"

Your reaction to this question about Starbucks might reveal more than you think. It might reveal your religious tradition's assumptions about the appropriate Christian stance toward culture. Consider some of the possible responses to this question.

- We should boycott all companies that have agendas that oppose Christian values. By doing so, we can put pressure on them to change their policies and agendas. We should use strategic activism to directly influence corporations to change their social agenda.
- Out of principle, we should at least try to limit our interaction with and cooperation with non-Christian companies. Realistically, this might not actually pressure them to change their policies, but at least we will stand on principle and avoid being corrupted by consumerism and secular values. As much as we can, we should support "Christian" businesses or at least those that stand for values similar to our own.
- We can continue to visit Starbucks so that we can build relationships with the baristas and other patrons in order to evangelize them. Our job is to

focus on "making disciples" rather than exerting pressure on businesses and changing culture.

- We can thank God for the coffee they make—he gave us the raw materials (e.g., coffee beans, cows for the milk, etc.) and made these people in his own image, with the ingenuity and creativeness to make such wonderful coffee. Plus, Starbucks is creating jobs, and based on universally accessible norms, some of their moral intuitions are to be applauded.
- Through reflecting on how the gospel shapes how believers participate in all cultural activities, we should encourage Christian entrepreneurs to open coffee shops and other businesses that lead to human flourishing.
- We should open Christian coffee houses to provide safe havens from corrupting pressures that come from being too embedded in secular culture.

Maybe this issue is not one that you have lost much sleep over. Still, the example shows that when it comes to how Christians should interact with the institutions and people around us, what seems like "common sense" to you is probably not actually so *common* for many other believers. Granted, all of these reactions are not necessarily mutually exclusive. Nevertheless, we typically each have an ingrained inclination to one or more of these responses, which is due to our own tradition—or perhaps due to the tradition we are reacting against. By "tradition" we mean a set of inherited communal practices and beliefs. Embedded in different Christian traditions is a larger story about what God is doing in the world and the church's role in it. Often these background stories are not explored in popular discourse. Instead, it is all too easy to assume our tradition is "obvious," without weighing into the biblical, theological, and practical concerns that have led to competing visions for understanding the relationship between the church and culture.

Culture, Religion, and the Early Church

Most people in the West can recognize at least some distinction between the general culture and religion. In contrast, traditional societies assume civil, social, and religious duties and norms to be intertwined.

Quite remarkably, in this ancient context, the early church emphasized both a respect for and a distinction from the political and cultural practices of the Roman Empire. The early Christians refused to offer

worship to any other "Lord." Christian leaders insisted that believers not
practice pagan worship, which was a part of political and cultural practices
within the empire. They also taught believers to respect government
officials and to be good citizens (Rom. 13:1–7; 1 Tim. 2:1–3; 1 Peter 2:13–17).

This balance, of both honor without veneration, led Tertullian to one of
the earliest defenses of religious liberty: "It is a fundamental human right,
a privilege of nature, that everyone should worship according to one's
own conviction. . . . It is assuredly no part of religion to compel religion. . . .
A Christian is enemy to none, least of all to the Emperor of Rome, who he
knows to be appointed by God, and so cannot but love and honor; and
whose well-being moreover [the Christian] must desire, with that of the
empire over which he reigns" (Tertullian, *To Scapula*, 1.2.). Concerning
a religious identity that was separate from their ethnicity or the wider
culture, historian Larry Hurtado has emphasized that "this distinctive early
Christian group is perhaps the earliest attempt to articulate what moderns
would recognize as a corporate *religious* identity that is distinguishable
from, not a corollary of, one's family, civic, or ethnic connection." (Hurtado,
Destroyer of the Gods: Early Christian Distinctiveness in the Roman World
[Waco, TX: Baylor University Press, 2016], 104.)

What Does the Bible Say?

What does the Bible say about the church's role in the broader culture? One
approach to this question could be to simply group passages together in support
of a particular posture toward culture. While this tactic might confirm those
who are already convinced of a particular tradition that they have indeed been
right all along, it will likely prove unpersuasive to others and leave you susceptible
to blind spots. The Scriptures address the subject of culture, but it is a little more
complicated than just gathering a group of passages to "prove" your position.

From her inception, the church has wrestled with her relationship to the
culture. The New Testament Scriptures themselves display a variety of postures
toward the broader world, and thus there is a growing consensus that the question "How should Christians approach culture?" cannot be answered by simply
citing biblical book, chapter, and verse numbers.

Take the relationship between the church and state as an example. Romans
13:1–7 teaches that God has instituted governments for positive reasons. In
particular, the government is to "bear the sword" and are servants of God to

"bring punishment" (Rom. 13:4). Governments, even pagan governments, like the ones Paul had in mind, have a positive role to play in the world. Revelation 19 casts the empire in a much more negative light as John uses the imagery of a "great prostitute" to describe the state. While there are some commonalities presented across the New Testament on this issue, D. A. Carson explains that "local conditions and complementary theological truths evoke disparate emphases."[1]

Niebuhr's Christ and Culture Taxonomy

The most seminal taxonomy of Christian responses to culture was proposed by H. Richard Niebuhr in the middle of the twentieth century. His five categories include:

Christ against culture: Culture is viewed negatively in this model. The church is to stand out from the culture and avoid being corrupted by withdrawing from it. Think of this model as standing on the far end on one side of a spectrum.

Christ of culture: Culture is viewed positively. God is at work outside his church and the church should look for ways to accommodate and come alongside the Spirit's work in culture. This model is on the complete other side of the spectrum as Christ against culture.

The following three models, all variations of what Niebuhr called *Christ above culture*, are more nuanced and mediate between the first two polar opposites.

The Synthesis: This view seeks to synthesize Christ and culture, by understanding God to be utilizing the best of culture to help us attain what we cannot on our own. Cultural law and divine law are viewed as two different realties. As Niebuhr himself writes, according to this view, "Culture discerns the rules for culture, because culture is the work of God-given reason in God-given nature. Yet there is another law [which] the rational man must discover and obey."[2]

---

1. D. A. Carson, *Christ and Culture Revisited* (Grand Rapids: Eerdmans, 2008), 171.
2. H. Richard Niebuhr, *Christ and Culture* (San Francisco: HarperSanFrancisco, 2001), 135.

Christ and culture in paradox: This understanding views Christians as dual citizens, members of both secular culture and the sacred community of Christ. Christians have a responsibility to each, but these responsibilities do not overlap.

Christ transforming culture: This approach emphasizes the responsibility of Christians to not only have a general role in the broader culture but more than this, to transform culture according to Christ.

While Niebuhr admitted that this taxonomy was in some sense artificial—life is always more complicated than theoretical models can display—he believed the transformational model was the ideal. While this Niebuhr's classifications have proved influential in discussions on the church and culture, critics have identified various legitimate concerns with his taxonomy.[3] While we are sympathetic to many of these critiques, adopting some kind of general taxonomy is needed to provide a sketch of how different traditions have addressed this question. Communicating to the uninitiated a new complex subject always carries the risk, if not the inevitability, of overgeneralization. For our purposes here, we have chosen to explain the various approaches by articulating three basic underlying narratives. For a fair taxonomy that is both clear and goes into more details, offering strengths and weaknesses of each approach, see Timothy Keller, *Center Church*, 194–232.

Or consider two passages from the Old Testament. In Jeremiah 29, the prophet sends a letter to God's people who had been exiled in Babylon and commanded them to take up residence, conduct productive lives, pray for their new home, and seek the general peace and prosperity of this pagan city. Jeremiah's instructions are different from other Old Testament texts that call the people of God to separate from their pagan neighbors. For instance, in Leviticus 20:26 we read: "You are to be holy to me because I, the LORD, am holy, and I have set you apart from the nations to be my own." Part of how one understands these particular passages and their relevance for today is rooted in how the biblical story as a whole is understood. The Bible is full of diverse genres that are held together by

---

3. See, for example, Carson, *Christ and Culture Revisited*; Craig A. Carter, *Rethinking Christ and Culture: A Post-Christendom Perspective* (Grand Rapids: Brazos, 2006); Angus J. L. Menuge, ed., *Christ and Culture in Dialogue: Constructive Themes and Practical Applications* (St. Louis: Concordia Academic Press, 1999).

a narrative framework. To understand and apply the Bible appropriately, we have to understand how the story line fits together.

The Scriptures are not simply giving us abstract truths or a comprehensive list of instructions for every possible contemporary situation. Rather, the Bible includes truth applied to concrete cultural and ecclesial situations of the human author's context. For this reason, among others, the Bible actually says different things on the appropriate posture toward culture. This diversity is not the same as a contradiction. A *contradiction* is when two things cannot both be true because they oppose each other; they are mutually exclusive. If I am married, I can't also be a bachelor. Saying otherwise would be a contradiction.

The Bible is not contradicting itself when it displays different stances to culture. Instead, it expresses a *legitimate diversity*—the type of diversity we should relish in and expect, given that God has inspired his Word to guide his people in real-life situations rather than in a theoretical existence abstracted from the messiness of life. Take the second example above. The nation of Israel was called to be a holy nation and a kingdom of priests. She was not to be corrupted by the pagan nations that surrounded her. The Mosaic Covenant instructed the nation how they were to fulfill this role. In one particular instance in Deuteronomy 23:6, which is semantically connected to Jeremiah 29, the people are commanded, as part of God's judgment, "not to seek the shalom" (holistic welfare or flourishing) of the Ammonites or Moabites.

As the story goes on, we discover that Israel failed repeatedly to live out God's calling to be a holy nation and eventually was cast into exile. Later in the story, in the passage we read from Jeremiah, a portion of God's people found themselves not in the holy land, but in a pagan land. How then shall they live? God uses the same expression as in Deuteronomy 23:6, but instead positively commands the people to "seek the shalom" of the city. The prophet Jeremiah in essence is saying, "Given this context and what God is doing in the world, you should think and act in this way. You should seek the prosperity of this pagan city." Just like any good story, there are different moves in the biblical plot.

There was no temple or tabernacle in Babylon for sacrifices to be made. God did not call them to wage war against the public idolatry of the foreign nation they were residing in (though, of course, they were to abstain from idolatrous worship). And yet in Jeremiah's commands we hear echoes of the earliest chapters in the biblical story: plant gardens, marry, multiply, and be a blessing to this foreign nation (see Gen. 1; 2; and 12). In other words, this is the same story with the same God at the center of it all.

There is *diversity* in the Christian story, which is one reason why it makes sense—not only for practical reasons but also for biblical reasons—to acknowledge, along with sociologist James Davison Hunter, that "as to a strategy for engaging the world, perhaps there is no single model for all times and places."[4] This is why, as we will see in our next chapter, much in cultural engagement hangs on wisdom and virtue rather than a list of rules or universal plan that we might extract from the Bible.

But there is also a *unity* in the Scriptures that binds all the stories of the world together by way of God's grand story.[5] This unity provides a framework for us to think and live within as we wait for the final, consummating stage of the story.

As we will see in the next section, the legitimate diversity has generated certain theological questions for the church as we wrestle with how to apply the Bible in our particular contexts. In the history of the church, a variety of different theological traditions have developed in response to the question of how Christians should relate to culture.

In light of the unity and diversity found in Scripture, one way to view different theological traditions and how they relate to culture is to understand how they tell the macro story of the Bible. Stories have different elements, and the Bible is full of many genres besides narrative—law, prophets, proverbs, poetry. And yet, essential to understanding the various genres and interweaving narratives of the Bible is a broader story that makes sense of the smaller elements. Beyond the practice of biblical interpretation, "story" is essential for daily communication and understanding the world around us. Alasdair MacIntyre makes this point in his seminal book *After Virtue*:

> I am standing waiting for a bus and a young man standing next to me suddenly says, "The name of the common wild duck is Histrionicus, histrionicus, histrionicus." There is a problem as to the meaning of the sentence he uttered: the problem is how to answer the question, what was he doing in uttering it? Suppose he just uttered such sentences at random intervals: this would be one possible form of madness. We would render his action of utterance intelligible if one of the following turned out to be true. He has

---

4. James Davison Hunter, *To Change the World: The Irony, Tragedy, and Possibility of Christianity in the Late Modern World* (New York: Oxford University Press, 2010), 276.

5. Richard Bauckham puts it like this: "While the Bible does not have the kind of unity and coherence a single human author can give a literary work, there is nevertheless a remarkable extent to which the biblical texts themselves recognize and assert, in a necessarily cumulative manner, the unity of the story they tell." Bauckham, "Reading Scripture as a Coherent Story," in *The Bible in the Contemporary World: Hermeneutical Ventures* (Grand Rapids: Eerdmans, 2015), 3. This diversity amidst the unity of the biblical metanarrative is one of the reasons why Bauckham refers to the Bible as offering a nonmodern, nontotalizing metanarrative. See also Richard Bauckham, *Bible and Mission: Christian Witness in a Postmodern World* (Grand Rapids: Baker, 2003).

mistaken me for someone who yesterday had approached him in the library and asked: "Do you know the Latin name of the common wild duck?" *Or* he has just come from a session with his psychotherapist who has urged him to break down his shyness by talking to strangers. "But what shall I say?" "Oh, anything at all." *Or* he is a Soviet spy waiting at a prearranged rendezvous and uttering the ill-chosen code sentence which will identify him to his contact. In each case the act of utterance becomes intelligible by finding its place in a narrative.[6]

Daily conversations and situations don't make sense without a larger narrative that provides context. In MacIntyre's example, one cannot understand what the young man on the bus is saying unless there is a story in place to make sense of his words. Similar to conversations in life, understanding how the Scriptures fit together and communicate our responsibility in relating to culture cannot be correctly understood without discovering how the different texts fit into the larger biblical story. The challenge is that different theological traditions have told the overarching biblical story differently. In the following section, we will look at three accounts of the biblical story, focusing on the relationship between God's people and culture. Our purpose is not to prescribe one of these three accounts, but rather to describe how the story is being told by different traditions.[7] These broad-brush summaries are meant to help you better identify the background assumptions that often are decisive yet unmentioned when Christians engage on particular issues.

Three Accounts of the Biblical Story Line and Culture

1. The Ongoing Cultural Mandate in the World[8]

As image-bearers, humans are called to live in relationship with God while obeying his commission to steward creation. As his vice-regents, who were called to "rule over" all creatures, we are to care for and cultivate creation (Gen. 1:28–30). Our relationship with our creator is related to our role in his creation. God created the world "good" and commanded his image-bearers to "fill the earth and subdue it" and to "rule over the fish in the sea and the birds in the sky and over every living creature that moves on the ground" (Gen. 1:28). Humankind

---

6. Alasdair MacIntyre, *After Virtue*, 3rd ed. (Notre Dame, IN: University of Notre Dame Press, 2007).

7. Each of the three stories below could be told with variations but still be close enough to align with the general category as it is represented here.

8. This approach is often referred to as Kuyperian or Neo-Kuyperian, named after Dutch theologian and politician Abraham Kuyper.

was to reflect God's rule in the world and mediate his blessings to the world.[9] Humanity has been given a "cultural mandate."[10] Though creation was good, it was incomplete. The world was full of potential, and God made humans with the mandate to develop creation's latent possibilities as his vice-regents. As Old Testament scholar Richard Middleton puts it, in Genesis 1 and 2 God gives his image-bearers a mandate that "involves representing and perhaps extending in some way God's rule on earth through ordinary communal practices of human sociocultural life."[11]

Yet humans turned away from God and the virtuous way he intended for us to fulfill his mandate. The root of the human predicament is that the creatures sought to have ultimate dominion and to subvert God's authority, forsaking moral innocence. This breach in our relationship with God resulted in universal implications for creation and our role in it. The task to cultivate and develop creation remains, but God's image and his creation mandate—which includes discovering, developing, and creating—has been marred. The mandate is now frustrated by idolatry, the power of sin, and the "principalities" of evil.

The gospel is the message of "good news" for how God has reconciled his image-bearers to himself by entering the world as a man, dying on the cross, and rising again to redeem sinners, defeat evil, and usher in the new creation. Those who are in Christ are restored to God, transformed by his Spirit, and called to make him known as we steward creation. This stewardship includes both understanding and caring for the world. According to this view, we are to work against the disorders and maladies of a fallen world while developing the potentialities which have been inherent within creation from the beginning.

As redeemed image-bearers, the people of God are to live out their vocations caring for all of creation in light of the revelation of Christ and reflecting the priorities of our risen Lord. We do not bring in the kingdom of Christ by offering such a vision, but we are to serve as a picture of the King's care for the world and a preview of the consummation of his kingdom. God promises that he will

---

9. By referring to humans as his image-bearers, Old Testament scholars point to the ancient practice of kings erecting statues of their own image in cities to remind the citizens who was ruling them.

10. In reference to Genesis 1, Old Testament scholar Richard Middleton explains, "The human calling as *imago dei* [image of God] is itself developmental and transformative and may be helpfully understood as equivalent to the labor or work of forming culture or developing civilization." *The Liberating Image: The Imago Dei in Genesis 1* (Grand Rapids: Baker Academic, 2005), 89. Humans were created for "organizing and transforming the environment into a habitable world," and Middleton notes that later, Genesis highlights "human cultural achievements and technological innovations such as city-building (4:17; 11:1–9) and nomadic livestock-herding, music, and metallurgy (4:20–22)." (Ibid., 89). Due to humans' unique role within the cosmic temple—imagery used in these opening chapters of Genesis—their divinely given task is to be both "cultural shapers" and "priests of creation," "actively mediating divine blessing to the nonhuman world," and after the world is corrupted by sin, "interceding on behalf of a groaning creation until that day when heaven and earth are redemptively transformed to fulfill God's purpose for justice and shalom" (Ibid., 90).

11. Middleton, *The Liberating Image*, 60.

one day dwell with a new humanity in a new creation (Rev. 21). As the physical resurrection of Jesus' body has prefigured, both the redeemed and creation itself will be renewed on the last day (Rom. 8:21), and a diversity of the artifacts of culture will be presented on the last day (Rev. 7:9; 21:24; Isa. 60). To live as fully human image-bearers, transformed by the Spirit, we are to reflect Christ and his coming in all areas of life while we await the day God will bring heaven to earth.[12]

2. The Cultural Mandate Fulfilled in Christ[13]

Similar to all the ongoing cultural mandate accounts of the biblical story, this view stresses the goodness of God's work in creating the world. Humans are uniquely created in the image of God, exercising dominion essential to bearing the image of God. Thus, as theologian David VanDrunen explains, "Humans were made for *cultural* activity, God gave them a cultural task that they were to pursue in faithful service to him."[14] So far this sounds basically like the previous narrative, but this tradition emphasizes that the role given by God to Adam was only a temporary means to a greater end. "The first Adam did not bear God's image in order to work aimlessly in the original creation but to finish his work in this world and then to enter a new creation and to sit down enthroned in a royal rest."[15] The task given to the first human was a "covenant of works" that was supposed to lead to rest from the activities given to cultivate and fill the earth.

The first Adam failed in achieving the rest through a "covenant of works." If he would have passed this first test, "the rest of us would still have come into existence and shared the glory of the world-to-come with him in the presence of God."[16] Human cultural activity still continues after the fall today, but our cultural activities will always lead to "sinful failure." Their end is "death and destruction." VanDrunen summarizes this retelling of the story:

> The story of human history told to this point is one of terrible tragedy. God created human beings with a high office, a noble calling, and a glorious destiny. Adam had a great cultural task set before him, which was to find focus in his workings and guarding the garden of Eden. Because he bore the divine likeness, the outcome of his royal work in this world should have been a royal rest in the world-to-come. But his failure to complete this task

---

12. J. Richard Middleton, *A New Heaven and a New Earth: Reclaiming Biblical Eschatology* (Grand Rapids: Baker Academic, 2014).

13. This tradition is often referred to as Two Kingdom Theology.

14. David VanDrunen, *Living in God's Two Kingdoms: A Biblical Vision for Christianity and Culture* (Wheaton, IL: Crossway, 2010), 40, 93.

15. Ibid., 40.

16. Ibid., 41.

plunged the human race into guilt, condemnation, and corruption. The
fallen race cannot undertake its cultural endeavors with a righteousness
acceptable to God, it finds the natural world largely uncooperative and
beyond its control, and it faces everlasting death as the only outcome of its
work in the world.[17]

The good news is that believers are justified by the new Adam, Jesus Christ.
Whereas the old Adam failed to fulfill the covenant, the new Adam was perfectly obedient. Jesus fulfilled the cultural mandate so that through faith in him
we can enter into the rest that the old Adam would have ushered in if he had
been obedient.

After the fall, God formally instituted two different covenants: the covenant
with Noah and the covenant with Abraham. The covenant with Noah was a
covenant with all of humanity, which established the common kingdom. The
common kingdom is the place of cultural activity, which Christians as well as
non-Christians find themselves working in. All worldly institutions outside of
the church are in this common kingdom. These are not spiritual activities per
se, and they are not directly related to the gospel. Cultural activities should be
conducted as a way that God providentially cares for the world in this temporary
fallen state, but they should not be overly spiritualized. Jesus Christ is the only
one who has or could fulfill the cultural mandate. The redeemed should not seek
to fulfill Adam's cultural task.

In addition to the common kingdom, followers of Christ are members of
the redemptive kingdom, which was formally instituted by the covenant with
Abraham. In contrast to the Noahic covenant, "The Abrahamic covenant . . .
concerns *religious faith and worship* (rather than cultural activities), it embraces a
holy people that is *distinguished* from the rest of the human race (rather than the
human race in common), it *bestows the benefits of salvation* upon this holy people
(rather than preserving the natural and social order), and it is established *forever
and ever* (rather than temporarily)."[18] The church is tasked to proclaim the saving
message of the Bible and exercise the various means of grace for salvation, rather
than to directly use Scripture to change temporal culture.

The coming new creation will replace the old creation, which will be annihi-
lated (2 Peter 3:1–7). Except for human bodies which will be resurrected, the rest
of the world will be destroyed, and new heavens and earth will be created by God.
Though this will be a physical new world, no cultural activities from the common
kingdom will last for eternity.

---

17. Ibid., 47.
18. Ibid., 82.

3. The Cultural Mandate Fulfilled inside the Church[19]

God created the world good. Humans were made in his image and given the mandate to steward and fill the earth, living in an obedient relationship to their Creator.[20]

The first humans rebelled against God, ushering in both separation from God and chaos in the world. Sin infected all of creation, perverting God's original intent for the world.

In his mercy, God called Abram out of paganism to create a distinct people, set apart from the world. It was through existing as a holy nation, a kingdom of priests with different laws and a different way of life, that God would be a blessing to the nations.

Similar to the story told in the Old Testament, God has called the New Testament church to be set apart, a city set on a hill to reflect his character to the world. The ethics of the gospel, as seen in Jesus' Sermon on the Mount, is antithetical to the natural ways of the world. To live out such commands, the church must view herself as a holy nation, resident aliens in the midst of a fallen world. This does not need to imply that the church in any way is neglecting its mission to the world. Instead, this is the way God's people bring redemption to the world because the church stands "in tension with the world in order to faithfully serve the world."[21]

Rod Dreher refers to his approach, which best fits within this third category, not as "escapism" or "inaction," but as a "strategic withdrawal."[22] Others, whose posture can look similar to Dreher's option, prefer the language of "separateness" rather than "withdrawal."[23] If this general story line includes the idea of a "cultural

---

19. This approach is commonly associated with Neo-Anabaptists.

20. While this opening part of the story is not necessarily directly at odds with the first two versions of the story, the opening scenes are not normally a matter of emphasis in this way of telling the story. See for instance the works John Howard Yoder, *The Christian Witness to the State* (Newton, KS: Faith and Life Press, 1964); *The Politics of Jesus*, 2nd ed. (Grand Rapids: Eerdmans, 1994); *Revolutionary Christian Citizenship* (Harrisonburg, VA: Herald, 2013); Rod Dreher, *The Benedict Option: A Strategy for Christians in a Post-Christian Nation* (New York: Sentinel, 2017); Stanley Hauerwas and William Willimon, *Resident Aliens: Life in the Christian Colony*, 25th anniversary ed. (Nashville: Abingdon, 2014).

21. Hauerwas and Willimon, *Resident Aliens*,182.

22. Dreher, *The Benedict Option*, xvii.

23. Despite the basic similarity, there seem to be some significant points of departure between those who share the key features of the story line described above. For example, see Jonathan Tran, "Trump and the Specter of Christian Withdrawal" in *Marginalia: The Los Angeles Review of Books*, https://marginalia.lareviewofbooks.org/trump-and-christian-withdrawal/. Tran carefully distinguishes between the approach of Hauerwas, which he refers to as "separateness," from Dreher's Benedict Option: "Hauerwas' work is best described as a theology of witness, where the political stakes have to do with the church as a distinct but not sequestered type of politics. Withdrawal gives all of that up. Because the drift of Dreher's *Benedict Option* is less witness, less about serving and influencing the world, and more about protecting Christianity's own moral integrity, it then makes withdrawal, insofar as it is a principled and strategic retreat, a live option for Christianity. Indeed, it has to since it sees the status of Christianity within the world as unidirectional and threatened, the world's viciousness threatening Christianity's moral righteousness, withdrawal the sole option if virtue is to survive. Hence, the Benedict *option*."

mandate," which is not often the language explicitly used in this way of telling the Christian story, we could say it must happen inside the church as the church cultivates its own culture for the world to see and be invited into. It could be said that within this telling of the story, the church *does* have a mandate to culture, but the immediate focus is not on extending the creational goods of the garden (Gen. 2), but on maintaining the garden within the church as a faithful public witness. The church can preserve a culture, an earthly foretaste of the coming kingdom, only if it guards the borders, not allowing the values and ideals of the fallen world to creep inside the walls of a redeemed counterculture. The life of the church ultimately serves the world. As the church preserves and nurtures a counterculture centered around Christ, inviting the world to come in and "taste and see," we wait for Christ to return to save his church and bring ultimate peace to the world.

Relevancy Story Lines?

More stories and variations of the three narratives explained above could be given. For example, in Tim Keller's helpful taxonomy, he includes the relevance model (*Center Church,* 194–232). This category is not, however, explained easily by way of summarizing one account of the biblical story. This is because those who fit into this approach are either less committed to tracking with the story line of Scripture, or they attempt to go beyond the story line, or are simply more pragmatic about the church's task within the culture. What binds together those within the "relevancy" category is that they see many positive things happening in the culture apart from the church or the gospel. They understand the church's role as coming alongside of culture and connecting with it for the sake of God's kingdom.

For instance, for some evangelicals, the focus is not so much on critiquing or transforming culture, but on using it to attract people to the Christian message. While the message should not change, it is argued that cultural institutions and products are positive—or at least neutral—instruments that can be used for the sake of the gospel. Church services and programs can be reimagined, given cultural changes, but the core message of Christianity should not change. The form is adaptable; the message is what is important and is the only thing that must be guarded as sacrosanct. This emphasis is not necessarily at odds with the biblical macro stories told in this chapter. Some cultural adaptation, also known as contextualization, is impossible to avoid and is affirmed and modeled in the Bible. What has proved to be controversial are the limits for contextualization.

Many have rightly questioned the notion that *form* can be so easily detached from *meaning*. For example, when the gospel is packaged with consumer driven marketing and services focused on entertainment, how is Jesus' message of repentance, grace, and taking up one's cross actually understood? At the very least, the limits for historic Christianity are transgressed when central doctrines are altered for the sake of better aligning with the spirit of the age. An example is classic liberal theology, which attempted to respond to modern skepticism toward the supernatural by shedding the miraculous to salvage the kernel of truth behind these premodern notions found in the Bible. When this move is made, undermining essential elements of Christianity, culture sets the terms for defining Christianity, and the distinctive nature of the gospel is lost.

For more on the limits and necessity of contextualization, see Joshua D. Chatraw and Mark D. Allen, *Apologetics at the Cross: An Introduction for Christian Witness* (Grand Rapids: Zondervan, 2018), ch. 9.

The Biblical Stories and How Grace Works

A lesson from this sketch of three different understandings of the biblical story line is that a simple "me and my Bible" approach to discerning a faithful approach to culture will not work. For one, we are all interpreting the Scripture through some kind of lens, some kind of tradition or story. Becoming cognizant of our own traditions and how they put the Bible together will allow us to be better interpreters and more open to potential shortcomings within our own theological traditions. This approach might even cause us to consider the possibility of converting to another Christian tradition. One has to continue to go back to the Bible and see which story makes the best sense, while recognizing how these three different stories might intersect and interlock at various points. And since these stories are certainly not always mutually exclusive, at the very least these alternative traditions should cause you to consider what insights can be gained from other approaches and how your own tradition might need to be tempered.[24]

---

24. A prime example of this is James K. A. Smith, *Awaiting the King: Reforming Public Theology* (Grand Rapids: Baker Academic, 2017). While Smith reads the biblical story as highlighting what we refer to as

Second, we've seen that the Bible displays legitimate diversity as its human authors are writing in different contexts to address particular concerns within their communities. This means that simply collecting all the passages that address the church's relation to the world and then directly applying them to today will not settle the issue. Making sense of how these texts fit into a larger story will prove to be important for navigating the diversity found within the Bible.

With this overview in place, we need to add one more element to the discussion. Theology—the study of God and the revelation of himself—involves not only proposing how these diverse texts actually fit together but also relates to theological doctrines that are reflected within the drama of Scripture. Introducing some pertinent theological concepts related to God's revelation of himself further "fills out" the distinctives within the three different interpretations of the story.

General Revelation

By way of general revelation, God universally reveals himself through his creation. Romans 1:19–20 is the classic New Testament passage illustrating general revelation: "What may be known about God is plain to them, because God has made it plain to them. For since the creation of the world God's invisible qualities—his eternal power and divine nature—have been clearly seen, being understood from what has been made." Or consider Psalm 19:1–4:

> The heavens declare the glory of God;
>   the skies proclaim the work of his hands.
> Day after day they pour forth speech;
>   night after night they reveal knowledge.
> They have no speech, they use no words;
>   no sound is heard from them.
> Yet their voice goes out into all the earth,
>   their words to the ends of the world.

One does not need a Bible or a prophet to look out and see the stars and the sky. The Bible tells us everything we see is the work of God's hands and is a revelation of himself. Yet how much sin clouds and even makes us blind to the meaning of this general revelation is a debated topic among theologians.

"the *ongoing* cultural mandate in the world," he applies insights from others, such as Hauerwas and Willimon, to "extend and revise" his own tradition—particularly what he sees as the propensity for Kuyperians to assimilate the deformative ideals of the wider culture.

Common Grace

Common grace is a broader doctrine that encompasses general revelation. Common grace is the mercy of God expressed through unmerited gifts given to people, irrespective of their personal faith or virtue. In his Sermon on the Mount, Jesus explains that God "causes his sun to rise on the evil and the good, and sends rain on the righteous and the unrighteous" (Matt. 5:45). Because of his common grace to humanity, God gives general revelation as a gift to all people. Every skill and ability by which individuals—from artists to athletes and comedians to surgeons—contribute to culture has been given by God, the giver of every good gift.

Particular Revelation

In contrast to general revelation, God gives particular revelation (or special revelation) to specific people at specific times. For instance, God spoke to Abraham, making a covenant with him (Gen. 12), spoke to the church by his Son (Heb. 1:1–2), proclaimed the gospel through Peter on the day of Pentecost (Acts 2), and speaks through Scripture to those who have access to the Bible. Jesus Christ is particular revelation *par excellence*, the very revelation of God himself.

Middle Grace

An important concept that is now receiving more attention in these discussions is middle grace. Theologian Peter Leithart, who coined the term, describes middle grace as a category that exists between special revelation and general revelation:

> Whatever moral consensus exists is thus not a product of pure "common grace" (devoid of all contact with revelation), nor of "special grace" (saving knowledge of God through Christ and his word), but what I call ... "middle grace" (non-saving knowledge of God and his will derived from both general and special revelation). To put it another way, because of the cultural influence of the Bible, unbelievers in America are more Christian than unbelievers in Irian Jaya. To put it another way, there is not and has never existed a pure "common grace" cultural situation.[25]

---

25. Peter J. Leithart, *Did Plato Read Moses?: Middle Grace and Moral Consensus* (Niceville, FL: Biblical Horizons, 1995), 4–5. "The Word of God has been so intertwined with our civilization that the two are nearly impossible to separate. Distinctly biblical moral precepts seem to the Western mind to be precepts of nature, accessible to every reasonable man with a modicum of common sense. The God in whom Western atheists disbelieve is the biblical God (not Baal or Kronos), and many relativists claim that the one absolute is that preeminent Pauline virtue, love. One ancient near eastern flood myth recorded that the gods sent a flood because the people swarming over the earth were so noisy that the gods could not sleep at night. To the extent that moderns find this quaint or appalling, to that extent biblical religion—not some abstraction called 'common grace'—has shaped our conception of what conduct is proper to God. What the West has held in common is precisely what is, theologically speaking, special" (Leithart, *Did Plato Read Moses?*, 19).

Not everyone emphasizing middle grace puts it in as strong terms as Leithart appears to in this quote. For many, some moral consensus could be possible through common grace. Nevertheless, the underlying concept behind middle grace is being increasingly affirmed by various authors, though different terminology is used to describe the idea. Human rights, universal benevolence, the dignity and worth of all people, and various assumptions that lie behind both modern science and Western liberal democracy are not simply a product of "common grace." Instead, these cultural and moral gains are historically contingent on special revelation being introduced into a culture.[26]

Theologians and their respective traditions typically agree that both general revelation and common grace exist. Given the existence of sin in the world, the debate is over how much weight we should give to common grace versus the need for special revelation in cultural activities.

Common Grace and Special Revelation

The cultural mandate being fulfilled inside the church has a low regard for common grace and emphasizes the church's role as being a light to the world, with means guarding her purity from the evils of a fallen world. Special revelation radically redirects all the values of the redeemed, so that the church will be in strong tension with the world around her. Through her words and deeds from outside of the culture, the church serves in a prophetic role, calling the world to repent and enter into the church. To return to our opening Starbucks example, here are some possible responses of how this tradition understands the biblical story line and these theological issues:

- We should open Christian coffeehouses to provide safe havens from corrupting pressures that come from being too embedded within secular culture.

---

26. For example, of scholars with varying religious commitments who stress Christian theology's unique impact on the current Western moral, social, and political assumptions, see John Gray, *Straw Dogs: Thoughts on Humans and Other Animals* (London: Granta, 2002), 3, 88; Jurgen Habermas, *Time of Transitions* (Cambridge: Polity, 2006), 150–51; Jurgen Habermas, *Religion and Rationality: Essays on Reason: God, and Modernity* (Cambridge: Polity, 2002), 149; Jurgen Habermas, et al., *An Awareness of What Is Missing*, 18–21; Oliver O'Donovan, *The Ways of Judgment* (Grand Rapids: Eerdmans, 2005), 309–12; Oliver O'Donovan, *The Desire of the Nations: Rediscovering the Roots of Political Theology* (Cambridge: Cambridge University Press, 1996), 226; James K. A. Smith, *Awaiting the King: Reforming Public Theology* (Grand Rapids: Baker Academic, 2017); Larry Siedentop, *Inventing the Individual: The Origins of Western Liberalism* (Cambridge, MA: Belknap, 2014), 245; Charles Taylor, *Sources of Self: The Making of the Modern Identity* (Cambridge, MA: Harvard University Press, 1989); Charles Taylor, *A Secular Age* (Cambridge, MA: Harvard University Press, 2007); Brian Tierney, *The Idea of Natural Rights: Studies on Natural Rights, Natural Law, and Church Law* (Atlanta, GA: Scholars Press for Emory University, 1997), 1150–1625; Nicholas Wolterstorff, *Justice: Rights and Wrongs* (Princeton, NJ: Princeton University Press, 2008), 311–61.

- Out of principle, we should at least try to limit our interaction with and cooperation with non-Christian companies. Realistically, this might not actually pressure them to change their policies, but at least we will stand on principle and avoid being corrupted by consumerism and secular values. As much as we can, we should support "Christian" businesses or at least those that stand for values similar to our own.

The cultural mandate fulfilled in Christ has a high regard for common grace over special revelation in cultural activities. While the other two stories do not completely discount common grace, they are not nearly as optimistic about the impact of common grace within the culture. Those who follow this story line place more of an emphasis on the ability of all humans, without the aid of special revelation, to excel in cultural activities. In support of this claim, they point out that special revelation is not needed for most cultural tasks. God provides the milk maids to milk cows, the auto mechanic to fix cars, and the doctor to diagnose and treat diseases. There is no special Christian or biblical way to perform such tasks. Therefore, the primary role of the church is to apply special revelation to proclaim spiritual realities and to practice the spiritual disciplines. Once again returning to our opening coffee illustration, two responses fit within this approach.

- We can continue to visit Starbucks so that we can build relationships with the baristas and other patrons to evangelize them. Our job is to focus on "making disciples" rather than exerting pressure on businesses and changing culture.
- We can thank God for the coffee they make. He gave us the raw materials (coffee beans, cows for the milk, etc.) and made these people in his own image, with the ingenuity and creativeness to make such wonderful coffee. Plus, Starbucks is creating jobs and, based on universally accessible norms, some of their moral intuitions are to be applauded.

The ongoing cultural mandate in the world emphasizes special revelation and middle grace as essential for justice, peace, and charity to spread in the world. While not necessarily discounting common grace, this view stresses that Western culture is still living off the "borrowed capital" of special revelation. Although the Bible does not give specific directions for most cultural activities, it does provide a lens or a "worldview" through which all cultural tasks should be viewed. The fruit of the proclamation of God's world and the practices of spiritual disciplines should lead to different ways—sometimes obvious and other times more tacitly—of pursuing vocations and cultural activity.[27] Finally, note how the two examples of reactions to the Starbucks test case that fit within this category share an emphasis on cultural involvement while having different postures toward culture.

- Through reflecting on how the gospel shapes how believers participate in all cultural activities, we should encourage Christian entrepreneurs to open coffee shops and other businesses that lead to human flourishing.
- We should boycott all companies that have agendas that oppose Christian values. By doing so, we can put pressure on them to change their policies and agendas. We should use strategic activism to directly influence corporations to change their social agendas.

Common Ground?

Within the field of cultural engagement, there is no shortage of disagreements. These differences stem from the larger story lines mentioned above and account for some of the diverging articles you will find in this book. It has not been our goal in this chapter to build a case for a particular story line, but rather to bring to the forefront the essential issues that often lie in the background of how you approach culture. Nevertheless, there are at least two areas of budding consensus that could provide for some potential common ground.

First, many Christian leaders in the past were slow to recognize the complexity of cultural issues. Too often we heard clichés like "It is not a race issue, it is a sin issue" and other maxims that simply implied changing individual "hearts and minds" through evangelism was *the* Christian strategy for solving larger cultural issues. Today many Christian thought leaders have begun to stress the complexity involved in cultural issues without undermining the need for and importance of personal conversion. More churches and ministries are recognizing that apparent one-dimensional, narrow approaches to cultural engagement are insufficient and ineffective. For instance, one current cultural issue is the prevalence of communities marked by alarmingly high rates of depression, rampant drug addiction, and a lack of stable family structures. It has been tempting for some to try to quickly isolate the "problem" and offer a solution. But thought leaders are more likely to look closely at such situations and find that these issues are complicated, involving religious, economic, systemic, and historical factors. Cultural issues are complex because each one involves holistic beings living in

---

27. For a practical outworking of this, see Timothy Keller with Katherine Aldsdorf, *Every Good Endeavor: Connecting Your Work to God's Work* (New York: Penguin, 2016).

multifaceted communities with problems that are interconnected. To respond to such challenges effectively, there is more interest in interdisciplinary approaches to cultural engagement. The second section of this book, with its diversity of authors from different fields and backgrounds, is intended not only to provide a range of different theological perspectives to engage with but also to encourage engaging with the cross-currents of different disciplines.

Second, more leaders across different traditions are emphasizing that the church's faithful witness in culture is directly related to the degree our character has been formed by gospel cultures that counteract the secular liturgies of our age. For instance, while James K. A. Smith's *Cultural Liturgy Series* and Rod Dreher's *The Benedict Option*—both of which garnered widespread attention—are different in significant and important ways, they agree that virtue-forming countercultures are essential for Christian faithfulness in our secular world. Our consciences and goals in life are formed, in large measure, by the cultures we are surrounded by, whether it be the media, our family, the place we work, our school, or the church we attend. One salient example of the power of culture to form us is the way the messages sent in Western culture have created the now ubiquitous mindset which holds self-fulfillment as the ultimate good. *New York Times* columnist David Brooks, who calls this phenomenon "The Big Me," explains how the same theme can be seen in everything from movies and popular TV shows to graduation speeches: "Follow your passion. Don't accept limits. Chart your own course. You have a responsibility to do great things because you are so great."[28] Embedded in these all-too-familiar clichés are notions of life, meaning, and the good. And what is most alarming about the "Big Me" mindset is that it doesn't just exist in the secular culture; it has seeped into Christian hearts and the culture of our institutions, propagating gospels of self-interest and self-trust.

The ethos of the gospel of Christ stands in sharp contrast to the default settings of the "Big Me" culture. The first will be last. The greatest will be a servant to all. The weak are strong. To live, you must first die. What seems like foolishness to the world is the wisdom of God—the gospel that saves us so that we might embody the coming kingdom.

As sociologist James Davison Hunter has pointed out, Christians in the past tended to focus on and primarily interact with things they see shifting on a daily basis—law, policy, statements made by politicians, and even the latest on their Twitter feeds. These changes, however, are only the tip of the iceberg: "The world has actually changed in deeper ways than what we can see and for reasons that are much more complicated than the rise in secularism. When people observe a

---

28. David Brooks, *The Road to Character* (New York, Random House, 2015), 7.

weakening in public virtue or traditional personal character, they tend to blame the artifacts of change and not the sources of change."[29] Hunter represents a growing consensus in emphasizing that the church should build strong virtue-forming communities of faith that prioritize the gospel and provide a glimpse of the values of the coming King and his kingdom.[30] It's to the cultivation of these kingdom virtues that we now turn.

---

29. James Davison Hunter, "The Backdrop of Reality," Cardus.ca, https://www.cardus.ca/ comment/ article/4617/the-backdrop-of-reality/.

30. Portions of this last section were adapted from Joshua D. Chatraw, "Cultural Engagement: Integration and Virtue," *Didaktikos* 1, no. 2 (2018).

chapter three

ENGAGING CULTURE VIRTUOUSLY

For the past half century or so, American Christianity, particularly evangelical-ism, has been immersed in a model of cultural engagement aptly termed "the culture wars." The metaphor of war is, like all figures of speech, more than merely a metaphor. The power of the image is such that it not only describes but also prescribes corresponding mindsets and tactics. As the explicitly—if not always consistently—Christian foundation of American culture has been corroded by increasing secularism, many Christians, particularly theologically conservative Christians, have allowed fears about *what* might be lost in the battle to over-shadow concerns with *how* we should engage in it. Too often, in the attempt to rescue the character of the culture in terms of its morality, we have neglected to preserve our own character, or virtue.

Indeed, even the important distinction between morality and virtue has been largely lost. In basic terms, morality distinguishes between right and wrong, while virtue, going all the way back to Aristotle, means simply *excellence*. Human virtue refers to the universal qualities of human character that make a human being excellent. Christian virtue refers to the characteristics the Bible says define the Spirit-led Christian, among these love, joy, peace, forbearance, kindness, goodness, faithfulness, gentleness, and self-control.

Knowing the difference between what is right and wrong is, as explained above, the realm of morality. The moral person, when faced with a choice between right and wrong, chooses what is right. Morality is derived from rules or laws, such as the Ten Commandments, that define good and evil. Even a post-Christian society such as ours has its own "rules" of morality, albeit based on changing values (such as for tolerance) rather than unchanging absolutes. In contrast to the moral person, the virtuous person has, by cultivating habits over time, developed the kind of character that embodies the various excellencies of human nature, such as courage, humility, patience, justice, prudence, temperance, and diligence. Virtue ethics is a field of moral philosophy that studies the way character leads to the ethical life in ways that approaches based on rules or outcomes cannot.

Virtue assumes *telos*, or purpose: the virtue of a racehorse is to run fast; the virtue of a saw is to cut well; the virtue of a human being is to excel in the qualities that make us human; the virtue of a Christian is to be Christlike. If someone thinks the purpose of a saw is to work in the same way a hammer does and uses it accordingly, he will find it to be less than virtuous, or excellent. Similarly, I cannot declare a pair of scissors to be excellent unless I know what they are for. Thus, an understanding of human virtue assumes a common belief in the chief end of human existence. Such a common belief was characteristic of previous ages and cultures (such commonly held views are not limited to Christian societies).

However, one defining characteristic of modernity is that we no longer believe in an essential purpose, or *telos*, for human existence. This is because purpose assumes design, and design assumes a designer. It is the very definition of secularism that such an assumption of a transcendent meaning or purpose is no longer held in common. Charles Taylor describes the transition to a secular society as the change from a culture "where belief in God is unchallenged and indeed, unproblematic, to one in which it is understood to be one option among others, and frequently not the easiest to embrace."[1] We no longer know what makes a person virtuous or excellent because we do not agree on what the purpose or meaning of being human is.

Yet if such a transcendent source of meaning does exist, we will seek to find and express it some way, even if we deny we are doing so. Alasdair MacIntyre argues in *After Virtue* that in an age that no longer professes belief in a unifying, transcendent *telos*, we still employ the language of virtue, but we do so not to name the excellences that characterize human essence but rather to name our personal preferences. MacIntyre calls this tendency emotivism, which he defines as the belief that "moral judgments are nothing but expressions of preference, expressions of attitude or feeling."[2] In other words, when an objective external source of meaning and purpose is replaced by internal subjective feelings, there is no basis other than emotion upon which to base both morality and virtue. And if our own moral judgments are based on our emotional and personal preferences, then we assume that the judgments of others are as well. Therefore, we have no basis for determining what makes another moral argument more valid than ours because all are equally subjective. And because emotivism is cloaked in the language of morality, MacIntyre argues, it becomes increasingly difficult to distinguish between true virtue and a "simulacra [imitation] of morality."[3]

---

1. Charles Taylor, *A Secular Age* (Cambridge, MA: Harvard University Press, 2007), 3.
2. Alasdair MacIntyre, *After Virtue: A Study in Moral Theory*, 3rd ed. (Notre Dame, IN: University of Notre Dame Press, 2007), 11–12.
3. Ibid., 2.

Even Christianity has been influenced by such developments, a development which contributes, at least in part, to some of the disagreements on the issues represented in this volume.

Despite the fact that Christians live in an age which is "after virtue," an age that no longer recognizes a common human *telos* toward which our virtues would be directed, Christians are still called to know and live according to that purpose and to cultivate those qualities that allow us to fulfill that calling with excellence. These are the qualities that reflect God's image in us. We simply can no longer presume that believers (or even the churched) ascribe to the transcendent human *telos* that was commonly assumed before the rise of secularity.

It is helpful to understand that virtues are traditionally understood as the mean between two extremes, an excess and a deficiency. For example, Aristotle finds courage to be the virtuous mean between rashness (excessive courage) and cowardice (deficient courage).[4] Similarly, Aristotle says that being truthful about one's abilities and accomplishments is the virtuous mean between boastfulness and false modesty.[5] The essence of virtue ethics is summed up nicely in the old adage that calls for "moderation in all things." (It is also captured in the King James Version's rendering of Philippians 4:5: "Let your moderation be known unto all men.") Whether we think the most biblical model for our relationship with the culture is to be at war with it, to engage it, to transcend it, or transform it, Christians are called to have virtuous character.

While philosophers throughout the ages have identified various virtues and categories of virtues, all of them are interdependent; one virtue cannot excel in the absence of other virtues. For example, an act of courage relies on prudence (another virtue) and must be directed toward a justice (yet another virtue) in order for it to constitute the virtue of courage. While the truly virtuous person possesses all of the virtues working with one another, some virtues are worthy of particular consideration within the context of cultural engagement.[6] (And by no means are the few listed here exhaustive of the virtues necessary for good cultural engagement.)

One of the first virtues necessary for the believer who seeks effective and God-honoring cultural engagement is diligence. The Bible describes diligence, in fact, as the foundation for the other virtues: "Giving all diligence, add to your faith virtue, to virtue knowledge, to knowledge self-control, to self-control perseverance, to perseverance godliness, to godliness brotherly kindness, and to

---

4. *Nicomachean Ethics*, 3.7.
5. Ibid., 4.7.
6. Some material here is drawn from Karen Swallow Prior, *On Reading Well: Finding the Good Life through Great Books* (Grand Rapids: Brazos, 2018).

brotherly kindness love. For if these things are yours and abound, you will be neither barren nor unfruitful in the knowledge of our Lord Jesus Christ" (2 Peter 1:5–8 NKJV).

The word "diligence" comes from a root word that means "care" and "attentiveness." One feature of these times when so much news and information is thrust before us minute by minute is that it is impossible to attend with care every single disaster, debate, or development. In the age of the "hot take," when everyone is expected to have an opinion on the issue of the day and silence is too often assumed to equal indifference, it is tempting to weigh in on everything, regardless of how little we actually know about the topic.

To be diligent, however, requires that we apply care and attention to the matters we choose to engage in. As Andreas Köstenberger explains, "Diligence requires thoroughness rather than superficiality." One mark of superficiality, Köstenberger notes, is being familiar only with sources whose point of view matches your own.[7] Diligence requires seeking out different points of view on a matter from various sources (discerning the reliability of the sources and the truthfulness of their conclusions). Of course, it is impossible to engage diligently on all (or even many) topics, simply because it is impossible to be knowledgeable about everything or even many things. Indeed, the impetus behind this book, in part, is the desire to help readers to be more diligent in engaging with the topics covered here (which are themselves selected out of a vast range of possible topics).

It is helpful in considering virtues to consider the vices that oppose them. The vice that opposes diligence is sloth. The book of Proverbs often contrasts these two qualities. For example, Proverbs 12:24 states, "The hand of the diligent shall bear rule: but the slothful shall be under tribute" (KJV). Sloth is often used interchangeably with laziness, but the early monastics offered keener insight into this vice. The Greek word for sloth, *acedia*, means "without care," what we would refer to today as "careless" or "apathetic." When we think about apathy or carelessness within the context of cultural engagement, two ways of exhibiting this vice are worth reflecting on. The most obvious understanding pertains to the sort of apathy associated with paying too little or no attention to an issue. But a less obvious as well as more sinister and pervasive form of *acedia* is along the lines of carelessness. Carelessness is not so much a lack of attention as much as it is a lack of sufficient attention. When we do something carelessly, the problem is not that we do not do the thing at all; it is rather that we do not do it well. In fact, this is why the chronic busy-ness that characterizes most days for many of us—the multitasking, the frenetic pace, the running to-and-fro that define life

---

7. Andreas J. Köstenberger, *Excellence: The Character of God and the Pursuit of Scholarly Virtues* (Wheaton, IL: Crossway, 2011), 95.

in the modern age—is, strangely enough, a manifestation of the vice of *acedia*. Nowhere is this vice more evident in cultural engagement than in our tendency to assume or adopt an opinion without diligent research and understanding. Less harmful, perhaps, but even more common is the practice of carelessly sharing an article on social media without reading it or vetting the source, something most of us are guilty of from time to time. It probably is safe to say that the "fake news" phenomenon is due almost entirely to a lack in the virtue of diligence.

No one can be an expert in everything. But we can choose to be more knowledgeable about some of the issues that most define and vex the current culture. To practice the virtue of diligence requires that we approach issues we choose to engage with the care and attention due them—and to refrain from ironclad pronouncements when that care and attention reveal our need for another virtue: humility.

Christian tradition has long held that pride is the root of all sin. Humility, the opposite of pride, therefore, is traditionally seen as the first virtue. At its core, humility is an accurate assessment of oneself and correspondingly, in cultural engagement, one's opinions and views as well as one's expertise (or lack thereof).[8] Assessment of humility first takes its measure of us as finite human beings in relation to the all-knowing God. Humility requires that our views concerning timeless issues and controversies of the day are to be measured by the enduring principles of God's unchanging Word.

We further gain humility when we measure ourselves—and the perspective of our times—against history and all the wise men and women who lived before us, whether decades, centuries, or millennia ago. Studying both the wisdom and the errors of the past is inherently an act of humility. We can, in so doing, see just how much philosophical and theological groundwork has been laid, making our own modern ponderings seem like tiny tips on massive intellectual icebergs built up over human history. Yet no era exists that doesn't feature some great moral blind spot (or a few spots), prompting the most honest question we can ask: Not "How could they not see?" But "What are we not seeing today?" Andreas Köstenberger observes, "Without humility, you will be blind to your own weaknesses, unaware of the obvious holes in your argument, and unable to be corrected by others. Humility allows a [person] to truly learn through submission to the evidence and correction by the insights of others."[9]

The Bible has a great deal to say about humility and about the pride that obstructs it. Over and over, the Bible tells us that God looks with favor upon the

---

8. For more on this topic, see Tom Nichols, *The Death of Expertise: The Campaign Against Established Knowledge and Why It Matters* (Oxford: Oxford University Press, 2017).

9. Ibid., 207.

humble. How we approach engaging culture generally, or engaging on specific issues, Christians must do so with a spirit of humility if we desire God's favor. God does not need us to be right as much as we need him to be pleased with us.

Integrity—generally defined as purity or wholeness—is a virtue that takes two distinct but not unrelated forms: moral and intellectual. Moral integrity is concerned with the way one's practices accord with one's beliefs. Intellectual integrity centers on the pursuit of truth, broadly, and therefore with the ways in which particular facts, knowledge, and beliefs connect to larger truths.

Both the content and the form of the Christian's engagement with culture must be marked by moral and intellectual integrity. Sadly, those who profess to believe one way yet act another, showing their lack of moral integrity, are not hard to find. There also is no scarcity of Christians who lack intellectual integrity, hiding behind anonymous social media accounts while claiming to "defend truth" in interactions on social media that are anything but gracious or humble. Unwillingness to engage opposing arguments suggests that the foundation of one's own point of view is too unstable to withstand the slightest shake from opposition. In fact, this book was met with a few raised eyebrows—even strenuous objections—for including this or that point of view because such a view is so clearly *wrong*. But integrity in cultural engagement pertains to not only what one believes but also why one believes it, how one applies and advances that belief, and the willingness to engage confidently with opposing ideas.

Such integrity requires far more than knowledge. Reading a book such as this offers a breadth of knowledge on a range of issues as well as various perspectives on those issues. Such knowledge is good, for as Köstenberger reminds us, "Ignorance is not a virtue." He adds, "Neither is knowledge, however, unless it is applied and put to proper use." Wisdom is the "application of knowledge to real-life situations."[10] It is the "ability to discern or judge what is true, right, or lasting; insight."[11] One can read and understand all the essays in this book on a topic and ten times more in order to be armed with knowledge. However, to judge and apply all that knowledge requires wisdom. As noted above, humility leads us to recognize our strengths and limitations; wisdom compels us to act on that knowledge by pressing on or holding back, accordingly.

We all know people who are characterized by wisdom—and those who are not. It might even seem that wisdom is something that some people have by nature—and other people do not. While it may be true that some people have inherent qualities, including wisdom, that are part of their makeup, the field of

---

10. Köstenberger, *Excellence*, 178.
11. *The Free Dictionary*, s.v. "wisdom," accessed February 8, 2019, https://www.thefreedictionary.com/wisdom.

virtue ethics holds that virtues can be acquired through intentional and repeated practice. Wisdom might seem like the most difficult virtue to attain, but it is helpful to think about the constituent parts of wisdom. These qualities might include reflectiveness, experience, knowledge, deliberation, and temperance. All of these are behaviors that can be practiced and cultivated by each of us and will lead to greater wisdom.

Even so, while human wisdom can be cultivated through practice, godly wisdom comes from God, and it surpasses all human wisdom. "But the wisdom that comes from heaven is first of all pure; then peace-loving, considerate, submissive, full of mercy and good fruit, impartial and sincere" (James 3:17). James 1:5 exhorts us, "If any of you lacks wisdom, you should ask God, who gives generously to all without finding fault, and it will be given to you." When God told Solomon to ask of him whatever he wanted, Solomon chose wisdom. And because Solomon chose so wisely (not to mention humbly), God gave him that and more—both wealth and honor (1 Kings 3:4–13). We should do likewise. In engaging culture, the Christian is to seek not only human understanding but also the wisdom that is a gift from God.

In addition to the virtues of diligence, humility, integrity, and wisdom that are available through common grace to all human beings, and in addition to the godly wisdom that comes only from God, the Christian is called to manifest the fruit of the Spirit. This fruit is especially essential to effective engagement with the culture because human culture is defined by a spirit of worldliness, not the spirit of the Lord. Some Christians eschew serious listening and interaction with others because they see the danger for the believer in being influenced by the culture rather than influencing the culture is real and ever-present. While the editors of this book do not agree with the separatist mentality, it is foolish to ignore or downplay the danger the believer has of being overcome by the spirt of the world rather than that of Christ. Sadly, everywhere we look, we can see this worldly spirit in those who engage culture in the name of Christ. We might go so far as to say that to engage in a way characterized by a spirit of worldliness while invoking the name of Christ is to take the Lord's name in vain. The best check and measure against this worldly spirit is not, we would argue, sequestering ourselves from the world, but rather is being filled with the Spirit. If we do not demonstrate in our engagement with the world (or with fellow believers) love, joy, peace, forbearance, kindness, goodness, faithfulness, gentleness, and self-control (Gal. 5:22–23), then our efforts are for naught. And even if we adopt the right position or espouse the right view, if we have not love, we are but a "clanging cymbal" (1 Cor. 13:1).

In *A Theology of Reading: The Hermeneutics of Love*, Alan Jacobs points to a famous passage in Augustine's *On Christian Teaching* in which the church father says that an imprecise meaning drawn from Scripture is not a pernicious or deceptive error if it is aimed toward building up love. Jacobs argues that this hermeneutics of love applies not only to Scripture but also to other kinds of reading. He explains, "The universal applicability of Jesus' twofold commandment makes Augustine's charitable imperative just as relevant to the interpretation of epic poems or national constitutions as it is to the reading of Holy Scripture."[12] Jacobs argues that "only if we understand this love of God and neighbor as the first requirement in the reading of *any* text can we fulfill 'the law of love' in our thinking, our talking, and our manner of working."[13]

Ultimately, engaging in culture is nothing more—and nothing less—than seeking the truth in order to love with a godly love.

12. Alan Jacobs, *A Theology of Reading: Hermeneutics of Love* (New York: Routledge, 2001), 11.
13. Ibid., 12.

part two

CONTEMPORARY ISSUES

chapter four

SEXUALITY

The words of the Bible on sexuality are unchanging—even if interpretation of those words is debated. In contrast, views on sexuality throughout various cultures and across history differ widely. In one's own culture and time, it is easy to think of the biblical view, particularly in the current political climate, as starkly contrasting with the cultural view. But it's important to consider the ways in which cultural views about sexuality have shifted and changed over time.

Though same-sex relations is only one topic among many within the current controversies surrounding issues of sex and gender, it serves as a fitting gateway to the articles in this section. For in the case of same-sex intercourse, we can't think simply in terms of "the biblical view" vs. "the cultural view" since the views within and across cultures vary quite dramatically.

Because debates about same-sex intercourse are so prominent today in both the church and the culture, it may seem surprising that the Bible explicitly addresses the subject only a few times in the Old and New Testaments. Some theologians, such as New Testament scholar Richard B. Hays, suggest the infrequency of the Bible's mention of the subject implies the topic is "a minor concern" in terms of biblical emphasis.[1] But this is likely because the male-female sexual bond as the source of image-bearing fruitfulness and as a type of the union of Christ and his church is woven throughout the scriptural narrative from Genesis to Revelation. This norm is assumed, and it is against this understanding that mention of counter practices occurs.

The Old Testament passages that address the topic include the story of Sodom and Gomorrah from Genesis 19. The men of the city of Sodom come to Lot's house, demanding that Lot give them his two visitors—angels who appear to be men—to have sexual relations with them. God destroys the city for its sin, which later in Ezekiel 16:49 is identified not as same-sex intercourse but pride, excess, and ease, as well as failure to assist the poor and needy. This story has

---

1. Richard Hays, *The Moral Vision of the New Testament: Community, Cross, New Creation: A Contemporary Introduction to New Testament Ethics* (New York: HarperCollins, 1996), 381.

been cited throughout church history, however, as a key passage in denouncing same-sex intercourse.

Levitical law is much more explicit than the story of Sodom and Gomorrah in condemning male sex with another male. Leviticus 18:22 and 21:13 prohibit a male lying with another male "as with a woman" and pronounce such behavior to be "an abomination." According to Hays, this "unambiguous legal prohibition stands as the foundation for the subsequent universal rejection of male same-sex intercourse within Judaism."[2]

In the New Testament, the most detailed and explicit condemnation of same-sex intercourse (both male and female) is found in Romans 1:18–32. This passage points to the transformative power of the gospel, contrasting this power to behaviors that manifest rebellion against God in refusal to acknowledge him. Such behaviors, which include homosexual behavior, are presented essentially as idolatry. According to this account, the consequences for such rebels is that God "gave them up" to their own lusts and passions, among which are numbered same-sex erotic acts.[3]

In 1 Corinthians 6:9–11, Paul offers a list of "wrongdoers" who "will not inherit the kingdom of God." Among these is a word often, but not always, interpreted as "homosexual." The problem in translation is that the categories for identifying a person according to sexual behavior or "orientation" did not then exist, as we will see below. Similar problems of translation exist in 1 Timothy 1:10 and Acts 15:28–29, although these passages are usually understood to include same-sex intercourse among those actions Scripture counts as disobedient, lawless, and contrary to the sound teaching of the gospel.

Regardless of any problems in translation, the Levitical laws make God's views of same-sex intercourse clear, and the creation account of Genesis provides a picture of the inherent complementarity of the sexual union.

While the male-female norm is central within the world of Scripture, knowledge of some of the surrounding culture makes clearer why any mention of same-sex intercourse at all was required in the biblical texts.

In the surrounding pagan cultures, same-sex intercourse (although not personal identification with homosexual practice) was often the norm. Many depictions and affirmations of same-sex erotic acts in art and literature from the ancient Greco-Roman world give a clear picture of their views. Plato, for example, in *Symposium* drew approving parallels between the art of conversation and the art of pursuing a boy sexually.[4] Within classical Greece and Rome,

---

2. Ibid.
3. Ibid., 383–87.
4. W. L. Bryan & C. L. Bryan, eds., *Plato the Teacher: Being Selections from the Apology, Euthydemus, Protagoras, Symposium, Phaedrus, Republic, and Phaedo of Plato* (New York: Scribner's, 1897), 129–31.

marital sex between a man and woman served primarily in the production of lawful heirs; sex between men—particularly an older male with a youth—was considered not only normal and healthy, but ideal, lauded in art, literature, and philosophy.

The categories of behavior (and corresponding moral judgments) within the ancient Greco-Roman world related not to homosexual or heterosexual acts, but to participants' active or passive roles. A vast vocabulary of Latin terms associated with various sexual practices, mostly gay, reveals very different categories for sexual behavior than those in either the Judeo-Christian world or the modern one. Roles in the sex act were expressions of conquest and power (or lack thereof), not morality or righteousness as in the biblical understanding. The approval of same-sex intercourse in this world was derived from a basis radically different from approval given in our society today.

Even in the Middle Ages, when the term "sodomite" was used to describe a person who engaged in same-sex intercourse, the term did not apply to a category of desire or attraction, but only to certain behavior, whether between persons of the same or opposite sex.[5] The categories of "homosexual" and "heterosexual" that are assumed today, in fact, did not emerge until the nineteenth century when they were developed from the newly emerging discipline of psychology. The development of these terms at this time reflected a modern epistemological shift, one increasingly rooted in science and one that sought medical and biological accounts of all human behavior.

However, such neat binary categories came to be rejected by postmodern theorists. Michel Foucault, for example, pointed to the constructedness of categories such as "homosexual" and "heterosexual," noting the inability of such categories to account for the wide range of sexual attraction, behavior, and identity throughout human history.[6] Social constructionists argue that there "is no given mode of sexuality that is independent of culture; even the concept and experience of sexual orientation itself are products of history."[7]

This jettisoning of rigid categories and the shift away from biological explanations in favor of felt experience and self-identification have brought the issues of gender identity, transgenderism, and even gender neutrality into any current day discussions that counter the traditional view now labeled as "heteronormativity."

With increased visibility and acceptance of gay and lesbian persons and

---

5. "Homosexuality," *Stanford Encyclopedia of Philosophy*, last modified July 5, 2015, http://plato.stanford .edu/entries/homosexuality/.

6. See Michel Foucault, *The History of Sexuality*, trans. Richard Hurley (New York: Random House, 1985).

7. "Homosexuality," *Stanford Encyclopedia of Philosophy*.

same-sex unions within the wider culture, the church's engagement with the issue has undergone fairly rapid shifts, whether dramatic or subtle, in the way Christians talk about and approach sexual minorities. Thus, just as occurred in ancient Greece and Rome, as well as in the Middle Ages and the nineteenth century, new vocabularies have been developed for dealing with these issues, including within the church.

Congregations and individual believers who fully embrace homosexual desire and behavior as acceptable to God call themselves "welcoming" or "affirming." The terms "Side A" and "Side B" further nuance the debate, with Side A expressing the view that God blesses same-sex desire and same-sex unions, and "Side B" expressing the view that gay Christians are called to lifelong celibacy. Other Christians would reject both Side A and Side B in arguing that same-sex desire itself is sinful and cannot be affirmed or part of one's identity as a believer—even within the context of celibacy.

From even this cursory review, it's clear that cultural attitudes and understanding of sexual identity, behavior, and practice have changed dramatically over time and likely will continue to do so. The Christian, however, is able to stand securely on the biblical vision for sexuality to critically engage changing understandings.

In the opening essay of this section, Todd Wilson connects the argument that sexuality is binary back to the first chapter of Scripture, the consensus of the church throughout history, and the image of God as revealed in creation. This is followed by an essay by Robert Gagnon, which offers an exegetical case for the biblical support for the male-female relationship as a necessary biblical prerequisite for marriage. Rosaria Butterfield's essay provides her first-hand account of how her conversion and faith transformed her life, ultimately leading her to walk away from her lesbian community and her career in order to follow Christ. Butterfield challenges us to rethink the way we love our LGBTQ neighbors and friends by ensuring that we share with them the full truth of the gospel. Michael Bird examines the cultural issues surrounding the gender debate, specifically considering the effects of the restrictive binary classification system that has governed the way we often discuss gender. Offering a sharp contrasting opinion from the other contributors, Matthew Vines urges Christians to reexamine the way we understand the controversy surrounding homosexual relationships, arguing that the interpretations that have shaped our understanding of this issue are not asking the right questions or framing the conversation within the monogamous, loving relationship between two same-sex individuals.

The closing two essays in this section address sexual dysphoria. Matthew Mason explains how the gospel speaks to issues surrounding gender dysphoria by reaffirming the inherent goodness of the created order and offering the promise of the restoration of all things. Finally, Mark Yarhouse and Julia Sadusky examine the issue of gender dysphoria from a psychological perspective, explaining the key terms, offering not only an examination of the significance of the issue in the field of psychology as well as an integrated approach for addressing the issue from a theological-psychological perspective.

MERE SEXUALITY

The Church's Historic Position

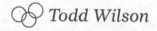 *Todd Wilson*

The Bible affirms that human beings are sexually differentiated, male and female, and this defines what marriage is and what sex is for. This vision of human sexuality is what I call "mere sexuality," a shorthand way to refer to the themes that have characterized the historic biblical vision of sexuality down through the ages. By calling this mere sexuality, I offer a nod to C. S. Lewis and his famous book with a similar-sounding title and want to say that this is what most Christians at most times in most places have believed about human sexuality—the historic consensus.

Does such a consensus exist? Yes, there is historic consensus about human sexuality that has been part of the church in each of its major expressions— Orthodox, Catholic, and Protestant. It's been around for centuries, from roughly the fourth to the middle of the twentieth century. And it has only seriously been called into question within the last forty to fifty years, with the liberalization of Christian sexual ethics in the foment of the 1960s sexual revolution.

This does not mean that there has been complete unanimity on every issue in the Christian tradition. There has been real diversity and even some divergence within the church. Yet despite these disagreements, the consensus I call mere sexuality has been surprisingly robust through the centuries, and we can identify its basic contours. They include a number of interrelated beliefs and convictions, but at the heart of mere sexuality, and the church's historic teaching on human sexuality, is the belief that sexual difference, being male or female, is both theologically and morally significant—it matters to God and it ought to matter to us.[1]

---

1. In his carefully researched book on the significance of sexual difference for the moral theology of marriage, *Creation & Covenant*, Christopher C. Roberts shows that for centuries there has been a Christian consensus on sexuality. He explains, "After an initial patristic period in which Christian beliefs about sexual difference were fluctuating and diverse, a more or less rough consensus on sexual difference existed from the

On the first page of the Bible we read that "male and female [God] created them" (Gen. 1:27). Immediately, then, we're confronted with both the canonical and theological priority of sexual difference in Christian thinking. It is essential to who we are, not accidental or peripheral, flexible or negotiable. Sexual difference is part of our nature as creatures. It is not something we create, like iPhones or automobiles. God has woven sexual difference into the fabric of creation. And because of this, our being male and female is integral to our calling as image-bearers, not least in that most basic of all human communities—the one known as marriage. As a result, we can't ignore or minimize the fact of our being either male or female without undermining our ability to flourish and find fulfillment.

And since our sexual difference is core to who we are, it will not be eradicated at the resurrection but persist for eternity, though in a fully glorified expression. Our resurrection bodies will be sexed bodies, just as Jesus' risen body is a sexed body. He is, and always will be, a crucified, circumcised Jewish male.

These are the basic contours of what has been a time-honored and widespread Christian consensus on sexual difference, with implications that touch virtually every dimension of our lives. This is what I'm calling mere sexuality, what most Christians at most times in most places have believed about human sexuality.

The Bible says having sexed bodies is essential to our identity, not optional. It's a gift we receive, not a choice we make. Or as Rosaria Butterfield says, "Christians are gender and sexuality essentialists."[2] But the Bible also says that our identity isn't reducible to one aspect of our sexuality, not even our sexual desires or attractions.

Contrast this with our culture's messaging which tells us that we are who we desire sexually—turning sexual desire into an idol that has power to name us in a way that should be left to God. The Bible connects our identity to what is called the *imago Dei*, or the image of God.[3] We find this expression in Genesis 1:26–27: "Then God said, 'Let us make mankind in our image, in our likeness, so that they may rule over the fish in the sea and the birds in the sky, over the livestock and all the wild animals, and over all the creatures that move along the ground.' So God created mankind in his own image, in the image of God he created them; male and female he created them."

fourth to the twentieth centuries" (pp. 185–86). He summarizes, "There is an ancient Christian tradition, from Augustine to John Paul II, which has believed and argued that sexual difference is significant" (p. 236).

2. Rosaria Butterfield, *Openness Unhindered: Further Thoughts of an Unlikely Convert on Sexual Identity and Union with Christ* (Pittsburgh: Crown & Covenant, 2015), 6. See also chapters 4–5 where she describes the nineteenth-century advent of the notion of "sexual orientation" and with it the transformation of personal identity.

3. Scholarly discussion of the image of God is vast. But for a helpful assessment, see John F. Kilner, *Dignity and Destiny: Humanity in the Image of God* (Grand Rapids: Eerdmans, 2015).

This is the first chapter of the Bible, and it is foundational to all the rest—not least our understanding of God and ourselves. On the sixth day God creates human beings, his culminating act of creation. In verse 26, God speaks in the first person, as though he's more heavily invested in the creation of humans than, say, grasshoppers or walruses or even supernovas. Then, in the next verse, God's clearly stated intention is given: "male and female he created them." This statement is grammatically parallel with being created in the image of God in the first two parts of the verse. What is the significance of this? It means that being male and female is essential to being created in God's own image.

Marriage, then, is a one-flesh union built on the sexual complementarity of male and female—a uniting of heart, mind, and body. This classic and historic Christian view of marriage has been the dominant view of marriage in Western culture—until recently.

We find this view of marriage in the opening pages of the Bible where we read these words: "That is why a man leaves his father and mother and is united to his wife, and they become one flesh" (Gen. 2:24). Notice that phrase "one flesh." According to the biblical and historic Christian view, marriage is a one-flesh union. It's not just an emotional bond or a relational connection you feel with someone. Rather, it's a specific kind of union—a one-flesh union. It is a union of heart, mind, spirit, and body.[4] I like the way author Kevin DeYoung puts it, "The ish [man] and the ishah [woman] can become one flesh because theirs is not just a sexual union but a reunion, the bringing together of two differentiated beings, with one made from and both made for the other."[5]

That's why Scripture refers to marriage as a "one-flesh" union, not a one heart or one spirit or one soul union. The uniting of bodies, of flesh, is essential, not optional. The language of "one flesh" is meant to be a very specific concrete reference to your flesh, your physical body. But, frankly, we should be even more specific. The one-flesh union here is not just a uniting of bodies in some general way, like exchanging hugs or holding hands. It refers to a coming together of two bodies in a very specific way. The old-fashioned term for this coming together is coitus, the less old-fashioned term is intercourse, and today we just call it sex. It's what church tradition and common law have for centuries seen as the consummation of the marriage. Men and women have one and only one bodily organ that has been specifically designed for a complement, and when these two organs—the male

4. While the primary emphasis of the phrase "one flesh" in Genesis 2:24 may not be sexual but familial (or as affirming scholar James Brownson says, "a lifelong kinship bond" [James V. Brownson, *Bible, Gender, Sexuality* (Grand Rapids: Eerdmans, 2013), 85–109]), I remain convinced that it does include a reference to the male-female sexual encounter, especially in light of the theme of nakedness and shamelessness in Genesis 2:25.
5. Kevin DeYoung, *What Does the Bible Really Teach about Homosexuality?* (Wheaton, IL: Crossway, 2015), 28.

and female sexual organs—come together to perform one unified and unifying act, they form a one-flesh union quite literally, physically, indeed even biologically.

This is a one-flesh union, a complete and total uniting of lives, and we have for centuries called this comprehensive union marriage. And within this view of marriage, sex is intended to unite two lives and create new life. Sex has both a unitive and procreative purpose.

But controversial implications follow from this. Put positively, all sexual activity ought to express and embody the one-flesh union we call marriage, for this is the God-given purpose of sex. Put negatively, any form of sexual activity that fails to express or embody a one-flesh union is out of step with the teaching of Scripture and outside of the will of God.

According to the Bible and the nearly unanimous consensus of the church—what I call "mere sexuality"—God says Yes! to the sexual difference of male and female, Yes! to the uniting of lives to form a one-flesh union called marriage, and Yes! to enjoying the unitive and procreative powers of sex—a divine hearty Yes! to it all. There's nothing wrong or sinful or disordered about any of this, and there's everything right and good and glorious about all of it.

But with this Yes! comes an equally resolute No! Because, according to the Bible and the nearly unanimous consensus of the Christian church, God says No! to any and every form of sexual activity outside of this one-flesh union called marriage. And let me hasten to add, God says No! irrespective of the sex of the people involved, whether same sex or opposite sex.

The Bible is clear, as has been the centuries-old teaching of the Christian church, that same-sex sexual activity is out of step with God's will for human beings. But the church has held this position not because it hates same-sex sexual activity, but because this is sexual activity outside of the one-flesh union of marriage. Biblically speaking, the sex of the two people engaging in the sexual act isn't the main issue. The main problem with same-sex activity is that it happens outside of the legitimate one-flesh union designed exclusively for the covenant of marriage. Simply put, sexual activity is inappropriate for anyone—male or female, same-sex or opposite-sex attracted—outside of the context of a one-flesh union we call marriage.

Todd Wilson (PhD, Cambridge University) is the president of the Center for Pastor Theologians, a ministry dedicated to helping pastors provide theological leadership to their churches. Todd has served as a pastor for fifteen years, the last decade as the senior pastor of Calvary Memorial Church in Oak Park, Illinois. He is the author and editor of more than a dozen books, including *Mere Sexuality* and *Galatians: Gospel-Rooted Living*.

AN EXEGETICAL CASE FOR TRADITIONAL MARRIAGE

✺ *Robert A. J. Gagnon*

A male-female prerequisite for marriage—and thus an opposition to all homosexual practice—can rightly be called a core value in biblical sexual ethics since it is a value held throughout Scripture.

A significant body of biblical texts speak specifically to homosexual practice.[1] Three sets of texts in particular can be singled out. First, there are the absolute prohibitions of sexual intercourse between a man and another male (whether a minor or adult) in Leviticus 18:22 and 20:13, alongside prohibitions of bestiality, incest, and adultery as capital offenses.[2] Second, Paul in 1 Corinthians 6:9 includes in his vice list of people who are self-deceived if they think that they will inherit God's kingdom both "soft men" (*malakoi*; i.e., men who feminize

---

1. For more information on the Bible and same-sex unions, see my 500-page book *The Bible and Homosexual Practice: Texts and Hermeneutics* (Nashville: Abingdon, 2001); my 50-page essay in *Homosexuality and the Bible: Two Views* (Minneapolis: Fortress, 2003), coauthored with Dan O. Via; my 150-page article "The Scriptural Case for a Male-Female Prerequisite for Sexual Relations: A Critique of the Arguments of Two Adventist Scholars," *Homosexuality, Marriage, and the Church: Biblical, Counseling, and Religious Liberty Issues*, ed. R. E. Gane, N. P. Miller, and H. P. Swanson (Berrien Springs, MI: Andrews University Press, 2012), 53–161; and my 110-page article "Why the Disagreement Over the Biblical Witness on Homosexual Practice? A Response to David G. Myers and Letha Dawson Scanzoni, *What God Has Joined Together? Reformed Review* 59.1 (Autumn 2005): 19–130, http://www.robgagnon.net/articles/ReformedReviewArticleWhyTheDisagreement. pdf]. See also articles at www.robgagnon.net, including "Is Homosexual Practice No Worse Than Any Other Sin?" and http://robgagnon.net/articles/homosexAreAllSinsEqual.pdf.

2. Sex with a menstruant is also mentioned (Lev. 20:18), but chapter 20 lists it as a second-tier offense along with incest other than between parent and child. There are a number of indicators in the literary context that show clearly that the sex laws in Leviticus 18 and 20 are dealing with moral offenses, not merely ritual infractions: (1) The forbidden sex acts in Leviticus 18 are specifically designated as "iniquity," or "sin," not just ritual uncleanness (18:25 KJV). (2) As one would expect of moral offenses, these sex laws do not permit absolution (viz., cleansing from defilement) merely through ritual acts like bathing. (3) Like the other sex offenses in Leviticus 18 and 20. (Except for the outlier case of sex with a menstruant, the sexual offenses treated in Leviticus 18 and 20 do not make the participants contagious to touch.) Unless otherwise noted, Bible translations are the author's own. (4) The sex laws in Leviticus 18 and 20 do not penalize persons who act without willful intent (note the culpability formula in ch. 20: "their blood will be on their own heads"). (5) An implicit rationale is given for each prohibition, showing that an unreasonable phobia is not in view. (6) The sex laws in Leviticus 18 and 20 are applied not just to Jews but to resident aliens (gentiles) as well.

themselves to attract male sex partners) and "men who have sex with men" (*arsenokoitai*; so also 1 Timothy 1:10).[3] Third, in arguably the most important of direct texts, Paul offered an unqualified description of homosexual practice in Romans 1:24–27 as an act "contrary to nature," in which both parties are "dishonored among themselves" and commit gross "indecency" by suppressing knowledge of the "natural use" (bodily design) of the other sex, ordained by the Creator and obvious to rational beings. To these can be added various other texts that less directly address homosexual practice.[4]

Various arguments have been unsuccessfully used to vitiate the force of these texts, including the following claims: that the Greco-Roman world was unaware that "the parts fit" male-to-female,[5] that committed homosexual relationships existed,[6] or that any forms of homosexual attraction might be traceable to biological factors.[7] Also untenable is the claim that opposition to homosexual practice in the ancient world was always predicated on misogyny: Because women were

---

3. This is a formulated in Jewish and Christian circles from Levitical prohibitions of same-sex male intercourse, using the term for "male" (*arsēn*) and "lying" (*koitē*) found therein. We know that first-century Jews like Josephus and Philo understood Leviticus 18:22 and 20:13 to apply to all sexual intercourse between males, whether committed or promiscuous and exploitative. On the terms *arsenokoitai* and *malakoi*, see *The Bible and Homosexual Practice*, 303–30.

4. Chief among these is a triplicate of narratives illustrating cataclysmic divine judgment for attempted or completed rape of males by males: Ham's act against Noah (Gen. 9:20–27), the sins of Sodom (Gen. 19:4–11), and the Levite at Gibeah (Judg. 19:22–25). Given the coercion involved, these are not ideal stories for indicting committing homosexual relationships. Yet neither are they irrelevant. The effect of each story is somewhat like telling a story about an incestuous rape: Understood contextually, such a story could not be viewed as an indictment of only coercive forms of incest. Rather, it must be treated as a multiple-offense story implicating both incest and homosexual practice. The same applies to the story about the offense at Sodom. In its literary context, history of interpretation (especially Ezek. 16:50; Jude 7; 2 Peter 2:6–10), and historical context in the ancient Near East, the story must be viewed as a multiple-offense narrative indicting both rape and sex between males. See further: "Why We Know That the Story of Sodom Indicts Homosexual Practice Per Se," http://robgagnon.net/articles/homosex7thDayAdvArticleSodom.pdf); *The Bible and Homosexual Practice*, 63–100. Another set of relevant passages are the series of texts that show scorn for men involved in homosexual cult prostitution (Deut. 23:17–18; 1 Kings 14:21–24; 15:12–14; 22:46; 2 Kings 23:7; Job 36:14; compare also Rev. 21:8; 22:15). Although their connection of homosexual practice with idolatry complicates their application today, such figures in the context of the ancient Near East were primarily criticized for their attempt to erase masculinity and serve as the passive partners in homosexual intercourse (*Bible and Homosexual Practice*, 100–110).

5. For example, the second-century physician Soranus referred to *molles*, "soft men" eager for penetration (i.e., the Latin equivalent for the Greek term *malakoi* in 1 Cor. 6:9), as those who "subjugated to obscene uses parts not so intended" and disregarded "the places of our body which divine providence destined for definite functions" (*On Chronic Diseases* 4.9.131). According to Thomas K. Hubbard, a classicist at the University of Texas (Austin), who has written the premiere sourcebook of texts on homosexuality in ancient Greece and Rome: "Basic to the heterosexual position [against homosexual practice in the first few centuries C.E.] is the characteristic Stoic appeal to the providence of Nature, which has matched and fitted the sexes to each other" (*Homosexuality in Greece and Rome: A Sourcebook of Basic Documents* [Berkeley: University of California Press, 2003], 444).

6. "A Book Not to Be Embraced: A critical appraisal of Stacy Johnson's *A Time to Embrace*," *Scottish Journal of Theology* 62, no. 1 (2009): 62–80 (part 3, http://robgagnon.net/articles/homosexStacyJohnsonSJT2.pdf); see also *The Bible and Homosexual Practice*, 347–61.

7. "Does the Bible Regard Same-Sex Intercourse as Intrinsically Sinful?" in *Christian Sexuality: Normative and Pastoral Principles*, ed. R. E. Saltzman (Minneapolis: Kirk House, 2003), 106–55,

seen as inferior to men, women should play only the passive-receptive role in intercourse and men only the active-penetrative role.[8] Often overlooked is the fact that Paul's rejection of homosexual practice partly echoes God's design at creation in Genesis 1:27 and 2:24.

It would be a mistake to argue that the limited number of texts that speak directly to homosexual practice indicate the Bible's relative disinterest in the topic. For one thing, infrequency of mention when it comes to sexual offenses can be a sign of the gravity of the offense (compare the comparable attention to incest and the rare mention of bestiality). For another, it is more accurate to say that the entire Bible is invested in a male-female foundation for sexual ethics, which is the affirmative flip side of prohibiting homosexual relationships.

Thus, every text in Scripture treating sexual matters (whether narrative, law, proverb, poetry, moral exhortation, or metaphor) always presupposes a male-female prerequisite for all sexual activity.

In general, we find a principle in Scripture that the more severe an offense, the earlier any loopholes are closed off. For example, men were given a pass on monogamy in ancient Israel, entitled to marry more than one wife concurrently (polygamy). Not until the New Testament is this license closed off. Loopholes that existed for close-kin marriages among Israel's patriarchs were closed off earlier than polygamy: already forbidden by the time of Levitical incest law (Lev. 18; 20). That suggests that incest is a more severe sexual offense than polygamy. The fact that Scripture never had to close off a loophole in the prohibition of homosexual practice is a testament to the fact that homosexual practice is the most severe intra-human, consensual sexual offense. It violates the very foundation of sexual ethics established in Genesis 1–2.

The most important texts in the Bible speaking to the issue of homosexual practice are those that address it indirectly in the broader context of a creation mandate. First among these is Jesus' interpretation of marriage in Mark 10:2–12 (with a parallel in Matt. 19:3–12). Because Christians confess Jesus as Lord, it is harder even for liberal Christians to dismiss Jesus' perspective by claiming that he either misunderstood the nature of marriage or lacked sufficient knowledge. Since Jesus here makes explicit appeal to Genesis 1:27 and 2:24, these two creation texts are the next most important texts.

---

specifically 140–52 (also online: http://robgagnon.net/articles/ChristianSexualityArticle2003.pdf). As Hubbard notes, "Homosexuality in this era [i.e., of the early imperial age of Rome] may have ceased to be merely another practice of personal pleasure and began to be viewed as an essential and central category of personal identity, exclusive of and antithetical to heterosexual orientation" (*Homosexuality in Greece and Rome*, 386).

8. "The Scriptural Case for a Male-Female Prerequisite for Sexual Relations," 127–29.

⚭ Jesus on Marriage

Many proponents of same-sex sexual unions look at Jesus' remarks on marriage and assert that they have nothing to do with homosexual practice, but address only the question of divorce and remarriage. In fact, while Jesus did not speak directly to the issue of homosexual practice,[9] he did predicate a prohibition of taking a new wife while the first one was still alive on a vision for marriage that presumes the necessity of a male-female foundation. For Jesus, the central texts in his Bible (Old Testament) outlining this vision were found in Genesis 1:27c ("male and female [God] created them") and Genesis 2:24 ("That is why a man . . . is united to his wife [woman] and they [or the two] become one flesh").

To understand the relevance of Jesus' remarks for homosexual practice, it is crucial to understand that Jesus' prohibition of remarriage after (invalid) divorce has implications for prohibiting polygamy as well.[10] Indeed, if Jesus categorizes as adultery a man taking a second wife after he has divorced the first, then taking a second wife while still married to the first is all the more an instance of adultery. In effect, remarriage after divorce is a serial version of concurrent polygamy: Instead of having two or more spouses simultaneously, one divorces a spouse before marrying another. The question before us is this: What was the moral logic of Jesus' position that having a second wife while the first is still alive constitutes adultery? Furthermore, what does this tell us about Jesus' view of homosexual practice?

New Testament scholar James Brownson, who has written an influential work promoting committed homosexual unions,[11] admits that Jesus' words do not serve only the purpose of prohibiting divorce and remarriage after divorce. Rather, they "presuppose that a man may not be married to more than one woman at the same time (polygyny)." Yet he insists that the "moral logic" under-pinning Jesus' citation of the "one flesh" union of Genesis 2:24 has nothing to do with the fact that man and woman are complementary sexes. It has nothing to do with an alleged image derived from Genesis 2:21–24 of male and female reuniting (woman being formed from the original human) and restoring their original "one flesh" unity. Rather, he contends, the "moral logic" behind Jesus' prohibition of remarriage after divorce concerns only the establishment of "one kinship group."[12] For Brownson the phrase "they become one flesh" in Genesis

---

9. There was no need for him to do so. No Jew in Jesus' day was advocating for homosexual relations, much less known to be engaging in such, and the Jewish Scriptures were clear on the issue.

10. In ancient Israel, the only acceptable form of polygamy was polygyny (multiple wives). Women were never allowed multiple concurrent husbands (polyandry).

11. James V. Brownson, *Bible, Gender, Sexuality* (Grand Rapids: Eerdmans, 2013).

12. Ibid., 32–33, 86, 88, 97.

2:24 means only that two people of any sex become kin, which in turn encourages a permanent union.

However, there is a big problem in Brownson's interpretation of Jesus' moral logic. One cannot arrive at a limitation of two persons to a sexual union by referring to "one kinship group" because kinship bonds can be of any number. Brownson is making a "not this . . . but that" out of a "both . . . and." I'm not saying that the phrase "become one flesh" does not refer to the establishment of legal kinship across bloodlines. It does. Yet it refers to something more. "One flesh" refers also to gender complementarity. Both complementarity and kinship are involved in the phrase "one flesh." Only in this way can Jesus arrive at a limitation of two persons to a sexual union.

It is not hard to discern Jesus' moral logic behind his claim that two and only two persons are allowable in a sexual union. The only thing in common between the short clause in Genesis 1:27c and the whole of Genesis 2:24 is the theme of two sexes: "male and female," "man" and "his wife [woman]." For Jesus, the God-ordained binary sexuality among humans was the basis for limiting the number of persons in a sexual union to two. Once the two sexual halves of the sexual spectrum are joined into a single sexual whole, a third partner (or more) is neither necessary nor desirable. In short, the twoness of the sexes is the foundation for the twoness of the sexual bond. A duality of sexes leads logically to a union consisting of two—one from each sex.

Clearly Jesus construes the phrase "male and female" not merely as a reference to everyone but as a distinct sexual unit or complementary sexual pair required for legitimate marriage. This is consistent with the fact that the precise expression "male and female" (*zakar uneqeba*), confined elsewhere in the Old Testament to Genesis 5–7, never means merely "all humans" but rather always denotes a sexual pair (Gen. 5:2; 6:19; 7:3, 9, 16; cf. Gen. 1:27–28). Only when "male and female" is understood as a self-contained, exclusive sexual pair does it provide a rational basis for limiting sexual unions to two persons. By implication, eliminating any relevance to the sexual binary logically eliminates a marital binary and opens the door to polyamory (more than one romantic relationship).

A Closer Look at Genesis 2:21–24

Jesus' understanding of "one flesh" in Genesis 2:24 as denoting not just kinship but also binary complementarity is consistent with the literary context for that verse. Genesis 2:21–23 stresses *four times* that God formed woman by *taking from* the human (*'adam*) a part of him. Man and woman are clearly being viewed as the two complementary parts of an original sexual whole. The image of two sexes coming from one flesh grounds the principle of two sexes becoming "one flesh." No one denies that the text also points to the similarity of woman as a fellow human being, in contrast to the animals who were not suitable "helpers" (2:18–20). Yet the fact that a new being is constructed out of material from the first human *that the latter no longer has* is also an obvious indicator of difference. The missing element is regained in the encounter with the woman built from what was removed.

Brownson alludes to the kinship formulas—"You are my own flesh and blood" and "I am your flesh and blood" (Gen. 29:14; Judg. 9:2; 2 Sam. 5:1; 19:11–12; 1 Chron. 11:1)—asserting that "there is not a hint of any notion of complementarity" in this phrase.[13] Yet he ignores both the very different context of Genesis 2:23a (union with an extraction, not an extension through reproduction), a difference confirmed by the unique wording, ". . . bone of [taken *from*] my bones and flesh of [taken *from*] my flesh." The fact that the precise expression "one flesh' does not appear anywhere else in the Old Testament or in subsequent Jewish literature in antiquity apart from a reference to marriage in Genesis 2:24 makes it unlikely to have been an expression for denoting covenant bonds outside of man-woman marriage. Moreover, the human immediately follows the statement of sameness in 2:23a with a statement of difference: "she shall be called *'ish-shah* [woman] for she was taken out of *'ish* [man]" (2:23b). The similar sounding names in Hebrew indicate as much difference within sameness as do the English terms "*wo*man" and "man."

Had the biblical author wanted to stress sameness alone and not male-female difference, he could have constructed the narrative to read that the woman too was created directly out of "dust from the ground (*'adamah*)." In the traditional Mesopotamian story of the creation of humanity we find something like that. In *Atra-hasis* seven human males and seven human females are formed separately from a mixture of clay and the flesh/blood of a slaughtered god. Both males and females are created in the same way and from the same material. Woman is not molded from material extracted from man, and so there is nothing missing from man.[14] A number of texts from early Judaism alluding to woman's creation from the "side" or "rib" of the first human highlight the woman *qua* woman as the missing element to man so far as sexuality is concerned (4 Macc. 18:7; *Apoc. Moses* 29:9–10; 42:2–3).

When Genesis 2:18 and 20 refer to God making for the first human a "helper," a term is added that can connote difference within similarity: *kenegdo*.[15]

---

13. Ibid., 30.
14. W. G. Lambert and A. R. Millard, *Atra-hasis: The Babylonian Story of the Flood* (Oxford: Oxford University Press, 1969), 54–65, Tablet I lines 189–305; also G ii 1–18; S iii 1–21. Cf. Bernard F. Batto, "The Institution of Marriage in Genesis 2 and in '*Atrahasis*,'" *Catholic Biblical Quarterly* 62 (2000): 621–31, esp. 628–30.
15. It consists of three elements: (1) a prefixed *ke-as*, *like*; (2) a substantive *neged* that everywhere else is a

Typical English translations of the phrase are "as one corresponding to [or suitable or fit for, suited to] him" or "his partner." An even better rendering given the context of the creation of a distinct but complementary sex, woman, is "his complement" (or "his counterpart" CSB).

Some Jews in early Judaism also depict the first woman not merely as the first human's "rib" but as his "side" in the sense of "half of the man's body."[16] There is good reason for understanding the Hebrew word *tsela'* as "side," indicating a more substantial extraction from the first human. Chief of these is the fact that all thirty-eight other occurrences of the word in the Old Testament mean "side" or something approximating it. Once it refers to the side of a hill (2 Sam. 16:13) and everywhere else the "side" of a piece of sacred architecture: the "side" of the ark, tabernacle, or incense altar (Exodus); or "sides" of various features of the Solomonic temple (1 Kings) or of the eschatological temple (Ezekiel). The implication is that the sexual bodies of man and woman in their interaction are sacred architecture (cf. 1 Cor. 6:19–20). Guarding the complementary design of man and woman matters. Homosexual practice represents a desecration of God's holy construction.

Robert A. J. Gagnon, PhD, has degrees from Dartmouth College (BA), Harvard Divinity School (M.T.S.), and Princeton Theological Seminary (PhD). He is a professor of theology at Houston Baptist University and the author of *The Bible and Homosexual Practice* and coauthor of *Homosexuality and the Bible: Two Views*.

---

preposition denoting a spatial *before, in the presence of,* often in the sense of situated *opposite*; and (3) a personal suffix *o, his.*

16. See Philo of Alexandria in his *Creation of the World,* 152; *Allegorical Interpretation,* 2.19–20; and *Questions and Answers on Genesis* 25; and an early rabbinic tradition recorded in *Genesis Rabbah,* 8:1; 14:7.

WHAT IT MEANS TO LOVE OUR LGBTQ NEIGHBORS

Rosaria Butterfield

If this were 1999—the year I was converted and walked away from the woman and lesbian community I loved—instead of 2018, a message about the holiness of LGBT relationships would have flooded into my world like a balm of Gilead. How amazing it would have been to have a Christian say out loud what my heart was shouting: "Yes, I can have Jesus and my girlfriend. Yes, I can flourish both in my tenured academic discipline (queer theory and English literature and culture) and in my church. My emotional vertigo could find normal once again."

Maybe I wouldn't need to lose everything to have Jesus. Maybe the gospel wouldn't ruin me while I waited, waited, waited for the Lord to build me back up after he convicted me of my sin, and I suffered the consequences. Maybe it would go differently for me than it did for Paul, Daniel, David, and Jeremiah. Maybe Jesus could save me without afflicting me. Maybe the Lord would give to me respectable crosses (Matt. 16:24). Manageable thorns (2 Cor. 12:7).

Today I hear the message of Christians who condone and support homosexual relationships—and a thin trickle of sweat creeps down my back. If I were still in the thick of the battle over the indwelling sin of lesbian desire, it is this message that would have put a millstone around my neck.

Died to a Life I Loved

To be clear, I was not converted out of homosexuality. I was converted out of unbelief. I didn't swap out a lifestyle. I died to a life I loved. Conversion to Christ made me face the question squarely: did my lesbianism reflect who I am (which is what I believed in 1999), or did my lesbianism distort who I am through the fall of Adam? I learned through conversion that when something feels right and good and real and necessary—but stands against God's Word—this reveals the

particular way Adam's sin marks my life. Our sin natures deceive us. Sin's decep-
tion isn't just "out there"; it's also deep in the caverns of our hearts.

How I feel does not tell me who I am. Only God can tell me who I am,
because he made me and takes care of me. He tells me that we are all born as male
and female image-bearers with souls that will last forever and gendered bodies that will either suffer eternally in hell or be glorified in the New Jerusalem.
Genesis 1:27 tells me that there are ethical consequences and boundaries to being
born male and female. When I say this previous sentence on college campuses—
even ones that claim to be Christian—the student protestors come out in the
dozens. I'm told that declaring the ethical responsibilities of being born male and
female is now hate speech.

Calling God's sexual ethic hate speech does Satan's bidding. This is Orwellian
nonsense or worse. I only know who I really am when the Bible becomes my lens
for self-reflection, and when the blood of Christ so powerfully pumps my heart
whole that I can deny myself, take up the cross, and follow him.

There is no goodwill between the cross and the unconverted person. The
cross is ruthless. To take up your cross means that you are going to die. As A. W.
Tozer has said, to carry a cross means you are walking away, and you are never
coming back. The cross symbolizes what it means to die to self. We die so that we
can be born again in and through Jesus by repenting of our sin (even the uncho-
sen ones) and putting our faith in Jesus, the author and finisher of our salvation.
The supernatural power that comes with being born again means that where I
once had a single desire—one that says if it feels good, it must be who I really
am—I now have twin desires that war within me: "For the flesh desires what is
contrary to the Spirit, and the Spirit what is contrary to the flesh. They are in
conflict with each other, so that you are not to do whatever you want" (Gal. 5:17).
And this war doesn't end until glory.

Victory over sin means we have Christ's company in the battle, not that we
are lobotomized. My choice sins know my name and address. And the same is
true for you.

A few years ago, I was speaking at a large church. An older woman waited
until the end of the evening and approached me. She told me that she was
seventy-five years old, that she had been married to a woman for fifty years, and
that she and her partner had children and grandchildren. Then she said something chilling. In a hushed voice, she whispered, "I have heard the gospel, and I
understand that I may lose everything. Why didn't anyone tell me this before?
Why did people I love not tell me that I would one day have to choose like this?"
That's a good question. Why did not one person tell this dear image-bearer that
she could not have illicit love and gospel peace at the same time? Why didn't

anyone—throughout all of those decades—tell this woman that sin and Christ cannot abide together, for the cross never makes itself an ally with the sin it must crush, because Christ took our sin upon himself and paid the ransom for its dreadful cost?

We have all failed miserably at loving fellow image-bearers who identify as part of the LGBT community—fellow image-bearers who are deceived by sin and deceived by a hateful world that applies the category mistake of sexual orientation identity like a noose. And we all continue to fail miserably. On the biblical side, we often have failed to offer loving relationships and open doors to our homes and hearts, openness so unhindered that we are as strong in loving relationships as we are in the words we wield. We also have failed to discern the true nature of the Christian doctrine of sin. For when we advocate for laws and policies that bless the relationships that God calls sin, we are acting as though we think ourselves more merciful than God is.

May God have mercy on us all.

This essay was adapted from an article originally published with the Gospel Coalition.

Rosaria Butterfield, PhD, is a former tenured professor of English and women's studies at Syracuse University. The author of The Secret Thoughts of an Unlikely Convert and The Gospel Comes with a House Key, Rosaria lives in Durham, NC. She is married to Kent Butterfield, pastor of the First Reformed Presbyterian Church of Durham.

GENDER AND SEX

Related but Not Identical

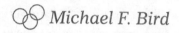 *Michael F. Bird*

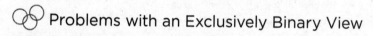 Problems with an Exclusively Binary View

One of the most complicated and contested topics in our contemporary culture are those related to gender, specifically gender identities in family, society, and various religious communities.

What has contributed to contemporary conflicts over gender is that Western culture has for the most part regarded gender as synonymous with biological sex. Consequently, genitalia and reproductive function were believed to indicate whether a person was *either* male *or female*. Gender was thought to be determined by something of the *body*, and its options were exclusively *binary*. Undergirding that was the biblical description of God creating humans as "male and female" (see Gen. 1:26–27; 5:1–2). The reduction of gender to biology and its binary limitations was thought to be warranted by divine revelation.

The first problem with the binary approach is there are biological and psychological factors that render a person's sexual differentiation far more complicated than being either male or female. For instance, there are people who are intersex, who have elements of both male and female reproductive organs, and even though one sexual organ and one set of chromosomes may predominate, such people still carry features of both male and female in their bodies. Similarly, even the XX and XY chromosomes do not fully determine one's sexual makeup since chromosomes can be influenced by various genes and environmental factors. For example, the maternal uterine environment can impact the sex development of an infant. In addition, gender dysphoria is the mental distress a person experiences when the assigned biological sex does not match his or her perceived gender identity, usually caused by a mixture of environmental factors and/or prenatal development. Thus, dividing people into either male or female does not reflect the full suite of human biology and psychology which seems to be far more complicated.

A second problem with the binary approach to gender is the fact that sex and gender are not the same thing. Sex is a person's reproductive capacity as male or female. Gender is more than sex. It pertains to the culturally constructed characteristics and expected behaviours assigned to the sexes and regarded as normative in a society. For example, boys wear blue and girls wear pink, men cook the BBQ while women make the salad, and males wear trousers while women wear dresses, etc. These cultural norms are not natural, intrinsic, or inherent to the sexes; rather, they are artificially constructed and to some degree imposed by one's cultural context.

Two further factors that have contributed to struggles over gender have been the largely patriarchal dominance of Western society and the tendency to essentialize gender—meaning to take traits natural to women and turn them into a negative (i.e., women are emotional rather than rational, and therefore suited to nurturing rather than leading). We have to remember that the story of the twentieth century, at least in Western countries, includes the slow advance of women's equality in political rights, the workplace, and in the family. It should be borne in mind that less than a hundred years ago, in many places, women could not vote, could not work in some occupations, could be discriminated against for being women, were subject to all forms of harassment, and were paid less than a male counterpart. Even marital rape was still legal. Some of these inequalities still persist today. The result is that in patriarchal societies, women are disempowered and victimized because of their sex and gender. One of the things that facilitated a belief in female inferiority and enabled widespread discrimination against women was essentializing their gender, taking what is natural about them and amplifying it as a negative. Women could be disparaged for being emotional rather than rational, empathetic rather than effective, or submissive rather than assertive. Of course, the same thing can be done to men, whereby maleness is associated with power, aggression, strength, and domination.

At the risk of gross generalization, we could say that the modern gender wars are the unfortunate fruit of a binary view of sex, collapsing gender into sex, stemming from the long history of patriarchal domination of women, and derived from cultural mores that essentialize gender.

In our own time, a diverse array of disciplines and discourses—feminism, womanism, gender theory, queer theory, intersectionality, etc.—have spawned various ideologies and legalities designed to deal with perceived abuses pertaining to gender. This has led to a mixture of profound insight into human existence and correction to gender-based injustices, but also spawned no little degree of confusion as to what it means to be a gendered human being.

⚭ When Gender Is Completely Divorced from Sex

While failing to distinguish gender from biological sex has, as we've seen, its own set of problems, one of the more problematic aspects of contemporary discourse about gender identity is that gender is often completely divorced from biological sex. As a result, gender identities have become peculiar social fictions that can be multiplied almost infinitely. While gender cannot be reduced to biological sex, to say that gender has nothing to do with biological sex is to open up a quasi-gnostic anthropology whereby a person's sense of self, their "identity" as it were, is completely disengaged from their embodied existence as a human. In other words, "I am not my body and my body is not me." This is why social media sites like Facebook list up to seventy-one different gender options that a user may select from to identify themselves. Among them are pangender, asexual, two-spirit, and neutrois. The underlying notion is that identity of any variety—sexual, ethnic, national, or ableness—is neither inherited nor determined by external factors, but rests entirely in the will of the individual. In practice it means that you can define yourself with any eclectic set of ethnicities, genders, sexual orientations, or abilities that you wish.

The whole notion of identity politics—whether related to gender or other features of human existence—while nobly intentioned and intending to meet real needs, has to be prevented from lurching into the absurdities of infinite plurality or artificial sameness.

First, the multiplication of gender identities and their accompanying sexual orientations runs the risk of collapsing under the weight of its own incredibility. Uttering the words "I identify as . . ." is not a legal pronouncement, nor can it effect an ontological change in a person's psychological and physical makeup. Claims to a particular identity are at most a statement about how a person wishes to be understood amidst the swirling mix of selves in an increasingly diverse society. Treating people how they wish to be treated is one thing, but catering to an infinite number of identities with peculiar hybridities and strange derivations is quite another.

Second, while gender is more than sex and biology, biology is still an important factor in one's gender. The fact is that every cell in the human body is encoded with male and female DNA. Plus there are real differences between men and women at the level of physical attributes and the neurobiological wiring of their brains. But it also has to be acknowledged that the difference between men and women often is no greater than the differences between men or the differences between women. Even so, we should recognize that differences between men and women do exist; they are God-given and good. They enrich the vast array of human experiences and arguably contribute to human flourishing. What that means is that cultural pressures to pursue an idealized form of human existence characterized by some kind of androgynous sameness should be resisted.

What Christians should take away is that God created humanity as male and female, yet the complexity and beauty of the divine design means that male and female sexes are *not an absolute binary, but more of a spectrum*. All people exist within the nodes of maleness and femaleness to some degree or another. This allows us to account for things like intersex and gender dysphoria, plus recognize how being male and female is not monolithic, and attributes can be shared between the sexes. In addition, as the apostle Paul said, in Christ there is no "male and female"; the gender binary is negated by the new creation, negated insofar as gender distinctions can no longer be utilized as a means to power and superiority over others (Gal. 3:28). That is not because gender somehow ceases to exist for the Christian, we do remain male and female after all, but our sex and its associated gender is transcended by our distinct Christian identity, namely, that we are baptized into Christ. The most determinative aspect of a Christian's identity is not genetics, genitals, gender, or sexual orientation, but participation in Christ's death and resurrection.

Michael F. Bird (PhD, University of Queensland) is an Anglican priest and biblical scholar. He teaches at Ridley College in Melbourne, Australia, and is the author of *Evangelical Theology* and *The Gospel of the Lord: How the Early Church Wrote the Story of Jesus*.

RETHINKING SAME-SEX RELATIONSHIPS

Matthew Vines

For the first fifteen hundred years of church history, all Christians believed that the earth stood still at the center of the universe. They also believed that the Bible clearly taught that to be true. After all, Psalm 93:1 says, "The world is established, firm and secure." Other verses describe the sun's motion, and no verses describe the earth as revolving around the sun.

But the invention of the telescope in 1608 cast doubt on that geocentric belief, and Galileo's discoveries presented a challenge to the traditional interpretation of the Bible. Despite early opposition from church leaders, Christians began to look at the relevant biblical passages differently, asking whether there was a way to interpret Scripture that squared with what they were learning to be true about the cosmos.

Today Christians acknowledge without controversy that the biblical authors wrote about the sun, the stars, and the moon based on how things appear from our vantage point. Their aim was to communicate clearly, not to teach about astronomy. New information about the solar system changed Christians' lens for interpreting Scripture, leading them to a more nuanced, accurate understanding of the text.

Many Christians today ask what right we have to reconsider an interpretation of Scripture about same-sex relationships that has been held for almost all of church history. I include the controversy about the solar system as a reminder that new information led Christians to rethink longstanding interpretations before. In our day, new information about a much more personal subject—sexual orientation—is leading many Christians to reconsider their interpretation of Scripture on same-sex relationships.

What is that new information? For most of church history, same-sex behavior was viewed as a vice of excess akin to gluttony or drunkenness. That view had ancient roots, from Plato's declaration that same-sex behavior was the product of "an inability to control pleasure" to John Chrysostom's assertion in his fourth-century commentary on Romans 1 that it "comes of an exorbitancy which endures not to abide within its proper limits."[1] Those ideas made sense at the time, given the fleeting, self-seeking forms of same-sex behavior that were most widely practiced in the biblical world: married men having sex with male prostitutes, slaves, or boys as an outlet for lustful self-indulgence.[2]

But the debate in the church today is about something different. It centers around long-term monogamous relationships of gay and bisexual Christians—followers of Jesus who have a different sexual orientation, not people who are abandoned to hedonism. Even many nonaffirming Christians acknowledge this major conceptual difference. Richard Hays, a New Testament professor, has written that sexual orientation "is a modern idea of which there is no trace either in the [New Testament] or in any other Jewish or Christian writings in the ancient world. . . . The usual supposition of writers during the Hellenistic period was that homosexual behavior was the result of insatiable lust seeking novel and more challenging forms of self-gratification."[3]

It wasn't until the twentieth century that same-sex attraction came to be widely understood as a permanent sexual orientation of a small minority of people. The existence of same-sex orientation doesn't resolve the question of how we should interpret Scripture on this topic, but as with the invention of the telescope four hundred years ago, this new information should affect the questions we ask when we approach the text.

When I came out to my dad, he believed that same-sex relationships were sinful. After all, he'd looked up what the Bible had to say about same-sex behavior, and every one of the six passages that referred to it was condemnatory. So in his view, "Is homosexuality a sin?" was an open-and-shut case. But once he began to learn more about what it means to be gay, he started to ask different questions in his study of Scripture. Instead of looking simply for references to any sexual behaviors between people of the same sex, he began to ask what the Bible had to say about the type of same-sex relationship I hoped to have one day—a committed, monogamous relationship that formed the basis of a family and a home.

---

1. Plato, *Laws*, 636B–D, quoted in Thomas K. Hubbard, ed., *Homosexuality in Greece and Rome: A Sourcebook of Basic Documents* (Berkeley: University of California Press, 2003), 252. John Chrysostom, *Homily 4 on Romans*, trans. J. Walker, J. Sheppard, and H. Browne, rev. George B. Stevens, in *Nicene and Post-Nicene Fathers*, 1st ser., vol. 11, ed. Philip Schaff (Buffalo, NY: Christian Literature, 1889), at New Advent, rev. and ed. Kevin Knight, www.newadvent.org/fathers/210204.htm.

2. The best treatment of same-sex behavior in ancient Rome was written by Craig A. Williams, *Roman Homosexuality*, 2nd ed. (Oxford: Oxford University Press, 2010).

3. Richard B. Hays, "Relations Natural and Unnatural: A Response to John Boswell's Exegesis of Romans 1," *Journal of Religious Ethics* 14, no. 1 (1986), 200.

What did the Bible say about a relationship between two men or two women like the relationship he's had with my mom for more than thirty years?

When he reread the story of Sodom and Gomorrah in Genesis 19 with that question in mind, the harrowing account of a threatened gang rape no longer seemed to speak to the same issue. Of the Bible's twenty references to Sodom and Gomorrah after Genesis 19, none described same-sex behavior as the sin of Sodom. Ezekiel 16:49 identifies Sodom's sin forthrightly: "Now this was the sin of your sister Sodom: She and her daughters were arrogant, overfed and unconcerned; they did not help the poor and needy." There are only two verses that connect Sodom to sexual immorality in general—2 Peter 2:7 and Jude 7—but not to same-sex behavior specifically. Moreover, the only form of same-sex behavior described in the Sodom story is a threatened gang rape, which is worlds apart from long-term, committed relationships.

Leviticus 18:22 and 20:13 prohibit male same-sex relations in clear terms. But while we should take the Old Testament law seriously, Christ was the end of the law (Rom. 10:4), and its many regulations and prohibitions have never applied to Christians. The same chapters also condemn sex during a woman's menstrual period as an abomination worthy of permanent exile (Lev. 20:18), but few Christians today regard that as a sin. The Old Testament even prescribes the death penalty to other things that most Christians don't treat as moral issues at all, like working on the Sabbath (Ex. 35:2) and charging interest on loans (Ezek. 18:13). So while the Old Testament is certainly important, it doesn't determine how Christians should view committed same-sex relationships.

The central New Testament text in this discussion is Romans 1:26–27, in which Paul condemns women who "exchanged natural sexual relations for unnatural ones" and men who "abandoned natural relations with women and were inflamed with lust for one another." While he refers to "lustful" behavior, nonaffirming Christians argue that his condemnation extends even to loving, committed same-sex relationships because he labels same-sex unions "unnatural." But Paul uses the same Greek word (*physis*) in 1 Corinthians 11:14 to say that long hair in men is contrary to nature, and most Christians interpret that verse as referring to cultural norms rather than God's universal design. The term "unnatural" was in common use among Greco-Roman writers before Paul to describe same-sex unions because such behavior violated conventional patriarchal gender roles: men were seen as being submissive and women were seen as being dominant.

In a culture in which women were regarded as inferior to men, for a man to take the so-called "woman's role" in sex was profoundly shameful. That's why any same-sex relationships that were accepted even in more permissive ancient societies had to be structured on strict hierarchical lines: a free man with an enslaved man, a man with a teenage boy, a free Roman citizen with a foreigner. The notion of two men of equal social status entering into a committed, monogamous relationship was not conceivable in a society so committed to upholding a patriarchal order.[4]

As Christians, then, we must ask this basic hermeneutical question to help us faithfully apply Romans 1 today: What is the status of patriarchy in the kingdom of God? If we affirm, based on the overall biblical witness, that women and men have equal status and that patriarchy should be overcome in Christ, then the patriarchal logic behind the Greco-Roman view of same-sex unions as "unnatural" does not provide a sound basis for rejecting all same-sex relationships today.

There is much more to be said on this topic, and these reflections only scratch the surface of the case I make in *God and the Gay Christian*. But regardless of your views, I encourage you to build meaningful relationships with LGBTQ Christians, to walk in our shoes, and to make space for us in your churches and homes. As important as theology is, when the church has caused this much pain and suffering to a group of people, our first response should be repentance and sacrificial love.

Matthew Vines is the author of *God and the Gay Christian: The Biblical Case in Support of Same-Sex Relationships* and the founding executive director of the Reformation Project, a nonprofit organization that works to advance LGBTQ inclusion in the church. He lives in Dallas, Texas.

---

4. See David M. Halperin, *One Hundred Years of Homosexuality: And Other Essays on Greek Love* (New York: Routledge, 1990), 1–40.

A THEOLOGICAL AND PASTORAL RESPONSE TO GENDER DYSPHORIA

Matthew Mason

s the Christian gospel good news for someone experiencing gender dysphoria? In the light of the gospel, how should Christians think about the issue and engage people who suffer in this way?

"Gender dysphoria" names the distressed condition of someone who feels that their body's biological sex does not match their true gender identity. Christians who engage the issue must remember two things: First, we are not so much speaking about an "issue" as speaking to and of people made in God's image and precious to him. We must speak with gentleness, understanding, compassion, and respect. Second, Christians are not free to draw their own conclusions and rest in their own judgments on this or any other ethical issue. In our speech and actions, we are responsible to the God of the gospel.

The resurrection, which lies at the heart of the gospel (1 Cor. 15:3–5), offers wisdom with which to engage these questions.[1]

Oliver O'Donovan has argued that Christian ethics depends on Christ's resurrection, because it must "arise from the gospel of Jesus Christ."[2] O'Donovan connects gospel and creation because in preaching Christ's resurrection, the apostles proclaimed "the resurrection of mankind in Christ; and in proclaiming the resurrection of mankind, they proclaimed the renewal of all creation with him."[3] God's good creation has been ruined by sin, but through Christ's death

---

1. For a more detailed account, see Matthew Mason, "The Wounded It Heals: Gender Dysphoria and the Resurrection of the Body," in Gerald Hiestand and Todd Wilson, eds, *Beauty, Order, and Mystery: The Christian Vision of Sexuality* (Downers Grove, IL: InterVarsity, 2017), 135–47.

2. Oliver O'Donovan, *Resurrection and Moral Order: An Outline for Evangelical Ethics*, 2nd ed. (Leicester: Inter-Varsity Press, 1994), 11; hereafter, *RMO*.

3. O'Donovan, *RMO*, 31.

and resurrection, creation will be restored and perfected. Thus, the gospel reaffirms the order inherent in creation, including the twofold embodied form of humanity as male and female (Gen. 1:27).[4]

In 1 Corinthians 15, Paul argues from the resurrection of Christ to the future resurrection of all believers (vv. 20, 23). Paul contrasts Christ and Adam (vv. 21–22) and establishes two things. First, there is an organic connection between Christ's resurrection and the resurrection of believers. Second, there is an organic connection between Adam's body in creation and Christ's body in the resurrection.

From verse 35, Paul answers the objection, "How are the dead raised? With what kind of body will they come?" He argues for continuity and transformation, using the analogy of sowing a seed (v. 37), and states that "God gives it a body as he has determined, and to each kind of seed he gives its own body" (v. 38). God has authority over the kind of body with which the dead are raised. He gives the form of the body, in conformity with his choice, not ours. The phrase "He has determined" translates an aorist tense verb that implies God gives the body he determined in creation.[5] Thus, someone born with a male body (by the Creator's choice) will be raised with that same male body. This fits what we know of Jesus' resurrection appearances. He was raised bodily (John 20:27; Luke 24:31, 37–43), and the tomb was empty. He did not leave his old body behind; he rose with the same male body the Father had prepared for him in the incarnation (cf. Heb. 10:5).

Even as Paul promises our bodies' glorious transformation (1 Cor. 15:53–54), he emphasizes their future continuity with the bodies we have now. Four times he states that it is *this* (Gk. *touto*) weak, frail, and dying body—the one God gave in creation—that will put on glory, honor, and immortality. This surely includes the body's male or female form (Gen. 1:27).[6]

The gospel therefore speaks a hard word in relation to gender dysphoria: We do not have absolute authority over our bodies and their sexual form. We live in a creation that is shaped by God's purposes, and we cannot decide for ourselves whether we are male or female. Our creator has decided for us, and the resurrection shows he is eternally committed to that decision. The sex of my body at birth will be the sex of my body when I am raised. Therefore, it defines my gender

---

4. On the male-female creation pattern, see Karl Barth, *Church Dogmatics* III/4 (Edinburgh, T&T Clark, 1964), 116–240; Julián Marías, *Metaphysical Anthropology: The Empirical Structure of Human Life*, trans. Frances M. López-Morillas (University Park, PA: Pennsylvania State University Press, 1971), 123–78; Matthew Mason, "The Authority of the Body: Recovering Natural Manhood and Womanhood," *Bulletin of Ecclesial Theology* 4, no. 2 (2017): 39–57.

5. Anthony C. Thiselton, *The First Epistle to the Corinthians* (Grand Rapids: Eerdmans, 2000), 1264.

6. Cf. Augustine, *City of God*, 22.17.

now. Put starkly, the resurrection of the body shows that gender reassignment is a rebellion against the moral order God has written on our bodies in creation. This also suggests that whatever reassignment treatment someone has undergone, his or her true sex has not changed. There is an underlying God-given and God-affirmed ontological reality.

This may sound hard, but it may also be a word of comfort and hope. Some who undergo gender reassignment regret their decision and desire to transition back.[7] This may prove impossible in this life. But the resurrection assures us that the Great Physician will remake us perfectly, in a moment, in the twinkling of an eye (1 Cor. 15:51–52).

This promise of the renewal and transformation is, for many, good news. But what of those who might recoil in horror at the message that the body they were born with is God's eternal design for them? Can this gospel be good news for someone who is so alienated from her body and its sex that she identifies as being of the opposite gender? By God's grace it can, because the resurrection does not leave us simply confronted by an objective reality; it "includes us and enables us to participate in it."[8] Resurrection means our renewal and reintegration as moral agents. The risen Christ does not only renew our bodies; by his Spirit he renews us to the very depths of our beings, even in the darkest and most troubled corners of our lives. This renewal is partial in this life. But in the resurrection, for believers, it will be complete. All brokenness and alienation will be healed, entirely, forever.

The transgender gospel of our age says, "Be true to yourself. Do whatever it takes to express the real you." Jesus, our creator and risen Lord, says, "Deny yourself. Take up your cross. Follow me." For those who experience gender dysphoria, this call to die may well include an agonizing struggle to be true to the body he gave them. But Jesus' gospel comes with an eternal promise: "For whoever wants to save their life will lose it, but whoever loses their life for me and for the gospel will save it" (Mark 8:35).

Matthew Mason is a fellow of the Research Institute of the Kirby Laing Institute for Christian Ethics, Cambridge, UK; a fellow of the St John Fellowship of the Center for Pastor Theologians; and a PhD student in divinity at the University of Aberdeen.

---

7. Walt Heyer, "I Was a Transgender Woman," *The Public Discourse*, April 1, 2015, http://www.thepublicdiscourse.com/2015/04/14688/.

8. O'Donovan, *RMO*, 101.

A CHRISTIAN PSYCHOLOGICAL ASSESSMENT OF GENDER DYSPHORIA

Mark A. Yarhouse and Julia Sadusky

Diagnostic Criteria

Gender dysphoria refers to "a marked incongruence between one's experienced or expressed gender" and biological sex.[1] There must also be evidence of distress or impairment in social, occupational, or other important areas of functioning.

A diagnosis of gender dysphoria can be given to children, adolescents, or adults. For a child to receive a diagnosis of gender dysphoria, there has to be "a strong desire to be of the other gender or an insistence that one is the other gender."[2] In addition, five of seven other criteria have to be met. These other criteria address strong preferences for cross-gender dress, roles, and activities, and rejection of gender typical dress, roles, and activities. A child may also express dislike of his or her own primary and/or secondary sex characteristics or express a desire for the primary and/or secondary sex characteristics of the other gender.

Different criteria apply to adolescents and adults than those which apply to children. An adolescent or an adult would experience strong desire to be of the other gender, or may believe they have the same emotional reactions of the other gender. There is also often a desire to be rid of one's primary and/or secondary sex characteristics or to have the primary and/or secondary sex characteristics of the other gender. An adolescent or adult needs to meet two of six criteria to receive a diagnosis of gender dysphoria.

---

1. The American Psychiatric Association (APA), *The Diagnostic and Statistical Manual of Mental Disorders*, 5th ed. (Washington, DC: APA, 2013), 452.
2. Ibid.

◎ Prevalence

Gender Dysphoria is a relatively rare phenomenon, but it is unlikely that it is as rare as current estimates suggest. *The Diagnostic and Statistical Manual of Mental Disorders*, fifth edition (*DSM-5*), cites prevalence estimates of 0.005–0.014 percent for biological males and 0.002–0.003 percent for biological females.[3] These estimates are problematic because they are based on adults seeking medical intervention from specialty clinics in Europe. They likely significantly underestimate the prevalence of gender dysphoria (which can exist along a continuum). In fact, many people with gender dysphoria do not seek medical interventions, such as hormonal treatment and/or sex reassignment surgery.

Transgender is an umbrella term for the many ways people experience, express, or live out a gender identity that is different from those for whom their experience of gender identity and their biological sex are congruent.[4] A higher percentage of people would identify as transgender than those who experience gender dysphoria (1 in 215 and 1 in 300, respectively).[5] Much higher percentages of transgender experiences have been reported in a recent Harris Poll Survey in which 3 percent of respondents age 18 to 34 identified as agender, 3 percent as genderfluid, 2 percent as transgender, 1 percent as bigender, and 1 percent as genderqueer.[6] Not everyone who identifies as transgender experiences gender dysphoria, and it may be helpful to distinguish emerging gender identities from gender dysphoria as such.

◎ Etiology

It is unclear what causes gender dysphoria. The most widely cited theory is referred to as the "brain-sex" theory and assumes a biological etiology. This theory is related to the observation that sex differentiation occurs at two different stages of fetal development. At one stage, there is a sex differentiation of the genitalia; at a later stage, there is a mapping of the brain toward male or female. The question that has been raised, according to the brain-sex theory, is whether, in rare instances, it is possible for the genitalia to map in one direction and the brain to map in the other direction.

---

3. Ibid., 454.

4. M. A. Yarhouse, *Understanding Gender Dysphoria: Navigating Transgender Issues in a Changing Culture* (Downers Grove, IL: InterVarsity Press Academic, 2015).

5. K. J. Conron, G. Scott, G. S. Stowell, and S. J. Landers, "Transgender Health in Massachusetts: Results from a Household Probability Sample of Adults," *American Journal of Public Health* 102, no. 1 (2012): 118–22; G. J. Gates, "How Many People Are Gay, Bisexual, and Transgender?" *The Williams Institute* (2011): 1–8, http://williamsinstitute.law.ucla.edu/wp-content/uploads/Gates-How-Many-People-LGBT-Apr-2011.pdf.

6. Harris Poll, "Accelerating Acceptance 2017," GLAAD, http://www.glaad.org/files/aa/2017_GLAAD_Accelerating_Acceptance.pdf.

Other theories consider the roles of environment and upbringing. These are based on correlational relationships between gender dysphoria and one's family and rearing environment, including parental wishes for a child of the other sex, parental support for gender variant behavior, and emotional, physical, and sexual abuse.

Still other theories would consider a combination of nature and nurture in the etiology of gender dysphoria.

 Treatment

As we consider treatment options, it can be helpful to distinguish between services offered to children and interventions offered to adolescents and adults.

Historically, there have been three approaches to children diagnosed with gender dysphoria: facilitating a resolution in keeping with one's biological sex, watchful waiting, and facilitating a cross-gender identity. The first, facilitating a resolution in keeping with one's birth sex, has been a focus of concern among transgender advocates and some mental health professionals, who believe such interventions can be shaming and harmful to a gender atypical child. In some states, legislation has been written to make efforts to change gender identity illegal.

Watchful waiting is often preferred by those who believe gender dysphoria resolves on its own in a high percentage of cases. This resolution has been cited in 75–80 percent of cases and may entail a nonbinary gender identity, a gay, lesbian, or bisexual identity, or presentation as a more masculine female or a more feminine male.[7]

Facilitating a cross-gender identity has also been a consideration. Proponents argue that it provides time for exploration of one's preferred gender identity and may reduce distress and behavioral acting out.

A more recent trend in treatment for older children is to suppress puberty at just the beginning of puberty through medical intervention. This can occur for up to two years, allowing an older child time to see if living as one's preferred gender is helpful in diminishing gender dysphoria. The child, now a teenager, can then decide whether to discontinue puberty suppression and form a gender identity in keeping with his or her biological sex or to continue on in his or her preferred gender identity.

It was noted that, in childhood, gender dysphoria tends to resolve on its own by the time a child reaches adolescence or early adulthood. Once a person

---

7. L. Edwards-Leeper, *Balanced Affirmative Mental Health Care for Transgender and Gender Non-Conforming Youth* (Portland, OR: Springer, 2016).

reaches later adolescence or adulthood, gender dysphoria does not tend to resolve. There do not appear to be established psychotherapeutic protocols to facilitate the resolution of gender dysphoria with one's biological sex. Many people who are diagnosed attempt, through trial and error, to manage their dysphoria through specific strategies (e.g., clothing styles, adjustments in hair and makeup, cross-dressing, etc.).

Some individuals will pursue cross-gender identification (a social transition) and/or medical interventions, such as the use of cross-sex hormones and/or sex reassignment surgery. The *DSM*-5 suggests that, after such interventions, a person may no longer meet criteria for a diagnosis of gender dysphoria. A 30-year longitudinal study, which provided some evidence that surgery may alleviate gender dysphoria, also noted that surgery did not appear to reduce the rates of concerns such as overall mortality, suicide attempts, and psychiatric hospitalizations.[8]

Three Frameworks

In our previous work, *Understanding Gender Dysphoria*, we offered three frameworks for understanding gender identity concerns: integrity, disability, and diversity.[9] The integrity framework is based on the theological understanding that there is an essential maleness and essential femaleness intended by God from creation. This lays the foundation for what is considered morally permissible sexual behavior (complementary male-female genital sexual intimacy in marriage). It also raises concern that adopting a cross-gender identity in some way impinges on the natural order and male/female distinctiveness.

The disability framework sees gender identity concerns as a variation that occurs in nature in rare instances. In this sense, the phenomenon is a nonmoral reality to be addressed with compassion. A Christian drawn to this framework would place greater emphasis on the effects of the fall on the created order.

The diversity framework interprets gender identity differences as signaling a people group that should be celebrated. In this sense, variations in gender identity that may be signaled by gender dysphoria represent a culture that should be recognized and valued. The diversity framework also provides a person with a sense of identity as part of the transgender (and broader LGBTQ) communities.

We recommend an integrated framework that draws on the best of each of the existing frameworks. A Christian psychology perspective on gender

---

8.   C. Dhejne, P. Lichtenstein, M. Boman, A. L. V. Johansson, N. Langstrom, and M. Landen, "Long-Term Follow-Up of Transsexual Persons Undergoing Sex Reassignment Surgery: Cohort Study in Sweden," *PloS ONE* 6, no 2 (2011), https://doi.org/10.1371/journal.pone.0016885.

9.   Yarhouse, *Understanding Gender Dysphoria*, 2015.

dysphoria recognizes the importance of the theological foundations provided by the integrity framework. The emphasis on God's creational intent (Gen. 1 and 2) provides a point of reference for identity and acknowledges norms regarding sex and gender. The disability lens acknowledges the reality of the fall (Gen. 3) and highlights the value of extending grace to those enduring conditions which were not within God's original plan. The diversity framework is strong in its attention to questions of identity and community. Although we disagree with certain applications of the diversity lens, it challenges the Christian community to consider how to better offer a sense of identity and community for people who experience gender dysphoria.

In practical care for people diagnosed with gender dysphoria, some are able to live and express a gender identity in keeping with their biological sex, although there may continue to be challenges related to that. Others utilize various strategies to manage their dysphoria. We recommend helping people manage their dysphoria in the least invasive way possible, identifying the most invasive ways as medical interventions, such as cross-sex hormones and surgical procedures.

Dr. Mark Yarhouse was recently named the Dr. Arthur P. Rech and Mrs. Jean May Rech Chair in Psychology at Wheaton College after serving as the Hughes Endowed Chair of Christian Thought in Mental Health Practice at Regent University. He is author of several books, including *Understanding Gender Dysphoria: Navigating Transgender Issues in a Changing Culture*.

Julia Sadusky is a candidate in the doctoral program in clinical psychology at Regent University where she served as research assistant in the Institute for the Study of Sexual Identity and completed clinical rotations in the Sexual & Gender Identity Clinic.

DISCUSSION QUESTIONS

1. In his article, Mason states that gender is determined by the biological sex given by God. How might people from Bird's perspective comment on this remark, and how might those from Yarhouse/Sadusky's tradition comment—especially in regards to the "brain-sex theory"?

2. How might someone from Vines's approach respond to Gagnon's use of 1 Corinthians 6:9, especially in regards to the phrase "soft men"? How would they respond to Gagnon's interpretation, and what might be theirs?

3. Butterfield and Vines both share personal testimonies in which they interpreted God's Word to mean two very different things for their lives. Where is it that the fundamental differences between their understandings of Scripture begin? In what definition or Scripture is the root of their differences in interpretation found?

4. Due to a difference in vocational background, Yarhouse/Sadusky and Mason use very different tones and language in their respective articles. Although these articles are very different, are there any areas in which the two agree or overlap? In which ways do the two languages find themselves at odds with each other?

5. Wilson's article concludes that any sexuality outside of a covenantal and committed marriage is, in his interpretation, outside of God's will for sexuality. How might Vines respond to this statement? On which point is it that Vines disagrees with Wilson, and how does each support their interpretation?

6. Vines uses the story of the telescope and Christians' reevaluation of the earth as the center of the universe to parallel the modern-day Christian's need to reevaluate a traditional orthodox view of marriage. He declares that the Bible refers specifically to illicit homosexual relations rather than committed, monogamous homosexual relationships, which are not condemned by Jesus or the Bible. How might Gagnon respond to this claim, especially in regards to the teachings of Jesus?

7. There are many terms used by all of the articles, and it is important to understand the way each author defines the terms they use. How are the terms

sexuality, marriage, biological sex, gender, gender dysphoria, and binary defined? Do any of the authors differ on their definitions?

8. In his article, Mason makes the following statement: "The gospel therefore speaks a hard word in relation to gender dysphoria: we do not have absolute authority over our bodies and their sexual form." What would Bird say is the problem or confusion found in this statement?

9. At the end of his article, Vines mentions that regardless of their doctrinal beliefs, Christians should welcome gay Christians into their churches with love because of the past history of discrimination and pain caused by the church. Butterfield is explicit, however, in her claim that to allow gay Christians to believe that their lifestyle is biblically condoned is the opposite of love, comparing it to a millstone tied around the neck. Is it possible to reconcile these two statements? Can a Christian welcome gay Christians into their church while also loving them the way that Butterfield expresses is crucial, or are the two perspectives mutually exclusive?

10. Yarhouse and Sadusky outline the different treatment methods available to individuals who suffer from gender dysphoria in their article. Does the church have a role to play in helping members seek or decide on treatment, and if so, what is it?

chapter five

GENDER ROLES

While Christians can and should look to the Bible for the foundations of gender roles, it is nearly impossible to develop an understanding and applications of this topic apart from cultural perceptions of manhood and womanhood. While biological sex and the roles connected to biological reality (i.e., physical strength, child bearing, etc.) are virtually unchanging, many roles connected to gender vary significantly depending on culture, historical moment, and technology. The historical oppression of women outside the church has profoundly affected the treatment of women inside the church, leading to significant confusion concerning which views about gender roles are based in Scripture and which are based in culture, with some proof-texts from Scripture used as support. The main thrust of the current questions surrounding gender roles within the church reflects a growing sense of inequality between men and women that came to a head in the late 1900s.

For most scholars, the central question is what roles women should hold within the church. According to Gregory Boyd and Paul Eddy, the central question is, "Is it appropriate for women to aspire to leadership roles within the church that will place them in positions of authority over men?"[1] While this question accounts for a large part of the theological debate, it does not fully account for the wider cultural debate surrounding gender roles. Of course, this question gets at the root of the 1 Timothy 2 passage, but it does not move beyond that to many of the other peripheral issues that continue to surround our biblical and cultural understanding of gender roles. For instance, it does not address the issues of male headship within the home as taught in passages such as Ephesians 5 and 1 Peter 3. And, more broadly, the question considers only the role of *women* in the church; it does not address what roles and duties men should actively fulfill in the church and home. This, in sum, is the problem. The focus of the debate is rooted in what women should and should not do within the church, rather than addressing the

---

1. Gregory A. Boyd and Paul R. Eddy, *Across the Spectrum: Understanding Issues in Evangelical Theology* (Grand Rapids: Baker Academic, 2002), 250.

issue holistically to consider how the people of God might work together in an orderly fashion to build the kingdom of God in a biblical fashion. Even so, at least two points of the biblical and theological debate are settled. First, both sexes are created in the "image of God" (Gen. 1:26–27) and "are of equal dignity, value, and worth."[2] Second, "since all Christians—male and female—have the Holy Spirit within them, all believers are gifted by God for ministry within the body of Christ."[3]

Two predominant positions hold sway within the contemporary church regarding the roles of the sexes within the kingdom of God: the complementarian view and the egalitarian view. While these two categories account for the broad classifications, there are further distinctions and divisions within them. It is important to note that these two categories are late twentieth-century developments and are therefore a very new development within church history.[4]

When the Council on Biblical Manhood and Womanhood first convened in 1987, the evangelical leaders of the time recognized the growing gender confusion and hoped to reestablish a secure foundation for gender roles based on sound theology, biblical interpretation, and careful scholarship. Scholars such as John Piper, Wayne Grudem, Wayne House, Dorothy Patterson, Thomas Schreiner, Susan Foh, and Andreas Köstenberger all fall somewhere within the complementarian spectrum which purports that the Bible teaches that "men and women are complementary, possessing equal dignity and worth as the image of God, and called to different roles that each glorify him."[5] People espousing the complementarian view believe men are called to be the leaders in the home and in the church while women have been designed by God to serve as man's "helper" and "partner."[6] To support this view, scholars most often point to the creation narrative, noting that God created Adam first, and Eve was designed to complement him both sexually and structurally. The issue, then, is not just authority, but responsibility within the created order. While Adam was given the ultimate responsibility to rule the earth, Eve was charged to help him as he fulfilled his responsibility. Thus, the relationship is one of complementing roles, where Adam leads under the authority of God while Eve follows Adam, helping him to fulfill his God-given responsibility of stewardship.

The egalitarian view proposes that leadership roles within the home and

---

2. Ibid.

3. Ibid.

4. Scot McKnight, "Revisionist History on the Term 'Complementarian,'" *Patheos*, March 2, 2015, http://www.patheos.com/blogs/jesuscreed/2015/03/02/revisionist-history-on-the-term-complementarian/.

5. The Council of Biblical Manhood and Womanhood, "History," Council of Biblical Manhood and Womanhood (website), https://cbmw.org/about/history/.

6. Boyd and Eddy, *Across the Spectrum*, 251.

church "are determined by gifting rather than by gender."[7] Egalitarians often examine the cultural elements of the debate in light of other cultural issues that exist in Scripture, issues such as slavery and polygamy, which, at various points in Scripture are discussed without being condemned. Boyd and Eddy, for example, explain that God has tolerated the fallen cultural norms for a time in order to eventually bring forth his ideal structure within the world. Thus, during the time the New Testament was written, God was working within the cultural norms regarding the patriarchal society, but as that system has been overthrown, much like slavery, women are now free to serve based on gifts rather than gender.[8]

Others argue that while cultural context is important in interpretation, the New Testament (e.g., 1 Tim. 2:12–13) grounds the distinctive roles in God's creation order itself and that the analogy with the practice of slavery or polygamy confuses categories since the New Testament, unlike with slavery and polygamy, explicitly affirms the distinction in roles between men and women.

Within the academy, the egalitarian movement has gained popularity in recent years, with prominent scholars such as N. T. Wright highlighting the cultural context surrounding those first-century passages.[9] Other scholars have sought to recast the debate, most notably Michelle Lee-Barnewall's *Neither Complementarian nor Egalitarian: A Kingdom Corrective to the Evangelical Gender Debate*, which attempts to reframe the terms of the debate as unity and reversal, rather than authority and equality.[10]

Among churches in America, surveys have indicated "a slow and steady rise of female pastors."[11] While some denominations allow for individual churches to decide on this issue autonomously, the majority of evangelicals[12] and the Roman Catholic Church remain committed to having only men in the role of "pastor" or "priest," while mainline denominations and many black and Pentecostal churches allow women to serve as ordained ministers.

The crux of the gender roles question is how to account for the cultural differences between the first-century church and the contemporary one and what role cultural context plays in biblical interpretation. The distance between the patriarchal Middle Eastern context of the early church and the contemporary global church is vast, and any position must work to interpret, apply, and obey

7. Ibid., 250.
8. Ibid.
9. See Tish Harrison Warren's use of Wright's work in support of egalitarianism below.
10. Michelle Lee-Barnewall, *Neither Complementarian nor Egalitarian: A Kingdom Corrective to the Evangelical Gender Debate* (Grand Rapids: Baker Academic, 2016).
11. Halee Gray Scott, "Study: Female Pastors Are on the Rise," *Christianity Today*, 2017, https://www.christianitytoday.com/women/2017/february/study-female-pastors-are-on-rise.html.
12. "What Americans Think About Women in Power," Barna, March 8, 2017, https://www.barna.com/research/americans-think-women-power/.

Scripture within the context of the fallen culture. This requires examining closely what the entirety of Scripture says about the nature of humankind, our bodies, our responsibilities, and our gifts so that each member of the body of Christ can use his or her gifts to the glory of God.

In the opening essay, Wendy Alsup, representing the complementarian position, explores how the fall affects how individuals experience gender internally, how the genders relate to one another externally, and how the gospel speaks to the issues surrounding the gender relationships. Representing a contrasting position, Tish Harrison Warren presents an egalitarian position for understanding how women and men should serve in the home and church in mutual submission to one another.

In relation to the question of women in the workforce, Owen Strachan encourages the church to reaffirm the biblical value of femaleness and maleness, thereby setting women free to work wherever God places them without allowing their value to be defined by cultural expectations. Katelyn Beaty, while also concerned with how the culture subtly shapes how we view such issues, views this issue differently from Strachan. Beaty argues that the Industrial Revolution rather than the Sexual Revolution did more to shape our modern views of the roles of men and women in the workforce. As such, she calls for churches to reshape the way they disciple men and women when it comes to working and child-rearing.

EQUAL BUT DIFFERENT

A Complementarian View of the Sexes

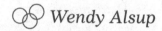 *Wendy Alsup*

> Then God said, "Let us make man in our image, according to our likeness. They will rule the fish of the sea, the birds of the sky, the livestock, the whole earth, and the creatures that crawl on the earth." So God created man in his own image; he created him in the image of God; he created them male and female. (Gen. 1: 26–27 CSB)

In the beginning, there was only primordial chaos and God. But into the darkness, God spoke light. Into the raging seas, God spoke land. On the land and in the sea, he spoke into existence an amazing array of plants and animals. From chaos, he brought order and life. Out of nothing, he brought everything. He then crowned his new creation with humankind who, unlike the plants and animals previously created, were made in his image. They were not gods. They weren't even angels. They were something new, and they were created specifically to reflect something about their creator God. He created one new species, but he made them of two distinct biological sexes, one male and the other female (see also Gen. 5:2). They were spiritual, and they were physical—eternal souls coupled with physical human bodies. They made up humankind. And all was good.

God created two distinct biological sexes, two distinct types of physical, human bodies, but culture shapes concepts of gender at every age in every location. Ellen Mandeville notes, "The term gender has morphed to mean the expectations a culture creates for males and females. One (*Oxford English Dictionary*) definition for gender says: 'The state of being male or female as expressed by social or cultural distinctions and differences, rather than biological ones.'"[1]

---

1. Ellen Mandeville, "Male and Female He Created Them," *Christ and Pop* Culture, December 7, 2015, https://christandpopculture.com/male-and-female-he-created-them/.

Though concepts of gender are influenced by time and culture, God created humankind with two distinct sexes in a way that transcends time and culture for the good of his creation. God's character is understood through the fullness of these two sexes, first by the overlap they share as humans, a starting point that cannot be overstated, and then by their distinctions as male and female. He created both man and woman in his image and, according to Genesis 2:18, created woman specifically to help (Hebrew *ezer*) the man in ways that suited, complemented, or went before him (Hebrew *neged*) in the image of the one true *ezer*, God himself.[2] The man and the woman were to work the garden together, but they were clearly not exactly the same. Though modern Western culture often seeks to diminish differences in men and women, understanding God's design of biological sex before the fall causes us to value the differences in the two sexes as we also value the qualities they share.

The problem is that Genesis 1 and 2, where God created man and woman in his image to reflect something of himself, are quickly followed by Genesis 3. We did not get to see how the differences in the male and female human played out in perfection. Instead, we see much in the rest of Scripture of how those differences played out after the fall, often with horrible consequences. The fall affected all of the human condition, including biological sex, both internally and externally. We experience internal disorder in our own sexual bodies and external disorder between the sexes, male and female. Understanding both internal and external disorders from the fall helps us understand the solution Jesus Christ brings and the subsequent hope we have for men and women working together in Jesus' name in our churches today.

The fall has affected male and female bodies internally with chromosomal abnormalities, infertility, dysphoria, and other forms of sexual dysfunction. The issue of gender discomfort, or the more serious mental health issue of gender dysphoria, should cause us to think through the relationship of our physical bodies to our spiritual and emotional bodies. Modern Western culture often distinguishes between the actual physical human body and the spirit within it, similar to the reasoning of gnostics who infiltrated the early church. Gnostics separated the realities of the human body from the spirit and believed they held special knowledge unknown to others that allowed them to disregard Christian ethics. The facts of biological sex, in that realm of thought, take a backseat to inner perceptions of sex. In contrast, in 1 Corinthians 6:12–20, the apostle Paul argues that both our bodies and our spirit are united to Christ, effectively crushing the gnostic view that our bodies are immaterial to our spiritual realities.

---

2. Deuteronomy 33:29 and fifteen other Old Testament verses refer to God as *ezer*.

Though we may feel at odds with culture's perceptions of gender inside and out-side our churches, our material bodies matter. I am a woman, not because I feel very feminine or perceive myself as a girly girl, but because my material body has the female genetic makeup and physical features that go with it. I am needed as a woman in my church, not because I fit a gender stereotype of femininity, but because God created me in his image as an *ezer*/helper that fits the needs of male image-bearers in my church.

The fall has affected male and female bodies internally, but it has also affected the male and female sex externally in the way that men and women relate to one another. While a variety of issues between the two biological sexes have played out over the years since the fall of humanity, there are also particular ways predicted in Genesis 3 that have consistently shown up generation by generation, including the generation and culture in which we now live.

Genesis 3:16 predicts that after the fall, the woman will have frustration in key areas of her life—childbearing and relationship with the man:

> He said to the woman:
>> I will intensify your labor pains;
>> you will bear children with painful effort.
>> Your desire will be for your husband,
>> yet he will rule over you. (CSB)

Woman was created with a particular emphasis on her strong help and alliance with the man in the image of God as *ezer* (Genesis 2:18), but after the fall, she will be frustrated in her attempts to strongly help the man, as the man responds with oppression to what should have been received with thankfulness. Man too will be frustrated in key areas of his life. He was created to work and keep the garden, but Genesis 3:17–19 shows that he will be vexed and troubled as the ground works against him in his effort.

The author of Genesis uses a Hebrew word (*teshuqah*) in Genesis 3:16, trans-lated into English most often as "desire."[3] In the course of translation history, some believed that it represented a sexual desire. It could also mean "turning" or "returning," in the sense that the woman turns toward her husband but is oppressed by him in return.[4] The standard definition in Hebrew lexicons and concordances is "longing" or "craving."[5] Genesis 3:16 then seems to reflect a

---

3. http://biblehub.com/hebrew/8669.htm.
4. Janson C. Condren, "Toward a Purge of the Battle of the Sexes and 'Return' for the Original Meaning of Genesis 3:16b," *JETS* 60, no. 2 (2017): 227–45.
5. James Strong, *The New Strong's Exhaustive Concordance of the Bible* (Nashville: Thomas Nelson, 1990), s.v. "tshuwqah."

desire or turning toward the man by the woman that now results in frustration and even abuse as he rules over her in return. Just as the man was created to work the ground but is now frustrated in his attempts, the woman was created to strongly help the man but is frustrated in her attempts. The long cultural problem between the two sexes has been our coping mechanisms, which differ generation by generation, to deal with these frustrations apart from the good news of Jesus and his redemption of both men and women.

The gospel speaks into both the inner struggles of our broken sexual bodies and the outer struggles between the two distinct sexes. Jesus' body was broken physically so ours could be healed. Some of us experience miraculous healing of various physical abnormalities during life on earth, but all of us are assured an eternity in perfectly resurrected physical bodies, as God first created Adam and Eve before the fall. In our churches and larger culture, we must recognize the very real issues that our broken bodies in our broken world experience in relation to biological sex. And we must point to Christ as the hope we have for redeemed sexual bodies both on earth and in eternity. Christ too is our source of help in inhabiting our broken bodies while they last on earth. He alone equips us to endure in hope as we confidently wait for him to return and make all things new.

This gospel equips us to navigate a culture in which our bodies tell us one thing about ourselves (that we are male or female) and our culture, Christian or secular, tells us another. My identity as a daughter of God isn't determined by outer cultural standards of hyperfemininity, nor should hypermasculinity define it for men. I am a woman because God created me that way, and my body matters to my faith. My identity in him equips me to look at the body he gave me and let him, not culture, define what it means to be a woman in his image.[6]

The interplay between two biological sexes created equally to image God, with overlap and distinctions in abilities and giftings, is necessary for the body of Christ, the church, not to simply function well, but to function at all. Interestingly, it is the interplay of the two distinct biological sexes redeemed in Christ that, in Ephesians 5, gives us some of our best imagery for understanding Christ's relationship with the church. Beyond the testimony of the gospel given by these two distinct but overlapping sexes in Christian marriage, we see from the long story of Scripture the necessity of both of these sexes for the essential functions of God's people. At the most basic level of human existence, both sexes are necessary for bearing new image-bearers into the world, an incredible,

---

6. A study of the Old Testament's use of the Hebrew *ezer* is helpful on this point. See Deuteronomy 33:29; Exodus 18:4; Psalms 10:14; 20:2; 33:20; 70:5; 72:12–14.

though often downplayed, function of these sexes. But whether individuals ever have biological children, the two sexes are integral in bearing and growing spiritual children. The importance of each sex is lost if we dismiss the distinct elements of their giftings or roles given in Scripture for doing the work of discipling the next generation of believers.

Consider Scripture's example. We have stories of the two sexes doing many of the same things. But we also have examples of them doing distinct things that the other sex does not. Both men and women were prophets/prophetesses, deacons/deaconesses, judges, and perhaps even apostles (depending on how you understand the reference to Junia in Romans 16:7). But only men were named priests in the Old Testament or elders in the New. Though both men and women were created in the image of God, according to Genesis 1, only woman was specifically named helper (Hebrew *ezer*) in the image of the one true helper, God himself. These distinct roles are as important as the overlapping ones for fully imaging God to a watching world.

In our churches, we undermine the value of the two biological sexes in two main ways. Many elevate the distinct elements of the two biological sexes while downplaying or ignoring any overlap. Others, often in reaction to the first group, downplay the distinct elements of the two sexes, focusing only on the overlap. But the gift of two biological sexes for imaging our creator to a watching world is found in both their distinct elements as well as their overlapping ones. Though churches at times have not navigated these two parts well, it is good and right that we value both and seek to use the gifts of men and women in the church in similar and different ways.

The good news of Jesus offers hope for reconciliation between the sexes, rejoicing in our shared humanity as we fulfill the call of Christ to go and disciple nations. In many cultures still today, both inside and outside of the church, women are systematically oppressed, harassed, denied education, and without basic freedoms that men and boys in those same cultures enjoy. Coping mechanisms apart from Christ at times rob men of their dignity in the image of God in response. Wherever the name of Christ is proclaimed and God is honored as creator, the basic shared human dignity of both man and woman should also be upheld. In Western cultures, later waves of feminism have encouraged an autonomy that protects women from male oppression but can also undermine the interdependent relationships between the sexes to which God calls us through the good news of Jesus. As believers engage culture, we can both uphold the dignity of womanhood and her necessary value in imaging God into the world along with the dignity of manhood and his necessary value in imaging God into the world. God created both male and female to reflect something of himself, and our hope in Christ equips us to once again, "be imitators of God" (Eph. 5:1) in our shared humanity as well as the distinctions between male and female. Our churches need both to function.

Wendy Alsup is the author of *Is the Bible Good for Women? Seeking Clarity and Confidence through a Jesus-centered Understanding of Scripture* and *By His Wounds You are Healed: How the Message of Ephesians Transforms a Woman's Identity.* She writes from her family farm in the Low Country of South Carolina and worships at New City Fellowship (PCA).

BOTH MEN AND WOMEN ARE CALLED TO LEAD

An Egalitarian View of the Sexes

◯◯ Tish Harrison Warren

Egalitarians believe that the Scriptures call men and women to work in collaboration and mutual submission with one another and that there is no role that women must be barred from in the home or the church. Though "egalitarianism" is a fraught and contested term, Christian egalitarianism, as opposed to secular "egalitarianism," denies the interchangeability of the sexes and affirms essential sex differences and the unique gift of both femaleness and maleness. It also affirms the full inclusion of women in the ministry of the church and in the flourishing of the home.

In this brief essay, my focus will primarily be on biblical arguments for women to be included in ordained ministry. Of course, these arguments intertwine with debates about women's roles in the home, but I cannot look at familial relationships with any depth in this brief essay. Instead, I will simply affirm that if relationships truly embody the kind of mutual submission Paul describes (Eph. 5:21), arguments about "egalitarianism" or "complementarianism" pale before the glory of a husband and wife striving to love and submit to one another in every way they can.

The biblical argument for women's ordination assumes a redemptive-historical approach to Scripture. Biblical egalitarianism is not based on highlighting a few "proof-texts" or countering a few "clobber passages" about women's silence or submission; instead it is rooted in a canonical approach to Scripture. In Genesis 1:26–28, men and women are both given dominion and care-taking responsibilities. There is no sign of hierarchy in the original relationship between man and woman—the woman is called man's "helper" (*ezer kenegdo*, Gen. 2:18), but this term in no way implies subjugation and is similar to *ezer*, which is most often used in the Old Testament to refer to YHWH himself.

After the fall, God's curse of Eve states that her husband will "rule over [her]" (Gen. 3:16). The original delightful and perfect unity between man and woman, marked by radical solidarity and mutuality (bone of my bone and flesh of my flesh), is shattered by the fall, marred by sin, and fissured by patriarchy.

Yet God does not abandon his original design but slowly works toward reconciliation between men and women. God clearly uses women as leaders in the Old and New Testaments—Deborah, Ruth, Esther, Rahab, Mary Magdalene, Priscilla, Tabitha, Phoebe, Lydia, Junia, and many others. Perhaps most notably, God chose women to be the first to testify to Jesus' resurrection. These were "apostles to the apostles," as they are called in the tradition. The elevation of women as leaders in both the Old and New Testaments and Jesus' treatment of women both hint at a redemptive biblical arc toward greater inclusion, empowerment, and dignifying of women, the restoration of the garden's unity and mutuality.

Through Christ, the church is to embody the New Creation. As an ethical community, we witness to the way things are meant to be and how they will one day be when Christ makes "all things new." Because of our identity as new creation, the fall's fractured unity between men and women is healed in Christ. We see this clearly in baptism. When the covenant sign of circumcision (for men only) was replaced by baptism (for men and women alike), it is clear that women and men are both equally incorporated into this new body of the church. In his discussion about circumcision giving way to the new creation of baptism, Paul proclaims that in Christ there is no "Jew nor Gentile . . . neither slave nor free . . . nor male and female" (Gal. 3:28). N. T. Wright argues that the reason Paul uses the particular phrase "male and female" (as opposed to the "nor" construction of the preceding phrases) is that he is quoting Genesis 1, highlighting how these hierarchical divisions wrought in human sin are reconciled in the new creation.[1] Christ restores the unity of God's original creative design; women and men are therefore included together as partners and co-laborers in every aspect of home and church.

But what about those passages, which, at first glance, certainly seem to preclude women from holding teaching authority in the church? A straightforward reading of 1 Timothy 2:11–15 in English, without any larger context for the passage, seems to ban women from any ecclesial service and even from speaking in church. But further study throws doubt upon the meaning of this passage. Theologian William Witt states, "The meaning of almost every word in this

    1. N. T. Wright, "Women's Service in the Church: The Biblical Basis," conference paper for the symposium "Men, Women, and the Church," St. John's College, Durham, September 4, 2004. *NT Wright Page*, http://ntwrightpage.com/2016/07/12/womens-service-in-the-church-the-biblical-basis/.

passage is subject to debate and disagreement."[2] N. T. Wright argues that "the crucial verse 12 need not be read as 'I do not allow a woman to teach or hold authority over a man.' . . . It can equally mean (and in context this makes much more sense): 'I don't mean to imply that I'm now setting up women as the new authority over men in the same way that previously men held authority over women.'"[3] He, with Catherine Kroeger and other scholars, argues that in the context of Ephesus, which was the center of a female goddess cult (of Artemis) in which only women were allowed to be priests, Paul is highlighting that the newfound freedom that women found in the gospel should not result in "domineering over" or subjugating men.[4]

Much of the debate around this passage results from uncertainty about the best way to translate *authentein* (have authority over), which is a hapax legomenon, a term used only once in Scripture, with very few extant examples from the same time period in extra-biblical literature. *Authentein* could be translated as "to domineer or usurp," which would not preclude women from any authority, but would only forbid the minimization of men in the new creation community.

The command in 1 Corinthians 14:34 that women "remain silent" is even less clear. Whatever this passage means, it cannot be that women literally must never speak or teach in church, since three chapters earlier, Paul addresses how women should dress when they prophesy in public in church. If those against women's ordination were to apply this passage consistently, without sneaking in some hermeneutical interpretation, they would have to prevent women from making announcements, singing hymns, passing the peace, or teaching Sunday school. Any interpretation of this passage other than one that requires entire silence from women introduces some level of hermeneutical expansion. Thus we must assume that universal silence from women is absurd, given the New Testament witness of women such as Junia, Priscilla, and Philip's prophesying daughters, not to mention Paul's instructions to women in other passages. We must conclude, at the very least, that Paul and the other New Testament authors do not make categorical statements about what roles women should have in the church irrespective of social context.

Historically, women's ordination to ministry has not been mainstream, although, as Kevin Madigan, Carol Osiek, and especially Gary Macy have shown, prior to the twelfth century it was neither as rare nor as aberrant as is usually

---

2. William Witt, "Concerning Women's Ordination: Speaking and Teaching," *Will G. Witt* (blog), October 2, 2014, http://willgwitt.org/theology/concerning-womens-ordination-speaking-and-teaching/.

3. Wright, "Women's Service in the Church."

4. Richard Clark Kroeger and Catherine Clark Kroeger, *I Suffer not a Woman: Rethinking 1 Timothy 2:11–15 in Light of Ancient Evidence* (Grand Rapids: Baker Academic, 1992).

thought.[5] There are at least five documented women episcopae in the early med ieval church, three of which cannot be explained away as women married to a bishop. These women were explicitly charged with, at a minimum, overseeing churches, both the upkeep of the building and the doctrine and discipline of the clergy in the church.[6]

Presbyterae are more regularly documented in the medieval West. Though these are commonly "priest's wives," they often had individual distinctive ministries. One graffito near Poitiers documents that "Martia the presbytera made the offering together with Olybrius and Nepos." Scholarly research indicates that this means the female presbyter Martia co-celebrated the Eucharist with Olybrius and Nepos.[7]

A tenth-century Frankish rite details how deaconesses are to be ordained, including the episcopal impartation of a stole, the sign for ordained clerical responsibility. The responsibilities entailed in this ordination included preaching, catechesis of young women, assistance with baptism, and in some instances service at the altar.[8] Lastly, it was common for abbesses to hear the confessions of nuns, to prescribe penances, and to absolve, as well as to preach and teach both men and women, even into the nineteenth century. The range of ministries engaged in by women quite clearly shaded into many of the roles often regarded as the unique preserve of ordained clergy today.[9]

And it is essential to note the unfortunate fact that the dominant reasoning behind the subjugation of women prior to the nineteenth century was the idea of the ontological inferiority of women. Epiphanius of Salamis, a fourth-century opponent of the ordination of women, sums up the commonly held belief that "women are unstable, prone to error, and mean-spirited."[10]

Though contemporary complementarians would generally insist that complementarianism is not based in a belief that women are ontologically defective, the historical argument for what's now deemed "complementarianism" is that women are, essentially and irredeemably, "less rational, more gullible, and more susceptible to temptation" than men.[11] We therefore must acknowledge that both complementarian and egalitarian arguments, which assert that women equally

5. See *Ordained Women in the Early Church: A Documentary History*, ed. Kevin Madigan and Carol Osiek (Baltimore: Johns Hopkins University Press, 2011); Gary Macy, *The Hidden History of Women's Ordination* (New York: Oxford University Press, 2007). Credit and appreciation goes to my husband, Rev. Dr. Jonathan Warren, for assisting in historical research for this essay.

6. Macy, *Hidden History of Women's Ordination*, 53–58.

7. Ibid., 60.

8. Ibid., 70–74.

9. Ibid., 80–86.

10. Epiphanius of Salamis, *The Panarion of Epiphanius of Salamis: Sects 47–80*, trans. Frank Williams (Leiden: Brill, 1994), 621.

11. William Witt, "Concerning Women's Ordination."

bear the image of God and are therefore ontologically equal to men, are "modern" innovations to historic belief.

It's clear that there is an overwhelming pastoral need for women in ministry. When the church does not give space for women's voices, women inevitably turn to voices outside of the church for spiritual instruction. Women, like men, need pastoral care, and we must speak honestly about the impediments to robust pastoral care and rigorous theological formation for women that complementarianism present. Confession of sin and pastoral counseling are made more difficult between members of the opposite sex, especially in the areas of sexuality and marriage. If women are to be holistically supported and discipled pastorally, all Christians must ensure that there are women set apart, equipped, and empowered by the church to do this work of pastoral care and leadership.

Tish Harrison Warren is author of *Liturgy of the Ordinary: Sacred Practices in Everyday Life* and a priest in the Anglican Church in North America. She serves as coassociate rector at Church of the Ascension in Pittsburgh. Her work has appeared in *Comment Magazine*, *The Point Magazine*, *The Well*, *Christianity Today*, and elsewhere.

THE BEAUTY OF CENTERING LIFE AROUND THE HOME

A Complementarian Perspective on Women and Work

 *Owen Strachan*

In a way, Karl Marx lost. After Marxism became a reigning social theory in the twentieth century, numerous regimes across the world collapsed, often in spectacular fashion, in the twentieth century.

But in another way, Marx won. What do I mean? Marx delineated people according to their economic class. Today, many people define themselves not according to their church, their home region, their family, or other traditional markers, but according to their job, their income, and their resulting social status.[1]

I begin here because I believe that redefining human identity along economic lines is a problem for men and women alike. We are enchanted beings, made in the image of God (Gen. 1:26–27). Human beings are complex creatures, but we are fundamentally stamped by eternity and created by God.[2]

Men and women share dignity and worth. Both were made for an active dominion-taking life. But as we see in Genesis 2 and 3, much of the woman's work is in the home and raising children. The childbearing ability of the woman signaled not simply the ideal delivery mechanism for offspring but also a major portion of her God-given calling.[3] God never moves away from this initial

---

1. For more on economic issues, see the helpful primer by Jay Richards, *Money, Greed, and God: Why Capitalism Is the Solution and Not the Problem* (San Francisco: HarperOne, 2010). For a searing look at how Marxist policies savaged a nation, see Jung Chang and Jon Halliday, *Mao: The Unknown Story* (New York: Anchor, 2005). Readers interested in a high-level philosophical analysis of some of the tenets of Marxist thought should see Roger Scruton, *Fools, Frauds and Firebrands: Thinkers of the New Left* (New York: Bloomsbury, 2015).

2. I am consciously echoing the famous words of Augustine: "You have made us for yourself, and our hearts are restless until they find rest in you." See *Confessions* 1.1.

3. Martin Luther speaks to this reality in his characteristically direct style: "The saintly women desire nothing else than the natural fruit of their bodies. For by nature woman has been created for the purpose of

plan. Throughout Scripture, women work unto the Lord as child-bearers and homemakers (Prov. 31; Titus 2:5). This is the normative call of God for most women; it is a culture-despised but God-enchanted way of life. There is much joy in it, albeit joy that eyes of unbelief struggle to see. We should not give up this vision of womanhood; we should raise our girls to inhabit it, whether single or married. We do not know what God will call them precisely to do, of course, but as we cultivate our daughters morally, intellectually, and spiritually, we cannot fail to ready them for motherhood, homemaking, and child raising.

Women do not all live the same life. The church has a long line of productive, faithful single women, and married women without children, and married women with adult children who have blessed the church and adopted a *coram deo* existence. In the apostolic era, women helped bankroll the apostles (see Joanna in Luke 8:3). In the modern missions movement, women like Lottie Moon gave their lives to take the gospel to the ends of the earth. In the late twentieth century, Elisabeth Elliot offered wisdom and biblical counsel to a generation of women bewildered by a secularizing culture.[4] Wherever we see women working unto God, striving to render excellent service to God and man, we give thanks.

In the twenty-first century, with this rich history in mind, here are three considerations for the intersection of womanhood and work.

First, we want women to see themselves in Godward terms, not cultural terms. Diverse factors—including secularism and feminism—have encouraged women to find their value in their job and their paycheck. Doing so sets women on a disenchanted trajectory for life that culminates in a secular eschaton of a personal kind—women "having it all" when they fashion a successful career while striking "life-and-work balance." Whatever precise role one plays in the world, women do well not to buy this conception of womanhood. We will be happy when we love and obey God, and locate our value in him, not in anything or anyone else.[5]

---

bearing children. Therefore she has breasts; she has arms for the purpose of nourishing, cherishing, and carrying her offspring. It was the intention of the Creator that women should bear children and that men should beget them." Martin Luther, *Luther's Works*, 5:355.

4. For a longer survey of the unique contributions made by women in biblical history, see Owen Strachan, "The Genesis of Gender and Ecclesial Womanhood," *9Marks*, July 1, 2010.

5. The figure in recent evangelical history who most elucidates the beauty and distinctiveness of womanhood is Elisabeth Elliot. See her *Let Me Be a Woman* (Carol Stream, IL: Tyndale Momentum, 1976). Elliot wrote this elsewhere: "The gentle and quiet spirit of which Peter speaks, calling it 'of great worth in God's sight' (1 Peter 3:4), is the true femininity, which found its epitome in Mary, the willingness to be only a vessel, hidden, unknown, except as Somebody's mother. This is the true mother-spirit, true maternity, so absent, it seems to me, in all the annals of feminism. 'The holier a woman is,' wrote Leon Bloy, 'the more she is a woman.'" See Elliot, "The Essence of Femininity," in *Recovering Biblical Manhood & Womanhood*, ed. John Piper and Wayne Grudem (Wheaton, IL: Crossway, 1991), 398.

When women know this and live by it, they are free—gloriously free—to plunge into whatever sphere of labor God has given them.[6]

Second, we want to raise girls to cherish their womanhood. Modern America encourages us to raise boys and girls the same way, with only the most minimal differences. But such gender-neutral parenting fails to honor the God-made distinctiveness of the sexes. Girls have far more estrogen than boys; boys have on average 1,000 percent more testosterone than girls.[7] This does not necessitate treating the sexes unfairly. We should encourage our girls to think hard, study well, and enjoy life.

We do not, however, raise our girls in exactly the same way we raise our boys. How interesting that, in our modern age, many young women have discovered the domestic arts their ancestors practiced—knitting, making delicious and healthy food, and loving home décor are all common hobbies of modern women.[8]

Whatever a woman's precise calling, we want her to undertake it as a woman—and know that there is no inadequacy or issue here. Women need not leave their womanhood behind to give God maximal glory through their living and working.

Third, we want to define work in biblical terms. I laugh when people ask me if my wife—a mother of three and homemaker—works. In truth, it is difficult to quantify the amount of work she does on a daily basis, whether it's teaching mathematics, sending flowers to struggling loved ones, bringing home Target bounty, or caring for the soul of a three-year-old child. All this is work, done out of a heart enraptured by Christ; all of it is doxological and obedient to God. Little of it is appreciated today by our Marx-influenced world. Whether the culture applauds or sneers, the church cannot fail to encourage women to value what the Bible pristinates. There is such a thing as biblical womanhood. It is distinctive and God-honoring. It is not prissy and tame; it is sacrificial and visceral, a daily death to self. Elisabeth Elliot captures well the kind of theological mindset that Christian women will need to adopt in order to work unto God in distinctly feminine ways:

6. My words here echo the seminal thought of Dutch theologian Abraham Kuyper and his concept of "sphere sovereignty." One need not buy every facet of this paradigm to appreciate and profit from it. See Kuyper, *Lectures on Calvinism: The Stone Lectures of 1898* (Peabody, MA: Hendrickson, 2008).

7. See Anne Moir and Bill Moir, *Why Men Don't Iron: The Fascinating and Unalterable Differences Between Men and Women* (New York: Citadel, 1999), 168. This book is filled with revelations about the differences between the sexes.

8. See, for example, Ruth La Ferla, "The Knitting Circle Shows Its Chic," *New York Times*, July 12, 2007; Michael Andor Brodeur, "The Cult of 'Fixer Upper,'" *Boston Globe*, January 3, 2017; Thomas Rogers, "How Food Television Is Changing America," *Salon*, February 26, 2010. These trends—and others like them—show that even in an age that downplays traditional gender roles, women still have interest in traditional pursuits.

The routines of housework and of mothering may be seen as a kind of death, and it is appropriate that they should be, for they offer the chance, day after day, to lay down one's life for others. Then they are no longer routines. By being done with love and offered up to God with praise, they are thereby hallowed as the vessels of the tabernacle were hallowed—not because they were different from other vessels in quality or function, but because they were offered to God. A mother's part in sustaining the life of her children and making it pleasant and comfortable is no triviality. It calls for self-sacrifice and humility, but it is the route, as was the humiliation of Jesus, to glory.[9]

When we understand work in panoramic perspective—seeing it as a common-grace gift of God, not our core identity—then women are freed to work with pleasure and satisfaction they've never previously known. They may earn a million dollars a year or they may earn precisely zero dollars for their domestic efforts. Money and titles are not the key. For Christians, and for Christian women, what matters most is obeying the Word and applying the Word faithfully to the situations, gifts, and opportunities God places before us.

There are many matters to sort out related to women and work. We need biblical wisdom to figure out what godliness looks like in a gender-neutral society, one that features uniquely high ages of first marriage for men and women, when many women are faced with complexities previous generations did not know.

Regardless of her personal situation, however, every woman must know what the right questions are.

The question she must answer is not, "Will she work?"

The question is truly this: "Who will she work for, and what will her reward be?"

Dr. Owen Strachan is associate professor of Christian theology at Midwestern Baptist Theological Seminary. At MBTS, he leads the Center for Public Theology. Strachan is the author of numerous books, including *Awakening the Evangelical Mind* and *The Colson Way*. He holds a PhD from Trinity Evangelical Divinity School, an MDiv from Southern Seminary, and an AB from Bowdoin College.

---

9.   Elisabeth Elliot, *Love Has a Price Tag: Inspiring Stories That Will Open Your Heart to Life's Little Miracles* (1979; Ventura, CA: Regal, 2005), 209–10.

WOMEN'S WORK IS IN THE HOME—AND OUT OF IT

Katelyn Beaty

More American women are working outside the home now than ever before. According to the US Bureau of Labor Statistics, as of 2014, about 6 in 10 women participate in the labor force, a majority of them full-time and year-round. Among mothers with children younger than six, 64 percent work outside the home, while 75 percent of moms with kids ages six to seventeen do the same. These numbers represent one of the most dynamic changes in Western culture in the past century as well as an opportunity for churches that want to offer work-faith resources for congregants.

Yet anecdotal research indicates that there remains a discipleship gap for many working women. In dozens of conversations for my book on women's work and vocation, a common theme emerged: Work as a topic of theological and pastoral concern is highly gendered.

Katherine Leary Alsdorf had been the CEO of several companies before she came to Christ at Redeemer Presbyterian Church in Manhattan. As a new Christian, she wanted to know what it meant to serve God at the office on Mondays as much as in church on Sundays. Yet when she asked a pastor if she could join the group of Christian CEOs who met regularly, he said, "It's all men, so why don't you find a group of women CEOs and form your own group?" Alsdorf noted that the other women CEOs she knew didn't go to church and might not feel welcome if they did. "For most career women in the church, it's been a challenging, pioneering time," she told me.

Even women who are not high-powered CEOs noted that their church women's small groups meet on weekdays—which assumes most women aren't working then—or that the faith-work programming is under the men's ministry. Other women are explicitly discouraged from professional work. Liz Aleman, a lawyer in California, shared a painful story of excitedly telling her pastor that she had gotten into law school, only to have him caution that no Christian man would want to marry a lawyer.

In other words, in many churches work is treated as masculine, while family and home are treated as feminine. Some Christian leaders see the work/home and attendant male/female dichotomy as biblically prescriptive. According to popular teachings on biblical manhood and womanhood, God made husbands to be breadwinners outside the home, while God made wives to be nurturers and caretakers at home.

Yet when we examine the words of Scripture, we find that these dichotomies are not rooted in the text but in powerful cultural and economic forces beyond it. As churches adjust to women's increased work outside the home, it's important to recount how vast changes over the past 300 years affected both industry and gender, so that we have a fully biblical understanding of both.

Nearly all women who have ever lived have labored to provide for their families and communities. The choice for women *not* to participate in the economic sphere is relatively new. Historically speaking, all women except for the elite—aristocrats or heiresses, say—had to work by the sweat of their brows on a farm or, later, in home-based workshops. Work was home and home was work, and men and women labored alongside each other to survive.

Colonial America, for example, had men and women "working side by side in a common enterprise," notes scholar Nancy Pearcey.[1] Women of this time cared for children (who themselves were seen as laborers) while spinning, weaving, sewing, gardening, preserving food, cooking, and making goods like candles and soap. Men were highly involved in child-rearing; Pearcey notes that sermons and manuals of the day told both husbands and wives to raise their children together. We should resist idealizing colonial life, given the backbreaking nature of survival. But we might envy the cohesion of daily life experienced by men and women of the time.

So what happened? Some Christians point to the feminist movements of the past century to explain the breakdown of the family, the denigration of motherhood, and many social problems. But in fact the Industrial Revolution more than the feminist movement reshaped how we do work as well as how we view gender. The Industrial Revolution—more than any specific biblical text—is the inspiration for the teaching that men are to be breadwinners and women are to stay at home with children.

Between 1780 and 1830, the United States made a seismic transition from an agrarian economy to an industrial economy. Factories replaced farms, eventually

---

1. Nancy R. Pearcey, "Is Love Enough? Recreating the Economic Base of the Family," *The Family in America* 4, no. 1 (January 1990), http://www.arn.org/docs/pearcey/np_familyinamerica.htm.

taking the most difficult and creative work of home life outside of it. Working-class men and women moved to cities to take up low-skilled factory work. But among the upper and emerging middle class arose a powerful ideology called "separate spheres." Alexis de Tocqueville, during his famed travels to the United States in 1835, observed, "In no country has such constant care been taken as in America to trace two clearly distinct lines of action with the other, but in two pathways that are always different."[2] The belief that "a woman's place is in the home" can be found in ancient Greek and Roman culture and traditional Judaism. But it became enshrined as moral and spiritual fact among relatively wealthy, white Americans in the nineteenth and twentieth centuries.

Separate spheres allowed such women to attend to raising children and to identify motherhood as their primary vocation. Indeed, many women across classes would prefer to stay home with young children; today, 56 percent of US women with kids under eighteen would prefer to stay home over going to work.[3] Especially given women's unique biological role in having and raising kids, separate spheres is an efficient way to organize a family economy for those who can choose it.

But there are costs. Many men today experience undue pressure to provide for a family on their own, all the while spending their days apart from their children. Women who have earned academic degrees and worked hard in their twenties often find few avenues back to the workforce after having children. Current conversations about "work-life balance," paid parental leave, and the unexamined value of caretaking all speak of a society trying to overcome the divides wrought by the Industrial Revolution.

Christian communities can speak a word of encouragement to women who work out of necessity, calling, or both. Work is a core aspect of what every image-bearer is made to do. The Bible opens with a description of God as a worker who invites his image-bearers to be like him and labor to care for the physical and cultural world. The Proverbs 31 woman in the Old Testament, and Joanna, Lydia, and Phoebe in the New, are positive models of "the presence of women in the economy of the ancient world," notes biblical scholar Lynn Cohick.[4]

Whether their work is done outside or inside the home, at an office or coffee shop or backyard, women need more resources for working "with all your heart, as working for the Lord, not for human masters" (Col. 3:23). Churches with

---

2. Alexis de Tocqueville, "How Americans Understand the Equality of the Sexes," in *Democracy in America*, revised ed., trans. Henry Reeve, vol. 2 (New York: Colonial, 1900), 222.

3. Lydia Saad, "Children a Key Factor in Women's Desire to Work Outside the Home," *Gallup*, October 7, 2015, https://news.gallup.com/poll/186050/children-key-factor-women-desire-work-outside-home.aspx.

4. Lynn Cohick, *Women in the World of the Earliest Christians: Illuminating Ancient Ways of Life* (Grand Rapids: Baker, 2009), 241.

strong work-faith programming for all congregants can profoundly shape cultures, transform institutions, and serve and love their neighbors well. Working women are a great untapped resource for the church—if only it has the eyes to see them.

Katelyn Beaty is author of *A Woman's Place: A Christian Vision for Your Calling in the Office, the Home, and the World* and former managing editor of *Christianity Today* magazine. She has written for *The New Yorker, The New York Times, The Atlantic,* and *The Washington Post* and lives in New York City.

DISCUSSION QUESTIONS

1. In the background of each of these positions is an assumed definition of both biblical manhood and biblical womanhood. Can you articulate the presupposed definitions that each view assumes as they engage this topic?

2. Beaty declares that concepts of women "are actually constructs of the culture following the Industrial Revolution." How do you think someone who holds Strachan's position would respond to Beaty's statements regarding the Industrial Revolution?

3. Alsup references in her article that "only men were named priests . . . or elders" as one of the distinctions between males and females. Consider 1 Timothy 2:11–15 and describe how each of the two contrasting views in this section understand this passage.

4. In his article, Strachan declares that Marxism and feminism have pulled women away from their instinctual, God-given roles and provided identity confusion. How do you think someone with Beaty's perspective might respond to that claim?

5. Strachan says that "in Genesis 2 and 3, much of the woman's work is in the home and raising children." What evidence do you see for this in Genesis 2 and 3?

6. In her article, Alsup says that as a woman she is an "*ezer*/helper that fits the needs of male image-bearers in my church." How do you think someone from Warren's tradition would respond to this description of women's role in the church?

7. Beaty discusses at length the overwhelming gap in the church for women who work. Warren, discussing this same idea, declares that when "the church does not give space for women's voices, women inevitably turn to the voices outside of the church," citing this as the reason churches need women pastors. How would someone who opposes Warren's view of women as pastors respond to both the problem posed by Beaty and the solution (women pastors) given by Warren?

8. In her article, Alsup briefly acknowledges a quote and definition of gender as a concept influenced by both culture and time (still holding that God-given biological sex transcends culture and time). In his article, however, Strachan seems to relate the presence of more estrogen and less testosterone to traditional "gender roles." Can you articulate the two different relationships between gender and biological sex assumed by these two articles?

9. Warren uses a reference to William Witt's writing to state that the historic roots of complementarianism are built on the belief that women are, quite simply, inferior to men. She acknowledges that contemporary complementarians do not agree with this belief, but still sees this history as a problem for contemporary complementarians. Is this a relevant point? Why or why not?

10. While each of these articles expresses a unique and sometimes contrasting perspective on the issue of gender roles, there also is overlap. From your reading, where did you find that the authors agree with each other?

chapter six

HUMAN LIFE AND REPRODUCTIVE TECHNOLOGY

Children are a blessing. This idea is taught and reinforced multiple places throughout Scripture. As early as the first chapter of Genesis, God blesses Adam and Eve, saying, "'Be fruitful and multiply and fill the earth and subdue it, and have dominion over the fish of the sea and over the birds of the heavens and over every living thing that moves on the earth'" (Gen. 1:28 ESV). Later, in Psalm 127:4–5, David explains, "Like arrows in the hand of a warrior are the children of one's youth. Blessed is the man who fills his quiver with them!" (ESV). When Scripture talks about children, it does so favorably and with the exhortation that Christians should love, cherish, and train these little ones. Yet, today and throughout church history, the church has wrestled with balancing this scriptural principal against changing cultural practices and attitudes regarding sex and reproduction.

Conflicting views within the church are reflected by varied interpretations of Onan's sin described in Genesis 38:9, where it states that he "spilled his semen on the ground" rather than impregnating his widowed sister-in-law, which was customary among the Israelites in such situations. The following verse says that the Lord saw Onan's act as wicked and put him to death. One traditional teaching is that Onan's sin was simply his attempt at "birth control," nonprocreative sexual relations. However, the biblical context suggests that Onan's sin was in willfully depriving his brother's widow of an heir, thereby to inherit his brother's property himself. This single biblical story reveals many of the complexities that have surrounded questions about birth control throughout the history of the church that persist today: is birth control itself sinful? If not, are there faithful as well as sinful reasons for practicing it? Are some methods and technologies in and of themselves sinful?

As technology has developed and family life has evolved and changed along with these advancements, such questions have grown even more complicated.

There is no manner of reproductive technology that is not mired in some form of moral dispute within the Christian church.

The Roman Catholic Church has long held that contraception runs counter to God's purpose for sex and marriage. Natural family-planning methods, which time female fertility and practice abstinence during that window of time, uphold the teaching that every sexual act must be open to life in order to be licit.[1] However, the Catholic Church's requirement (based on the examples of Jesus and Paul) that priests be celibate—denying not only sexual relations but also natural families—was viewed by Protestant Reformers as a distortion of the full counsel of Scripture.

In "History of Contraception in the Protestant Church," Allan Carlson argues, in fact, that at the root of the Reformation was Luther's driving desire to reform the church's attitude toward marriage and childbearing, bringing it more fully in alignment with Scripture's teaching that children are a blessing. Carlson notes, "Church tradition held that the taking of vows of chastity—as a priest, monk, or cloistered sister—was spiritually superior to the wedded life. In consequence, about one-third of adult European Christians were in Holy Orders." This attitude meant that fewer and fewer children were being born to Christian parents, a problem that Luther addressed often in his writings.[2] Luther fought against this mindset, both in word and in deed, as Carlson explains: "In short, Luther's fierce rejection of contraception and abortion lay at the very heart of his reforming zeal and his evangelical theology. His own marriage to Katherine von Bora and their brood of children set a model for the Protestant Christian home, one that would stand for nearly four hundred years."[3]

Similar to Luther, Calvin also rejected the use of contraception while emphasizing fellowship and continence as important purposes for sex within marriage. Kathryn Blanchard summarizes how theological reflection on marriage progressed in the centuries that followed the initial break from Rome:

> Although Protestant views of marriage shifted toward an emphasis on fellowship (and away from procreation) in the centuries after Calvin, Christian views on birth control (at least as committed to writing by male theologians) remained largely unchanged until the end of the nineteenth century. Religious objections to birth control were largely underdeveloped. . . . It was not until there began to be an active and vocal social

---

1. "A Healthy Marriage with Catholic Natural Family Planning," Beginning Catholic, http://www.beginningcatholic.com/catholic-natural-family-planning.
2. Allan Carlson, "History of Contraception in the Protestant Church," *Bound 4 Life*, https://www.bound4life.com/history-of-contraception-in-the-protestant-church/.
3. Ibid.

movement (first among women, and followed by religious supporters) for birth control at the turn of the twentieth century—amidst industrialism and its formation of the kind of "family" unit we now recognize—that the Catholic Church was forced to make a more extensive argument against it.[4]

Widespread Protestant acceptance of birth control emerged from a mix of cultural and ethical concerns at the Lambeth Conference of the Church of England (1930). At Lambeth the Anglican bishops decisively voted that when there was a "morally sound reason," the use of contraceptives was permittable given that they are not used out of "selfishness, luxury, or mere convenience." This resolution set a trend for similar Protestant statements. It was in this post-Lambeth context that Karl Barth, arguably the most important theologian of the twentieth century, wrote on marriage and parenthood. Blanchard summarizes his position, which finds certain parallels with the luminary of the Reformed tradition:

> Barth's position is not so far from Calvin's, in that it first recognizes the goodness of marriage in itself, as a godly vocation regardless of whether or not it is biologically procreative. Second, he affirms that children are from God, who is sovereign over nature and whose own freedom implies that children are not (against what he sees as the Catholic overemphasis on nature) a necessary function of natural processes. And last, Barth recognizes that begetting children requires a couple's conversation with God with regard to their parental vocation in the world—that is, may they have biological children, or should they be elders in some other way? The Christian's response is an act of free conversation; even if some find contraception objectionable, Barth says, "they must not make their repugnance a law for others." The divine command might take different forms for different people in different times and places. The ongoing struggle for Christians (and it should be seen as a struggle) is to discern what that command is and what their free response to it should be.[5]

A legal and cultural turning point occurred in 1965 when the US Supreme Court in the landmark case Griswold vs. Connecticut struck down state laws against contraception as a violation of marital privacy. The right to privacy established in this case was cited later in the 1973 Roe v. Wade ruling, which legalized abortion on demand.

---

4. Kathryn D. Blanchard, "The Gift of Contraception: Calvin, Barth, and a Lost Protestant Conversation," *Journal of the Society of Christian Ethics* 27, no. 1 (2007): 239.

5. Ibid.

By the middle of the twentieth century, "virtually all Protestant churches," like the surrounding culture,

> embraced contraception and (somewhat less frequently) abortion as compatible with Christian ethics. Pope Paul VI's courageous opposition to these acts in the 1968 encyclical, *Humanae Vitae*, won broad condemnation from Protestant leaders as an attempt to impose "Catholic views" on the world. Even leaders of "conservative" denominations such as the Southern Baptist Convention would welcome as "a blow for Christian liberty" the 1973 Roe v. Wade decision of the U.S. Supreme Court that legalized abortion as a free choice during the first six months (and in practice for all nine months) of a pregnancy. Not a single significant Protestant voice raised opposition in the 1960's and early 1970's to the massive entry of the U.S. government into the promotion and distribution of contraceptives, nationally and worldwide.[6]

By the time many Christians realized that the church had surrendered moral ground, the cultural shift had already found solid footing that was not easily unsettled or reversed. Today more conservative Christians have begun to raise awareness regarding the secularism that pervades the church's discussions on marriage and sex.

Of course, not all reproductive technologies are geared toward preventing pregnancy and birth. Many of the most recent innovations in reproductive technology assist the infertile to have children. Yet, these technologies too are mired in moral complexities. Scott Rae summarizes the controversy surrounding reproductive technologies this way:

> The new reproductive technologies give great hope to infertile couples and make many new reproductive arrangements possible. They also raise many difficult moral issues. Artificial insemination by husband is considered moral, but artificial insemination by donor raises questions about a third party entering reproduction. In vitro fertilization is acceptable within limits: the couple should ensure that no embryos are left in storage and that the risk of selective termination is avoided. Commercial surrogate motherhood raises problems because it is the equivalent of selling children, can be exploitative of the surrogate, and violates a mother's fundamental right to raise her child. Even altruistic surrogacy raises questions about the degree

---

6. Carlson, "History of Contraception in the Protestant Church."

of detachment the mother must have from her unborn child to successfully give it up after birth.[7]

The numerous ethical, legal, and moral dilemmas surrounding each of the reproductive technologies used today leads John Piper to conclude that "the wisest and most compassionate course of action in all these matters is to stay close to the natural processes of reproduction, which God designed—basically keeping eggs and sperm in our bodies."[8] In this way, John Piper is reinforcing to a limited degree the long-held Catholic respect for "natural law," which emphasizes "the continuity between procreation and parenthood."[9]

Even among Christians, the default position is often the pursuit of producing a child at any moral (and financial) cost without sufficient and informed consideration of the moral and ethical dilemmas inherent in many of these technologies. While the church has become outspoken in recent decades on abortion, it still remains largely silent on assisted reproduction, leaving couples to navigate murky medical and moral waters alone. A recent book by Matthew Arbo, however, addresses these complicated issues with the skill of a moral ethicist and the care of a pastor/theologian. Arbo cautions that Christians need to be adequately informed about all that reproductive technologies such as IUI and IVF entail in order to begin to weigh the ethical questions surrounding their use. However, many well-intentioned Christians step blindly into these complicated processes at the prompting of medical professions before taking stock of the potential ethical boundaries that might later be crossed. Too often, even Christians fall into the pragmatism of thinking the ends justify the means.[10]

The Bible's teaching that children are a blessing has, for many in the church, been taken to mean that they are also a right. The church now finds itself grappling with the moral and ethical quandaries that have developed from this neglect.

Stephen and Brianne Bell open this section sharing their own story of struggling with infertility and ultimately pursuing IVF in order to conceive their first child. Through their story, the Bells acknowledge the many controversies surrounding their decision, but ultimately uphold that they sought to bear children in accordance with God's plan for Christians. In contrast, Jennifer Lahl argues that the Bible clearly speaks to the issues of infertility and procreation and

---

7. Scott Rae, "Reproductive Technologies," CRI, http://www.equip.org/article/reproductive-technologies/.

8. John Piper, "Do Reproductive Technologies Oppose God's Design?" *Desiring God*, February 28, 2018, https://www.desiringgod.org/interviews/do-reproductive-technologies-oppose-gods-design.

9. Rae, "Reproductive Technologies."

10. Matthew Arbo, *Walking through Infertility: Biblical, Theological, and Moral Counsel for Those Who Are Struggling* (Wheaton, IL: Crossway, 2018), 82.

that Christians should listen to these stories in order to form God-centered views on the designed purpose, plan, and place for procreation. Assuming the same position as Lahl, Charles Camosy explains how consumerism has influenced the reproductive technologies by treating our children and reproductive capacities as goods to be bought and sold.

Integrating her own story, Ellen Painter Dollar explains how the Bible, as a story, speaks to the nuanced issues surrounding reproductive technology and encourages Christians to become people who listen generously to the stories of individuals who have encountered reproductive challenges and unplanned pregnancies in order to gain a more nuanced biblical view on these topics. In contrast to Dollar's argument, Karen Swallow Prior and Kenneth Magnuson make clear their denunciation of abortion, while disagreeing on how to talk about abortion within a culture in which the practice is so common and widely accepted. Prior urges Christians to choose their rhetoric carefully when addressing the issue of abortion so that the truth spoken in love can be heard above the noise of inflammatory speech. In an exception to the normal pattern in this volume, Kenneth Magnuson responds specifically to Prior's article, arguing that the rhetoric, context, and definitions surrounding the issue of abortion need careful consideration and attention so that the debates on this issue can remain simultaneously uncompromising and compassionate.

IN VITRO FERTILIZATION IS PRO-LIFE

Stephen and Brianne Bell

Studies have shown that infertility affects one in eight couples, according to the Centers for Disease Control and Prevention.[1] We were in our mid-thirties when we decided to start a family after two years of marriage. We tried on our own for over a year (experiencing at least one chemical pregnancy) before Brianne's OB-GYN introduced her to Clomid, an estrogen modulator that induces ovulation, but which also resulted in painful ovarian cysts. We were then referred to a reproductive specialist.

After our first meeting with the doctor, we felt hopeful, excited, and confident. We went through various screenings and testing that included a semen analysis, blood work to check the reproductive hormones, and a hysterosalpingogram (HSG) to check for uterine abnormalities. All the testing came back normal, so we began with a few rounds of Letrozole and had three intrauterine inseminations (IUI). IUI involves placing sperm directly into the uterus to facilitate fertilization by increasing the number of sperm that reach the Fallopian tubes.

Through the Letrozole and the IUI we became pregnant several times, all of which resulted in early loss. It was at this point that we began to discuss the possibility of in vitro fertilization and embryo transfer (IVF-ET), which extracts the eggs, retrieves a sperm sample, and then manually fertilizes them in a laboratory dish. We both agreed that we would try everything medically possible to have our own children before we would attempt other options such as adoption or surrogacy. We were also very blessed to have our parents' help with the financial costs, which were admittedly prohibitive.

---

1. "Reproductive Health: Infertility FAQs," *CDC*.gov, March 30, 2017, https://www.cdc.gov/reproductive health/infertility/index.htm/.

Based on our doctor's recommendation, we decided to do IVF-ET with PGD (preimplantation genetic diagnosis) testing because of our recurrent miscarriages. PGD is a procedure in which one or more cells are removed from each embryo and used for genetic diagnosis. The embryos are then selected for uterine transfer based on the outcome of the testing. Once the eggs were removed, a single sperm was injected into each egg, a procedure called intracytoplasmic sperm injection (ICSI), to increase the chances of fertilization.

The process of IVF is not only emotionally exhausting but it's also physically demanding. The many medications required come with side effects and some resulted in mood swings, headaches, and nausea. The injections were not painful, but they were time consuming. Brianne was quite sore after the egg retrieval. Once the process was complete, we ended up with five embryos, which received normal genetic diagnosis and were cryopreserved. Our first frozen embryo transfer resulted in our beautiful, spunky daughter, Caroline. Another frozen embryo failed to implant last year, while a third embryo transfer was successful, and Brianne will be giving birth to another daughter in about a month. Two additional embryos remain cryopreserved.

The most common ethical objections to IVF among many Christians seem to fall under two main categories. First, IVF and other reproductive technologies encourage participants to play God, seizing his prerogative to create life and seeking to manipulate circumstances (such as infertility) outside their control. Second, IVF creates an excess of embryos that are either frozen until they're finally donated (equivalent to giving away one's children?) or eventually all transferred to the mother. Should participants allow for the possibility that more embryos are created than they're prepared to give birth to?

Rod Dreher, in his recent work *The Benedict Option: A Strategy for Christians in a Post-Christian Nation*, devotes an entire chapter to the seductive dangers of the worldview of "Technological Man," the autonomous self so valorized by modernity for uncritically embracing the gifts of technology with no regard for ethical consequences. The most important consideration is for humans to be free to pursue individual happiness and satisfaction through the means made available by science and technology. As Dreher puts it,

> Beginning with nominalism [in the fourteenth century] and emerging in the early modern era [there was a growing belief that] nature had no intrinsic meaning. It's just stuff. To Technological Man, "truth" is what works to extend his dominion over nature and make that stuff into things he finds useful or pleasurable, thereby fulfilling his sense of what it means to exist. To regard the world technologically, then, is to see it

as material over which to extend one's dominion, limited only by one's imagination.[2]

Dreher argues that a majority of individuals in the West, including many Christians, subscribe to this belief system (whether they would acknowledge it or not), which is powered by the twin engines of emotivism and Moral Therapeutic Deism. While emotivism would discard the imperatives of faith and reason in favor of impulsivity and human choice, Moral Therapeutic Deism preaches subjective happiness and material comfort as the central goals of life. Such a worldview places no limits on what we can do with our bodies, since the most important considerations are that we are happy and comfortable from one moment to the next. For Dreher and Christian opponents of reproductive technologies like IVF, the problem is that "[w]e have made biology subject to human will. . . . Reproductive technology extends the mastery of procreation by liberating conception from the body entirely."[3]

We regularly see such abuses of reproductive technology today, from the controversial to the utterly unacceptable. Celebrity couples like John Legend and Chrissy Teigen have used PGD testing to select the sex of the embryo they wished to be transferred.[4] *Slate* magazine highlights an Australian company called Baby Bee Hummingbirds, which converts unwanted frozen embryos (referred to by some as "frosties" or "snowbabies") into earrings and jewelry by cremating embryos into ash that preserves their DNA. The company's founder, Amy McGlade, promises to lovingly transform these embryos into "sacred art" for a cost between $80 and $600.[5] As one Catholic blogger quoted in the article tweeted in outrage, "If we value kids only to serve us, of course they can be made into jewelry if they no longer serve our needs alive." A recent *USA Today* article explores the controversial practice of gene editing through such recent discoveries as CRISPR-Cas9, "a powerful gene-editing tool that gives scientists the ability to make precise edits of single strands of DNA. . . . CRISPR could be used to erase and replace mutations that make some susceptible to a wide range of conditions, from AIDS to the Zika virus."[6]

2. Rod Dreher, *The Benedict Option: A Strategy for Christians in a Post-Christian Nation* (New York: Sentinel, 2017), 219–20.

3. Ibid., 221.

4. Monica Kim, "Should you select your child's gender? The debate surrounding Chrissy Teigen's IVF reveal," *Vogue*, February 26, 2016, http://www.vogue.com/article/chrissy-teigen-ivf-gender-selection-controversy -explained.

5. Ruth Graham, "Just how creepy is 'embryo jewelry,' exactly?" *Slate*, May 5, 2017, http://www.slate .com/blogs/xx_factor/2017/05/05/embryo_jewelry_is_creepy_but_how_creepy.html.

6. Mike Feibus, "CRISPR gene editing tool: Are we ready to play God?" *USA Today*, July 24, 2017. https:// www.usatoday.com/story/tech/columnist/2017/07/24/crispr-gene-editing-tool-we-ready-play-god/490144001/.

However, just because a technology or human advancement can be illicitly exploited, does that mean that conscientious Christians should actively avoid technologies such as IVF that increase the chances of human conception? IVF functions merely as a means of increasing the probability of an embryo's viability in the mother's womb, not a Promethean attempt to literally create human life and steal fire from the gods. We must also remember that humans have always manipulated nature to achieve their ends, not all of which are harmful and transgressive. As one friend of ours from church mused, "Is it considered playing God when plants are genetically modified to grow more rapidly? Or when animals are crossbred to create something that has specific characteristics that are desirable for certain functions?"

God created humans with curiosity and a drive to understand and create. Indeed, many theologians would argue that God's command in Genesis 1:28 entails an endorsement of the inherent good to be found in the work of culture and human advancement: "Be fruitful and increase in number; fill the earth and subdue it. Rule over the fish in the sea and the birds in the sky and over every living creature that moves on the ground." Although this work of dominion can be exploited and abused, leading to a culture of death rather than one of life (as abortion technologies have demonstrated), it can just as well facilitate increased fruitfulness and human flourishing.

When we elected to begin fertility treatments, we understood it not as a faithless choice that circumvented God's sovereign control over our bodies and defied his clear requirements in Scripture, but as a fulfillment of his command to joyfully bear his image and conceive and bear godly offspring made in his image as well. As another college friend recently encouraged us, "[Your decision] could be viewed as an act of faith to . . . persevere in seeking God to fulfill one of the fundamental callings, purposes, and commands associated with your very existence."

For those who would argue that such logic twists scriptural truth to rationalize an act that God explicitly forbids, consider why contraception is generally accepted in Protestant circles (discouraging fertility and human flourishing), while reproductive technologies are viewed as harmful and transgressive. Our mindset was always one of prayerful expectancy and hope beyond hope rather than temporizing or arrogantly seeking to wrest control from God over the outcome.

We'll confess that the second objection regarding what to do with the remaining embryos has been the most challenging for us. Since Stephen is now 44, and Brianne is turning 40 this year, it's unlikely that we'll seek to have two additional children after Caroline's sister is born. Obviously, we would never consider simply discarding them (or turning them into jewelry!), so that leaves us with the option of donating them to a childless couple or eventually transferring all of them one at a time to Brianne and leaving the rest to God. One couple in our church who also pursued IVF and has given birth to twins plans to pursue this latter option, but will forgo all the shots, injections, and medicine each time a new embryo is transferred. Donating the embryos to an anonymous couple certainly remains an option, but now that we have Caroline, it's painful to think of potential children somewhere in the world, looking very much like she does, with our DNA, growing up in another family. And what if the parents are unbelievers, or, God forbid, cruel to those children? Those are the thoughts that keep us up at night. Yet in this, as in all areas in life, we hold fast to God's character as revealed in his word and are comforted—he will always actively demonstrate lovingkindness, his mercies are new every morning, and he is the author of life.

Stephen Bell (PhD, Indiana University of Pennsylvania) teaches literature at Liberty University and has been a member of the English graduate faculty since 2014.

Brianne Bell (MEd, University of Virginia) worked in the Lynchburg City School system as a second-grade teacher until Caroline was born, when she became a full-time stay-at-home mom.

THE CASE AGAINST IN VITRO FERTILIZATION

Jennifer Lahl

Now when Rachel saw that she bore Jacob no children, she became jealous of her sister; and she said to Jacob, "Give me children, or else I die."

Genesis 30:1 NASB

First comes love and then comes marriage, but what happens when there is no baby carriage?

The grief and sadness of the barren womb, infertility, has been with us since the beginning of time. In fact, the first account of the barren womb is presented in the first book of the Bible, in the story of Sarai, Abram, and Hagar.

Now Sarai, Abram's wife, had borne him no children. But she had an Egyptian slave named Hagar; so she said to Abram, "The LORD has kept me from having children. Go, sleep with my slave; perhaps I can build a family through her."

Abram agreed to what Sarai said. So after Abram had been living in Canaan ten years, Sarai his wife took her Egyptian slave Hagar and gave her to her husband to be his wife. He slept with Hagar, and she conceived.

When she knew she was pregnant, she began to despise her mistress. Then Sarai said to Abram, "You are responsible for the wrong I am suffering. I put my slave in your arms, and now that she knows she is pregnant, she despises me. May the LORD judge between you and me."

"Your slave is in your hands," Abram said. "Do with her whatever you think best." Then Sarai mistreated Hagar; so she fled from her. (Gen. 16:1–6)

One has to wonder, since infertility has been with us since the beginning, and the issue of surrogacy and its negative aftermath are spoken of in the Bible so explicitly and early, why is it that Christians today are uninformed on the ethics of assisted reproductive technologies (ART) in general, and specifically on the use of in vitro fertilization (IVF), egg donation, sperm donation, and surrogacy?

Perhaps it's because we don't speak of or teach about the barren womb in light of these modern technologies. When was the last time you heard a sermon preached on God's purposes for the barren womb and infertility? Our churches typically have annual celebrations around Mother's Day and Father's Day, and every infant dedication or baptism is a major church festivity. But what about those who desire children, who long for children, yet are unable to conceive and bear an infant? What is our response to them?

◯◯ A Primer

We are told in Scripture that children are gifts from God, a reward and a blessing. Children are fearfully and wonderfully made by God, knit together by him in their mother's womb. Children are made by God; they are begotten by human beings. In the Roman Catholic tradition, the sacrament of marriage has the goal of producing children, allowing the husband and wife to participate in the begetting process as cocreators with God.

It is the Lord in his sovereignty and omniscience who opens and closes the womb (1 Sam. 1:5). No one has a right to a child. No one has a right to any blessing or reward from God. Of course, few people struggling with infertility approach it with the idea that God owes them a child foremost in their mind. However, what I have seen over and over in my work are actions and attitudes that seem as if, implicitly, they are owed a child, and if that child doesn't come naturally, the use of these new technologies is uncritically accepted. The justification I often hear is that God has given us these new technologies, and therefore we are permitted to benefit from them.

How are we to view the possible use of ART in light of the biblical truth that it is the Lord who opens and closes the womb? What about third-party assistance through egg donation, sperm donation, or surrogacy? I suggest we look toward a medical model of healing and restoring fertility if and when possible. This differs from circumventing infertility or bypassing infertility through technological means. To state it another way, we cross a bright ethical line when we remove eggs or sperm from the body and become technological makers rather than begetters.

As one ethicist has pointed out, there are at least thirty-eight ways to make a baby today.[1] Many, if not most of those involve taking eggs and sperm out of

---

1. Joe Carter, "38 Ways to Make a Baby," *First Things*, September 28, 2011, https://www.firstthings.com/web-exclusives/2011/09/38-ways-to-make-a-baby

the human body and into the lab. And certainly, all forms of third-party reproduction that do not involve adulterous sex involves making new life outside the
human body.

In addition, ART via IVF—creating embryos in the lab—is in no way a
pro-life approach. The loss of embryos from IVF is but one very real concern for
Christians who oppose the taking of human life. The most recent CDC data on
ART, from 2015, shows more than 91,000 IVF cycles started leading to more
than 59,000 embryos transferred, resulting in 26,708 positive pregnancies but
only 21,771 live births. The 59,000 embryos transferred (which, notably, is far
less than the number of embryos created during these processes), resulted in only
21,771 live births.[2] This is far from pro-life.

In a nutshell, the issue here is that this moves the procreation of children
from the domain of begetting to the domain of human manufacturing of children. In fact, we no longer speak of begetting or procreation, but of starting new
life in a laboratory, outside the human body.

I can write at length about the consequences that flow from the making of
human life in the lab, but I want to suggest that there is something deeper to be
considered here, namely God's intention for children to come into the world
through the physical uniting of a man and a woman. This is a deep issue to which
most people have given far too little consideration.

But some have.

Oliver O'Donovan writes, "When procreation is divorced from its context in
man-woman relationship, it becomes a project of marriage rather than its intrinsic good; the means to procreation become the instrumental means chosen by the
will, rather than themselves being of the goods of marriage."[3] C. S. Lewis warns
of "the power of Man to make himself what he pleases . . . the power of some
men to make other men [or our children] what they please."[4] The late Christian
ethicist Paul Ramsey goes even further with his condemnation of the use of IVF,
stating, "I must judge that in vitro fertilization constitutes unethical medical
experimentation on possible future human beings (without their consent) and
therefore it is subject to absolute moral prohibition."[5]

For couples facing infertility, roughly one third of infertility is due to issues
with the woman's body, roughly one third is caused by issues in the man's body,

    2. Saswati Sunderam et al., "Assisted Reproductive Technology Surveillance—United States, 2015,"
Surveillance Summaries 67, no. 3 (February 16, 2018): 1–28, https://www.cdc.gov/mmwr/volumes/67/ss/
ss6703a1.htm.
    3. Oliver O'Donovan, *Begotten or Made? Human Procreation and Medical Technique* (Oxford: Oxford
University Press, 1984), 39.
    4. C. S. Lewis, *The Abolition of Man* (New York: HarperOne, 2001), 59.
    5. Paul Ramsey, "Shall We 'Reproduce'? The Medical Ethics of In Vitro Fertilization," *Journal of the
American Medical Association* 220, no. 10 (1972): 1346–50, doi:10.1001/jama.1972.03200100058012.

and about a third is due to unknown reasons—tests are simply not able to find the cause. Still, there are many things that can be done to assist a husband and wife to achieve conception apart from ART: low-dose hormone therapy to regulate ovulation or help with low hormone levels (male and female), treating blocked Fallopian tubes or endometriosis, assistance with tracking and timing ovulation, and more. Other lifestyle factors sometimes come into play—healthy eating, maintaining a healthy weight, stopping smoking, decreasing alcohol consumption, etc. Age is often a factor as more couples postpone childbearing for graduate school, career, and other pursuits. In short, the biological clock is real, especially for women.

Perhaps we need to reorient our thinking about what a family is. God said that it was not good for Adam to be alone in the garden and so created Eve. Adam and Eve were a family. God's blessings come to us in many forms, and that form is not always children. Sometimes we are called to direct our desires to nurture the next generation in other ways. I am not aware of any church that has too many volunteers for the nursery or for other children's activities. Many older adults—single and married—find themselves lonely and would be greatly ministered to by a visit, a phone call, a card. The point is that perhaps some are called to a broader vision of what it means to nurture and to care.

The pain of infertility is real and it cuts deep. In no way do I diminish it. However, as with all desires, there are limits to what we may and may not pursue in meeting those desires. Moving eggs and sperm into the lab crosses an ethical line, changing procreation to technological making. All Christians would do well to think harder about ethical options available for treating infertility and about other options in situations where infertility cannot be overcome. When the baby carriage doesn't come, we need to be prepared to minister to those for whom God has something else planned.

Jennifer Lahl is the founder and president of the Center for Bioethics and Culture and an award-winning documentary filmmaker, making films in the space of assisted reproductive technologies, and the exploitation of women and children. She practiced nursing for over twenty years and has an MA in bioethics.

REPRODUCTIVE BIOTECHNOLOGY AS A PRODUCT OF CONSUMERISM

Charles Camosy

Readers may know that my own Christian tradition of Roman Catholicism interprets the command to "be fruitful and multiply" to mean that there is an inherent, God-given connection between sexuality and procreation. His gift of new human life comes from the sexual unity of two people becoming one flesh. This not only means that married persons should not close themselves off to that gift, but it also means that we must not take it upon ourselves to try to obtain children apart from this sexual union. Children are a blessing from the Lord, not something that we are owed. Technology may licitly be used to improve the chances that a sexual union produces a child, but it may not be used to produce children in ways that thwart God's plan. Such acts, most obviously when children are created via in vitro fertilization (IVF) with gametes (egg and sperm) not belonging to one or both of the parents seeking a child, are morally problematic. They turn children into the result of a human technological project, sought by the self-centered will, rather than ends in themselves, unconditionally welcomed as gifts from God.

Much attention has been given to the wrongness of these acts. Less attention has been focused on the social structures of sin that facilitate them. One could write a very long piece on how reproductive biotechnology relates to structural racism, ageism, sexism, or ableism—but in this short piece I will focus on consumerism. Consumerism has played a foundational role in forming Western culture at nearly every level. It permeates and drives the processes by which sex has been disconnected from openness to new life, and the processes by which attempts to have children are disconnected from sex. Consumerism forms potential parents, for instance, into the kind of people who believe they must achieve a certain kind of financial and autonomous lifestyle before having children. Such potential parents are often structurally coerced into waiting until a point in their lives when IVF is their best hope for having children.

But the consumerism driving reproductive biotechnology can also have a dramatic effect on others connected to the IVF process. For example, a surrogate mother paid for the use of her womb so another person or couple can have a child. One American company, Circle Surrogacy, estimates that it costs over $100,000 to hire a surrogate mother through them (not including purchase of donor eggs), and less than $40,000 goes to the surrogate mother.[1] Still, that is a substantial sum of money, which leads to de facto exploitation of poor women by biotech corporations. The exploitation becomes even more significant when, driven by a desire to grab more market share, these companies seek poor women in the developing world who will gestate a child for less money.

There can be legal problems with surrogacy. In many Western countries (including the US) it is the surrogate mother who has rights to the child until there is a legal handing over of the child to the couple who paid her for gestational services. Consider "Margaret," a 42-year-old single mother who has two other children, who changed her mind and had a dramatic confrontation with the biological parents for whom she was working:

> They may not be my eggs but I grew these babies inside me. I nourished them to birth and went through a life-threatening emergency caesarean to have them. I would be devastated if they are taken away from me now. The law regards me as their mother and I regard them as my children.
>
> When it became clear to me that this couple, who are both professionals, saw this as just a business arrangement, and me as some sort of incubator, I changed my mind and decided to keep the children.[2]

Also consider the case of a couple who had paid another woman to carry their biological child to term, but then learned that the child likely had Down syndrome and asked that the surrogate mother have an abortion. When the surrogate mother refused, the case was put into "legal limbo."[3] Once the parents who paid for the surrogacy backed off and made it clear they would not take the child,

1. "Estimated Program Expenses for Gestational Surrogacy with Egg Bank (2012 USA)," Circle Surrogacy, http://www.circlesurrogacy.com/index.php/costs/egg-bank-egg-sharing-surrogacy/costs-gs-bank-us.

2. Jo Knowsley, "Surrogate Mother Says 'Sorry, but I'm Keeping Your Babies,'" *Daily Mail*, December 2006, http://www.dailymail.co.uk/femail/article-423125/Surrogate-mother-says-Sorry-Im-keeping-babies.html#ixzz1oY1dulCk.

3. *National Post*, http://life.nationalpost.com/2010/10/06/couple-urged-surrogate-mother-to-abort-fetus-because-of-defect/.

the surrogate mother had an abortion anyway because she felt that raising this disabled child would put a burden on her current family. The US legal tradition is understandably confused about what to do when we treat our children and reproductive capacities as things to buy and sell, but structural consumerism is pushing our reproductive practices in precisely this direction.

Things get even more problematic when eggs needed for IVF are procured from an outside source. Many college-educated women reading this book will be familiar with advertisements enticing undergraduate women to sell their eggs. Given the consumerist forces in play, they don't want eggs from just any woman.

In a process akin to that of college admissions, Tiny Treasures requires all prospective donors to mail copies of their SAT scores and college transcripts with their applications, both of which have direct bearing on the amount of compensation received. The agency suggests first-time donors receive between $2,000 and $5,000, but students who qualify as "Extraordinary Donors"—those with SAT scores above 1250, ACT scores above 28, college grade point averages above 3.5 or those who have attended Ivy League universities—receive between $5,000 and $7,000 for their services.

A classified ad in the *Columbia Spectator* from "a stable NYC Ivy League couple" seeks an Ivy League student, between 5-foot-7 and 5-foot-10 tall, of German, Irish, English or Eastern European descent. Compensation was listed as $25,000.[4]

A study of 100 advertisements in 63 colleges across the United States found that 21 specified a minimum requisite SAT score. Half offered more than $5,000, and among this group, 27 percent specified an "appearance requirement." The bigger the money, the choosier the client: Above the $10,000 level, most ads "contained appearance or ethnicity requirements."[5] One advertisement in the *Stanford Daily* newspaper offered a whopping $100,000 for a suitable woman's eggs.[6]

But what to do if the price is too high or commercial selling of the eggs is illegal? One company has the solution: go on an egg-buying and/or IVF vacation.[7] They offer seven-to-ten-day stays in places like Cancun, Ukraine, Panama,

4. *Yale News*, http://www.yaledailynews.com/news/2005/mar/22/egg-donor-ads-target-women-of-ivy-league/.
5. William Saletan, "The Egg Market," *Slate*, March 29, 2010, http://www.slate.com/articles/health_and_science/human_nature/2010/03/the_egg_market.html.
6. Marilee Enge, "Ad Seeks Donor Eggs for $100,000, Possible New High," *Chicago Tribune*, February 10, 2000, http://articles.chicagotribune.com/2000-02-10/news/0002100320_1_egg-donor-program-infertile-ads.
7. See, e.g., "International FIV Patients," Advanced Fertility Center Cancun, https://www.fertilitycentercancun.com/international-patients.html.

and South Africa where there are "high quality clinics" which offer "a broad range of ethnic donors, equivalent services and success rates, and at a drastically reduced cost."

And many of the egg donors are desperate. For example, tens of thousands of immigrants from the Soviet Union live in Cyprus, and "local Russian-language newspapers often place advertisements seeking 'young healthy girls for egg donation.'" Sometimes "women from Russia and Ukraine fly in just to donate eggs" because they "desperately needing the money for rent and utility bills." Some women even depend on this "as their main source of income, going through the process of being injected with hormones at least five times a year."[8] However, given the desire on the part of the clinics and the umbrella businesses to make as much money as possible, many of these women are not told about the serious health risks.

Much more could be said about the relationship between consumerism and reproductive biotechnology. (Similar problems, for instance, are created by the sperm donation industry.[9]) But these issues should at least give us pause and, perhaps, lead to questions about whether embryos, gestational services, and gametes (egg and sperm) are the kinds of things that ought to be part of a consumerist marketplace.

Charlie Camosy is associate professor of theology at Fordham University, where he has taught since finishing his PhD at Notre Dame in 2008. He is the author of four books, including *For Love of Animals* and *Beyond the Abortion Wars*. He serves on the board of Democrats for Life.

8.   Antony Barnett and Helena Smith, "Cruel Cost of the Human Egg Trade," *The Guardian*, April 30, 2006, https://www.theguardian.com/uk/2006/apr/30/health.healthandwellbeing.

9.   Jacqueline Mroz, "One Sperm Donor, 150 Offspring," *New York Times*, September 5, 2011, http://www.nytimes.com/2011/09/06/health/06donor.html?pagewanted=1&_r=1&ref=health; "'I Didn't Want Children to Die': A Mother's Mission to Save Sperm Donor's 35 Kids Never Told about His Fatal, Genetic Illness," *Daily Mail*, http://www.dailymail.co.uk/news/article-2111623/Sperm-Donors-35-Kids-Never-Told -About-Fatal-Genetic-Illness.html?ito=feeds-newsxml.

A BROAD APPROACH TO REPRODUCTIVE ETHICS

⊘ *Ellen Painter Dollar*

I became interested in reproductive ethics when, fifteen years ago, my husband and I underwent preimplantation genetic diagnosis (PGD, which is in vitro fertilization, or IVF, with the added step of genetic screening) to try to conceive a child who would not inherit my genetic bone disorder, osteogenesis imperfecta (OI). When the wrenching decisions required by the PGD process forced us to address theological and moral questions raised by reproductive technologies, we found little help in existing Christian resources. Academics and theologians made impressive arm's-length arguments that failed to engage with the stories of actual people facing reproductive decisions in all their messy reality.

I was living that reality. I loved our two-year-old daughter just as she was. She had inherited my disorder, and I wished she didn't have the painful disorder that, in many ways, made her who she is (and made me who I am). I believe it is a parent's primary duty to love their child without condition, but I was now putting a condition on our second child's birth, namely, that he or she not have OI. I grieved over how genetic-screening technology supports our culture's devaluing of people with disabilities. I worried about how such devaluing could chip away at the progress disabled people have made in demanding equal rights and inclusion. I also understood that our choice to use PGD could contribute to that backward movement.

The moral and theological questions surrounding reproductive issues, such as abortion, prenatal diagnosis, and reproductive technologies, are wide ranging. They include the ethics of testing, manipulating, and/or destroying human embryos; how an unprecedented level of choice and control over reproduction may commodify or devalue human lives; the implications for disabled people and our culture of screening out disabling genetic conditions; and to what lengths we ought to go to relieve suffering—of women facing the physical, emotional, and practical toll of unplanned pregnancies; of children born to parents who lack the resources to provide adequate care; of couples who want to become parents but can't conceive; of parents who learn that their unborn baby has a serious anomaly; of people with genetic conditions that cause significant pain, impairment, or premature death; and of disabled people who suffer more from exclusion and prejudice than from their condition.

Addressing such questions is hard. It's hard because science and dry logic are inadequate tools for addressing one of the most fundamental, intimate, and emotion-laden human endeavors. It's hard because reproductive choices involve at least two human beings whose best interests don't always clearly align and with whose current and future well-being we are rightly concerned. It's hard because the guidance we get from Scripture is far from prescriptive; the Bible doesn't tell us whether abortion, prenatal diagnosis, IVF, or PGD are right or wrong.

My own views on these issues are nuanced, continually evolving, and, above all, reflective of the practical realities of human reproduction. For example, while I do not consider abortion a morally neutral act or a good thing, I support abortion rights. For all of human history, women have gotten pregnant unintentionally and have sought ways to end their pregnancies, often at the expense of their safety or their lives. When abortion is not legal, it becomes unsafe, but women seek it anyway. I care about those women, as well as the children they conceive, as people made in God's image. I believe the Christian mandate to care for "the least of these" means that we have a duty to provide a solid safety net for vulnerable women and children, including good health care, quality child care, safe housing, economic opportunities, and protection from abuse, thus addressing some of the reasons why women choose abortion. I have some significant moral and theological concerns about reproductive and genetic technologies, but I also recognize that such technologies are here to stay. The focus of my work in this area, therefore, has been helping Christians to ask good questions and have informed conversations about the unprecedented choices available to prospective parents.

While the Bible lacks crystal clear "do this, don't do that" language about reproductive decisions, there are several biblical ideas that speak directly to our conversations about reproductive ethics.

Stories Matter

The Bible is not a rule book; it's a story—the story of God's relationship with God's people, God's continual effort to call us back to our identity as beloved children made in God's image, and God's showing us what living out of that identity looks like. The biblical story is, like all stories involving human beings, full of complexity, nuance, inconsistency, and surprises.

Anytime we examine reproductive issues through a theological lens, we must engage with people's stories, understanding that those stories in all their complexity, nuance, inconsistency, and surprise will complicate our discourse but also deepen it.

This is not to argue for a shallow relativism in which each individual decides what is best for his or her situation, without regard for larger moral, theological, or communal realities. But our God is a personal God for whom each person's story matters, and so it should for us. People's stories are particularly vital when we're talking about having (or not having) babies—one of the most intimate, life-changing human endeavors that engages body, mind, and spirit.

The first and most important step in discussing a Christian perspective on reproductive issues is to listen, long and well, to the stories of people who have made difficult and complex reproductive decisions. Listen to the story of women who have had abortions—those who have regretted their abortion, and those who have not. Listen to parents whose unborn child received a troubling diagnosis. Listen to those who chose to terminate the pregnancy, and those who didn't. Listen to those for whom IVF succeeded, and those for whom it failed. Listen to couples who grieved their inability to conceive a child. Listen to those who chose not to try assisted reproduction, those who adopted, and those who decided God was calling them to something other than parenthood. Listen to parents who held their infant as she died of a genetic disorder, and then turned to PGD to conceive another child who wouldn't meet the same fate. Listen to people who are living full lives with a genetic disorder like mine. Listen to parents who have knowingly, willingly, and joyfully welcomed children with a variety of genetic conditions into their families through birth or adoption.

Just as in the Bible, the stories of God's people serve as a primary source of wisdom, guidance, and perspective when we're asking what it looks like to become the people God made us to be.

Bodies Matter

Christianity is prone to being over-spiritualized, emphasizing intangible spiritual gains over tangible physical realities. People suffering through terrible circumstances are encouraged to look on the bright side, because surely their minds and spirits are being enriched with wisdom and insight during this trial. For example, decades after anesthesia was discovered, Christian clerics argued against its use, believing that great physical pain was sent by God to strengthen our spirits and/or punish us for sin. Medieval theologians went to great lengths to describe Jesus' birth without referring to his mother's body and the visceral realities of childbirth.[1] Christians often treat sexuality more as a dangerous temptation or an inconvenient nuisance than a vital and good God-given quality of human beings.

But Christianity is a material faith, which doesn't mean it's consumerist (focused on getting and having more stuff), but simply that it's rooted in the material. God's first act in the biblical narrative is to create something from nothing. God's ultimate act of salvation is to become incarnate as a man in a body who ate, drank, slept, bled, and died. The central act of worship for many Christians involves eating and drinking real food and real drink.

When we're talking about reproductive ethics, we must remember that in Christianity, the material world matters and bodies matter. The body of a child growing inside its mother matters, and that mother's body—the ways it will grow and stretch and hurt and break in nurturing that child before, during, and after birth—matters too. The pain, physical and otherwise, caused by infertility and miscarriage matter. The bodies of people with genetic disorders like mine know pain, impairment, and struggle, and they also know strength, contentment, and joy—and all of it matters.

Just as we oversimplify when we deliberate over reproductive questions without considering real people's stories, we also oversimplify when we fail to consider the miraculous and wrenching realities of human bodies that bear other human bodies.

Community Matters

The biblical story is primarily about relationships—between God and God's people, and among people from disparate backgrounds—and about the transforming power of love, as summed up in the two great commandments to love God and neighbor. Pressing moral questions about reproductive decisions won't be answered by divisive debates that vilify "the other side." They will be answered by love.

In the end, what helped me and my husband to figure out what to do about our childbearing dilemma was the love of our community. We had honest and hard conversations with people who cared about us. Some of these people had a clear opinion about the ethics of PGD, but while they were up front about what they believed, they were also willing to listen, consider perspectives they

---

1. For more on theological views of pain and pain relief, particularly pain relief in childbirth, see Melanie Thernstrom's *The Pain Chronicles: Cures, Myths, Mysteries, Prayers, Diaries, Brain Scans, Healing, and the Science of Suffering* (New York: Farrar, Straus and Giroux, 2010); Randi Hutter Epstein's *Get Me Out: A History of Childbirth from the Garden of Eden to the Sperm Bank* (New York: Norton, 2010). Rachel Marie Stone also addresses theological perspectives on childbirth pain and idealized accounts of Jesus' birth in *Birthing Hope: Giving Fear to the Light* (Downers Grove, IL: IVP Press, 2018).

didn't share, and respond with love, not judgment, when we made decisions they wouldn't have made. When I've been asked what advice I'd offer to people who are in the position we once were, of having to make a fraught reproductive decision, I keep coming back to this: Take some time—before visiting the clinic or doctor or genetic counselor for the first time if possible—to discuss decisions with people in your community whom you trust. Read or listen to the stories of others who have faced similar situations. Tell your own story, again and again if necessary, to people you trust to receive it graciously.

As poet Wendell Berry has written for parents, "The only way is hard."[2] My grappling with tough reproductive decisions was hard, as is living with a painful, limiting disorder and loving my daughter through days of agony and despair caused by her experience with the same disorder. Ultimately, my husband and I did one cycle of PGD, which failed, and decided not to do another. We eventually conceived and bore two more children, a girl and a boy, neither of whom has OI. Loving them through their days of agony and despair is hard too—no one gets a pain-free life.

Were my husband and I right or wrong to pursue PGD? Were we right or wrong to abandon it? The short answer is that I don't know. Our story is simply our story. Living that story, I broadened my understanding of disability, limitation, choice, suffering, and the legacies we leave our children, but I've been unable to reach a firm conclusion concerning whether reproductive technologies such as IVF and PGD are acceptable for Christians under some circumstances, and not under others. That's why I won't end this chapter by telling readers the "right" answers to the many ethical and theological questions around human reproduction. I have opinions, but they continue to change and develop the more stories I hear and conversations I have. Coming to a single right answer is both impossible (there are many answers that we can back up with Scripture, Christian tradition, compassion, and logic) and less important than asking good questions, listening well to people's stories, and promoting compassionate, generous dialogue.

Ellen Painter Dollar has written about disability, ethics, and faith for online and print media, and is the author of *No Easy Choice: A Story of Disability, Parenthood, and Faith in an Age of Advanced Reproduction* (Louisville, KY: Westminster John Knox, 2012). She currently manages an Episcopal church office in Connecticut.

2. Wendell Berry, "The Way of Pain," in *The Selected Poems of Wendell Berry* (Berkeley, CA: Counterpoint, 1999), 113.

PRO-LIFE IN WORD AND DEED

∞ *Karen Swallow Prior*

In 2015, a drifter named Robert Lewis Dear killed three people during a shooting spree in a Colorado Springs Planned Parenthood facility. At the time, it was not clear whether Dear's attacks were fueled by opposition to abortion (or anything beyond being "mentally disturbed" as he was described in one news story), but unidentified sources told NBC News his rants to police included the phrase "no more baby parts," taken as a reference to the undercover video exposé of Planned Parenthood's fetal tissue sales. Eventually, Dear was declared incompetent to stand trial and was sent to a state mental hospital.

This incident, like other occasional acts of violence against abortion facilities and providers, raised the recurring question about the role played by rhetoric in the ongoing national debate around abortion. Some activists and politicians use such events to blame the language of opposition to abortion—which has a long history—for this recent act of violence.

Colorado governor John Hickenlooper said the shooting might have been caused by "inflammatory rhetoric we see on all levels."[1] He called for those debating abortion to "tone down the rhetoric."[2] The CEO of Planned Parenthood in the Rocky Mountains claimed that "extremists are creating a poisonous environment that feeds domestic terrorism in this country."[3] From opposite sides of the political spectrum, presidential candidates Bernie Sanders and Ben Carson cast some blame for the shooting on "bitter rhetoric"[4] and "hateful speech,"[5] respectively.

---

1. "Comments for: Colorado governor urges toned-down abortion debate after rampage," *BDN,* https://bangordailynews.com/2015/11/29/news/nation/colorado-governor-urges-toned-down-abortion-debate-after-rampage/comments/.
2. "Colorado Springs Shootings: Calls to Cool Abortion Debate," *BBC,* November 29, 2015, http://www.bbc.com/news/world-us-canada-34958284.
3. Sabrina Siddiqui, "Republicans Reject Link between Anti-Abortion Rhetoric and Colorado Shooting," *The Guardian,* November 29, 2016, http://www.theguardian.com/us-news/2015/nov/29/colorado-springs-shooting-planned-parenthood-mike-huckabee.
4. Jason Easley, "Bernie Sanders Calls Planned Parenthood Shooting a Consequence of Republican Rhetoric," *Politicus USA,* November 28, 2015, http://www.politicususa.com/2015/11/28/bernie-sanders-calls-planned-parenthood-shooting-consequence-republican-rhetoric.html.
5. Marcy Kreiter, "Planned Parenthood Shooting: Ben Carson Calls Abortion Debate 'Hateful

It would be easy to dismiss such charges—words are not deeds. But in fact Christians should recognize the power of words to bring good or ill: "The tongue has the power of life and death, and those who love it will eat its fruit" (Prov. 18:21). An earlier passage in Proverbs tells us, "The words of the reckless pierce like swords, but the tongue of the wise brings healing" (Prov. 12:18). Calling abortion what it is will bring good. Doing so without the temperance of love will bring harm.

Rallying for the defunding of Planned Parenthood isn't inflammatory rhetoric; it's political engagement. Videos depicting the self-damning words and actions of Planned Parenthood officials isn't yellow journalism; it's investigative reporting. Referring to abortion providers as "abortion ghouls," clinic volunteers and workers as "deathscorts" or "bloodworkers," and women who obtain abortions as "murderers" is worse than inflammatory: it is un-Christlike. [Calling legal abortion "murder" when it isn't (it is, to our shame, lawful) is to say what isn't true, at least in a civil (not church) context.]

To clarify: I am unwavering in my belief that according to God's law, abortion is murder, despite its current definition in civil law and in my belief that God hates the shedding of innocent blood. Having volunteered seventeen years at crisis pregnancy centers and offering help to women outside abortion clinics for ten years, I was trained not to use the word "murder" in trying to persuade them to choose life. I continue to believe this is wise counsel. I continue to work toward the day when our civil laws on abortion accord with God's law.

The purpose of language, its God-given raison-d'être, is to reveal truth, eternal and unfailing. It needs not the props of exaggeration or distortion of our feeble words. The truth about abortion demands no inflammation or embellishment. It is, rather, the purveyors of abortion who must veil the truth with charms. The hurt abortion causes to women and children and society can be communicated in plain terms.

For those who deny the reality of abortion, however, even the plain truth inflames. Thus we cannot ascribe to inflammatory language alone the attacks against abortion clinics. (In fact, the violence perpetrated against abortion providers peaked, according to figures in a report by NARAL Pro-Choice America, in the 1990s, before social media. It's entirely possible that the outlet social media provides for communicating dissent has helped lessen clinic violence.) Nor can we apologize for speaking the plain truth in love. Indeed, there is no love absent truth.

Still, human language has its limits. Humanity's brokenness is mirrored in the imperfection of our words, so often inept, ill-chosen, or misunderstood. "Human speech," writes Gustave Flaubert, "is like a cracked pot on which we beat out rhythms for bears to dance to when we are striving to make music that will wring tears from the stars."[6] Especially in situations as consequential as a pregnancy formed in crisis, a child to clothe and feed and love, it's important to get our words (as well as our actions) as right as we possibly can. When human lives are at stake, our language must reach not the bears but the heavens.

Consider the language Jesus used (and didn't use) in his interaction with the woman of Samaria at the well as recorded in John 4. When the woman tells Jesus that she has no husband, Jesus responds by saying he knows she has had five husbands and that the man she is with is not her husband. Here Jesus is truthful in pointing out her sin, but he does not call her a name based on her sin. He does not call her "Adulterer!" or "Fornicator!" Here Jesus provides an example of calling out sin for what it is without identifying a person with her sin by naming her with it.

As we affirm the truth that abortion ends a precious human life, we cannot do or support wrong—wrong words or wrong deeds—to achieve right. We are to pursue God's good in God's way: "There is a way that appears to be right, but in the end it leads to death" (Prov. 14:12). This is our duty both to God and to our society. Not as Bernie Sanders said, because of the "unintended consequences" of such language, but because Scripture teaches that temperate words are good in and of themselves: "The hearts of the wise make their mouths prudent, and their lips promote instruction. Gracious words are a honeycomb, sweet to the soul and healing to the bones" (Prov. 16:23–24).

If we are characterized by such language—and deeds that match it—we need not strain to distance ourselves from the Robert Lewis Dears of the world in a posture of defensiveness. And when our enemies malign us anyway, we will find ourselves already poised to love them in return. Christians have the power, through the perfect Word and our imperfect but careful words, to bring healing rather than harm.

This piece was adapted from an article that first appeared on ChristianityToday. com on December 1, 2015. Used by permission of Christianity Today, *Carol Stream, IL 60188. The original title of the article was "Loving Our Pro-Choice Neighbors in Word and Deed."*

---

6.   Gustave Flaubert, *Madame Bovary*, ed. Leo Bersani, trans. Lowell Bair (New York: Bantam, 2005), 187.

Karen Swallow Prior is an award-winning professor of English at Liberty University. She earned her PhD in English at SUNY Buffalo. Her writing has appeared at *The Atlantic*, *Christianity Today*, *The Washington Post*, *Vox*, *First Things*, *Sojourners*, *Think Christian*, and other places. She is a senior fellow at the Trinity Forum, a research fellow with the Ethics and Religious Liberty Commission of the Southern Baptist Convention, a senior fellow at Liberty University's Center for Apologetics and Cultural Engagement, and a member of the Faith Advisory Council of the Humane Society of the United States.

ON WHETHER ABORTION IS MURDER

The Questions of Rhetoric and Reality

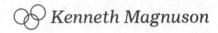 *Kenneth Magnuson*

Thinkers such as Karen Swallow Prior have written that referring to women "who obtain abortions as 'murderers' is worse than inflammatory: it is un-Christlike."[1] Prior does not encourage Christians to back down from opposition to abortion. Indeed, she asserts that to speak the truth in love includes and requires such opposition. Yet some pro-life advocates have critiqued her approach. Why? These advocates contend that abortion is murder, so to speak the truth in love requires that we call abortion murder.

How should we respond? To begin with, it seems that some of the criticism misses the point of Prior's exhortation. She doesn't deny the horror of abortion. Indeed, she affirms that "human lives are at stake," that "abortion ends a precious human life," and even that "according to God's law, abortion is murder." But the main concern of her essay centers on how Christians ought to engage our pro-choice neighbors, including abortion-minded women, in a way that reveals truth, transforms hearts and minds, and saves lives.

Prior's essay raises important issues. First, our words and their tone matter. What we say and how we say it communicates our convictions about truth as well as our concern for people, as we seek to engage our neighbors and speak on behalf of unborn babies. Our words and their tone may soften hearts or harden them, win people over or drive them away, or may be perceived as the overflow of love or hate. We should seek to win opponents with persuasive words of truth spoken in love, for truth unveils and enlightens. Part of that truth is that abortion

---

1. Karen Swallow Prior's original essay appeared in *Christianity Today* online in December 2015, entitled, "Loving Our Pro-Choice Neighbors in Word and Deed," http://www.christianitytoday.com/women/2015/december/loving-our-pro-choice-neighbors-in-word-and-deed.html.

"ends a precious human life," which is why many insist on calling it murder and why some reacted strongly against Prior's essay. It is worth probing the point of disagreement. Yet, as we do, we ought to recognize that how we speak to and about one another, as cobelligerents on behalf of the unborn, also matters. Where we disagree, we ought to seek clarity and understanding with grace and goodwill.

Second, context matters. Prior's exhortation grew out of years of volunteering in crisis pregnancy centers and sidewalk counseling at abortion clinics. To call abortion murder in that context, she suggests, is counterproductive and inappropriate. We ought to listen to those who have been on the front lines of the abortion issue. We may speak to a woman in crisis one way, to our neighbors making pro-choice arguments another way, and to abortion providers who show a grotesque indifference to the lives of unborn children yet another way. Jesus spoke the truth in love. At times, as with the Samaritan woman (John 4) and the woman caught in adultery (John 8), he was gentle, yet straightforward, without minimizing sin. At other times, he could be harsh in his confrontation, as he was with the Scribes and Pharisees in Matthew 23, calling them "hypocrites," "blind guides," "serpents," and a "brood of vipers." We might, therefore, question whether it is "un-Christlike" to confront with harsh words (at least at times) those pushing and profiting from abortion.

Third, definitions matter, and this brings us to the question at the center of the controversy. Is Prior right to say that we should not call abortion murder? In one sense, given the legal and cultural context of the debate, it can be confusing, unproductive, and polarizing to call abortion murder. We may rightly hold the conviction that, morally speaking, abortion is murder because it is the willful, premeditated killing of an innocent human being. Yet the law says that abortion is not murder. Wrong as that might be, the law is a teacher, and the legal status of abortion affects how many people in our culture understand it and how they will respond to those who call abortion murder.

At the same time, truth-telling compels us to challenge legal definitions that hide the truth. In the most contested statement in Prior's essay, she asserts, "Calling legal abortion '*murder*' when it isn't (it is, to our shame, lawful) is to say what isn't true, at least in a civil (not church) context." Here she accepts a definition of murder as an unlawful killing, yet this statement lends itself to confusion, and it concedes too much. Her quotation marks, underlining, parenthetical comments, and the fact that she is considering women in crisis pregnancies all qualify her assertion that we should not call abortion murder. She believes it is unnecessary and unhelpful to call abortion murder, for she is confident that the truth itself is sufficient, and that "the truth about abortion demands no inflammation or embellishment." Indeed, she says, "the plain truth inflames." But if, according to God's law, abortion is a case of murder, then to call it murder is not saying "what isn't true," nor is it an exaggeration or embellishment of the truth. Rather, it is the plain truth, which inflames.

If abortion in God's view is murder, then how should we best reflect that moral truth in our speech? Perhaps it is best to speak in a gentler manner when engaging and seeking to minister to women who have had an abortion or are abortion-minded. Yet in the broader debate, we ought at least to assert that it is the law that says what isn't true, for by making it legal, the law declares that abortion is not murder, when it is.

When civil law conceals the truth, it should not prevent us from speaking the truth, at least as a prophetic voice. By Prior's reasoning, though not by her words, we should not call the fetus a living and fully human being, since abortion laws deny that it is! (Yet our laws underscore a major point of contradiction, for fetal homicide laws declare that the fetus is a living human being, since killing the fetus is not only wrong, but an unjustified homicide. The law permits abortion, but not fetal homicide, based solely on the will of the mother, not on the status of the human being who is killed. It defies moral and legal logic.)

In the 1980s, CNN's primetime show *Crossfire* featured debates between conservative host Pat Buchanan and liberal host Michael Kinsley. Kinsley frequently challenged pro-life advocates, asking them if they thought abortion was murder, since they considered the unborn child fully human. By forcing them to acknowledge the logical conclusion of their view of the unborn, he thought he could back them into a corner and challenge their credibility. Yet he also conceded a significant point: if the unborn are fully human, then abortion must be a form of murder.

The early church fathers consistently condemned abortion as the killing of a human being, and some called it murder (e.g., Didache, Athenagorus, Clement of Alexandria, Tertullian, Mark Minucius Felix, Hippolytus, and Cyprian).[2] The German theologian and ethicist Dietrich Bonhoeffer uses plain, prophetic language about abortion. He writes, "To kill the fruit in the mother's womb is to injure the right to life that God has bestowed on the developing life. Discussion of the question whether a human being is already present confuses the simple fact that, in any case, God wills to create a human being and that the life of this developing human being has been deliberately taken. And this is nothing but murder."[3] He adds that we cannot hide this truth, that the mother feels the weight of it, and that society too bears much of the guilt. He acknowledges that

2. For quick reference, see David W. Bercot, ed., *A Dictionary of Early Christian Beliefs* (Peabody, MA: Hendrickson, 1998), 2–3.

3. Dietrich Bonhoeffer, *Ethics*, Dietrich Bonhoeffer Works, vol. 6 (Minneapolis: Fortress, 2005), 206.

there may be many factors that lead to abortion, but nothing changes the fact that it is murder.

In the right context, we should not shy away from that point.

The original version of this article first appeared online on the Ethics and Religious Liberty Commission's website in December 2015 and is entitled, "Is Abortion Murder? Rhetoric in the Abortion Debate."

Ken Magnuson is professor of Christian ethics at Southern Seminary in Louisville, Kentucky, where he also serves as director of The Commonweal Project on Faith, Work and Human Flourishing. He received his PhD in theological ethics from Cambridge University (UK). His current book project is an introduction to Christian ethics.

DISCUSSION QUESTIONS

1. In his article, Charles Camosy describes in specific and great detail the "social structures" of consumerism that contribute to the "morally problematic" issue of IVF. Is there room in his argument to accommodate Dollar's compelling argument that "stories matter" and complicate the issue, or must holding his position negate her assertion?

2. The Bells admit that the issue of what to do with extra embryos created through IVF is a "challenging" issue. How would someone from the tradition of Lahl or Camosy likely respond to the Bells' ending resolution that they will simply trust the sovereignty of God in this element of their story?

3. In each of these articles, the authors enter their presentation with presumed definitions for a couple of things, namely: what is meant by "author of life," when life actually begins (conception, implantation, or later), what qualifies an act as "murder," and what actually constitutes "playing God." Articulate how each author defines each of these ideas and explain how their respective articulations affect their interpretations of both science and Scripture.

4. Prior includes in her admonition for compassionate language in the pro-life community that it is incorrect to call abortion "murder" because our court system does not deem it to be so. In his article, Magnuson acknowledges the need for compassionate rhetoric while disagreeing with Prior, saying that to call abortion "murder" is not harsh rhetoric but simply the truth. How are each of these authors defining the word "murder," and how would each interact with the other's definition?

5. In her article, Dollar declares that Scripture is not prescriptive when it comes to reproductive technology, including IVF and abortion. How might Lahl and Magnuson interact with these claims?

6. In what ways does the Bells' article exemplify Dollar's claim that "stories matter," and how does the personal nature of their article contribute to the discussion?

7. The Bells claim that IVF simply increases the odds of "an embryo's viability in the mother's womb" and does not "literally create human life." Lahl,

however, declares that technologies like IVF take the act of procreation from "begetting" to "making" and cross an ethical line. What are the underlying premises in each of the arguments, and where do they differ?

8. While disagreeing on some elements of the pro-life Christian's presentation and posture regarding abortion, both Prior and Magnuson agree that according to God's Word, abortion is the ending of a human life. How might someone from Dollar's position, especially in light of two of her points—stories matter and bodies matter—interact with Prior's and Magnuson's respective postures?

9. Camosy gives a detailed description of the corruption and exploitation that has been created in the world surrounding IVF, specifically in regards to the selling and pricing of gametes (egg and sperm). In their article, however, the Bells ask if Christians are forced to avoid technologies just because there is a chance that the technology could be exploited. How might these arguments be weighed against each other?

10. Magnuson replies to Prior's article and says that to avoid using the term "murder" when talking with abortion-minded women might be a more compassionate practice, but in the "broader debate," to shy away from that term is to abandon our responsibilities as Christians. Are any responsibilities being abandoned if the term is avoided, as Magnuson and Prior suggest, in interactions with women who are considering or have had abortions?

chapter seven

IMMIGRATION AND RACE

Revelation 7:9 provides a picture of the future glorified kingdom consisting of "a great multitude . . . from every nation, tribe, people and language." This eschatological vision of a diverse population united by a common devotion to God is foundational to understanding the good of human diversity. Regularly in John's vision of the future kingdom, imagery is used to point hearers back to the origins narrative in Genesis 1 and 2. And yet, interestingly, in contrast to John's apocalyptic vision, in these two opening biblical chapters, humans are only explicitly differentiated by male and female. Yet this single differentiation was clearly not God's final word on diversity within the human race. Plurality and unity, which is also present in the triune God, is a characteristic of God's created order. The bookends of the scriptural narrative, while affirming diversity, teach us that racial strife and ethnic discrimination are the direct consequence of human sin. Moreover, the opening and closing scenes of the biblical story promise that the shalom present in Genesis 1 and 2 will culminate in the uniting of humanity around God's throne in the age to come.

Yet when it comes to modern conceptions of race, scholars have concluded that "no concept truly equivalent to that of 'race' can be detected in the thought of Greeks, Romans, and early Christians."[1] This is not to say that xenophobia, prejudice, slavery, and oppression did not exist in the ancient world. But racism as we understand it today was not a category within ancient thinking. Race was, rather, a somewhat fluid concept in Greco-Roman civilizations and in early Christianity. Race could be defined by such features as religious and other cultural practices and was not entirely determined by ethnicity. Other factors, such as kinship, were also large determiners in whether someone was Greek or Roman.[2]

But with the modern age and the rise of European political power came the expansion of global exploration and opportunities for exploitation of

---

1. George M. Fredrickson, *Racism: A Short History* (Princeton: Princeton University Press, 2002), 17.
2. Denise Kimber Buell, *Why This New Race: Ethnic Reasoning in Early Christianity* (Chichester: Columbia University Press, 2008), 40–43.

foreign lands and people. While slavery had always existed throughout human history—not always or even often based on racial differences—modern slave trafficking relied on these developing racist ideologies (such as the claim that racial differences were signs of inferiority or superiority) to support and defend it, even by those within the church. With novel interpretations, the Bible was used by Christians to defend slavery and white supremacy. For example, "The interpretation of Numbers 12:1 that sees Miriam and Aaron deprecating black Africans is a product of modern assumptions read back into the Bible. Looking at the biblical sources without the skewing prism of postbiblical history provides no such reading of the text. There is no evidence here that biblical Israel saw black Africans in a negative light."[3] Such ideologies and assumptions have persisted long after the abolition of the slave trade.

Despite the justification of slavery by many Christians (as well as their participation in it), other Christians throughout the eighteenth and nineteenth centuries led the opposition to the slave trade: Quakers, Anglicans, and evangelicals such as William Wilberforce and Hannah More. Abolitionists in Great Britain employed an incrementalist approach to ending human trafficking. This approach whittled away at the trade, one piece of legislation at a time, thus avoiding the kind of civil war that took place in America decades after the slave trade ended in England. Is it possible that the residual racism that continues in the United States to this day is due at least in part to the collateral effects of the national divisions that come with civil war, but not with a democratic, incrementalist approach that persuades everyone (or most everyone)?

The treatment of African-Americans following the Civil War led not to utter freedom, but to years of more subjection to bigotry and oppression. In the post-Civil War South, a new kind of servitude developed through a convict-leasing system in which prison systems provided black convicts to plantation owners in the form of enforced labor. Simply arresting and imprisoning black Americans for petty offenses created a ready supply of cheap labor.[4] In addition, Jim Crow laws segregated blacks and whites from the late nineteenth century through the civil rights era of the 1960s. Many African-Americans are alive today who were subject to great injustices, contradicting the claim made by some that racism is "a thing of the past." To the contrary, the effects of centuries of oppression and racism have not come undone in one or two generations. The systemic racism that is inherent within any nation founded on slave labor and a declaration of

---

3. David M. Goldenberg, *The Curse of Ham: Race and Slavery in Early Judaism, Christianity, and Islam* (Princeton: Princeton University Press, 2003), 28.

4. "Bodies of 95 black prisoners forced into labor in 1800s found in Texas," AL, July 28, 2018, https://www.al.com/news/index.ssf/2018/07/bodies_of_95_black_prisoners_f.html.

equality for all that does not include all is much more complex and difficult to trace than either racist attitudes and actions by mere individuals or those codified by law. During World War II, racism on a national scale was institutionalized once again with the internment of Japanese Americans in prison camps in their own country. Even then, the church was largely silent.[5]

The inability or unwillingness of the majority race to recognize the indirect (even beyond the direct) effects of systemic racism has resulted in recent years in heightened tensions around race issues. These tensions have manifested most recently in the Black Lives Matter movement and the policy debates around immigration. Immigration policies, like slavery, have historically been closely tied to the needs (real or perceived) within the American labor force.[6] Furthermore, the rise of globalism and domestic terrorism has produced countervailing movements toward nationalism and border security. The widely reported statistic that 81 percent of white evangelicals voted in the 2016 election for the candidate who ran on these issues has brought an identity crisis within American evangelicalism and the broader church.

Sadly, the story of the white church in America is one of too much silence too much of the time. Yet, ironically, the Christian faith of those who came here as slaves or as refugees is refreshing and enlivening the American church as a whole. "The triumph of African-American history is the flourishing of the gospel in black communities," Mark Noll says. "To African Americans, Christianity has brought comfort, consolation, and even power, to the surprise of the representatives of the dominant society, who more often expected it to bring passivity, complacency, and servility."[7] Many immigrants bring their Christian faith with them. Latino immigrants range from Catholics to Pentecostal to Baptist. Some churches have been planted in the US by Latin American churches.[8] While it is still true as Rev. Dr. Martin Luther King Jr. famously said, that Sunday is "the most segregated hour" of the week in America, race relations promise to shift, and by the grace of God, hopefully improve as the church continues to face its old festering wounds and receive the healing that comes only from repentance and reconciliation.

This section opens with an article by Walter Strickland II explaining the two forms of racism that typically occur and arguing that both forms need to be taken seriously to bring about reconciliation and healing. Then Lisa Fields argues that

---

5. Mark A. Noll, *A History of Christianity in the United States and Canada* (Grand Rapids: Eerdmans, 1992), 442.

6. M. Daniel Carroll R., *Christians at the Border: Immigration, the Church, and the Bible*, 2nd ed. (Grand Rapids: Brazos, 2013), 9–12.

7. Noll, *A History of Christianity in the United States and Canada*, 542.

8. Carroll, *Christians at the Border*, 9–12.

American evangelicals have fallen short of proclaiming and displaying the full gospel message when it comes to issues surrounding race, thereby hindering the efficacy of the gospel to the marginalized and misused people of different ethnic and racial origins. Offering a different emphasis, Ron Miller draws on history, his own experiences as a man of color, and Christ's teachings, reminding Christians that our first allegiance is always to God and his kingdom, and thus our first response to racial divides should always be to bridge them with the gospel.

The final two essays in this section concentrate on the topic of immigration. Sharing their own personal stories of immigration, Y. Liz Dong and Ben Lowe explain how Scripture encourages Christians to care for the immigrants, who are often vulnerable and marginalized. These immigrants are individuals loved by God, and the gospel message speaks to them as it does to us. Joshua Chatraw explains that much of the conservative and liberal rhetoric surrounding immigration reform is largely hyperbolic and unhelpful, relying on biblical proof-texting and sweeping generalizations to make destabilizing and inflammatory arguments. He calls for Christians to be more conscientious and measured in our approach to the complicated issues surrounding immigration.

DIAGNOSING RACE AS A TWOFOLD PROBLEM

 Walter Strickland II

R ace and racism have generated longstanding fissures in American's cultural landscape. The contemporary environment has produced some beacons of hope—the election of America's first black president and a growing black middle class—yet racial tension persists. While the era of President Barack Obama was thought to be the dawn of a post-racial America that promised a rejuvenated hope for racial reconciliation, it witnessed the formation of the largest black protest movement since the civil rights and Black Power movements—namely, #BlackLivesMatter. The evangelical response to claims of racial injustice has been divided, with some showing empathy and others dismissing the claim of injustice by insisting that #AllLivesMatter. How can claims of racial discrimination and its absolute denial coexist, especially among those who share similar biblical worldviews?

Manifestations of Racism

Confusion about the state of race in America is complicated because racism manifests itself in two ways, namely, "individually" and "systemically" (or structurally). Both forms must be resolved to have genuine hope for racial reconciliation and unity. Until racism is identified and resolved on both accounts, proponents from each side will continue to talk past one another and develop divergent, and at times conflicting, solutions to the problem because they perceive racism as fundamentally different issues. A theologically informed exploration of both types of racism serves to overcome blinders generated by cultural context and offer potential solutions.

Individual Racism

Individualists understand racism as something that is overt and is done by one individual to another.[1] As a result, racism and discrimination are matters of thinking, mental categorization, attitude, and discourse.[2] Individualists presuppose the notion of free-will individualism, which assumes that the success or failure of an individual is not determined by societal structures, and the determining factor of success is individual hard work or the lack thereof. As a result, individualists are often middle or upper-middle class, and are usually upwardly mobile.

In *Divided by Faith*, Michael Emerson and Christian Smith argue that white evangelicals are more likely to adopt an individualist concept of racism than whites in the society at large.[3] White evangelicals make sense of their lives with an anti-structural realism that individualizes a problem like racism and reduces it to unhealthy interpersonal relationships.[4] The reason for this is white evangelicals do not want there to be a race problem, and many have few relationships with minorities who grapple with structural racism. Individualists distance themselves from racism by relegating it to extreme cases like the Ku Klux Klan or other hate groups.

In addition, there is a theological reason undergirding this tendency toward an individualist view of racism. The notion that everyone is responsible for their sin and that all people must make a personal decision to follow Christ as Savior intensifies the evangelical's propensity toward an individual view of racism. The individual emphasis in verses like Romans 10:9 are pillars in evangelical thought that uphold individual accountability while omitting a distinction between individual and structural realities.

The individualist concept of racism, although arrived at honestly, is a powerful means of reproducing structural racism. Because perception is often reality, an effective way to perpetuate a biased system is to deny its existence.[5] Consequently, individualists rarely attribute their success to privileges granted by systems; their success is credited to individual prowess and hard work that others are assumed to lack.

Structural Racism

For structuralists, racism is much more difficult to define and diagnose because it is not expressed in discrete actions or words. While structuralists

---

1. George Yancey, *Beyond Racial Gridlock: Embracing Mutual Responsibility* (Downers Grove, IL: IVP, 2006), 20.
2. Richard Delgado and Jean Stefanic, *Critical Race Theory: An Introduction* (New York: NYU, 2012), 21.
3. Michael O. Emerson and Christian Smith, *Divided by Faith: Evangelical Religion and the Problem of Race in America* (New York: Oxford University Press, 2001), 89.
4. Ibid.
5. Ibid., 89–90.

affirm that thoughts, attitudes, and words are important, they contend that racism is the means by which the systems, organizations, and enterprises grant privilege and power to some and disadvantage others. The structuralist notion of racism rests upon the idea that humans are affected by the social structures in which they live.

The doctrine of creation helps bring the ambiguity of systemic racism into sharper focus. At the climax of the creation account, God declares that his creation is "very good" (Gen. 1:31). Although God declared its goodness, it did not mean it was complete. In a real sense, humanity has been appointed by God to have lordship over the earth in order to carry out his will "on earth as it is in heaven" (Matt. 6:10). In this, people are given the charge to develop the hidden potential that God injected into creation via the work of their hands. This includes stewardship of material creation (fashioning wood into houses and ice into igloos), but also developing immaterial creation (organizations, economies, and enterprise). In the same way that humanity reflects its creator, God, the work of our hands embodies the best and worst of fallen humanity, including the structures upon which society rests.

Since structural racism can be perpetuated unknowingly, those who most easily identify systemic injustice tend to be those who are influenced by its ill effects, namely, the most vulnerable citizens in society. Structuralists are commonly part of a nonmajority culture that comes with a deeply rooted feeling of voicelessness that is exacerbated when minorities are underrepresented in positions of power. This underrepresentation makes it difficult for the needs of under-resourced communities to be made known to those who shape society's structures and systems.

The complex nature of structural racism can be seen in public transportation. Inequitable public transportation has restricted many who are often typecast as being lazy and unwilling to work from having access to stable employment. One example of this emerged when New Orleans was being rebuilt in the aftermath of Hurricane Katrina that devastated parts of the city in 2005.

A 2015 study showed that the population of New Orleans's St. Claude neighborhood, a poor and minority-populated community, was 81 percent black and had an average household income of $29,029. According to a 2014 study conducted by Ride New Orleans, 86 percent of the city's population had returned to the city after Katrina, but only 36 percent of its transit service operations had been restored. Low income neighborhoods like St. Claude tend to be the communities without a restored public transportation system. In contrast, bus lines catering to tourist destinations like Canal Street and St. Charles had been restored because they are profitable for the city. Yet the communities who need public transportation to meet their basic needs, such as rides to work, school, and medical facilities, have been neglected, and the economic interests of others has been prioritized.[6]

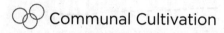 Communal Cultivation

The twofold appearance of racism—individual and systemic—should not be a surprise to the student of Scripture because the origin of both types of racism are located in the biblical text. Moving forward, the affluent must have the humility to admit that their view of the world is not flawless, but is obscured by a set of lived experiences. Having blind spots generated by human limitations is not sinful, but to assume that one does not "see through a glass, darkly" (1 Cor. 13:12 KJV) is tantamount to having a god complex. God has granted humanity resources to overcome our limitations, one of which is the people of God who can help us to identify our areas of blindness. As a result, Christians are better equipped to live a life of faithfulness in community, especially when the community is representative of different ages, stages of life, races, and socioeconomic demographics. People of various types must be proactively included in both examining and establishing the structures that comprise our lives so that the love of God for all people is captured in every structure of society.

Dr. Walter R. Strickland II serves as associate vice president for Diversity and assistant professor of systematic and contextual theology at Southeastern Baptist Theological Seminary in Wake Forest, NC. His research interests include contextual theology and African-American religious history. He holds a PhD in theology from the University of Aberdeen.

---

6. Facts from the New Orleans bus transportation example come from Corinne Ramey, "America's Unfair Rules of the Road," *Slate*, February 27, 2015, http://www.slate.com/articles/news_and_politics/politics/2015/02/america_s_transportation_system_discriminates_against_minorities_and_poor.html.

THE CHALLENGES OF RACISM WITHIN EVANGELICALISM

Lisa Fields

On July 4, 1776, thirteen united states of America made a declaration that "all men are created equal, that they are endowed by their creator with certain unalienable Rights, that among these are life, liberty and the pursuit of happiness."[1] However, America failed to live up to these ideas with their treatment of Africans and Native Americans. Their declaration did not match their practice. This disconnect does not just appear in American history but evangelical history as well. This article will explain how evangelicalism has historically failed to live up to God's creational intent on matters of race and will provide a framework for future racial engagement.

It is important that evangelicalism be defined before it can be critiqued. Timothy Larsen defines an evangelical as:

> an orthodox Protestant who stands in the tradition of the global Christian networks arising from the eighteenth-century revival movements associated with John Wesley and George Whitefield; who has a preeminent place for the Bible in her or his Christian life as the divinely inspired, final authority in matters of faith and practice; who stresses reconciliation with God through the atoning work of Jesus Christ on the cross; and who stresses the work of the Holy Spirit in the life of an individual to bring about conversion and an ongoing life of fellowship with God and others, including the duty of all believers to participate in the task of proclaiming the gospel to all people.[2]

---

1. United States, and Thomas Jefferson. *The declaration of independence, Encyclopedia Britannica* (1952), 85.

2. Timothy Larsen and Daniel J. Treier, *The Cambridge Companion to Evangelical Theology* (Cambridge: Cambridge University Press, 2007), 1.

By Larsen's definition of an evangelical, it can be assumed that evangelicalism is a movement of people who have adopted these beliefs. One of the most important doctrinal positions within evangelicalism is the authority of Scripture. As the declaration of independence is an authoritative document in the United States of America, the Bible is the authoritative book in evangelicalism. Both the Declaration and the Bible have a similar premise: all people are equal. This put white evangelicals in conflict with the practice of slavery in America. On the one hand, white evangelicals affirmed the Bible; on the other hand, many benefited from an institution that contradicted the teachings of that book.

George Whitefield, one of the founders of evangelicalism, argued for the authority of Scripture but also for the introduction of slavery in Georgia. This background is important to keep in mind as one seeks to understand the intersection of racism and evangelicalism. While it is appealing and more palatable to detach racism from the evangelical movement, it is also almost impossible to do so. Michael Emerson and Christian Smith note in their book *Divided by Faith: Evangelical Religion and the Problem of Race in America* that Whitefield "further petitioned for the introduction of slaves by arguing that God has created the Georgia climate for blacks, that the large investment in the colony would be lost without increased production, that the orphanage would not survive without the benefit of slaves, and, consistent with his calling, the unsaved would become saved."[3] Whitefield believed "God allowed slavery for larger purposes, including the Christianization and uplifting of the heathen Africans."[4] Whitefield preached that God could free Africans from sin, but lobbied to keep them enslaved to white men. These words and others from the lives of evangelical founders like Whitefield cannot be detached from the formation of American evangelicalism.

It is important to remember that movements with racist roots will often bear racist fruit. This racist fruit still poisons souls today. Many African-Americans struggle to accept the whole counsel of God because of the ways in which evangelicals misused it. In *Jesus in the Disinherited*, Howard Thurman discussed his summers with his grandmother in Daytona Beach, Florida. He noted that he would read the Bible to her, but she would never let him read any of the Pauline epistles. When he finally mustered enough courage to ask her why, she responded:

During the days of slavery, the master's minister would occasionally hold services for the slaves. Old man McGhee was so mean that he would not let a Negro minister preach to his slaves. Always the white minister used as his

---

3. Michael O. Emerson and Christian Smith, *Divided by Faith: Evangelical Religion and the Problem of Race in America* (New York: Oxford University Press, 2001), 26.
4. Ibid., 27.

text something from Paul. At least three or four times a year he used as a text: "Slaves, be obedient to them that are your masters . . . , as unto Christ." Then he would go on to show how it was God's will that we were slaves and how, if we were good and happy slaves, God would bless us. I promised my Maker that if I ever learned to read and if freedom ever came, I would not read that part of the Bible.[5]

Thurman's grandmother's response is not unique. Many African-Americans struggle to accept the authority and sufficiency of Scripture because of the ways in which it was misrepresented by white evangelicals. One should not be surprised that some young African-Americans view the Bible as a tool of oppression instead of a guide to true freedom. Some African-Americans have rejected the Bible altogether because of the ways it was used against slaves, claiming that it is "a white man's religion." When one disconnects their orthopraxy from their orthodoxy, it bears the strange fruit of irrelevance. It is ironic, then, but not inconceivable, that a movement with a core value of evangelism has become an obstacle to evangelism in the African-American context. The history of the founding members of evangelicalism has created an apologetics problem for African-Americans who seek to lead other African-Americans to Christ. Black cults, such as the Hebrew Israelites, the Moors, and the Nation of Gods and Earths, have used the mismanagement of Scripture by white evangelicals to their advantage.

It is almost impossible to understand and engage the racial issues in evangelism apart from its problematic history. Racism, slavery, and oppression are skeletons in the evangelical closet and cannot be overcome until they are honestly addressed. The old tale that "time heals all wounds" is a lie. Time cannot heal what is not confronted and discussed. This is the very nature of the gospel message. The gospel confronts the sinful nature of humanity and requires confession and repentance to have a right standing with God. There is no reconciliation without confession. If evangelicalism cannot be honest about its dark past, it will never see wholeness in its future.

Honesty is not just important when one is discussing the dark history of evangelicalism but also when one is referring to the contributions of Africans in the formation of Christian doctrine. Many times the contributions of Africans are not highlighted. Many white evangelical spaces do not emphasize the African ancestry of those who defended the doctrines they affirm. It is important that evangelicals highlight the fact that Tertullian, Athanasius, and Augustine of Hippo were African. These historical facts not only create a place at the table for those of African descent, but they also take away the ammunition in the arsenal of black cults. When white evangelicals give an honest rendering of history, people will be able to differentiate between human sin and God's intent. While some white evangelicals have struggled to live up to God's creational intent on matters of race, it's important that evangelicals not let past sins hinder them from future progress. They must work hard to reflect what they affirm and remember that "we are all created equal."

Lisa Fields (MDiv, Liberty University) is the founder and president of the Jude 3 Project. She has spoken at evangelism, apologetic, and biblical literacy events at universities and churches. Lisa also hosts a secular podcast for young professionals called Brunch Culture.

OUR ONGOING RACE ISSUE

Idolatry as the Primary Problem

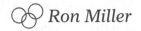 *Ron Miller*

In 2016, I toured Appomattox Court House National Historical Park, a short driving distance from my home in Lynchburg, Virginia. As I gazed upon the room in the McLean House where General Ulysses S. Grant drafted the terms of surrender that General Robert E. Lee accepted, I thought back to the gravity of that moment and was suddenly struck by a feeling of melancholy.

Five days after the surrender at Appomattox, President Abraham Lincoln, the architect of a gracious peace that promised "malice toward none, with charity for all,"[1] was gunned down at Ford's Theatre in Washington, DC, by a deranged Confederate sympathizer, and the goodwill Lincoln had hoped to engender was shattered. Everything that followed those fateful days—Reconstruction, the reign of domestic terror for blacks (especially in the South), the civil rights movement, and the racial conflicts of today—are all by-products of that moment in history.

As we stand right now, I cannot help but ask, "Why, after such incredible sacrifices—over 678,000 dead and over 469,000 wounded—are we still struggling with the issue of race in America?"

Americans have long looked to government to bring about racial harmony, but in the more than fifty years since the passage of the 1964 Civil Rights Act, race relations have ebbed and flowed like the tide, eroding the good intentions of the law as both sides of the racial divide play a zero-sum game.

Some believed the election of Barack Obama to the presidency of the United States would usher in a "post-racial" America in which blacks would finally ascend to their rightful place alongside their fellow Americans, and whites

---

1. "Second Inaugural Address of Abraham Lincoln: Saturday, March 4, 1865," *The Avalon Project: Documents in Law, History and Diplomacy*, Yale Law School Lillian Goldman Law Library, 2008, http://avalon.law.yale.edu/19th_century/lincoln2.asp.

would be absolved for the sins of slavery, institutionalized discrimination, and racism. Public opinion polls reflected some of the most optimistic beliefs on race in decades.[2]

Fast-forward to today, and it's clear that blacks, by most objective economic measures, did not realize the recovery for which they'd hoped, and whites did not get the absolution they sought as they continue to be blamed for systemic racism. Eventually, the smoldering tension between law enforcement and the black community erupted into a wildfire with several highly publicized shootings of young black men by white police officers, extending the historic perception of systemic injustice against people of color. Numerous public opinion polls show that race relations in America are at their lowest point in decades.[3] President Obama, as eloquent and measured as he was on the topic of race, could not bridge the racial divide. The rise of Donald Trump to the presidency and the undercurrent of white resentment of minorities that some say aided his unexpected victory pours salt into wounds which were never bound up as President Lincoln had hoped. The ghosts of Appomattox continue to haunt us years into the twenty-first century.

What about the church? Racism, after all, is a moral problem, and the church exists to promote and preserve morality.

The Christian church, however, does not have clean hands when it comes to race. The very existence of predominantly black denominations in America stems from the refusal of white Christians to worship alongside their black brethren. Southerners used the Bible to justify slavery, prompting Frederick Douglass to proclaim, "Between the Christianity of this land and the Christianity of Christ, I recognize the widest possible difference."[4] Dr. Martin Luther King Jr. called the white church "a weak, ineffectual voice with an uncertain sound" and "an arch-defender of the status quo."[5]

The schism between churches transcends worship style or rituals. Polls have identified "divergent perceptions on race among black and white Christians"[6] who claim to worship the same Savior but curse each other with the same tongue from which their worship comes. As Jesus' brother James exclaimed, "My brothers, these things ought not to be so" (James 3:10 ESV).

2. Frank Newport, "Americans See Obama Election as Race Relations Milestone," Gallup.com, November 7, 2008, http://www.gallup.com/poll/111817/americans-see-obama-election-race-relations-milestone.aspx.

3. Carrie Dann, "NBC/WSJ Poll: Americans Pessimistic on Race Relations," NBC News, September 21, 2017, https://www.nbcnews.com/politics/first-read/nbc-wsj-poll-americans-pessimistic-race-relations-n803446.

4. Frederick Douglass, "Appendix," *Life of an American Slave* (Boston: Anti-Slavery Office, 1845), 118, http://docsouth.unc.edu/neh/douglass/douglass.html.

5. Martin Luther King Jr., "Letter from Birmingham Jail," in *Why We Can't Wait*, ed. Martin Luther King Jr. (New York: Signet Classics, 1963), 77–100.

6. Morgan Lee, "Behind Ferguson: How Black and White Christians Think Differently About Race." *Christianity Today*, August 21, 2014.

If black and white churches are not one in Christ, then they cannot be the moral conscience of a nation riven by race. This division is the consequence of what I call "the invisible sin," the sin of idolatry. The word brings up images of golden calves, but an idol is not necessarily a totem or symbol. Racial identity, politics, culture, family, heritage, even a nation can be an idol. Anything that takes precedence over Jesus Christ is an idol that violates the first commandment the Lord gave to Moses, "You shall have no other gods before me" (Ex. 20:3 ESV).

Lawrence Ware, a black pastor who teaches at Oklahoma State University, expressed his frustration with the perceived equivocations of the nation's largest Protestant denomination on issues of race by declaring, "I love the church, but I love black people more. Black lives matter to me. I am not confident that they matter to the Southern Baptist Convention."[7]

As a person of color, black lives matter to me as well, and I understand that this statement, as controversial as it has become, has at its heart a plea for acknowledgment of equal value with the rest of humanity.

However, my faith in Jesus Christ is the organizing principle around which I order my life, and the church, whatever form it takes and whatever its failings, is his bride for whom he gave his life. The church is us, all who call Jesus Lord and Savior, black, white, and every shade or ethnicity in between, and to love anything or anyone more than Christ and his church is to violate the First Commandment, which is repeated in various forms throughout Scripture:

> Jesus replied: "Love the Lord your God with all your heart and with all your soul and with all your mind. This is the great and first commandment." Matthew 22:37–38 (ESV)
>
> Jesus said, "Whoever loves father or mother more than me is not worthy of me, and whoever loves son or daughter more than me is not worthy of me. And whoever does not take up his cross and follow me is not worthy of me." Matthew 10:37–38 (ESV)

Does this exclude loving your family, or loving black people, white people, or anyone else we hold dear? Of course not. What it does, however, is give precedence to our love of Jesus Christ and, by extension, those who love him as we do:

> While Jesus was still talking to the people, a man told him that his mother and his brothers were standing outside, asking to speak to him. Jesus replied to him, "Who is my mother, and who are my brothers?" Pointing to his

---

7. Lawrence Ware, "Why I'm Leaving the Southern Baptist Convention." *The New York Times*, July 17, 2017.

disciples, he said, "Here are my mother and my brothers! For whoever does the will of my Father in heaven is my brother and sister and mother." (Matt. 12:46–50 ESV)

The sad thing we as Christians often fail to realize is that when we put Christ in his rightful place on the throne of our hearts, he promises to provide the good and worthy things that matter to us. Jesus said, "But seek first the kingdom of God and his righteousness, and all these things will be added to you" (Matt. 6:33 ESV).

That includes the emphasis on black lives that Mr. Ware seeks. After all, it was Jesus' disciple John who emphasized: "If anyone says, 'I love God,' and hates his brother, he is a liar; for he who does not love his brother whom he has seen cannot love God whom he has not seen" (1 John 4:20 ESV).

You can't love Jesus and hate your fellow Christian. Those two passions cannot reside in the same space, and anyone who worships the Lord while denigrating his or her black or white brother and sister is deceiving themselves. If we truly want racial harmony and to repudiate the rage of the "alt-right" or the more radical elements of the Black Lives Matter movement, black and white Christians need to put aside their idols, whether they are movements or people, and put Christ first.

When Jesus prayed for us before his crucifixion, it was his fervent desire that, in a world which would hate and persecute us, we would be as one under him:

[My prayer is not] for these only, but also for those who will believe in me through their word, that they may all be one, just as you, Father, are in me, and I in you, that they also may be in us, so that the world may believe that you have sent me. The glory that you have given me I have given to them, that they may be one even as we are one, I in them and you in me, that they may become perfectly one, so that the world may know that you sent me and loved them even as you loved me. (John 17:20–23 ESV)

How beautiful that our Savior prayed so passionately for us to the Father even before we were conceived! It moves me to see into the heart of Jesus and to know how much it meant to him that we become one in his name. That is why I have made it my life's goal to bring the church together across the racial divide and model the love of Christ to an unbelieving world.

I hope that those in the church who are truly devoted to Jesus Christ will ignore the idolatrous forces that seek to tear Christ's church apart, whether they are "alt-right," Black Lives Matter, progressive, conservative, or whatever phrase or acronym one wants to use to describe them. Let us honor the prayer Jesus made for us before he went to the cross to secure our salvation. Let us have no other gods before him.

Ron Miller is the interim dean of the Helms School of Government at Liberty University and author of the book *SELLOUT: Musings from Uncle Tom's Porch*. The married father of three is dedicated to biblical reconciliation across cultures and denominations and is an elder at Mosaic Church in Lynchburg, Virginia.

WHY CHRISTIANS SHOULD BE PRO-IMMIGRANT

Y. Liz Dong and Ben Lowe

A recent survey of American evangelicals found that only 12 percent say their views on immigration are primarily influenced by the Bible.[1] The vast majority—a whopping 88 percent—say that the media, family and friends, and previous encounters with immigrants are more influential for them on this issue than the Word of God.

This is a troubling sign of the health of our churches today. One of the defining traits of evangelical Christianity is that the Bible is our ultimate authority for Christian belief and living.[2] Given how much Scripture says on the topic of immigration, it appears that much of American evangelicalism may not be very evangelical any more.

What Does the Bible Say?

The Bible does not prescribe a particular set of immigration policies for the United States or any other country outside of Israel during biblical times. It does, however, lay out God's heart for immigrants and the values that should define how we view and respond to immigration issues.

Gēr, the Hebrew word for sojourner (also foreigner, depending on the translation), appears ninety-two times in the Old Testament. God specifically and repeatedly calls his people to care for foreigners who, as newcomers to the land and its social systems, can easily fall victim to marginalization and injustice (e.g., Lev. 23:22; Ezek. 22:7, 29). After all, as God often reminds the Israelites, they

---

1. "Evangelical Views on Immigration," LifeWay Research, 2015, http://lifewayresearch.com/wp-content/uploads/2015/03/Evangelical-Views-on-Immigration-Report.pdf.
2. "What Is an Evangelical?" National Association of Evangelicals, https://www.nae.net/what-is-an-evangelical/.

were once foreigners too (e.g., Ex. 22:21; 23:9; Lev. 19:34). Scripture often links the foreigner with three other groups of uniquely vulnerable people: the orphan, the widow, and the poor (e.g., Deut. 10:18–19; Ps. 146:9; Jer. 22:3; Mal. 3:5). This biblical call for justice for the sojourner remains urgently relevant. To give just one example, a disproportionate number of human trafficking victims today are immigrants, particularly those lacking legal documentation.[3] This fact highlights just how vulnerable immigrants are.

Another recurring theme throughout the Bible is that of hospitality. Romans 12:13 exhorts us to "practice hospitality," and Hebrews 13:2 commands us to "not forget to show hospitality to strangers." The Greek word for hospitality used in these verses is *philoxenia*, which means "love of strangers." Jesus modeled this for us throughout his earthly ministry as he welcomed diverse and marginalized peoples into his presence, including widely hated foreigners such as Samaritans (e.g. Luke 17:11–19), Romans (e.g. Matt. 8:5–13), and other gentiles (e.g., Mark 7:24–30).

In addition to welcoming the stranger, Jesus lived as an immigrant himself. Due to Herod's genocidal decree after the visit of the Magi, Jesus' family fled as refugees to Egypt and lived there until the murderous king's death (Matt. 2:13–16). Toward the end of his ministry, Jesus identified directly with the stranger, teaching that those who fail to welcome strangers in their midst will face judgment, and that anyone who welcomes a stranger is in fact welcoming Christ himself (Matt. 25:31–46).

The Bible has much more to say here, and multiple books exist for unpacking these and other Scriptures in greater depth.[4] Our overall point is that immigration is a thoroughly biblical concern. God cares specifically and deeply for immigrants and calls us to as well.

⊗ Remembering Our Own Stories

As we rely on the Scriptures for guidance, we remember that we are all ultimately sojourners in this world (Heb. 11:13). Most of us in the United States today are also ultimately from foreign-born families who came to America either by choice or by force (as in the case of slaves). Remembering our heritage helps us

---

3. "Uniquely Vulnerable: The Nexus between Human Trafficking and Immigration," Faith Alliance Against Slavery and Trafficking," 2014, https://s3.amazonaws.com/media.cloversites.com/33/336bad01-3ae4–41f0-aaab-dde25ca8746f/documents/Uniquely_Vulernable_the_nexus_between_human_trafficking_and_immigration.pdf.

4. See Matthew Soerens, Jenny Yang, and Leith Anderson, *Welcoming the Stranger: Justice, Compassion & Truth in the Immigration Debate* (Downers Grove, IL: IVP, 2009); M. Daniel Carroll R., Ronald Sider, and Samuel Rodriguez, *Christians at the Border: Immigration, the Church, and the Bible* (Grand Rapids, Brazos, 2013).

identify with and have compassion for our immigrant neighbors today. This is very personal for both of us.

I, Ben, moved with my family to the United States at the age of sixteen. Born and raised as a missionary kid in Singapore, I received US citizenship at birth through my American father. My Malaysian mother, however, spent fifteen years navigating America's often frustrating naturalization process before finally being granted citizenship. Though my family faced challenges along the way, we were greatly blessed with the relationships and resources needed to transition into the United States. We became part of largely immigrant churches and have been involved in welcoming new immigrants and refugees into our communities ever since.

I, Liz, immigrated to the US as a child with my family on valid visas. We were on track to apply for permanent residency when our immigration attorney made a serious error that left me without proper status. I suddenly found myself undocumented at the age of twelve, even though my family tried to do everything right. It was difficult for me to come to terms with my new "identity," along with the shame that it carried and the practical limitations of not being able to drive, work, or go to college. As my world seemed to close in, God used this immigration debacle to open my eyes to a whole other reality shared by millions of my undocumented neighbors. I found myself in the shadows of society along with them—seeing their faces, hearing their stories, and sharing their lives, which were now all part of my life too. I came to understand that documented and undocumented immigrants are much more alike than different in our aspirations and work ethic. I realized that my family was very privileged to have the means to come with visas and afford a reputable immigration attorney (albeit one who was very negligent in my case). My experience as an undocumented immigrant has been formative in my coming to know Jesus Christ and experiencing his love for me made tangible by the church. I am committed to extending this same love and hospitality to others.

◯◯ Mission on Our Doorsteps

As God has worked in both our lives through our experiences—as immigrants and as those working with immigrants and refugees—so he is also at work through the migration of peoples throughout the world. This presents a tremendous missional and discipleship opportunity for the church. While much of the church's missions focus has been on sending out workers to serve all over the world, people from all over the world are also coming to us. They are now our neighbors, classmates, and colleagues. The International Mission Board estimates that the US has more unreached people groups (361) within its borders than any other country except China and India.[5]

Moreover, many immigrants are already Christians when they arrive. This includes refugees fleeing religious persecution. Where these fellow believers are welcomed into American churches and denominations, they are helping to bring a new vitality to their communities. Timothy Tennent, President of Asbury Theological Seminary, observes,

> The fastest growing churches in North America are the new ethnic Churches[. . .] Increasingly, we are going to see the emergence of major new ethnic congregations across our country filled with Korean, Chinese, Hispanic and African peoples. This represents our greatest hope for the renewal of the Church in our country.[6]

God is building his kingdom through the diaspora of people (Acts 17:26), and we get to join him by welcoming the stranger in our midst.

Not If but How

According to Jesus, loving God and loving our neighbors are inseparable (Matt. 22:36–40; Mark 12:28–31). We are all called to love our neighbors as ourselves—including our immigrant neighbors—regardless of their current legal status or our individual political affiliation or opinions. As Pastor Rick Warren, author of *The Purpose Driven Life*, has said, "A good Samaritan doesn't stop and ask the injured person, 'Are you legal or illegal?' before reaching out to help."[7]

So the question for us today is not *if* we should respond to immigration issues, but *how* we can respond faithfully. Practical ministry to and with immigrants—including language instruction, legal support, community integration, and more—are valuable ways for us to show Christ's love at an interpersonal level. We also recognize, however, that our immigration system in the United States is broken and outdated. It perpetuates the exploitation of undocumented immigrants, the separation of families through deportation and severe visa backlogs, and the inconsistent enforcement of the rule of law. As a result, loving our immigrant neighbor also means working together—through coalitions such as

5. J. D. Payne, *Strangers Next Door: Immigration, Migration and Mission* (Downers Grove, IL: InterVarsity, 2012), 63.

6. Timothy C. Tennent, (2011). "What Is the Global Church?," *The Asbury Herald* 121, no. 3 (Winter 2011): 5. https://asburyseminary.edu/wp-content/uploads/Winter2011Herald.pdf.

7. Rick Warren, quoted in USA Today, 2009, http://content.usatoday.com/communities/Religion/post/2009/09/rick-warren-lords-prayer-compassion-illegal-immigration/1#.WU6lL2jyvIW.

The Evangelical Immigration Table and ministries such as World Relief—to tackle systemic issues and advocate for just policies (Prov. 31:8), even if we may differ on exactly what policies are the most just.

In all of this, we pray. We praise God for welcoming us exiles into his kingdom and uniting us at the foot of the cross. We thank God for our immigrant neighbors and the ways they enrich our lives and communities. We pray for the burdens they carry and the challenges they face. We seek to recognize and repent from the ways that sins such as fear, selfishness, apathy, and racism have kept us and our churches from loving them as ourselves. And we continually ask for God's Spirit to empower us and God's Word to ground us, that we may more faithfully see one another through the eyes of Christ and welcome the stranger as if we were welcoming Jesus himself.

Y. Liz Dong works in immigration advocacy with World Relief and the National Immigration Forum. Her writing and work have been featured in *TIME*, *Christian Post*, *WORLD*, and other publications. She is the cofounder of Voices of Christian Dreamers and a graduate of Northwestern University and the University of Chicago.

Ben Lowe is the author of *Green Revolution*, *Doing Good Without Giving Up*, and *The Future of Our Faith* (with Ron Sider). He is a graduate of Wheaton College (IL) and is ordained in the Christian and Missionary Alliance. For more info: benlowe.net.

REFRAMING THE IMMIGRATION DEBATE

The Need for Prudence Rather than Proof-Texting

◯◯ Joshua D. Chatraw

Ever since immigrants first began arriving in the newly formed United States of America in the late 1700s and federal restrictions on immigration were first set in place in the late 1800s, immigration policy has become a heated topic.[1] In recent decades, the debates have only intensified: the increasing impact of globalism, the rising number of unauthorized immigrants,[2] the continued demand for low-wage labor, the humanitarian concerns created by refugees fleeing war-torn countries, and the threat of worldwide terrorism have brought the anxiety and anger of many to a head, as seen in the inflammatory rhetoric of the 2016 presidential election.

Unfortunately, when Christians have weighed in on the immigration debate, their conversations are often riddled with biblical proof-texting and sound bites—whether they use Scripture commanding compassion for foreigners to argue for liberal policies or Scripture emphasizing the government's role in protection to argue for restrictive policies. While both sides hold elements of truth, both can and have been oversimplified and used to accuse the other side of being unjust or unlawful, or worse, xenophobic or anarchistic.

On the one hand, consider, for example, a well-known pastor's use of the Old Testament book of Nehemiah to argue in favor of building a wall across

---

1. A special thanks to my former assistant, Micailyn Geyer, for her help researching for this essay.
2. The illegal immigrant population rose from 3.5 million in 1990 to a peak of 12.2 million in 2007. Following the Great Recession, it has leveled off to around 11 million. Until recently, the majority of illegal immigrants were from Mexico, but in 2016 they accounted for only half. Jens Manuel Krogstad, Jeffrey S. Passell, and D'vera Cohn, "5 Facts About Illegal Immigration in the U.S.," April 27, 2017, http://www.pew research.org/fact-tank/2017/04/27/5-facts-about-illegal-immigration-in-the-u-s/.

the southern border of the United States: "God instructed Nehemiah to build a wall around Jerusalem to protect its citizens from enemy attack. You see, God is NOT against building walls!"[3] While in one sense, there is some truth here—God was not against the Israelites building a wall to defend themselves against enemy attack—his analogy is problematic, to say the least. Even setting aside the question of whether the United States can be so simply compared to ancient Israel, the posture this analogy takes misrepresents Christianity. The tone of this sort of analogy along with the rhetoric of some ("deport them all!" and "build a wall to shut them all out!") can shape an atmosphere in which immigrants begin to feel like our enemies—perhaps even encouraging us to start thinking that way. There is now a mindset, even among some Christians, that equates the word "immigrant" with the word "felon," "terrorist," or "freeloader."

Most immigrants, however, are none of these things, and painting them as such is wrong. Most, including those who are here illegally,[4] are just normal people trying their best to care for their families.[5] Christians in particular should be the last to allow overblown rhetoric to foster within them an ungenerous or hostile spirit. In countless biblical texts, God commands Christians to be compassionate toward the poor, the outcast, and the foreigner and to seek to give them real, tangible assistance.

Historically, animosity toward the foreigner—the "other"—has been all too common. Because of all the hateful rhetoric that has been used against immigrants, some dismiss any conservative approach to immigration policies as, at best, selfish and lacking in compassion, and at worst, xenophobic and racist. While these might be accurate descriptions in some cases, those who indiscriminately level such accusations must be willing to reflect on the actual concerns held by many Americans. It is far too easy to "take the moral high ground" and look down on the many Americans who, concerned about the current situation, are wary of more open policies. Though proponents of conservative policies may not always express their concerns well or with appropriate levels of compassion, a conservative position on immigration needs to be understood as it is best articulated.

Many Christians appeal to the biblical support for citizens to respect the laws of the land as well as for the government to maintain order and protect those citizens. A high regard for the law of a nation is essential for a society to maintain

---

3. TIME staff, "Read the Sermon Donald Trump Heard Before Becoming President," *TIME*, January 20, 2017, http://time.com/4641208/donald-trump-robert-jeffress-st-john-episcopal-inauguration/.

4. In this essay I am using the terms "illegal," "unauthorized," and "undocumented" synonymously.

5. This is not to endorse people entering the country illegally or to ignore the possible dangers undocumented immigration can present; it is merely to observe the inaccuracy of picturing all (or even most) unauthorized immigrants as hardened criminals or terrorists.

order (though, of course, in a democracy the people are supposed to have some say in what those laws will be). Governments provide laws as God's ordained means to provide stability to a society. As Michael Walzer has argued, regulating membership through admission and exclusion is essential in preserving "communities of character"—that is, "historically stable, ongoing associations of men and women with some special commitment to one another and some special sense of their common life."[6]

In the same way a mother ought to look out for her own children first, a nation has a heightened obligation to care for its own citizens. In other words, if one accepts a narrative concept of personhood, as Harvard professor Michael Sandel suggests, then "our identity as moral agents is bound up with the communities we inhabit," and thus, we have "a special obligation for the welfare of our fellow citizens by virtue of the common life and history we share."[7] This does not mean government leaders and policies should be unconcerned or spiteful toward immigrants. By analogy, as Christians we are to cultivate stable and thriving families so we become the home into which other children in the neighborhood are welcomed and, consequently, want to visit and maybe even be adopted. A flourishing society—like a flourishing family—displays *order, solidarity,* and *hospitality.*

As Christians, we are called to speak with moral clarity to shape the conscience of America's immigration policy. However, if we allow self-interest groups and government officials on both sides of this issue to cloud needed conversations with caricatures, reductionistic theories, and appeals solely designed to rally their base, our society's sense of solidarity and structure will be damaged, destroying the integrity of the very place in which immigrants are seeking refuge. Yet a respect for law and the importance of solidarity should not be used to prop up the status quo and certainly not for justifying "solutions" that result in separating children from their parents, any more than the biblical texts advocating compassion for the stranger mean, therefore, we should have open borders. Things are more complicated than that.

Actual Policy Is Complicated

In actuality, the situation is messy. On the one hand, the United States bears some of the blame for the current situation. As Darrell Bock observes, for the past thirty years or so since the most recent policy has been in place, the US has not only enforced policy weakly and inconsistently but has also done a lot of

6. Michael Walzer, *Spheres of Justice* (New York: Basic Books, 1983), 62.
7. Michael Sandel, *Justice: What's the Right Thing to Do?* (New York: Farrar, Straus, and Giroux), 2009.

"eye-winking," even "encourag[ing] people to come and establish themselves."[8] Because of this, "several generations of undocumented and illegal people have been and are here, often with our initial acceptance."[9] Compounding the situation is the fact that there has been no clear, reliable way for immigrants to gain citizenship once they are already in the US temporarily with a visa. Forty percent of all illegal immigrants were once legally in the country (as visitors, students, or temporary workers) with visas, but were unable to extend their visas, so they chose to break the law to stay.[10] In light of how poorly the US has handled its immigration policies and the fact that many illegal immigrants and their families have been firmly established in the US for years,[11] suddenly deporting illegal immigrants en masse isn't a viable option. It would be inhumane.

On the other hand, conservatives have legitimate questions and concerns. For instance, do immigrants take away jobs and drive down wages?[12] If this possibility had a negative effect primarily on the upper-class Americans, then some might write this off as simple greed. However, this monetary concern is likely felt most acutely by many lower-class American families.

Also, unauthorized immigration raises concerns about our vulnerability to national security breaches and other illegal activities. Regardless of who immigrants are, where they are coming from, or whether they have posed a significant threat thus far, it is extremely unwise and dangerous to admit *anyone* into our country through lax enforcement if we have no idea who they are.

In seeking to show compassion to immigrants longing to get into the United States, we must not neglect to consider our fellow citizens.

---

8. Darrell L. Bock, *How Would Jesus Vote: Do Your Political Positions Really Align with the Bible?* (New York: Howard, 2016), 80.

9. Ibid.

10. Mark R. Amstutz, *Just Immigration: American Policy in Christian Perspective* (Grand Rapids: Eerdmans, 2017), 3; of the 11 million aliens living in the United States illegally, about 40 percent arrived legally but stayed when their visas expired. Bryan Roberts, Edward Alden, and John Whitely, *Managing Illegal Immigration in the United States: How Effective Is Enforcement?* (New York: Council on Foreign Relations, 2014), 32.

11. The Pew Research Center affirms this: a rising share of illegal immigrants have lived in the US for at least a decade (66 percent of adults in 2014 as compared to 41 percent in 2005). See Krogstad, "5 Facts."

12. There is disagreement over whether immigrants actually take away jobs and drive down wages. David Brooks and Reihan Salam, both conservatives, suggest that immigrants do not. Mark Amstutz, however, while acknowledging there is disagreement, suggests that they do and adds that what most scholars do agree on is that "the economic benefits of unlawful migration accrue disproportionately to the wealthier citizens." See Amstutz, *Just Immigration*, 68. Overall, immigrants, regardless of legal status, work in a variety of different jobs, and do not make up the majority of workers in any US industry. Lawful immigrants are most likely to be in professional, management, or business and finance jobs (37 percent) or service jobs (22 percent). Illegal immigrants, by contrast, are most likely to be in service (32 percent) or construction jobs (16 percent) and are overrepresented in farming (26 percent of all workers in the US) and construction (15 percent of all workers in the US). Illegal immigrants account for 5 percent of the total US workforce. See Krogstad, "5 Facts."

Moving Beyond Proof-Texting

While the Christian faith does not provide specific policy instructions for a twenty-first-century Western society, it does offer "ultimate perspectives, broad criteria, motives, inspirations, sensitivities, warnings, and moral limits"[13] that can help structure the analysis of public affairs and inspire and guide action. Rather than attempting to proof-text specific immigration policies with biblical passages in an attempt to invoke divine authority for specific legislation, it is more important to interject morals and values relevant to the conversation. As David Brooks has suggested, the best approach on immigration policy is to recognize the need for a balanced realism: "There is no one and correct answer to the big political questions. Instead, politics is usually a tension between two or more views, each of which possesses a piece of the truth. Sometimes immigration restrictions should be loosened to bring in new people and new dynamism; sometimes they should be tightened to ensure national cohesion. Leadership is about determining which viewpoint is more needed at that moment. Politics is a dynamic unfolding, not a debate that can ever be settled once and for all."[14]

We must seek to improve current legislation with cooler heads, measured words, and a greater awareness of historical, cultural, and political realities—recognizing that legitimate concerns from both sides of this issue need to be balanced and weighed. In short, "such a time as this" calls for theological prudence rather than biblical proof-texting. The need of the day is sympathetic listening rather than inflammatory rhetoric. Christians who have concerns with more liberal approaches to immigration must find approaches to communicate God's love for the vulnerable and the downtrodden, whether they be stranger or citizen.

Joshua Chatraw (PhD, Southeastern Baptist Theological Seminary) serves as the director for New City Fellows and the resident theologian at Holy Trinity Anglican Church in Raleigh, North Carolina. His books include *Apologetics at the Cross*, *Truth in a Culture of Doubt*, and *Truth Matters*. He is a fellow with the Center for Pastor Theologians and has served in both pastoral and academic posts during his ministry.

13. John C. Bennett, *Foreign Policy in Christian Perspective* (New York: Charles Scribner's Sons, 1966), 36.
14. David Brooks, "What Moderates Believe," *The New York Times*, August 22, 2017, https://www.nytimes.com/2017/08/22/opinion/trump-moderates-bipartisanship-truth.html?mcubz=0.

DISCUSSION QUESTIONS

1. As Fields discusses in her article, many African-Americans still have difficulty in accepting the authority of the Bible because of how it was used as an oppressive tool. In his article, Chatraw states how unproductive it is to oversimplify and proof-text Scripture for the purpose of advocating for one's political views on immigration law. Understanding the harm done by slave owners by proof-texting Scripture, how might similar biblical proof-texting on the issue of immigration result in harm toward immigrants?

2. Miller states that the only way for us to receive true harmony in terms of race relations is to put Christ first. Strickland discusses the difference between individual and structural racism. Since structural racism "is not expressed in discrete actions or words," how can it be fought by "putting Christ first"?

3. In their article, Dong and Lowe discuss the biblical implications of hospitality and how Jesus modeled loving the stranger. How would the notion of hospitality affect the issues of both individual and structural racism discussed in Strickland's article?

4. In Miller's article, he discusses that despite how many people believed the election of President Barack Obama would lead to a "post-racial" America, it has clearly not yet come about. Chatraw's article, then, examines the polarized views of Christians on immigration and the harm that has been created by this polarity. How has the polarization of views on immigration affected the racial divide in America?

5. Dong and Lowe state that 88 percent of evangelicals "say that the media, family and friends, and previous encounters with immigrants are more influential for them on this issue [of immigration] than the Word of God." At the same time, both Fields and Chatraw discuss the harm that misuse of Scripture has done in race relations and immigration opinions. How can someone avoid both ignoring Scripture on the one hand and abusing Scripture for personal gain on the other?

6. Dong and Lowe address the large number of unreached people groups in the US because of immigration and the opportunity this poses for evangelism.

How might someone with a different view on immigration respond to the claim that more immigrants offers us more opportunities for evangelism and church renewal? How do you think Dong and Lowe would address this response?

7. Fields discusses how a "movement with racist roots will often bear racist fruit." Integrating this discussion with Strickland's discussion of individual and structural racism, how has the existence of predominantly white and black churches, as referenced by Miller, been impacted by racist roots and individual and structural racism?

8. Chatraw explains the issue of using inconsiderate rhetoric when referring to immigrants, such as "felons," "terrorists," or "freeloaders." How might Miller's discussion of idolatry speak to this inherent hostility that many Christians seem to hold toward immigrants?

9. Dong and Lowe discuss the need for us to be involved in "practical ministry" with immigrants, while Fields writes that "there is no reconciliation without confession." How can one integrate Fields's call for confession with Dong and Lowe's encouragement toward engaging in practical ministry?

10. Chatraw describes the long and complex history of "animosity toward the foreigner." With this upsetting history in mind, as well as Strickland's assertion that structural racism "can be perpetuated unknowingly," is it reasonable to hope for reconciliation, and if so, how can these two obstacles be addressed with hope?

chapter eight

CREATION AND CREATURE CARE

Scripture is clear that God declared his creation to be "very good" (Gen. 1:31) and that God commanded humans to "rule over" the other creatures (Gen. 1:28), placing them in the land to "work" and "take care of" it (Gen. 2:15). What has been less clear over the course of human history since the fall is what form that rule and care should take. Just as the forms of rule (or "dominion" as other translations render the word) that human beings have over one another through various types of governments and social contracts vary greatly, so too do our understandings of how Christians should steward creation. The tension between human care over and control of creation reflects a parallel tension between God's lovingkindness toward humanity and his sovereignty over us. But when sin entered the world, God's plan for the relationship between human beings and the rest of creation, like everything else, was affected by the fall. The "original harmony of creation" was ruptured at three levels, one scholar explains: woman from man, human animals from nonhuman animals, and humanity from the earth and soil.[1]

The Christian tradition concerning creation care has been influenced not only by Scripture but also by two pagan philosophical schools that predate Christianity. The first influence is Neo-Platonism, which is characterized by a dualism that sets human beings apart from the rest of creation in ways that go beyond the clear implications of *imago Dei* and privileges the spiritual realm over the material physical one. The second influential school of thought stems from Plato's student Aristotle, who espoused a hierarchical, rather than dualistic, view of all of creation. Aristotle conceived of all of creation as existing along a *scala naturae* or, as it later came to be called, the Great Chain of Being,[2] which positions each category of created things within a hierarchy based on each being's

---

1. Ellen Davis, *Getting Involved with God: Rediscovering the Old Testament* (Cambridge: Crowley, 2001), 74.
2. For more history on the Great Chain of Being, see Arthur O. Lovejoy, *The Great Chain of Being* (Cambridge: Harvard University Press, 1971).

complexity and capacity for reason: God, angel, humanity, animals, plants, rocks, with countless subcategories in between. The problem with both of these views, if they are not chastened by a biblical framework, is that they are, ultimately, anthropocentric rather than theocentric.

The Christian understanding of the relationship between the Creator and creation—the belief that God created the world out of nothing and exists above and apart from it—led to a way of thinking about humanity's relationship, in turn, to the natural world that departed dramatically from that of the earlier pagan philosophers. James Hannam explains that both Greek philosophers and early Christians studied nature not for its own sake but, in the case of the philosophers, as an extension of natural philosophy, and of the Christians, as a means of understanding God and theology:

> Medieval Christians were not deliberately trying to make progress toward science as we know it today. They were simply studying God's creation so that they could become better theologians and Christians. In that sense, their motives for doing science were no different from those of earlier eras. It was just that the metaphysical background to Christianity turned out to be uniquely conducive to successfully understanding the working of nature.[3]

Many scholars credit this particular Christian understanding of the relationship of God to creation and, in turn, of humanity to creation, for the beginning of the empirical mode and, subsequently, of modern science. With the modern scientific age came a mastery over creation—from the microscopic to the telescopic, from the nuclear to the galactic levels—that the ancients could hardly have imagined. And with the wonders wrought by such knowledge and technology also came more possibilities of greater harm to all of creation. This potential for harm became more dramatically evident during the Industrial Age and the massive destruction of the world wars that followed.

For millennia, human beings had met the natural and supernatural world with superstitions or humanistic philosophies. The spread of Christianity helped advance a dominionistic relationship toward creation that, while radically reducing disease, pain, and suffering, eventually caused increased environmental destruction and animal suffering in the later twentieth and early twenty-first centuries. This has led many to begin to question just how far dominion should go and at what cost. For example, some would argue that factory farming and

---

3. James Hannam, "How Christianity Led to the Rise of Modern Science," *Christian Research Journal* 3, no. 4 (2015), https://www.equip.org/article/christianity-led-rise-modern-science/.

human slavery both spring from extreme views of dominion over the earth—and bear the bitter fruit of great suffering.

In 1966, historian Lynn White gave a famous lecture (later published), "The Historical Roots of Our Ecologic Crisis," in which he claimed that Christianity (which he calls "the most anthropocentric religion the world has seen") was the cause of an ecological crisis. Since that landmark argument, many notable Christian thinkers, scientists, and theologians (including Francis Schaeffer, John Stott, and Richard Bauckham)[4] have made attempts to restate and refine a more nuanced biblical understanding of stewardship, including a less anthropocentric view of creation in favor of a theocentric one.

In the lead essay of this section, Jonathan A. Moo argues that issues surrounding climate change provide Christians with the distinct opportunity to demonstrate God's plan for the natural world and our interaction with it. Thus, Moo reminds Christians that, because we are accountable to God for our stewardship of the earth, we should acknowledge the challenges of climate change and exercise our power to help mitigate those challenges. Yet, while not necessarily being at odds with the theology expressed in Moo's essay and acknowledging the reality and complexity of climate change, Timothy Terrell cautions Christians against rushing toward government intervention on this issue, explaining that the issues of the global climate are too large and complex for one national government or assembly of governments to undertake with equanimity.

Joel Salatin's essay challenges Christians to see how their support of factory farming and the industrial fast-food industry are "life disrespecting." By prioritizing God's order in creation, we serve as faithful stewards of creation and avoid potential health risks that result from disregarding creation's divinely ordered patterns. On the other side of this issue, Tom Pittman argues that, contrary to popularized belief, organic farming is no more environmentally sustainable or nutritionally valuable than factory farming. Moreover, Pittman asserts that factory farms feed more people more efficiently, thereby caring for the people and the environment in a way that frees individuals to follow God's calling into diverse fields.

Finally, Christine Gutleben briefly looks at Scripture, denominational trends and statements, and historical evangelical involvement in animal welfare to support her claim that evangelicals have championed the movements and organizations that have promoted and encouraged care for animals.

---

4. Francis Schaeffer and Udo Middelmann, *Pollution and the Death of Man* (Wheaton, IL: Crossway, 1970); John Stott, *The Radical Disciple: Some Neglected Aspects of Our Calling* (Downers Grove, IL: IVP, 2014); Richard Bauckham, *Living with Other Creatures: Green Exegesis and Theology* (Waco, TX: Baylor University Press, 2011), 18.

CLIMATE CHANGE IS A CHRISTIAN ISSUE

Jonathan A. Moo

Why Do We Disagree about Climate Change?

UK climate scientist Mike Hulme claims that we disagree about "climate change" because it is as much a cultural and social issue as a scientific one.[1] We interpret climate change according to contrasting visions of the world and our place within it. For some, climate change represents the greatest threat to life on earth and all that is wrong about our industrialized, globalized society. For others, climate change is a minor issue that has been overhyped by the media, scientists, and politicians eager to chase money or attention. For still others, climate change is simply a technological problem to be fixed with better technology.

Whatever perspective we adopt, the idea of climate change has become an inescapable part of our culture, reason enough for a book on Christian cultural engagement to give attention to it. Yet climate change is significant in another way. The notion that human beings might play a role in affecting the atmosphere of the entire earth has become a dramatic example of the inseparability of human culture and "nature." It prompts fresh questions about what we value and humanity's role and responsibilities in the world. Climate change thus represents potentially more than just a practical challenge that demands an informed Christian response. It also provides an opportunity to articulate and live out what a distinctive Christian vision of the world as God's creation means for how we relate to God, our human neighbors, and the rest of the natural world.

---

1. Mike Hulme, *Why We Disagree About Climate Change* (Cambridge: Cambridge University Press, 2009).

◯◯ What Is the Science of Climate Change?

Katherine Hayhoe, a leading North American climate scientist and evangelical Christian, is all too aware of the sharp disagreements that her academic work prompts among fellow Christians. So she often reminds her audiences of the need to separate the science of climate change from the political and ideological debates that surround the subject.[2] Though such debates are necessary and important when it comes to interpreting the significance of scientific data and deciding how to respond, too often Christians remain mired in uninformed disagreements about the scientific evidence itself. The facts by themselves can't tell us how to act, yet Christians must be concerned with truth-telling and making decisions that are informed by the facts. Scripture reveals a wondrous and ordered creation in which God entrusts human beings with significant responsibility to rule and care for the earth and other creatures, and such rule requires knowledge and wisdom.[3] The ability to study and understand the world through science is thus a gift that enhances both our appreciation of God's glory as revealed in creation and our knowledge of how to live faithfully. Just as we use medical science to help us know how best to care for people's physical health, so too must we use the natural and physical sciences to help us know how to care for the earth and its inhabitants.

Our understanding of the earth's climate has improved dramatically in recent decades, although the basic physics has been understood for a long time. The effect of greenhouse gasses in keeping our planet warmer than it otherwise would be has been known for nearly two centuries, and in 1896 the Swedish scientist Svante Arrhenius calculated the potential impact that increasing the concentration of these gases might have on global temperatures. But it is relatively recently that scientists have been able to quantify more precisely what role human-caused increases of greenhouse gases play within the wide array of other factors that also influence the earth's climate. The result is growing certainty that the human factor is highly significant in the warming that the planet is currently undergoing.

When scientists attempt to model the climate of the past, they find that models which include all known variations in "natural" factors match the observed data very closely. But unless their models also include the increase

---

2. See her blog, http://katharinehayhoe.com, and book, Katherine Hayhoe and Andrew Farley, *A Climate for Change: Global Warming Facts for Faith-Based Decisions* (New York: FaithWords, 2009).

3. Adam's naming of the animals in Eden (Gen. 2:19–20) is an early biblical example of the need to know the creatures over which humankind is given rule; and King Solomon's wisdom includes knowledge of the natural world: "He spoke about plant life ... animals and birds, reptiles and fish" (1 Kings 4:33).

in atmospheric greenhouse gasses that have been caused by human activity (mostly the burning of fossil fuels and land-use changes since the industrial revolution), it becomes impossible for them to account for the recent warming of the earth. The human fingerprint on recent changes in the climate, as well as on the associated melting of arctic ice and acidification of the oceans (which absorb much of the carbon dioxide that is emitted when we burn fossil fuels), has become unmistakable. Scientists are now more confident than they could have been even several years ago about the impact that human activity is having on the climate.[4]

Of course, the earth's climate has always changed over time, sometimes dramatically. So even if human activity is playing a major role in changing the climate in our day, why does it attract so much concern? The main reason is that the warming of the planet that is under way and expected to continue well into the future is happening at a rate unprecedented in human history and is having far-reaching and long-lasting effects on all of life that will become more pronounced the more the earth warms. Some of these effects are benign; but, taken as a whole, a rapidly warming planet poses profoundly negative risks to human societies and all life on earth. In fact, on current trajectories, the challenges associated with climate change are likely to be the most significant of any we face this century. What is especially disheartening is that, although everyone will be affected, climate change disproportionately harms those living in poorer countries who are the least able to adapt and who have contributed the least to the historic burning of fossil fuels.

How Do Christians Interpret Climate Change?

Biblical Christianity provides a distinctive interpretation of what climate science reveals about humankind's impact on the climate. On the one hand, it should not be surprising that those who are called to rule within creation as God's image-bearers (Gen. 1:27–28; Ps. 8) and to whose fate the entire creation is bound (Rom. 8:20–21) might have a dramatic effect on the earth. That this effect can be negative is a sad feature of much of the prophetic literature of the Old Testament, where we read often of the land itself and other creatures suffering as a result of

---

4. For an accessible introduction to climate change, see Joseph Romm, *Climate Change: What Everyone Needs to Know* (Oxford: Oxford University Press, 2016); for a more in-depth introduction, see John Houghton, *Global Warming: The Complete Briefing*, 4th ed. (Cambridge: Cambridge University Press, 2009). For recent reports summarizing the science of climate change and its effects, see the IPCC reports at http://www.ipcc .ch; and, for a recent focus on impacts in the United States, D. J. Wuebbles et al., *Climate Science Special Report: Fourth National Climate Assessment, Volume I* (Washington, DC: U.S. Global Change Research Program, 2017).

human sin and injustice (e.g., Isa. 24; Hos. 4)—a theme the apostle Paul universalizes and applies to the entire creation in Romans 8:19–22.

But, we might ask, in what sense can the burning of fossil fuels be sin? After all, surely it is a gift to have stored energy buried in the earth that is now able to provide (for a time) cheap and plentifully available fuel for human progress and development—including indirectly even the technology that has enabled our current knowledge of the earth's climate.

On this point, Christianity must in fact acknowledge the great good that can be accomplished through human ingenuity and technology. Even Noah, the quintessential biblical example of someone caring for and preserving other life on earth, used technology—an ark—to save the animals. Rather than demonizing technology, we do better to foster a biblical vision that exposes the ambiguities of human culture and technology, that reminds us that power can be used for good or for evil, and that even potentially benign activities can become sinful when pursued limitlessly and heedlessly. For every Noah's ark, there is a Babel; for every New Jerusalem, a Babylon. The question for us, in light of what we have now learned about the impact of our actions, is what is required of us as followers of Christ in this time and place?

⊖ How Do Christians Respond to Climate Change?

Biblical Christianity enables us to question the assumptions of our culture about what is good, to see beyond business as usual, and to imagine alternative ways of being in the world. Most importantly, followers of Jesus seek to heed his call to love God and to love our neighbors as ourselves (e.g., Mark 12:30–31). To love God must include loving and caring well for the beautiful and wonderfully diverse creation that he made and values and for which he has given us significant responsibility. To love our neighbors requires that we care for the world of which they and we are a part, that we pay attention to the ways in which our collective actions affect the ability of others to live and flourish. The biblical demands of justice (e.g., Isa. 1:17; Mic. 6:8) and equality (2 Cor. 8:13–14) mean that those of us in richer countries who have benefited most from the burning of fossil fuels must be most prepared to follow the example of Christ and be willing to sacrifice for the sake of our global neighbors. Certainly, there can be no excuse for seeking simply to protect our own way of life if that way of life is now contributing to the suffering of others.

For those who in Christ are being renewed in the image of their Creator (Col. 3:10), traditional Christian virtues such as prudence, justice, temperance, courage, and above all faith, hope, and love must be lived out in fresh ways in a world facing anthropogenic climate change—that is, caused by human activities. Individuals and churches and communities need to support and actively promote technologies, initiatives, and policies that aim at climate change mitigation, adaptation, and resiliency. Such support must also include activism and engagement with the messiness of politics, where important decisions with wide-reaching ramifications are made. Yet biblical Christianity is suspicious of totalizing narratives and encourages humility to accept that we are always more ignorant than we know. Whatever the circumstances, it challenges us to stand with the oppressed, the poor, and the weak—and sadly, the refugee crises likely to result from climate change will provide plenty of opportunities for Christians to find practical ways to love their global neighbors. Precisely because Christianity limits transcendence to God alone, it prompts a pragmatism that is unwilling to worship any particular economic or environmental ideology but seeks to imagine how the kingdom of God is to be lived out here and now, while always entrusting our ultimate hope to God in Christ.

Biblical Christianity thus recalls us to a realistic assessment of our powers and our place in creation. In humility and in recognition of the limits of our knowledge and power, we do our work in the time given to us in ways that preserve and sustain creation's dynamic resilience, its hospitable climate, its mosaic of changing landscapes, and the creatures we share this world with, including above all our human sisters and brothers. Our model and example is Christ, who not only shows us what it truly is to bear God's image, to love and to sacrifice, but who in the incarnation and resurrection binds himself to creation and brings about the reconciliation and restoration that we could never bring about on our own.

Jonathan Moo (PhD, University of Cambridge) is associate professor of New Testament and environmental studies at Whitworth University in Spokane, Washington. He has published a number of essays and books, including the coauthored *Let Creation Rejoice* and *Creation Care: A Biblical Theology of the Natural World*.

THE NEED FOR CAUTION IN ADVOCATING FOR CLIMATE CHANGE POLICIES

Timothy D. Terrell

Climate science is complex, and our understanding of what is going on with the planet's atmosphere changes as new data and new methods of forecasting become available. Thus, Christians should enter into any research or discussion of climate change with care and humility.

In attempting to navigate these issues, Christians should stand for integrity and truth in the scientific process, and for justice and wisdom in policy making. It is appropriate to call a society to repentance for poor stewardship and violation of our neighbors' rights. We must also insist that any government policy making follow a process that acknowledges human limitations and moral fallibility and respects other social institutions and spheres of authority. We should question policies that through misguided action add to the burdens of the poor and the weak.

Ethics, Stewardship, and Climate

Policy made with good intentions is not necessarily good policy. Often, governmental responses to a perceived environmental problem are fashioned without good information about the causes or effects of environmental change. Unfortunately, Christians weighing in on environmental policy have sometimes brought more confusion than clarity, and often have underestimated the problems accompanying environmental regulation. Stewardship means being able to make wise choices among multiple uses of the natural world, and Christian thinking on this has often been vague about how those choices should be made.

Inevitably, we are confronted with trade-offs in climate change policy.

How do we weigh the costs of reducing emissions from our consumption and production processes against the costs of adaptation? And, since government regulation and markets both have their own set of problems and limitations, we should think carefully about the choice between the two. Moral policy making involves thinking about what government should do as well as considering the likely impacts of various courses of action.

∞ Ethics and the Limits of Government

The primary function of civil government is to promote justice—to punish those who do evil and commend those who do good (Rom. 13:4; 1 Peter 2:14). Biblical justice is simply the consistent application of God's law (Ezek. 18:5–9; John 5:30). When human action on the environment clearly violates the rights of another person, any government response should acknowledge the general principles of biblical justice, among which are due process (e.g., Deut. 19:15–19; Matt. 18:15–17), impartiality (Lev. 19:15), proportionality (Ex. 21), and rights to individual life and property (Ex. 20:13–15; Acts 5:4). Where global environmental change is occurring, applying these principles can be difficult. Skeptics of climate change policies might well ask a few questions:

How much climate change is due to human activity, versus natural fluctuations?[1]

Climate change can benefit some (e.g., through longer growing seasons or lower winter heating costs) while harming others. Who is hurt, who is helped, and who, precisely, deserves the blame or the credit?

Is it just to place heavy restrictions or penalties on a person because of theoretical future harms of uncertain magnitude to which he (and billions of other people) might contribute?

Is it proportional to impose policies that, for example, require an average family of four to lose about $1,200 a year of income, and risk job loss, for a reduction of 0.02°C in global average temperature by the end of this century?[2]

Do the wealthy in industrialized countries have the right to tell a poor family in a developing country that providing life-changing (and truthfully, life-saving) affordable electricity is too risky?

It is also clear that the civil government is one among several social institutions, and it must respect the realms of the family, the church, and the individual.

---

1.   David R. Legates and G. Cornelis van Kooten, "A Call to Truth, Prudence, and Protection of the Poor 2014: The Case against Harmful Climate Policies Gets Stronger," *The Cornwall Alliance for the Stewardship of Creation*, September 2014, http://www.cornwallalliance.org/wp-content/uploads/2014/09/A-Call-to-Truth -Prudence-and-Protection-of-the-Poor-2014-The-Case-Against-Harmful-Climate-Policies-Gets-Stronger.pdf.

2.   Ibid.

These limits are a kind of divine safeguard against the tendency of power to corrupt. Before we entrust to this government a new authority to handle a perceived environmental problem, we must first ask, "How might this intrude upon the other spheres of social authority?" This is true even if (and perhaps especially if) the civil government seems to be the only social institution powerful enough to address the problem. Mankind's fallenness may require governance, but that governance is also affected by sin. The greater the capacity for coercion from a governmental institution, the more caution is warranted in adding to the institution's power and reach.

◯◯ Ethics and the Consequences of Policy

While policies that reduce emissions of carbon dioxide are appealing to those who are concerned about climate change, there are several problems. Goals for emissions reduction are set by policy makers who are likely to be more influenced by politics than by what is best for the population. For example, curtailing coal usage confers significant financial gains on coal's alternatives—primarily natural gas. The support of some firms for political intervention may be a disguised effort to squelch competition. And sometimes, the scientific research process that may inform policy makers' decisions has been corrupted.[3] This is hardly a recipe for wise, ethical policy.

More disturbing, we have seen that the results of misguided climate change policy can be devastating for the poorest and weakest on this planet. Policies that drive up energy prices—particularly the cost of reliable electric power—can slow the escape from poverty in the most desperately poor nations on earth. Well over 1 billion people live without electricity across the world, and, according to the World Health Organization, "around three billion people cook and heat their homes using open fires and simple stoves burning biomass (wood, animal dung and crop waste) and coal."[4] About four million deaths a year—mostly women and children—result from respiratory illnesses and other diseases caused by these smoky cooking fires. In addition, gathering and hauling fuel for these fires means less time that could be spent gaining an education or working for money that could better their lives in other ways. The World Health Organization also points out that when access to electricity is limited, the poor turn to kerosene lamps and other lighting sources, which carry the risk of burns and poisoning.

---

3. Ross R. McKitrick, "Bias in the Peer Review Process: A Cautionary and Personal Account," in *Climate Coup*, ed. Patrick J. Michaels (Washington, DC: Cato Institute, 2011), http://rossmckitrick.weebly .com/uploads/4/8/0/8/4808045/gatekeeping_chapter.pdf.

4. "Household Air Pollution and Health," World Health Organization, May 8, 2018, http://www.who .int/mediacentre/factsheets/fs292/en/.

Is a policy that creates such costs for an uncertain benefit consistent with "love your neighbor" (Mark 12:31)?

The impact of climate policies on environmental quality may not be positive when the ripple effects are taken into consideration. "People cut down our trees because they don't have electricity," observed Ugandan Gordon Mwesigye. "Our country loses its wildlife habitats, as well as the health and economic benefits that abundant electricity brings."[5]

In the long term, pursuing economic growth can yield reductions in the emissions of many pollutants. A poor but growing economy may generate higher levels of pollution, but eventually will reach a stage where further economic growth is linked to reductions in pollution. For example, one study indicated that once an economy reaches an income level between $6,200 and $16,100, further economic growth tends to be associated with lower sulfur dioxide emissions.[6] For carbon dioxide, the turning point seems to be higher than other emissions—between $37,000 and $57,000. The developing world has a long way to go to reach this turning point, and consequently, climate change estimates are linked to how much economic growth occurs in the developing world. A slowdown in economic growth rates resulting from some climate change policies and other environmental policies can cause an economy to linger in a higher poverty stage of development, with consequently higher levels of sulfur dioxide, particulates, and other air and water pollutants—not to mention the other hazards of poverty. As economist Cornelis van Kooten has pointed out, "To mitigate climate change one needs to force the vast majority of humankind to continue living in abject poverty. Preventing climate change does not help the poor, it dooms them! Poverty simply kills more people than climate."[7]

◯◯ Toward a Biblical View of Climate Policy

While climate science improves, we may rely on certain principles that do not depend on a determination of the causes or extent of global climate change. First, as we have seen, the use of governmental power should follow biblical principles of justice, respecting its boundaries with environmental issues as with other social problems. Second, climate change policies may be distorted by political

---

5.   Roy Spence, Paul Driessen, and E. Calvin Beisner, "An Examination of the Scientific, Ethical, and Theological Implications of Climate Change Policy," *Interfaith Stewardship Alliance* (2005): 10–11, https://www.cornwallalliance.org/docs/an-examination-of-the-scientific-ethical-and-theological-implications-of-climate-change-policy.pdf.

6.   Bruce Yandle, M. Bhattarai, and M. Vijayaraghavan, *Environmental Kuznets Curves: A Review of Findings, Methods, and Policy Implications*, PERC Research Studies RS-02–1a (Bozeman, MT: Property and Environment Research Center, 2004).

7.   Legates and Kooten, *Call to Truth*, 47.

favor-seeking and biased science, so a level-headed skepticism is warranted when evaluating different policy proposals. Third, when trying to address long-term climate change, we should be on the lookout for unintended consequences, such as ripple effects on other kinds of environmental problems and prolonged global poverty.

Christian thinking on this issue should reflect a consistent and robust application of our faith. It should recognize our responsibilities to wisely steward our resources, love our neighbors and "remember the poor" (Gal. 2:10). It should acknowledge the limitations of our knowledge and the reality of our fallenness. And it should trust the sovereignty of a good Creator.

Timothy Terrell (PhD, Auburn University) is T. B. Stackhouse Professor of Economics at Wofford College. He is a senior fellow with the Mises Institute and serves on the editorial staff of the *Quarterly Journal of Austrian Economics*. His research includes works on environmental regulation, property rights, and the ethics of market systems.

GOD CARES FOR THE ANIMALS—SO SHOULD WE

Joel Salatin

As a Christian environmentalist, I straddle the tension between creation worshippers who demonize the religious right for their supposed hatred of the environment and the Creator worshippers who poke fun at the "tree huggers." While this probably is a little exaggerated, it often feels like I am stuck between conservative Christians elevating dominion except for human babies and the environmentalists elevating conservation except unborn babies.

Many years ago I was asked to help edit an animal welfare protocol for an animal welfare advocacy group, the Humane Society of the United States. When I noticed they thought it was inhumane to abort a calf embryo after the second trimester, I made a marginal note that certainly none of those authors thought an equivalent human baby abortion would be inhumane. It caused a stir and they never asked my opinion on anything else. The faith community looks at this hypocrisy with almost speechless incredulity.

By the same token, when Christians stop off for Happy Meals or Chick-fil-A on their way to a Sanctity of Life rally, the nonfaith community looks at this hypocrisy with equal incredulity. To the environmental community, these industrial fast-food chains represent egregious life-disrespecting paradigms. They find reconciling the two equally and indescribably hypocritical.

In classic Jesus-speak, let's look at the log in our own eye before disparaging the splinter (or log) in their eye. We Christians can't do anything about their hypocrisy, but we can sure do something about ours. Let's start with a broad statement: God owns us, the world, the universe, everything. It's all his stuff.

Why does it exist? I have no idea of all the thoughts in the mind of God, but I suggest one reason is to be an object lesson of spiritual truth. You and I can't see God and the rest of the spirit world. But creation offers a wonderful practical backdrop on which to present spiritual truth. It starts in Genesis with

God creating order out of chaos. God is ordered; He has a plan—for you, for me, for humanity, for the universe. Many of the issues confronting our secularizing culture is symptomatic of dysfunctional chaos: breakdown of marriage, the family, biblical norms, honesty, work.

Part of that order is patterns. We see that in seeds bearing after their kind. Species uniqueness is part of order and pattern. Blurring of kinds is chaos (read: Genetically Modified Organisms). We see differentiation in animals, like herbivores, carnivores, and omnivores. When the US Department of Agriculture took farmers like me to free steak dinners for thirty years to teach us a new scientific method to grow cheap beef by feeding dead cows to cows, I abhorred it not because I didn't like science or the USDA, but because I could find no pattern in nature as God created it where herbivores eat carrion.

Of course, the scientific community—and many Christians—laughed at me as a Luddite, anti-science Neanderthal, but thirty years later, the disorder bore fruit with bovine spongiform encephalopathy (mad cow disease). God's order can be circumvented for a while, but sooner or later, it will exact its toll. Environmentalists would say, "Nature bats last."

Baby boomers who grew up in the 1950s and '60s remember a day when "food allergies" was not even a phrase in the cultural lexicon. We didn't know the words camphylobacter, lysteria, E. coli, and salmonella. We might have known one or two obese people; perhaps one with diabetes; nobody with autism. When you don't treat your spouse right, your marriage tanks. When you don't treat the food system right, your health tanks.

The heavenly commendation of faithfulness to me, as a farmer, can only come if my farm illustrates God's truth. In other words, when visitors leave the farm, they should say, "We just saw redemption, abundance, beauty, neighborliness, respect for life." Does cramming 5,000 pigs in tiny cells in a building respect the pigness of the pig? Is it beautiful? Is it child friendly?

On our farm, we began raising pigs not to sell, but to do meaningful work: aerate compost. In fact, we call them pigaerators. Rather than using expensive and energy-intensive mechanical compost turners, we place corn in the pile and the pigs seek it out, aerating the material like giant egg beaters. These pigs are not just tenderloin and bacon; they are co-laborers in our great land-healing ministry. And it fully honors the physiological distinctiveness of the pigs—allowing them to express their gifts and talents. Environmentalists would use the word "diversity"; I say gifts and talents.

I've argued with many Christians who say farming does not have a moral dimension; factory farming, chemicals, whatever, it's just a choice someone makes. But 1 Corinthians 10:31 says, "Whatever you do, do it *all* for the glory of God" (my emphasis). God does not segregate spheres into moral and amoral. He's interested in all of it, from the lilies of the field to the hairs of our heads to whether or not a sparrow falls.

That doesn't mean we walk around on pins and needles and turn this into some sort of works-based cult, but it does mean we need to wrestle with what the spiritual dimensions are in the minutest corners of our lives. Does it matter if we use Styrofoam at the church potluck? Does God want a world clogged with landfills full of material that won't decompose? At least paper can be composted to return to his economy, which, by the way, runs on carbon.

The sun offers daily free energy, bathing the planet in abundance, that plants convert into physical structure, inhaling CO_2 and exhaling O_2. The plant lives, dies, decomposes, and regenerates through the energy deposited through the decomposition process. What a marvelous picture of spiritual life that can only occur through death. How do we live for him? We die to ourselves. How do we lead? We serve others. The most fundamental ecological principle is that in order to have life, something must die.

When we take the life of that carrot or chicken, that life is sacrificed that we may live. The whole notion that we can fertilize crops with synthetic chemicals circumvents this entire ecological foundation. And when that's how we grow things, our children don't have a context for how life occurs. Sanitizing the cross is a short step from sanitizing the cycle of life.

I would suggest that we give that sacrifice sanctity by how we treat its life. If we disrespect the chicken or the carrot in life, that cheapened existence denigrates the sacrifice. Does God care about soil erosion? Does he care that we humans—many of us Christians—have created through our agricultural runoff a dead zone the size of New Jersey in the Gulf of Mexico? If we were the servants given the talents in the famous parable of stewardship, would we pass the test?

The commons are the resources God (nature) placed here: air, soil, water. As a result of how we farm and how we eat, are we increasing the commons or depleting them? All of us would agree that the good steward, the faithful servant, would increase the commons. Is what we believe in the pew showing up on our menu? When manure spills kill the fish, odors stink up the neighborhood, and mono-cropping depletes the soil, what does that say about our care of God's stuff?

The fact that daring to ask the question in the average church jeopardizes our Christian credentials indicates how much moral equity the faith community has lost on this issue. We, dear folks, should be the ones carrying the creation stewardship banner. We should be the ones known for caring, for humbly caressing God's stuff. Today is the day to soften our hearts before God on this issue, to ask, "What would Jesus do?"

Joel Salatin and his family operate Polyface Farm in Virginia's Shenandoah Valley, producing salad bar beef, pigaerator pork, pastured poultry, rabbit, lamb, and forestry products all sold direct to 5,000 families, 50 restaurants, and other specialty stores. He is the editor of *Stockman Grass Farmer* magazine and has authored 12 books, including *You Can Farm* and *Folks, This Ain't Normal*.

EFFICIENT FARMING IS GOOD STEWARDSHIP

 *Tom Pittman*

I am a computer scientist, not a nutritionist or an economist, but I can read numbers and do the math.[1] I also read my Bible carefully. Computers are an unforgiving environment, so to make them work properly, I also must be very careful with my data. It gets to be a habit that spills over into everything I do. I like to think my spiritual life has benefited from that care.

This topic began for me in 2013, about the time the November *Christianity Today* ran what seemed to me a fuzzy article extolling the spiritual benefits of killing your own chicken on a (not quite "organic") "sustainable, GMO-free, free-range" farm somewhere in Ohio. Whenever somebody claims, "This (activity) is more spiritual than that one," I need to give due diligence to determine whether I should adjust my own spiritual life to encompass the claimed benefit, or if the claim is really nothing more than "I like my secular tradition more than your secular tradition." After substantial research, I decided the chicken farm article fell into the latter category. Let me explain.

"The earth is the Lord's and everything in it";[2] we are only stewards of what God has entrusted to our care. Depleting the ground is bad stewardship and contrary to the biblical notion that we are only stewards. However, adding chemicals to the ground to improve crop yield and reduce labor costs does not necessarily deplete the ground.[3] Organic farming methods also add chemicals to the ground,

---

1. The research that led to this essay is described in more detail on my website (including its link to my WebLog), see Tom Pittman, "Thanking God for Factory Farms and Processed Foods," *Tom Pittman's WebLog*, December 20, 2013, http://www.ittybittycomputers.com/Essays/FactoryFarm.htm.

2. Psalm 24:1 (see also 1 Cor.10:26, 28; Ex. 9:29; 19:5; 1 Chron. 29:11).

3. I found several sites pointing out that "organic" does not imply "sustainable." Most of these writers favor organic, so you need to parse out their arguments to see that conventional farming methods are actually more productive in a sustainable way. See Henry I. Miller, "How College Students Are Being Misled About 'Sustainable' Agriculture," *National Review*, May 4, 2017, https://www.nationalreview.com/2017/05/organic-farming-not-sustainable/; "Are Organic and Non-GMO Farming More Sustainable

but these "organic" chemicals are less effective, so for the same effect, they must be used in greater quantities than the nonorganic chemicals.[4]

I lived in California near where they grow carrots. A farmer there told me there are no organic carrots, because if you don't use pesticides, the nematodes eat them.[5] Twenty years later, I now see "organic" carrots in the grocery store, so they actually did use pesticides. A government website states:[6] "7 CFR 205.601 Synthetic substances allowed for use in organic crop production." There's another page for nonsynthetics, some of each listed chemical causing harm to organisms.

Organic food is widely considered healthier, but is it really? I was unable to find anything more than unsubstantiated opinion to say so; all the scientific data seems to suggest that there is no discernible nutritional difference.[7] Sure, long obscure chemical names sound less than appetizing, but they wouldn't be there if the scientists could discover that they caused harm. Unlike recreational drugs (including alcohol and tobacco and sugar), all those chemicals certainly haven't harmed most Americans; we now live to be almost double the life of our ancestors from a century ago who had no such additives in their food.

Then there's that "sustainable" word. If you don't damage the topsoil, then all the farms are sustainable, but the total yield (people fed) over a hundred years or more is maybe 25 percent higher for conventional factory farms than for "organic" factory farms,[8] and a lot higher than nonfactory farms where people and animals do the work instead of machines. Right now the US exports more food than we import.[9] If we converted every acre of present American crop land to organic farming, those exports would cease, and many people whose country experiences food shortages would suffer. We might be able to feed all the American people without imports—especially if we converted some wilderness

Than Farming Using GMO's?" Genetic Literacy Project, https://gmo.geneticliteracyproject.org/FAQ/organic-non-gmo-farming-sustainable-farming-using-gmos/.

4. Christie Wilcox, "Mythbusting 101: Organic Farming > Conventional Agriculture," *Scientific American*, July 18, 2011, https://blogs.scientificamerican.com/science-sushi/httpblogsscientificamericancom-science-sushi20110718mythbusting-101-organic-farming-conventional-agriculture/.

5. I no longer live near carrot farmers, but I found a couple corroborating (public) websites. See T. L. Widmer, J. W. Ludwig, and G. S. Abawi, "The Northern Root-Knot Nematode on Carrot, Lettuce, and Onion in New York," Cornell University, http://vegetablemdonline.ppath.cornell.edu/factsheets/RootKnot Nematode.htm.

6. "Synthetic Substances Allowed for Use in Organic Crop Production," Cornell Law School, https://www.law.cornell.edu/cfr/text/7/205.601.

7. Wilcox, "Mythbusting 101."

8. Bryan Walsh, "Whole Food Blues: Why Organic Agriculture May Not Be So Sustainable," *TIME*, April 26, 2012, http://science.time.com/2012/04/26/whole-food-blues-why-organic-agriculture-may-not-be-so-sustainable/.

9. I was unable to find solid figures for US food exports, but the fragments here are suggestive of the facts. See Daniel Workman, "United States Top 10 Exports," World's Top Exports, February 8, 2018, http://www.worldstopexports.com/united-states-top-10-exports/.

areas and national parks into productive farmland.[10] But is that a good use of our national resources?

While there is not a big difference in acreage between organic food and what the rest of us eat, the main difference is labor. Pretty much everyone agrees that organic farming is labor-intensive, but few sources will tell you how much. I found one farmer[11] who gave real numbers: "If you took my size of acres of operation and farmed it conventionally, it would probably only have one operator, and we are involving three people on a full-time basis." Organic requires three times the labor as conventional farming (for him). And in a culture where manual labor is required for organic farming, moving away from machines and chemicals would likely cause a massive labor shortage.

If you forced all the farms to grow only organic produce, you could not find enough workers willing to do it at a union-wage scale, let alone what family farms are willing to pay their kids and grandchildren. The cost of labor would be astronomical, and organic food in the stores would cost not double what factory farm food costs, but ten times as much.[12] We would be importing food from majority-world "cash crop" factory farms to feed our own starving masses. This is not a Christian way to do things, because God cares about "widows and orphans," essentially people who cannot take care of themselves.

Fortunately, in the US organic food—like private jets, fast cars, atheism, Marxism, and "fair-trade" coffee—is a luxury enjoyed by a tiny minority of very wealthy people who can afford it, and their preference does not harm the rest of the economy.

Two hundred years ago, before the invention of factory farm methods and processed foods, nearly everybody in the whole world (kings and entitled nobility excepted) spent most of their time getting food out of the ground (or out of the sea) and preparing it to eat. In the poorer countries of the world, that is still true, but not here. Everybody here benefits from factory farms and processed food, because vast numbers of people are freed up from bondage to getting barely enough to eat, so that many of us can exercise God's Second Great Commandment and make

---

10. The author of this website is pro-organic, but he makes some telling admissions, if you look for them. In particular, "With lower-yielding organic farming, . . . the existing farmland can feed [9.6 billion people in 2050] if they are all vegan, [but only] 15% with the Western-style diet based on meat." John Reganold, "Can We Feed 10 Billion People on Organic Farming Alone?" *The Guardian*, August 14, 2016, https://www.theguardian.com /sustainable-business/2016/aug/14/organic-farming-agriculture-world-hunger.

11. Alison Dirr, "Organic Farming: Reduced Chemical Costs, Increased Labor," American News, July 31, 2012, http://articles.aberdeennews.com/2012–07–31/news/32967117_1_conventional-farmers-organic-crops -organic-food.

12. My "ten times" figure is somewhat speculative, based on the mathematics of market economics, but no American government would survive long enough to let it get that far. We'd repeal any laws requiring 100 percent organics faster than we repealed Prohibition (starvation is a more critical problem than sobriety) and probably also throw the borders open to imported stoop labor and maybe even some people otherwise disinclined might go for the higher wages, or all of the above. See Note [9] for actual numbers supporting my speculation.

the world a better place. Many people squander their wealth on riotous living and reverting to the wasteful food-processing efforts of their great-grandparents, but there is enough wealth left over to enable vast numbers of people to create more wealth, making this the richest country in the whole world—so that even our poor (as defined by the Federal Poverty Level index)[13] have more income than half of the world's population.[14]

In the first century, the Roman highway system facilitated the propagation of the gospel throughout the Roman Empire. Fifteen hundred years later, the printing press and renewed literacy disseminated the Reformation insights to people previously locked out by unintelligible Latin liturgy. In the last century and a half, the industrial revolution—and by extension, the mechanization of farms and food processing—has liberated millions of people from the drudge of producing food to eat, which, like the previous technological advances, also enables us to pay for missionaries to the rest of the world and to reproduce the Bible and evangelistic materials in different languages in (belated) obedience to the Great Commission. I wanted to be a part of what God is doing, but God told me no, not as a missionary. God is using our technology and American wealth to spread the gospel. So as a technologist, I see that as what God called me to do.

And I thank God for factory farms and processed food,[15] so I can eat and be clothed and still have time left over to write Bible translation software and essays like this one, if that helps other people to see that God is good.

Tom Pittman (PhD, University of California at Santa Cruz) is the author (with James Peters) of *The Art of Compiler Design*. His more recent work includes mentoring a high school autonomous car project, DNA analysis software, and an extended journey into natural language translation based on the technology in his PhD dissertation.

---

13. "Federal Poverty Guidelines," *Families USA*, February 2017, http://familiesusa.org/product/federal-poverty-guidelines.

14. Glenn Phelps and Steve Crabtree, "Worldwide, Median Household About $10,000," *Gallup*, December 16, 2013, http://news.gallup.com/poll/166211/worldwide-median-household-income-000.aspx.

15. This essay extols the benefits of factory farms and processed food to me personally and to the American economy as a whole. It should not be taken as a recommendation to any other particular person, other than for giving thanks to God for these benefits.

ANIMAL WELFARE AS A CHRISTIAN ISSUE

◯◯ Christine Gutleben

Christianity has a rich history of compassion toward animals. For centuries, Christian thinkers have expressed a concern for animals rooted in the biblical mandate to "care for the least of these" (Matt. 25:40). Two of the most consequential animal welfare organizations in the world were formed and guided by Christians: The Royal Society for the Prevention of Cruelty to Animals (SPCA) in the United Kingdom and The Humane Society of the United States. In that sense, the Christian principles of compassion, mercy, and stewardship are the bedrock of the modern animal welfare movement.

Christian compassion for animals is also evident in statements issued by faith leaders and the governing bodies of denominations. These statements are theological expressions rooted in concern for God's creatures and define a faith community's set of beliefs around animals. Every major Christian tradition has official statements on animals.

The influence of individual Christians who have sought to raise awareness of animal welfare issues within their faith traditions, the growth in relevant scholarship, and the influence of Christian ecology and sustainability concerns have also shaped the recent history of Christian perspectives toward creation.

While the scope of Christian concern for animals is extensive, we will explore the premise for animal welfare in Scripture, some important trends across the range of Christian denominations evident in denominational statements, and Christian involvement in the foundation of the animal welfare movement.

◯◯ The Bible

In Genesis, the Bible teaches that God created the animals, blesses them, makes covenants with them, and calls them good.

From the garden of Eden, to Noah's Ark, to the Peaceable Kingdom, the Hebrew Scriptures contain many references to animals and our responsibilities toward them. Proverbs 12:10 is perhaps the clearest of these references: "The righteous care for the needs of their animals, but the kindest acts of the wicked are cruel."

We learn in Genesis that dominion cannot be understood apart from stewardship. God gives us dominion over creation—but it is still his creation. He remains the owner and sustainer. We are therefore stewards of a world that is not our own.

The New Testament contains fewer references to animals, but importantly, it assumes the foundation of the Hebrew Scriptures. In Matthew 10:29–31 we are told, "Are not two sparrows sold for a penny? Yet not one of them will fall to the ground outside your Father's care. And even the very hairs of your head are all numbered. So don't be afraid; you are worth more than many sparrows." As theologian Barrett Duke suggests, "Jesus wanted his listeners to understand that God is emotionally invested in that sparrow. He cares about what happens to it; he just cares more about what happens to people. Once we acknowledge that God is emotionally invested in birds, i.e., animals, as well as humans, we are now talking only about a difference in the degree to which he is, not whether or not he is."[1]

The Bible conveys God's concern for his creatures over and over again. It also demonstrates, through his relationship to creation, how we should treat them.

The History

The modern animal welfare movement began in early nineteenth-century England. The evangelical parliamentarian and abolitionist William Wilberforce believed that animal cruelty and other social vices had a coarsening effect on one's soul. Wilberforce understood that tolerating animal cruelty made it easier to tolerate human cruelties, even slavery.[2]

On June 16, 1824, Wilberforce, the Reverend Arthur Broome, and others established the first modern animal welfare organization, The Society for the Prevention of Cruelty to Animals, or the SPCA. They agreed that two committees would be formed, one to enforce the first animal welfare law passed two years earlier, and the other to oversee "the publication of articles and sermons to

---

1. Barrett Duke, "10 Biblical Truths About Animals," *The Ethics and Religious Liberty Commission*, January 5, 2015, https://erlc.com/resource-library/articles/10-biblical-truths-about-animals.

2. M. J. D. Robert, *Making English Morals: Voluntary Association and Moral Reform in England 1787–1886* (Cambridge: Cambridge University Press, June 2004).

effect a change in the moral feelings of those who had the control of animals."[3] Wilberforce believed that sensitivity to animals could best be awakened through faith. Eventually, the society Wilberforce helped to found received royal blessing, and became the Royal Society for the Prevention of Cruelty to Animals (RSPCA).

The Humane Society of the United States (HSUS), now the largest animal welfare organization in the United States, has frequently acknowledged the important role of faith in animal advocacy since its founding in 1954. The HSUS's first chairman of the board, Robert Chenoweth, said during his first annual presentation to membership, "Our faith is that there is a God who created all things and put us here on earth to live together. Our creed is that love and compassion is due from the strong to the weak."[4]

Two presidents of The HSUS, John A. Hoyt and Paul G. Irwin, were clergy, and their leadership in day-to-day operations spanned thirty-five years, more than half of the organization's existence. Hoyt was a Presbyterian minister who described his work as a ministry that benefited both animals and people. In 2007, The Humane Society of the United States formally established a Faith Outreach program.[5]

Statements

Official statements on animals from major denominations and faith leaders reflect extant and evolving Christian perspectives on animal welfare.

Catholicism and Animals

The Roman Catholic Church is the world's largest Christian denomination, representing more than half of all Christians and nearly 80 million Catholics in the US.

According to the *Catechism of the Catholic Church*, animals may be used to serve human purposes, but these uses have limitations since "it is contrary to human dignity to cause animals to suffer and die needlessly."[6] Pope Francis reiterated this teaching twice in his encyclical letter, *Laudato Si.*[7] The recurring

---

3. Edward Fairholme and Wellesley Pain, *Century of Work for Animals: The History of the R.S.P.C.A., 1824–1924* (Billing and Sons, LTD, 1924), 55.

4. Robert J. Chenoweth, *The First Annual Report by the Chairman of the Board to members of The National Humane Society* (November 3, 1955), HSUS Archive, Gaithersburg, Maryland.

5. "Faith Outreach," Humane Society, Humanesociety.org/faith.

6. The Holy See, *Catechism of the Catholic Church* (Vatican City: Libreria Editrice Vaticana, 1993), 2417–18.

7. Pope Francis, Encyclical Letter *Laudato Si'* of the Holy Father Francis on Care for Our Common Home (Vatican City: Libreria Editrice Vaticana, 2015), 92, 130.

use of this statement by Pope Francis leaves no question as to the value of animals beyond their usefulness to humankind.

Laudato Si is full of references to animals that underscore the idea that caring for animals and creation is essential to a faithful life. Pope Francis writes, "Living our vocation to be protectors of God's handiwork is essential to a life of virtue; it is not an optional or secondary aspect of our Christian experience."[8]

Historically, major Catholic figures like St. Thomas Aquinas (1225–1274) and St. Francis of Assisi (1181–1226) affirmed the value of animals: "All creatures . . . come from the intention of . . . God . . . in order that His goodness might be . . . represented by them."[9] Francis is said to have preached to the animals, rescued them from danger, provided them with food and comfort, and extolled their virtues. The lives of other saints provide similar examples of kindness to animals as an expression of religious faith.[10]

Mainline Protestantism and Animals

The four largest mainline Protestant denominations in the US are the United Methodist Church (UMC), the Evangelical Lutheran Church in America (ELCA), the Presbyterian Church U.S.A. (PC [USA]), and the Episcopal Church (TEC), which together total roughly 15 million members nationwide. The authority and structure of these denominations vary, relying on both local and national governing bodies.

The United Methodist Church "[supports] regulations that protect the life and health of animals, including those ensuring the humane treatment of pets and other domestic animals, animals used in research, and the painless slaughtering of meat animals, fish and fowl" and "the conservation of all animal species with particular support to safeguard those threatened with extinction."[11]

Sixty percent of all mammals on the earth are livestock,[12] so it is common for denominations to single out the industrial use of animals for food in their commentaries. The UMC "support(s) a sustainable agricultural system . . . a system where agricultural animals are treated humanely and where their living conditions are as close to natural systems as possible."[13]

---

8. Ibid, 217.

9. Thomas Aquinas, The 'Summa Theologica' of St. Thomas Aquinas, Part 1. Fathers of the English Dominican Province, trans. (London: R&T Washbourne, 1912), 255.

10. Thomas of Celano, *The Lives of Saint Francis of Assisi*, trans. A. G. Ferrers Howell (London: Methuen, 1908), 58–60, 77, 297. *The Church and Kindness to Animals* (London: Burns & Oates, 1906).

11. United Methodist Church, *The Book of Discipline of the United Methodist Church* (Nashville: United Methodist Publishing House, 2012), 51.

12. Nadia Murray-Ragg, "60% of All Mammals on Earth Are Livestock, Says New Study," LiveKindly, May 28, 2018, https://www.livekindly.co/60-of-all-mammals-on-earth-are-livestock-says-new-study/.

13. Ibid, 123.

The UMC can trace its concern for animals back to the teachings of the denomination's founder, John Wesley (1703–1791), who noted that "Nothing is more sure, than that as 'the Lord is loving to every man,' so 'his mercy is over all his works.'"[14]

The Evangelical Lutheran Church statement on creation explains that "God's command to have dominion and subdue the earth is not a license to dominate and exploit. Humane dominion (Genesis 1:28; Psalm 8), a special responsibility, should reflect God's way of ruling as a shepherd king who takes the form of a servant (Philippians 2:7), wearing a crown of thorns."[15]

The ELCA traces its origins to Martin Luther (1483–1546), who observed that "God's entire divine nature is wholly and entirely in all creatures, more deeply, more inwardly, more present than the creature is to itself."[16]

According to the Presbyterian Church, "Human Stewardship is not a dominion of mastery, it is a dominion of unequivocal love for this world."[17] It acknowledges that "there is increasing recognition that all the creatures with whom we share the planet have value in their own right" and notes that "the people of God are called to . . . reflect God's love for all creatures."[18]

The PC (USA) has its roots in the writings of John Calvin (1509–1564), who said that we treat creation as though we constantly hear God whispering, "Give an account of your stewardship."[19]

The Episcopal Church issued a set of resolutions in 2003, "Support Ethical Care of Animals." They "encourage its members to ensure that husbandry methods of captive and domestic animals would prohibit suffering in such conditions as puppy mills, and factory farms."[20]

While these statements are a very small representation of each tradition's consideration of animals, they touch on recurring themes: God loves animals, they belong to him, they have worth beyond their usefulness to us, and humans have dominion over them but with great responsibility.

---

14. John Wesley, "Sermon 60: The General Deliverance," The Works of the Rev. John Wesley, AM, vol. VI. John Emory, ed. (London: Wesleyan Conference Office, 1878), 242, 245.

15. Evangelical Lutheran Church in America, "A Social Statement on Caring for Creation: Vision, Hope, Justice," (1993), 2–3.

16. Martin Luther, *Luther's Works*, vol. 37, ed. Helmut T. Lehmenn (Philadelphia: Muhlenberg, 1959), 60.

17. National Council of Churches, "Past Denominational Statements, PCUSA, UPCUSA, PCUS: Stewardship" (1984), 6:5.

18. Presbyterian Church (USA), "The Constitution of the Presbyterian Church (U.S.A.) Part II: Book of Order 2015–2017" (Louisville, KY: Office of the General Assembly, 2015), W-7.5003.

19. John Calvin, *Institutes of the Christian Religion*, vol. II, Henry Beveridge, trans. (Edinburgh: T&T Clark, 1863), 35.

20. The Episcopal Church General Convention, "Resolution #2003-D016: Support Ethical Care of Animals," *Journal of the General Convention of . . . The Episcopal Church*, Minneapolis, 2003 (New York: General Convention, 2004), 253.

In 2010, Barna Group found that 93 percent of senior leaders of Catholic parishes and Protestant churches agreed that humans have a responsibility to treat animals humanely.[21] This near unanimous agreement is likely due to the steady reinforcement of Scripture and doctrine concerning animals.

Evangelicalism and Animals

In the United States, Evangelicals are a diverse group of Protestant Christians. Depending on what criteria are used to define this group, the number of Evangelicals can range from 25 to 35 percent of the US population.[22] Most members of the Southern Baptist Convention (SBC), a Protestant denomination comprised of nearly 16 million members, consider themselves Evangelical.

The SBC does not issue statements that are binding on member churches, but post confessions of faith and annual resolutions. While asserting that humanity is "the crowning work of His creation,"[23] the SBC clarifies that humans may use animals, but that human dominion has limitations: "God designed us with a dependence on the natural resources around us and has assigned us a dominion of stewardship and protection. . . . Our God-given dominion over the creation is not unlimited . . . all persons and all industries are then accountable to higher standards than profit alone."[24] In 2006, the convention resolved to "renew [its] commitment to God's command to exercise caring stewardship and wise dominion over the creation."[25]

The Reverend Billy Graham, one of the SBC's best-known leaders, grew up on a dairy farm, where he developed an appreciation for animals. "God is concerned about our care of every part of His creation—including animals," Graham once observed. "After all, He made them, and ultimately they belong to Him."[26]

In 2015, three Evangelical leaders drafted and released "An Evangelical Statement on Responsible Animal Care," signed by more than 100 Evangelical leaders. The statement is the first of its kind, "resolv[ing] to rule and treat all animals as living valued creatures, deserving of compassion, because they ultimately belong to God."[27]

---

21. Barna Group, "How American Faith Influences Views on Animals" (Humane Society of the United States, 2010).

22. The majority of surveys report numbers in this range. However, Barna Group reveals a lower number of just 8 percent of the population. Barna Group, *Survey Explores Who Qualifies as an Evangelical*, January 2007.

23. Southern Baptist Convention, "Basic Beliefs: Man," http://www.sbc.net/aboutus/basicbeliefs.asp.

24. Southern Baptist Convention, "Resolution: On the Gulf of Mexico Catastrophe" (2010), http://www.sbc.net/resolutions/1207/on-the-gulf-of-mexico-catastrophe.

25. Southern Baptist Convention, "On Environmentalism and Evangelicals" (2006), http://www.sbc.net/resolutions/1159/on-environmentalism-and-evangelicals.

26. Billy Graham, "Does God Care about Animals," Answers by Billy Graham, May 13 (2010), https://billygraham.org/answer/doegod-care-about-animals/.

27. *An Evangelical Statement on Responsible Animal Care for Animals*, www.everylivingthing.com.

Upon the release of the Evangelical statement on animals, Lifeway Research, the research arm of the Southern Baptist Convention, found that 89 percent of Protestant pastors agreed that Christians have a responsibility to speak out against animal cruelty.[28]

 ## Conclusion

Christian communities, leaders, and ordinary Christians have grappled with the question of animals and their treatment for centuries. Scripture, history, and church doctrine all offer glimpses into Christian perspectives on animal welfare along with the development of campaigns and programs by Christian laity.

In recent years, a rising concern for animals and their protection has resulted in the creation of position statements, statements of doctrine, and other expressions of concern. These sources, each in their own way, illustrate the meaning of *imago Dei*. Humans are given the dignity of responsibility for animals because we are a reflection of God and his mercy. Far from being a trivial matter, our treatment of animals is a reflection of our very nature as beings made in God's image.

Christine Gutleben is the former senior director of the Humane Society of the United States (HSUS) Faith Outreach program. Christine created the HSUS Faith Advisory Council and coproduced the film *Eating Mercifully*. Christine received her master's degree from the Graduate Theological Union and its affiliate, the Dominican School of Philosophy and Theology.

---

28. Lifeway Research, "Pastor Views on Animal Welfare," The Humane Society of the United States, 2015.

DISCUSSION QUESTIONS

1. In his article, Moo says that "richer countries who have benefited most from the burning of fossil fuels must be most prepared to follow the example of Christ and be willing to sacrifice for the sake of our global neighbors." How might someone from Terrell's position respond to this statement concerning Christians' obligations to those in developing countries regarding climate change?

2. In his article, Salatin refers to the strange dichotomies that exist in both the pro-life and pro-choice arena, causing each side to see the other as hypocritical. How might someone from Pittman's position respond to this comparison of the value placed on human lives and animal lives?

3. In his article, Pittman begins by stating that it is inaccurate to declare that one way of killing a chicken is "more spiritual" than another way to kill a chicken. How might someone from Gutleben's position respond to this statement, especially taking into account the history of Christian animal care and William Wilberforce in particular?

4. Pittman discusses at great length the logistics and pragmatics associated with farming, while Salatin discusses the doctrinal implications and natural patterns set into creation. Is it possible to balance both views, or must they oppose each other? If so, how would it be done?

5. Moo mentions that climate change has become an issue of culture and society rather than science alone. What are some examples of the way that different cultures, backgrounds, and demographics could shape a person's perception of the issue?

6. Both Salatin and Pittman refer to the concept of stewardship in their articles. For Pittman, this involves stewarding the time, talents, and other personal resources of people. For Salatin, this involves stewarding nature, creation, and the patterns of growth set in place by God. What are the underlying assumptions and definitions that cause these two positions to emphasize the same concept yet arrive at such different results?

7. Gutleben discusses at length the various statements made by multiple church denominations regarding the humane care of animals. Do the actions and teachings of present-day churches and Christianity reflect these statements well, or do the statements come as a surprise?

8. It can often feel as if the facts of each of the articles contradict each other. For example, Pittman states that adding chemical fertilizer to the soil does not necessarily deplete it, while Salatin states that it does. Terrell declares that the poor will suffer from policies regarding climate change, while Moo states that the poor will suffer if the climate change is not taken more seriously. How can a Christian account for all of these seemingly contradictory "facts," and how does this happen in the first place?

9. Moo discusses the importance of stewardship in caring for the climate—referencing that humans were given the task to care for creation. How might Terrell respond to this concept of stewardship? Who would Terrell say is responsible for that stewardship, and who is not?

10. In many of these articles, the authors stress the same concept while arriving at totally separate conclusions. Some of these concepts include loving your neighbor, stewardship, responsibility, caring for creation, and humane treatment. How does each author define each of these terms, and how does it affect their position on the issue?

chapter nine

POLITICS

For most of us in contemporary America, politics is not a topic that exists in the broad universal and philosophical sense. Rather, it is a topic of morning news shows, news feeds, sound bites, social media posts, and dinner-table discussions. It is too easy to fail to see that politics for all of us—Christian and non-Christian alike—exists in a deeply embedded cultural context that permeates everything else we do each day and that extends beyond the borders of states and nations.

The relationship of the church to the *polis* (the Greek term for *city* or *state*, from which we get the word *politics*) is varied and unclear because the history of the church to the state in which it finds itself is as varied as the governments that have existed throughout human history. The first-century church emerged within a society in which being a Christian could be perceived as treasonous and illicit. Just a few centuries later, the situation was reversed when Christianity became the official religion of the Roman Empire. From the two poles of this dialectic eventually emerged the American experiment, founded on ostensibly Judeo-Christian principles, key among them being both religious liberty and inalienable human rights.

Clearly, the relationship of the church to politics depends on the time, place, and society in which members find themselves. Even so, biblical principles concerning the Christian's citizenship in this world and the kingdom of God are unchanging, though the application of those principles has been understood in various ways. Throughout history, Christians have engaged the political sphere in a myriad of ways, from the separation of early Christian monasticism[1] to the political activism of the Moral Majority in the United States in the late 1900s.[2] To help Christians find a way forward, some, such as Rod Dreher, look to Christian history to see how Christians have engaged the political culture in times past. Others look not to the past but to contemporary global models—thus

---

1. "Monasticism," *New Advent*, http://www.newadvent.org/cathen/10459a.htm.
2. Doug Banwart, "Jerry Falwell, the Rise of the Moral Majority, and the 1980 Election," *Western Illinois Historical Review* 5 (2013), http://www.wiu.edu/cas/history/wihr/pdfs/Banwart-MoralMajorityVol5.pdf.

the recent increasing acceptance of socialism among Millennial Christians.[3] The methods Christians have taken to engage the political sphere have adapted with and adjusted to the cultural norms as the church is always seeking to find its voice within its context.

With such a wide array of political contexts, the first great task Christians must overcome in the political discussion is the tendency to see "politics" only in terms of our own national context. As James Davison Hunter explains, "For conservatives and progressives alike, Christianity far too comfortably legitimates the dominant ideologies and far too uncritically justifies the prevailing macroeconomic structures and practices of our time." But for Hunter, the critique needs to go deeper:

> The moral life and everyday practices of the church are also far too entwined with the prevailing normative assumptions of American culture. Courtship and marriage, the formation and education of children, the mutual relationships and obligations between the individual and community, vocation, leadership, consumption, leisure, "retirement" and the use of time in the final chapters of life—on these and other matters, Christianity has uncritically assimilated to the dominant ways of life in a manner dubious at the least. Even more, these assimilations arguably compromise the fundamental integrity of its witness to the world. Be that as it may, the way in which Christians assimilate to the political culture is just an extension of its assimilation to all of culture and the ways of life it lays down as normal. Its lack of critical distance and reflection about politics is an extension of its failure to critically reflect about the rest of the world they inhabit."[4]

In other words, the broader political systems reflect the culture that surrounds them, and thus the legislation and leaders that flow from those systems are already reflective of the broader culture. Within such an understanding, the role of the Christian in politics becomes, at once, much clearer and more obscured. Christians are not bound to the harsh "fundamentalist" and "secularist"[5] categories but are called to move beyond those categories.

However, as history shows, there is no "one size fits all" political form and

3. Thaddeus John Williams, "Christian Millennials and the Lure of Socialism, Part One: How Biblical Concern for the Poor Can Turn to an Unbiblical Understanding of People," *The Good Book* Blog, December 21, 2016, https://www.biola.edu/blogs/good-book-blog/2016/christian-millennials-and-the-lure-of-socialism-part-one-how-biblical-concern-for-the-poor-can-turn-to-an-unbiblical-understanding-of-people.

4. James Davison Hunter, *To Change the World: The Irony, Tragedy, & Possibility of Christianity in the Late Modern World* (Oxford: Oxford University Press, 2010), 184–85.

5. N. T. Wright, *Surprised by Scripture: Engaging Contemporary Issues* (New York: HarperCollins, 2014), 166.

therefore no one "Christian" form of engagement in politics. N. T. Wright makes this point when he explains that Jim Wallis's book *God's Politics: Why the Right Gets It Wrong and the Left Doesn't Get It* carries the opposite meaning in the United Kingdom than it does in the United States where the terms *left* and *right* have opposite connotations.[6] This humorous example calls attention to the fact that, as the title of Wright's chapter aptly suggests, the Christian view of politics is "too small."[7] Wright states,

> The church will do to the rulers of the world what Jesus did to Pilate in John 18 and 19, when he confronted the ruler with the news of the kingdom and truth, deeply unwelcome and indeed incomprehensible though both were. And part of the way in which the church will do this is by getting on with and setting forward those works of justice and mercy, of beauty and relationship, which the rulers know in their bones ought to be flourishing but which they seem powerless to bring about. But the church, even when faced with overtly pagan and hostile rulers must continue to believe that Jesus is the lord before whom they will bow and whose final judgment they are called to anticipate. Thus the church, in its biblical commitment to "doing God in public," is called to learn how to collaborate without compromise (hence the vital importance of the theory of the common good) and to criticize without dualism.[8]

Regardless of time, place, or culture, Wright argues, "Holding governments, especially powerful governments, to account . . . is a central part of the church's vocation" in the realm of politics.[9]

Some Christians throughout the history of the church have held governments to account as elected officials, some as participants, some as protestors, and many as martyrs. The tricky part is knowing what the church's call is in its particular presence within a particular time and place.

Robert P. George's short essay opens this section by arguing that the best way to reform American politics is to return to the original founding values that formed the nation. Rod Dreher takes a much different approach, arguing that the window for values-led voting has closed, leaving this class of voters homeless and without a strong ethical political voice. Thus, Dreher encourages Christians to look to the Benedict Option as a way to maintain a voice in the cultural

---

6. Ibid., 164.
7. Ibid., 171.
8. Ibid., 178.
9. Ibid., 179.

and political world without compromising the values undergirding that voice. Responding directly to the broader vision for engagement in a post-Christian America presented by Dreher in his book *The Benedict Option* (rather than just Dreher's specific essay in this volume), Nathan Finn presents his own Paleo-Baptist vision of Christian political engagement, arguing that this view promotes a more robust ecclesiastical and missional avenue to engage politically.

Vincent Bacote's contribution visits the thought of Abraham Kuyper to gesture toward a way Christians today can organize their work and faith in a coherent and complementary manner, thereby encouraging Christians to acknowledge the pluralism of worldviews and remain engaged in political and social spheres. And finally, Michael Wear's essay argues that when we rightly understand the purpose of political parties, we are liberated to reengage in the parties as a means to influence American politics in a more effective and efficient manner.

A CONSERVATIVE VISION FOR POLITICAL REFORM IN AMERICA

◯◯ Robert P. George

Our beloved country is, alas, in trouble and badly in need of reform. At the heart of our woes is what has so often been at the heart of our woes whenever we have had woes, going all the way back to the original sin of slavery—infidelity to our nation's founding principles. Those principles include our formal constitutional commitments as well as the moral and cultural norms, practices, and understandings that those commitments presuppose for their intelligibility and force and without which they cannot long endure. The promise of America remains great, but in many crucial areas, we have gone astray. If America is to fulfill her promise, things must be turned around. It will not be easy, nor can it be accomplished without sacrifice; but it can be done.

We must renew our national commitment to limited government and the rule of law. This will include the restoration of the constitutional separation of powers and the recovery of the principle of federalism. More broadly, we must demand respect for the principle of subsidiarity, the idea that the issues ought to be addressed at the lowest or most local level possible, not only for the sake of individual liberty (though that is certainly very important), but also for the sake of the flourishing of vitally important institutions of civil society. Those institutions begin with the family and religious and other private associations that: (a) assist the family in forming decent and honorable citizens—people who are fitted out morally for the burdens and responsibilities of freedom; and (b) play indispensable roles in the areas of health, education, and welfare, including the provision of social services and assistance to those in need.

We must also restore to its rightful place the democratic element of our republican system, by reversing the outrageous usurpations of legislative authority regularly and indeed routinely committed by the executive and judicial departments. Such reform will, substantively, enable us to make critically needed gains in the direction of restoring in law and culture even more fundamental principles, beginning with the sanctity of human life in all stages and conditions; marriage as the conjugal union of husband and wife; and respect for religious freedom and the rights of conscience; along with other basic civil liberties. Social liberalism is riding high, especially after eight years of extremely aggressive promotion by a president who was willing to stretch and even breach the constitutional limits of executive power at every turn, in order to institutionalize his socially liberal values and weave them into the fabric of our law and public institutions (including the military). But what he and the courts have done can be undone. It is a matter of political will—the willingness to "pay any price and bear any burden" to accomplish what is needed in the cause of moral-cultural renewal.[1]

Economic reform must also be given its due in an overall agenda of reform. Corporate welfare and crony capitalism (of the sort that, for example, creates regulatory barriers preventing upstarts from competing with large established firms that can more easily absorb compliance costs) are blights on the honor of our nation. Moreover, there is a problem of plutocracy, which the left derides while frequently taking advantage of it, and the right denies or ignores, supposing that the cultural and political power of big business is just the free market doing its thing. Economic inequality is not in itself unjust, and any truly effective effort to eliminate it would give us tyranny in no time flat. But justice does require that we maintain fair terms of competition and cultivate conditions for large-scale upward social mobility. A sound system will be one in which upstart firms can compete fairly with the big dogs, and hard work, initiative, and the willingness to take investment risks are rewarded.

In the area of national security, where many of our most urgent and frightening challenges lie, a renewed sense of American exceptionalism—one that would be massively advanced by moral reform and rededication to our constitutional principles—would serve us well. American exceptionalism is often misunderstood. It is not a claim that we, as Americans, are superior people. Rather, it is a claim that the principles of our founding are unique and valuable principles. It is an affirmation that the American people are not bound together as a nation by blood or soil but rather by a shared commitment to a moral-political creed: "We hold these truths to be self-evident, that all men are created equal, that they are endowed by their Creator with certain unalienable rights, and among these are life, liberty, and the pursuit of happiness."[2]

---

1. For more on a defense of traditional morality in the face of its modern assailants, see Robert George, *Conscience and its Enemies: Confronting the Dogmas of Liberal Secularism* (Wilmington, DE: ISI, 2016).

2. For more information concerning political morality, see Robert George, *In Defense of Natural Law* (New York: Oxford University Press, 2001).

This creed is what has rallied Americans in the past to the defense of our country. It can once again strengthen us to stand up to the evildoers who threaten us, and it can inspire us to make the sacrifices that—make no mistake—will have to be made if we are to defeat them. The evildoers have confidence that they will prevail over us, despite our overwhelming military power, because they believe in something and we believe in nothing; because they are spiritually and morally rigorous and we are soft and self-indulgent; because they are willing to fight and die and we are not. Our survival against them depends entirely on whether these beliefs about us are true or false. Whether they are true or false is up to us. A central goal of any reform movement worthy of the name will be to make it the case that these beliefs about us are false. If they are true, then we are doomed, and doomed with us is the noble experiment in morally ordered liberty bequeathed to us by the founders of the American republic at our country's birth.

This was adapted from an article first published on firstthings.com on July 4, 2016. The original title was "What a Would Reform Agenda Look Like."

Robert P. George is McCormick Professor of Jurisprudence and director of the James Madison Program in American Ideals and Institutions at Princeton University. A graduate of Swarthmore College, Professor George holds MTS and JD degrees from Harvard University and the degrees of DPhil, BCL, and DCL from Oxford University.

POLITICAL ENGAGEMENT ACCORDING TO THE BENEDICT OPTION

✇ *Rod Dreher*

Like the people of other Western democracies, Americans are living through a political earthquake shaking the foundations of the postwar order. Growing hostility toward Christians, as well as the moral confusion of values voters, should inspire us to imagine a better way forward. The Benedict Option, my broader Christian vision for a cultural strategic withdrawal inspired by the Rule of St. Benedict,[1] calls for a radical new way of doing politics, rooted in a hands-on localism. This localism is based on pioneering work by Eastern bloc dissidents who defied Communism during the Cold War. A Westernized form of "antipolitical politics," to use the term coined by Czech political prisoner Vaclav Havel, is the best way forward for orthodox Christians seeking practical and effective engagement in public life without losing our integrity, and indeed our humanity.

As recently as the 1960s, with the notable exception of civil rights, moral and cultural concerns weren't make-or-break issues in US politics. Americans voted largely on economics, as they had since the Great Depression. The sexual revolution, however, changed all that. The religious right began to rise in the Republican Party as the secular left did the same among the Democrats. By the turn of the century, the culture war was undeniably the red-hot center of American politics. Today, however, the culture war as we knew it is over. The so-called values voters—social and religious conservatives—have been defeated and are being swept to the political margins. The nation is fracturing along class lines, with large numbers on both the young left and populist right challenging the free market globalist economic consensus that has united US politics for generations.

---

1. Rod Dreher, *The Benedict Option: A Strategy for Christians in a Post-Christian Nation* (New York: Sentinel, 2017).

Where do the erstwhile values voters fit in the new dispensation? We don't, not really. The 2016 presidential campaign made it clear—piercingly, agonizingly clear—that conservative Christians are politically homeless. To be sure, Christians cannot afford to vacate the public square entirely. The church must not shrink from its responsibility to pray for political leaders and to speak prophetically to them. The real question facing us is not whether to quit politics, but how to exercise political power prudently, especially in an unstable political culture. The times necessitate attention to the local church and community, which don't flourish or fail based primarily on what happens in Washington. They also require an acute appreciation of the fragility of what can be accomplished through partisan politics. Yuval Levin, editor of *Nation Affairs* magazine and a fellow of Washington's Ethics and Public Policy Center, contends that religious conservatives would be better off "building thriving subcultures" than seeking positions of power.[2]

Though orthodox Christians have to embrace localism because they can no longer expect to influence Washington politics as they once could, there is one cause that should receive all the attention they have left for national politics: religious liberty. Religious liberty is critically important to the Benedict Option. Without a robust and successful defense of First Amendment protections, Christians will not be able to build the communal institutions that are vital to maintaining our identity and values.

Lance Kinzer, a ten-year Republican veteran of the Kansas legislature, is living at the edge of the political transition Christian conservatives must make. Kansas Republicans, anticipating court-imposed gay marriage, tried to expand religious liberty protections to cover wedding vendors, wedding cake makers, and others. Like many other Republican lawmakers in this deep-red state, Kinzer expected that the legislation would pass the House and Senate easily. Instead, the Kansas Chamber of Commerce came out strongly against the bill. Kinzer had already decided to leave state politics, and the ensuing debacle over religious liberty legislation confirmed that he had made the right decision. It wasn't simply exhaustion with the political process but more a recognition that given "the reality of the cultural moment," it was more important to shore up his local church community than to continue his legislative work. He did not, however, leave politics entirely. He now travels around the country advocating for religious liberty legislation in state legislatures, fulfilling the first goal of Benedict Option Christians: to secure and expand the space within which we can be ourselves and build our own institutions.

---

2. Yuval Levin, *The Fractured Republic: Renewing America's Social Contract in the Age of Individualism* (New York: Basic, 2016), 165.

✹ Antipolitical Politics

It might sound strange to call the Rule of Saint Benedict a political document, but it is nothing less than a constitution governing the shared life of a particular community. Benedict Option politics begin with the recognition that Western society is post-Christian and that absent a miracle, there is no hope of reversing this condition in the foreseeable future. Christians must turn their attention to something different. Part of the change we have to make is accepting that in the years to come, faithful Christians may have to choose between being a good American and being a good Christian.

We must now face a question that will strike many of us as heretical, according to our patriotic civic catechism. Because it prescribes government of the people, liberal democracy can be only as strong as the people who live under it. The question before us now is whether our current political situation is a betrayal of liberal democracy or, given its core principles of individualism and egalitarianism, liberal democracy's inevitable fulfillment under secularism. If the latter is true, then the need emerges not for the second coming of Ronald Reagan or for a would-be political savior, but for a new—and quite different—Saint Benedict.

What kind of politics should we pursue in the Benedict Option? If we broaden our political vision to include culture, we find that opportunities for action and service are boundless. Christian philosopher Scott Moore says that we err when we speak of politics as mere statecraft. "Politics is about how we order our lives together in the polis, whether that is a city, community, or even a family."[3]

Václav Havel, a Czech playwright and political prisoner, discusses this concept of "living in truth" and gives Christians much to learn from. Consider, says Havel, the greengrocer living under Communism, who puts a sign in his shop window saying, "Workers of the World, Unite!" He does it not because he believes it, necessarily. He simply doesn't want trouble. What if the greengrocer stops putting the sign up in his window? What if he refuses to go along to get along? He will lose his job and his position in society, but by bearing witness to the truth, he has accomplished something potentially powerful. He has said that the emperor is naked. And because the emperor is in fact naked, something extremely dangerous has happened: by his action, the greengrocer has addressed the world. He has shown everyone that it is possible to live within the truth. He becomes a threat to the system—but he has preserved his humanity. And that,

---

3. Scott H. Moore, *The Limits of Liberal Democracy: Politics and Religion at the End of Modernity* (Downers Grove, IL: InterVarsity Press, 2009), 15.

says Havel, is a far more important accomplishment than whether this party or that politician holds power.[4]

The answer, then, to preserving one's humanity, is to create and support "parallel structures" in which the truth can be lived in community. A good example of what this better life could look like comes from the late mathematician and dissident Vaclav Benda. A faithful Catholic, Benda believed that Communism maintained its iron grip on the people by isolating them, fragmenting their natural social bonds. Benda's distinct contribution to the dissident movement was the idea of a "parallel polis"—a separate but porous society existing alongside the official Communist order. At serious risk to himself and his family (he and his wife had six children), Benda rejected ghettoization. He insisted that the parallel polis must understand itself as fighting for "the preservation or the renewal of the nation community in the widest sense of the word—along with the defense of all the values, institutions, and material conditions to which the existence of such a community is bound."[5]

From this perspective, the parallel polis is not about building a gated community for Christians but rather about establishing (or reestablishing) common practices and common institutions that can reverse the isolation and fragmentation of contemporary society. In other words, dissident Christians should see their Benedict Option projects as building a better future not only for themselves but for everyone around them. As the West declines into spiritual acedia, there will be more and more people who are seeking something real, something meaningful, and yes, something wholesome. It is our mandate as Christians to offer it to them.

No matter how furious and all-consuming partisan political battles are, Christians have to keep clearly before us the fact that conventional American politics cannot fix what is wrong with our society and culture. The politics of the Benedict Option assume that the disorder in American public life derives from disorder within the American soul. Benedict Option politics start with the proposition that the most important political work of our time is the restoration of inner order, harmonizing with the will of God—the same telos as life in the monastic community. Everything else follows naturally from that.

Here's how to get started with the antipolitical politics of the Benedict Option. Secede culturally from the mainstream. Turn off the television. Put the smartphones away. Read books. Play games. Make music. Feast with your

4. Václav Havel, "The Power of the Powerless" (1979), trans. Paul Wilson, in *The Power of the Powerless*, by Václav Havel et al. (London: Hutchinson,1985), 27–28.
5. See Vaclav Benda, "The Parallel *'Polis,'*" in *Civic Freedom in Central Europe* (London: Palgrave Macmillan, 1991), 35–41.

neighbors. It is not enough to avoid what is bad; you must also embrace what is good. Times have changed dramatically, and we can no longer rely on politicians and activists to fight the culture war alone on our behalf. We faithful orthodox Christians didn't ask for internal exile from a country we thought was our own, but that's where we find ourselves. We are a minority now, so let's be a creative one, offering warm, living, light-filled alternatives to a world growing cold, dead, and dark.

Adapted from chapter 4, "A New Kind of Christian Politics," in Rod Dreher, The Benedict Option: A Strategy for Christians in a Post-Christian Nation *(New York: Sentinel, 2017).*

Rod Dreher is a senior editor at *The American Conservative*. Rod has written and edited for the *New York Post*, *The Dallas Morning News*, *National Review*, among others, and his commentary has been published in *The Wall Street Journal*, *Commentary*, and other publications. His books include *How Dante Can Save Your Life* and *The Benedict Option*.

A PALEO-BAPTIST VISION

The Priority of the Local Church and Mission

 Nathan A. Finn

I n 2017, Rod Dreher published his bestseller *The Benedict Option: A Strategy for Christians in a Post-Christian Nation.*[1] Dreher argues for a strategic withdrawal of Christians from public life for the sake of nurturing their own faith communities and preparing for future reengagement when American culture is in ruins and people are longing for a better way. David Brooks called *The Benedict Option* "the most discussed and most important religious book of the decade."[2]

Dreher frequently blogged about the Benedict Option before the book's publication, so Christian leaders have been discussing his proposal for about five years. Many have offered alternative proposals, drawing on historic figures such as William F. Buckley, Francis of Assisi, Abraham Kuyper, and William Wilberforce. In this essay, I offer my own friendly alternative to the Benedict Option. It is covenantal, congregational, countercultural, catholic, and commissioned. I call my proposal the Paleo-Baptist Option. The Paleo-Baptist Option offers a way to navigate post-Christian America that is more deeply rooted in local churches and more intentionally missional than the Benedict Option.

The Rise and Decline of the Paleo-Baptist Vision

The Baptist movement began in the first half of the seventeenth century.[3] The Paleo-Baptist vision, which developed during the first two hundred years of the

---

1. Rod Dreher, *The Benedict Option: A Strategy for Christians in a Post-Christian Nation* (New York: Sentinel, 2017).

2. David Brooks, "The Benedict Option," *New York Times* (March 14, 2017), https://www.nytimes .com/2017/03/14/opinion/the-benedict-option.html.

3. For an overview of Baptist history, see Anthony L. Chute, Nathan A. Finn, and Michael A. G. Haykin, *The Baptist Story: From English Sect to Global Movement* (Nashville: B&H Academic, 2015).

Baptist movement, focused on local churches and cultivated an identity that was covenantal, congregational, countercultural, and commissioned.

Early Baptists formulated their views of salvation and the church in covenantal terms. To be a Christian was to participate in the eternal covenant of grace through repentance and faith. Congregations were regenerated communities wherein professing believers voluntarily covenanted together in membership. Believers' baptism was considered the sign of the new covenant and represented the individual's covenant commitment to individual and communal discipleship. To fall into persistent unrepentant sin was to transgress the church's covenant and possibly evidence that you weren't really a partaker of the covenant of grace.

Early Baptists practiced congregational polity. They believed that every local church is a microcosm of the church universal and that it is the responsibility of the entire membership to exercise spiritual oversight over one another. Churches are kingdom embassies, church members are kingdom citizens, and every kingdom citizen takes ownership of the King's agenda. While Baptist congregations set apart individuals to serve as pastors and deacons, they argued that all believers were called to the ministry of proclaiming the gospel in word and living out its implications in deed.

They were countercultural, though not like the Anabaptists who rejected the legitimate authority of magistrates or embraced pacifism. Baptists desired to see Christians hold government office, they professed loyalty to the Crown, many fought during the English Civil War, and a few even sat in Parliament. Nevertheless, Baptists were countercultural in that they rejected the establishment of the English state church. They wanted a nation governed by Christian principles, but they advocated liberty of conscience, arguing that one is ultimately accountable to God alone for his or her religious convictions.

The earliest Baptists embraced a form of Free Church catholicity. In their confessional statements, they echoed the ecumenical creeds in formulating their views on the Trinity and Christology. The Orthodox Creed (1678) commended the ancient creeds to General Baptist congregations. The Second London Confession (1689) argued strongly for a universal visible church, of which Baptists are but one part. Calvinistic Baptists also understood themselves to be a part of the "Protestant Interest," the transcontinental Reformed-Lutheran bulwark against the encroachments of Roman Catholicism.

Finally, Baptists understood themselves to be a commissioned people, though this emphasis came along 150 years after the Baptist movement began. Though early Baptists were committed to evangelism and church planting, the seventeenth century was not a time of widespread missionary work by Protestants. By the early eighteenth century, General Baptists had imbibed deeply of Enlightenment skepticism and were drifting into heresy. Particular Baptists, influenced by hyper-Calvinist rationalism, often downplayed evangelistic urgency. Near the end of the Evangelical Awakening in Great Britain, key Baptist theologians offered evangelical rationales for evangelism and foreign mission. The key verse became Matthew 28:19–20, which Baptists interpreted as a binding command on every generation of believers.

With the exception of an emphasis on mission, among American Baptists these Paleo-Baptist priorities were either lost or redefined during the nineteenth and twentieth centuries. Many Baptists embraced a radical form of biblicism that divorced Scripture from any form of tradition, rejecting all creeds (and sometimes even denominational confessions) in principle. Baptists increasingly interpreted their historic principles through the lenses of Enlightenment individualism and Jeffersonian democracy. By the twentieth century, spokesmen were arguing that the Baptist tradition is quintessentially American because of the Baptist commitment to democracy and church-state separation.

Then the world began to change. While Baptist elites resonated with mid-century Supreme Court decisions that codified secular interpretations of church-state separation, grassroots Baptists became increasingly persuaded that America was a Christian nation that had lost her way. The moral turbulence of the 1960s contributed to a growing sense of dread. Many evangelicals who were experiencing this sort of cultural angst, including millions of Baptists, signed on with the emerging Religious Right, became active in the Republican Party, and sought to reclaim America for God. That so many Baptists wanted America to be a Christian nation demonstrates the massive gap between Paleo-Baptist priorities and modern Baptist views of public engagement.

Paleo-Baptists in Post-Christian America

Baptists in America must reclaim the Paleo-Baptist vision and commend it to all faithful believers in our post-Christian nation. For Paleo-Baptists, local churches are countercultural communities of disciples who covenant to walk together for the sake of worship, catechesis, witness, and service. To those like Dreher who are drawn to neo-monastic movements, Paleo-Baptists would say that a covenantal understanding of church membership accomplishes the same goal, but applies it to all members. When membership is restricted to professing believers, churches become the most natural context for theological and moral formation and intentional discipleship. In this vision, congregations embody the best of classical monastic priorities, but they are part of the warp and woof of meaningful church membership rather than a special form of discipleship reserved for the truly committed.

The time is ripe for what Timothy George calls an "ecumenism of the trenches" as modeled in initiatives such as Evangelicals and Catholics Together and The Manhattan Declaration.[4] Paleo-Baptists should be willing to link arms with other believers in as many ways as we can, with integrity, without retreating from our own tradition's core distinctives. The encroachment of militant secularism necessitates the mortification of all forms of sectarianism, denominational idolatry, and party spirit. Paleo-Baptist congregations shouldn't confuse themselves with the GOP at prayer, but rather as countercultures for the common good. Churches are missional bodies that equip members and work alongside other believers to spread the good news, serve the needy, and cultivate human flourishing. This missional component remains a significant lacuna in the Benedict Option.

While the Paleo-Baptist vision represents an alternative to the Benedict Option, Baptists have much to learn from Dreher in one key area. Dreher argues that faith communities should form believers in the Great Tradition of classical Christianity. While early Baptists were committed to a form of catholicity, it's fair to say this has never been a strong suit among Baptists. Nevertheless, I'm encouraged by the growing number of Baptists embracing the ecumenical creedal tradition, more closely observing the Christian calendar, celebrating communion more frequently in corporate worship gatherings, and learning from the spiritual practices of brothers and sisters in other ecclesial traditions. These Paleo-Baptists are intentionally embracing a greater sense of catholicity without backtracking one bit on their Baptist identity.[5] Baptists will thrive in post-Christian America if we self-consciously frame ourselves as an ecclesiological renewal movement within the Great Tradition of catholic Christianity.

Conclusion

The Paleo-Baptist Option offers a way forward for Baptists and other "baptistic" evangelicals as we seek to live faithfully in post-Christian America. Even traditions that disagree with some Baptist distinctives can embrace a more intentionally covenantal, congregational, countercultural, and commissioned outlook and adapt these priorities to their contexts. In this sense, all American believers

---

4. Timothy George, "Evangelicals and Others," *First Things* (February 2006), https://www.firstthings.com/article/2006/02/evangelicals-and-others.

5. For a representative group among Southern Baptists, see The Center for Baptist Renewal, http://www.centerforbaptistrenewal.com/.

can develop certain "Paleo-Baptist instincts" in response to militant secularism. More important than passing on Baptist identity to the next generation is passing on the faith once and for all delivered to the saints (Jude 3). While Paleo-Baptists believe historic Baptist distinctives are essentially correct and ought to be embraced, defended, and commended to others, only the faith shared by all Christian believers everywhere will fuel our spiritual maturity, empower us for Christian witness, motivate us for humble and sacrificial service, and help us to think rightly about God and his world and live rightly before God in his world.

This essay is adapted from Nathan A. Finn, "Baptists and the Benedict Option in American Babylon," Canon and Culture *(March 22, 2016), http://www.canonandculture.com/baptists-and-the-benedict-option-in-american-babylon/. See also Nathan A. Finn, "Baptists and the Benedict Option in American Babylon,"* Christianity in the Academy *13 (2016): 156–67.*

Nathan A. Finn (PhD, Southeastern Baptist Theological Seminary) serves as provost and dean of the University Faculty at North Greenville University. He is most recently coeditor of *A Reader's Guide to the Major Writings of Jonathan Edwards* and *Spirituality for the Sent: Casting a New Vision for the Missional Church.*

A KUYPERIAN CONTRIBUTION TO POLITICS

◯◯ Vincent Bacote

K uyperian" and "neo-Calvinist" refer broadly to an approach to a holistic
Christian faith rooted in the life and work of Abraham Kuyper. Kuyper was a
theologian, pastor, journalist, and politician who ultimately became prime min-
ister of the Netherlands (1901–1905). He gave leadership to a movement labeled
"Anti-Revolutionary" because of its contrast to the commitments of the French
Revolution. As put succinctly by David Koyzis:

> After the generation of war and instability set off in 1789 finally ended
> with Napoleon's defeat in 1815, many Europeans, especially those still loyal
> to the gospel of Jesus Christ, set about attempting to combat the ideological
> illusions the Revolution had engendered. This entailed breaking with the
> modern preoccupation—nay, obsession—with sovereignty and recovering
> a recognition of the legitimate pluriformity of society. . . . Recognizing that
> the only source of unity in the cosmos is the God who has created and
> redeemed us in the person of his Son, Christians are freed from the need to
> locate a unifying source within the cosmos.[1]

The themes and dispositions that emerged from Kuyper and his fellow anti-
revolutionaries led to an approach to Christian public engagement that neither
marginalized the institutional church nor encouraged ecclesiastical dominance
of public affairs. Instead, while the church gives priority and emphasis to the
work of Christian formation by means of proclamation of the Word and obser-
vance of the sacraments, Christians formed in and by the church are encouraged
to participate in the public realm in the diverse domains of education, business,

---

1. David Koyzis, "Happy AR Day! a holiday to counter Bastille Day," *Kuyperian*, July 20, 2017, http://
kuyperian.com/happy-ar-day-holiday-counter-bastille-day/.

voluntary associations, and politics. Christian participation in these domains is not directed by clergy, though the influence of Christian formation ought to influence the approach of Christians to the various public domains. Equally important, as Christians acknowledge God as the sole authority and should resist the need to identify and impose a unifying worldview within the marketplace of worldviews/ideas, they can acknowledge a worldview pluralism expressed in the emergence of institutions such as schools and political parties rooted in a variety of perspectives.

Kuyper's idea of "sphere sovereignty" is important here. In this view God is sovereign over the entire creation, but there is also a derivative sovereignty distributed across social spheres such as the family, schools, and the state. Each sphere operates distinctively (e.g., one ought not run a family like a business), and the pluralism of spheres also allows for a diversity of worldviews, manifested concretely in a diversity of public institutions.

Among the important theological dimensions of this approach to public life is a prominent theology of creation not in tension with redemption. While some expressions of Christian faith render salvation as an escape from a fallen creation, a Kuyperian approach to politics emphasizes creation as reclaimed by God, and never regarded as a lost cause. The doctrine of common grace is important in the latter regard. For Kuyper, common grace is the theological permission for Christians to move out of their enclaves into the public square with the purpose of being responsible stewards of the creation. In common grace God acts to preserve the created order after sin's entry into the world. The divine generosity that preserves the world makes it possible to continue to obey the first command to rule the world well, what some call either the creation mandate or cultural mandate (Gen. 1–2). In light of the reality of fallenness, while engagement in the world remains proper to humans, it is a more complicated enterprise. It is equally important to emphasize the possibilities that remain for participation in God's world while also maintaining a humble disposition due to the ever present challenges of a world that is good though fallen. The implications for politics are significant; while there may be ways that human life is developed or enhanced by the stewardship of political life, no policy or system will ever be perfect or best for everyone all around the world.

A Kuyperian approach to politics must also highlight what Kuyper called "the antithesis." This term refers to Kuyper's emphasis on the idea that because Christians are people who have experienced the special grace of salvation and who are regenerated by the Holy Spirit to perceive, think, and act in a way different from non-Christians, the result ought to be approaches to cultural and political engagement rooted in Christian principles. In politics during Kuyper's lifetime, this distinctiveness was notable in the development of the Anti-Revolutionary Party, which reached its zenith when he became prime minister in 1901 (though it is important to note Kuyper needed a coalition with other parties for this achievement). As with common grace, the antithesis must be tempered by humility; a regenerated heart does not lead to a mindset and political practice with crystal clear vision. We see through a glass darkly, and the process of sanctification is a long road with many twists.

For some, the fact that Kuyper became prime minister betrays that his approach has theocratic intentions even though he espoused a pluralistic public square. While he certainly made statements that expressed his desire for the Netherlands to be a country that operated according to God's divine ordinances, the following words make his understanding of "Christian nation" clear:

> Terms such as "a Christian nation," "a Christian country," "a Christian society," "Christian art," and the like, do not mean that such a nation consists mainly of regenerate Christian persons or that such a society has already been transposed into the kingdom of heaven . . . in such a country special grace in the church and among believers exerted so strong a formative influence on common grace that common grace thereby attained its highest development. The adjective "Christian" therefore says nothing about the spiritual state of the inhabitants of such a country but only witnesses to the fact that public opinion, the general mind-set, the ruling ideas, the moral norms, the laws and customs there clearly betoken the influence of the Christian faith. Though this is attributable to special grace, it is manifested on the terrain of common grace, i.e., in ordinary civil life. This influence leads to the abolition of slavery in the laws and life of a country, to the improved position of women, to the maintenance of public virtue, respect for the Sabbath, compassion for the poor, consistent regard for the ideal over the material, and—even in manners—the elevation of all that is human from its sunken state to a higher standpoint.[2]

To seek Christian influence in political life is not to pursue a theocratic, totalitarian agenda that threatens all who refuse to "get with the program." Instead, the Kuyperian approach at its best encourages us to seek ways of leavening society with Christian influence, constantly engaging the various aspects of public life with the aim of incremental transformation. This has to be a long-term commitment to navigate the peaks and valleys that attend cultural engagement

2. Abraham Kuyper, "Common Grace," in *Abraham Kuyper: A Centennial Reader*, ed. James D. Bratt (Grand Rapids: Eerdmans, 1998), 198–99.

and the political process. The goal, then, is not the Christian conquest of society, but sustained, faithful, and distinctive public engagement.

While a Kuyperian approach to politics emerged from a specific context in Europe and has had some influence in the West, this does not mean that the Kuyperian approach to politics is limited to environments with some form of democracy. Instead, just as the practical dimensions of Kuyper's approach were intended to address his immediate situation, the aim today and beyond must be to consider how to encourage and pursue political engagement in light of the opportunities and limitations of each political situation. In some cases, this means opportunities to be in the center of political life while in others it may be limited to extremely local efforts to facilitate human flourishing.

The Kuyperian political tradition at its best is a recognition of and response to our opportunity for political life as stewards of God's creation, the encouragement to seek creative ways for God's truth to be translated into expressions of the public good, and the humility to recognize that even our best contributions are penultimate and subject to refinement or revision.

Vincent Bacote (PhD, Drew University) is associate professor of theology and director of the Center for Applied Christian Ethics at Wheaton College in Illinois. He is the author of various publications, including *The Political Disciple: A Theology of Public Life*. An occasional bassist, he lives with his family in Glen Ellyn, Illinois.

CHRISTIAN AND DEMOCRAT

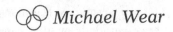 *Michael Wear*

The task of defending any political party, the task of defending political parties at all, is not an easy one these days. National approval of both the Democratic and Republican parties is low. Party polarization is at an all-time high. It seems clear, obvious even, that political parties are the problem with our politics.

The conversation about what it means to be a Democrat or a Republican has been undercut and distorted by the fact that no one seems all too happy that political parties exist in the first place. What might surprise people is that what they dislike most about our political parties is exacerbated by their decision not to participate in them. At a time when partisan identity is taking up so much space in our politics and in our lives, it is essential to reposition the role of the political party in our minds before any fruitful effort advocating for a particular political party can be made.

We have not invested such meaning into what a political party is and what it means to affiliate with one because of the nature of a political party, but because of what is in the interest of political parties and other political actors who benefit from them. That is to say, political parties demand our allegiance not because it is their right, but because it is in their interest.

America's founders, with their great confidence in and reliance on human rationality, were so wary of political parties because they understood how parties can undercut rational, independent thinking. In Federalist Paper Number Ten,[1] we learn that America's founders themselves (in this case, the paper was written by James Madison) were concerned about the threat that faction and polarization pose to democracy and rational thinking.[2]

---

1. James Madison, "The Federalist Papers: Number 10," November 23, 1787, *The Avalon Project,* http://avalon.law.yale.edu/18th_century/fed10.asp.

2. Madison explained why factions are formed: "As long as the reason of man continues fallible, and he is at liberty to exercise it, different opinions will be formed. As long as the connection subsists between his reason and his self-love, his opinions and his passions will have a reciprocal influence on each other; and the former will be objects to which the latter will attach themselves." "The Federalist Papers: Number 10," November 23,

The capacity for political parties to take up a defining place in our identity and to drive how we view our neighbors has been expanded by the increasing sophistication of political technology and the pervasiveness of political media. Politicians and political parties can reach deeper into our lives than ever before, and they ask not just for our vote but for our loyalty. Political parties and campaigns will take your loyalty based on your view that they embrace policies that will best advance the common good of our nation, but they will take it any way they can get it. If emotional appeals, cultural affinities, or simply the demonization of the alternative is sufficient, that will work too. If those methods prove to be more powerful than positive arguments for particular policy approaches, then a political party's interests will drive their strategy in the direction of a politics of identity, emotion, and feeling.

What we need to understand, what politicians, strategists, and even America's foreign adversaries understand, is that our politics is both driven by and guiding our emotions. Candidates are now treated as brands, with campaigns focused not on advancing ideas, but on presenting a candidate voters will "identify with" in a personal way.[3]

This is the difficult truth: the state of our politics and our political parties reflects our desires, our longings, our souls. There are structural components of our political system—for instance, how campaigns are financed and how election seasons are structured—that incentivize the worst of our politics, but I would like you to consider these realities as not just problems we must fix, but problems we have created. The structures and institutions that provoke such cynicism exist the way they do in large part because of our contributions, or lack thereof, to them. Most of what we dislike about our politics is a result of the very demands American citizens imposed on the political system, to varying degrees, in the past.

With this context in place, we are better prepared to consider political parties and the value of joining one.

1787, *The Avalon Project*, http://avalon.law.yale.edu/18th_century/fed10.asp. The essay goes on to explain the safeguards a republican form of government provides to constrain the effects of factionalism—that in a larger society it will be difficult for all who share a common interest to "invade the rights of other citizens" to "discover their own strength, and to act in unison with each other." These safeguards seem undermined by modern technological advancements.

    3.   In an article titled "How Big Data Broke American Politics," Chuck Todd explains that "Big Data—a combination of massive technological power and endlessly detailed voter information—now allows campaigns to pinpoint their most likely supporters. These tools make mobilizing supporters easier, faster and far less expensive than persuading their neighbors." https://www.nbcnews.com/politics/elections/how-big-data -broke-american-politics-n732901. Or consider how Russian operatives exploited America's most tender divides in order to provoke greater turmoil that advanced Russian interests and American political and social destabilization. They bought Facebook advertisements that were "slickly crafted to mimic and infiltrate U.S. political discourse while also seeking to heighten tensions between groups already wary of one another." https:// www.washingtonpost.com/business/technology/russian-operatives-used-facebook-ads-to-exploit-divisions -over-black-political-activism-and-muslims/2017/09/25/4a011242-a21b-11e7-ade1-76d061d56efa_story .html?utm_term=.8abb6ae87f4f.

Political parties are vehicles that organize politicians and the voters who support them. Their purpose is to represent a distinct outlook or political disposition, to appeal to voters on the basis of that outlook, and to provide institutional support to that party's elected officials and members. An obvious observation about political parties, though perhaps it is not so obvious given the rhetoric surrounding them, is that parties hold no actual control over the political convictions of their registered members. Party membership no more requires or implies that you agree to every position the party's current platform advocates than a gym membership requires that you will use every piece of equipment in the gym. No, you sign up for a gym membership because you believe you have an obligation to yourself (and perhaps to society) to stay fit, and because you need access to an institution that is dedicated to providing a vehicle for individuals to take action in the limited arena of exercise, and provides that vehicle by pooling the resources of other individuals who share the same general desire. You might choose a specific gym over other gyms for a range of reasons, both personal and more substantive. And, of course, your reasons for joining the gym will be different from the reasons of many others who chose the same gym. In fact, your reasons might be singular. Yet you're all there together, your individual contribution affecting and affected by your fellow members and the gym's leadership.

It might seem ludicrous, even offensive, to compare gym membership to party membership—the comparison is not a total one, to be sure—but one reason we might be so offended is because of the unjustified importance we place on partisan identity. Unfortunately, party polarization is a defining feature of not just modern politics, but of modern life. Partisanship is at an all-time high.[4] This polarization does not just infect policy making and political decision making, but our communities, our relationships, and our souls. Political identity is now reflected in our friendships and romantic lives, where we live and the media we consume.[5] As we have already discussed, this benefits political parties, but it fails the country.

The proper response would seem to be that we should withdraw from political parties. If we rob them of our influence, we rob them of their influence, right? This idea is actually being tested right now. Withdrawal from political

---

4. Niraj Chokshi, "U.S. Partisanship Is Highest in Decades, Pew Study Finds," *The New York Times*, June 23, 2016, https://www.nytimes.com/2016/06/24/us/politics/partisanship-republicans-democrats-pew-research .html.

5. A 2012 study, Bill Bishop's 2008 book, *The Big Short*, contends that Americans are increasingly geographically segregated—we choose to live near people who think the way we do. Over the last fifty years, we have seen an 800 percent increase in the percentage of Americans who would be upset if their child married someone who belonged to a different political party than they do. In 1960, only 5 percent of American adults felt this way. In 2010, 40 percent of American adults said they would be deeply upset. https://hbr.org/2017/05/ research-political-polarization-is-changing-how-americans-work-and-shop.

parties is not radical; it's passé. We have reached the highest percentage of adults who identify as political independents in the last few years. This has not brought about a surge of independent thinking. As political scientist Julia Azara has observed, "While parties as organizations are weak, parties as ideas—partisanship—is strong."[6] As both political parties are increasingly left with only "true believers," and as those parties have at the same time been weakened in terms of the strength and levers available to them as institutions, the parties have become more polarized, not less.

Azara argues that this has developed, in part, because "while party organizations are concrete, partisanship as an idea is abstract. Partisan identity tells us who shares our beliefs, and it helps to make political meaning, conveying important truths about the world through symbols. It is in these cracks of abstraction that truly pathological politics grows."[7]

To withdraw from political parties does not undermine this pathology; it affirms it. While party withdrawal weakens the institution of the party in some ways, it actually strengthens the idea of the party.

You join a political party to influence that party, not for the party to influence you. Political parties certainly want you to think that's not the case—it's much easier for their officials to lead if they can convince you that they define who is a "real Democrat" or a "real Republican" and who is not. But our political parties can change our views only if we give them that power.

Withdrawal is not working. To withdraw from our political parties is to unilaterally forgo one of the primary levers we have of influencing the direction of our government. Party participation is not an identity statement. It is a choice about how to use your power as a citizen.

What we need is a reinvestment of and from people, as they are, into political parties. Our politics will improve when Americans view political parties not as sources of identity but as a mediator for political influence that exists to receive and reconcile our opinions and perspectives, not to serve as sources for our opinion, perspective, or identity.

Now, with proper thinking about political parties, we can consider why a Christian would affiliate with the Democratic Party. What should be clear by now is that while we can make a case for why Christians should be Democrats, what we never want to suggest or argue for is that "the Democratic Party is the party for Christians" or that "all Christians should be Democrats." These kinds

6. Julia Azari, "Weak Parties and Strong Partisanship Are a Bad Combination," *Vox*, November 23, 2016, https://www.vox.com/mischiefs-of-faction/2016/11/3/13512362/weak-parties-strong-partisanship-bad-combination.

7. Ibid.

of arguments place a moral burden on politics that is unjustified and can amount to spiritual manipulation.

A person might choose their political party on the basis of personal interest or familial and personal history and experiences. I believe these are fine motivations for choosing your political party. As Christians, we should view politics as an essential form of loving our neighbors.[8] Your decision to affiliate with a political party should not be motivated solely by your personal interests, affinities, and experiences, but by a consideration of others' interests. Of course, such consideration can never be total or perfect. Party affiliation will never reflect a perfect consideration of others' interests because others' interests are regarded and served differently by each political party. This guidance to be other-centered in politics is primarily about the orientation of one's own heart, not another rhetorical weapon to bully others regarding their political decisions.

I am a Democrat for all of these reasons. I grew up in a family that was not overly political, and definitely not partisan, but the most important people in my life were Democrats. My grandfather, who I was very close to, was an FDR-Democrat (Franklin Delano Roosevelt), and that had an impact on me.

I am a Democrat because my first political interest was in the civil rights movement and the continuing work of civil rights leaders addressing racism in our laws and in our society. While I do not agree with all who claim to speak on behalf of the cause of civil rights all of the time, racism is odious to me, and I am sensitive to any efforts to undermine voting rights, for instance.

I am a Democrat because, once I became a Christian in the early years of the twenty-first century, I came to understand that while my views on some social issues would be at odds with many in my party, my reshaped, Bible-informed views on issues like immigration reform, criminal justice, civil and human rights, poverty, and so many other political issues were more closely aligned with the Democratic Party's approach at the time.

I am a Democrat because, as a child, for a relatively brief period, my family relied on the Supplemental Nutritional Food Program that Republicans often want to cut and Democrats fight to protect. I no longer rely on that program, but I know that millions of families do today.

I am a Democrat because I believe we have a responsibility to steward our environmental resources, and that economic gain does not always justify environmental degradation.

---

8. For more on the topic of how Christians should think about politics, see Michael Wear, *Reclaiming Hope: Lessons Learned in the Obama White House About the Future of Faith in America* (Nashville: Nelson, 2017).

I am a Democrat because I believe our immigration policies should err on the side of compassion and family preservation.

I am a Democrat because I believe that the government has a role to play in helping families thrive and, in particular, that family breakdown is not just an outflow of cultural norms but the result of incentives and disincentives that are baked into our economy and governmental policies.

All of these positions flow out of my faith, but I try not to confuse my motivations for what is ultimate and true. History is littered with examples of well-intentioned policies producing the opposite effect or resulting in unintended consequences. We simply do the best we can in applying the values we derive from Scripture and the Christian tradition, while leaving room for other Christians who prioritize other values or are led to different policy conclusions motivated by the same basic values we share.

To argue that you can join a flawed political party if you judge that action is the best way to steward your influence for the good of your neighbors is not to make an argument for relativism. It is to acknowledge that politics is, inherently, relative. It is the very nature of our system of government, which is at least as comprehensible to God as it is to us. Our choices are not entirely our own but are shaped by our fellow citizens and by institutional processes like those of our political parties.

You can be as faithful as a Republican as you are as a Democrat and vice versa. Really. What is required is that you never make an idol of your political party or subsume your conscience to the dictates of that party. One of the reasons our political parties have become so extreme is because we have starved them of ideological diversity. Christians are well-positioned to find the motivation to both engage institutionally in our political parties while maintaining ideological independence. Again, we do not join political parties for community or identity, but because political parties are vehicles that channel and mediate our political ideas.

You should join a political party because political parties play a crucial role in the functioning of government, which is of great importance to our communities and the well-being of our neighbors. My case for the Democratic Party is not that it is a perfect option for Christians or *the* Christian party, but it is, considering the times we are in and the state of the parties, the best party for Christians in my judgment. That is about all the weight I am willing to place on such a decision, as important as it is. In such a polarized time, our parties and our nation would benefit from people willing to make commitments that are tinged with ambivalence.

We should be wary of those who pretend the future we hope for can be realized if only our politics was more dogmatic, who wish to load onto politics the expectation that we might perfectly express ourselves through it, and who turn a question like party membership into a matter of religious dogma. Instead consider politics as a penultimate forum where we can love our neighbors, pursuing justice where we can, until the God of justice comes in his perfect glory to set all wrongs to right.

Michael Wear, founder of Public Square Strategies, is the author of *Reclaiming Hope: Lessons Learned in the Obama White House About the Future of Faith in America*. He writes for *The Atlantic, Christianity Today,* and *USA Today,* among others. Michael serves on the board of Bethany Christian Services and is a senior fellow at the Trinity Forum.

DISCUSSION QUESTIONS

1. In each of these articles, the authors begin their discussion with presupposed definitions for certain terms such as Democrat, Republican, politics, and others. Are there any discrepancies between the articles on any of these definitions of terms?

2. Dreher uses the 2016 election as proof that in the polarizing split of the two main political parties, conservative Christians no longer have a place. How might someone from Wear's tradition disagree with him and respond to this statement?

3. Bacote discusses the importance of stewardship in regards to Christians' role in politics, using it as the motivation for Christians' active involvement in the political arena. How might Dreher disagree on Bacote's interpretation of stewardship, and where might Dreher say that Christians should act out stewardship in regards to politics?

4. Wear declares that Christians must not view political parties as an identity, but as a means to be involved in the politics of the day. Is this reasonable or even possible in today's political climate, and if so, how does a Christian avoid their witness being hurt by other members of their chosen political party who might hold beliefs that hurt or contradict the Bible?

5. How does each of these articles define the Christian's role as "steward" in relation to politics?

6. What are the main distinguishing factors between the Paleo-Baptist Option and the Benedict Option?

7. How might someone from Dreher's tradition respond to the following sentence from Finn's article on the Paleo-Baptist option: "In this vision, congregations embody the best of classical monastic priorities, but they are part of the warp and woof of meaningful church membership rather than a special form of discipleship reserved for the truly committed"?

8. Wear discusses the fact that he is part of a political party but strongly disagrees with many of the other adherents on certain issues—citing religious liberty and abortion. How might someone from Dreher's tradition respond

to Wear or to anyone who was part of a party with which they disagreed on major tenets?

9. In his article, George declares that the solution to America's politic issues is found in returning to the foundation of the United States of America, and that the original principles on which our country was founded are Christian principles in and of themselves. How might someone from Dreher's tradition respond to this?

10. How might Finn and Dreher comment on the concept of "American Exceptionalism"?

chapter ten

WORK

We need not look any further than Genesis 1 to understand that Christians are called to work; it's part of God's original design. Genesis 1:28 tells us, "God blessed them and said to them, 'Be fruitful and increase in number, fill the earth and subdue it. Rule over the fish of the sea and the birds in the sky and over every living creature that moves on the ground.'" Before the fall, before work became toil, Adam and Eve labored side by side caring for and cultivating the garden as loving and joyful stewards.

Accepting work as an essential part of the Christian calling, however, does not make understanding the Christian's relationship to work any simpler outside of the garden. Work, and the Christian relationship to work, like everything, is distorted by the fall. Genesis 2:15 reads, "The LORD God took the man and put him in the garden of Eden to work it and take care of it." After the fall, God tells Adam that the gift he was originally given—the gift of a plentiful garden and good work—has now been replaced by, as Genesis 3:17–19 says, "painful toil," "thorns and thistles," and "the sweat of your brow." The labor of the woman—her work in childbearing—will also be accompanied by pain and suffering (Gen. 3:16). Work was initially a fruitful gift, but is now a source of "painful toil" (v. 17).

Since work was part of God's initial design and plan, it also falls under God's ongoing plan for humankind. Work is harder after the fall, but it is still good. This idea of the inherent goodness of work is at odds with the classical notion expressed in the Latin word for work (*negotium*), which comes to English as our word *negotiate*. The word *negotiate* in Latin means the negation or removal of *otium or work*, which is to say *leisure*. In this understanding, work is not a positive endeavor, but rather the negation of a positive state. This connotation emphasizes even further the idea of work itself as a curse rather than a blessing. Indeed, in the ancient world, leisure was a privilege of the elite, and labor was the obligation of the masses.

When Jesus chose his disciples, he called them to leave their earthly work in order to follow him, what contemporary Christians term "full-time ministry."

However, the apostle Paul offered an example of a minister who engaged in secular work, tent making, in order to support his mission of advancing the gospel and building the church. In later centuries, the early church carved out a class of people whose work required retreat from the world to a monastic life where copying manuscripts, praying and worshiping regularly, and studying Scripture formed their labor. (The word "liturgy," in fact, means "the work of the people." Thus worship should be understood as a kind of work.)

Martin Luther radically critiqued the medieval division between work in and for the church and work outside the church (sacred and secular) with his doctrine of vocation. Before the Reformation, the idea of vocation (or calling) was limited to holy vocations or callings: one was called out of the secular world and into the ministry. But Luther and other Reformers sought to recover a biblical view that understands all morally and biblically licit work as a way to fulfill every Christian's calling to love God and serve neighbors.[1]

Today some Christians pursue vocations within the ministry where they find their financial and physical needs being met as servants within the church. But most Christians pursue vocations outside of the church as bankers, teachers, electricians, plumbers, lawyers, and other lay positions, and this is where the tension arises. It is not difficult to see how the pastor of the local church serves the kingdom of God through his work. However, it can be difficult for the electrician, for example, to see how his work wiring a new house is, in and of itself, kingdom work. Luther's doctrine of vocation has yet to take hold in some contemporary thinking about work.

Lesslie Newbigin's description of the dualism that exists in post-Enlightenment society, written over twenty-five years ago, is still, in large measure, accurate: "It is assumed that there are statements of what is called 'fact' which have been—as we say—scientifically proved; to assert these is not arrogance. But statements about human nature and destiny cannot be proved. To assert them as fact is inadmissible."[2] Though the rise of "alternative facts" to persuade is an interesting political and public relations phenomenon, the distinction between "facts" and "values" is typically assumed. The public sphere operates with what is assumed to be "objective, scientific facts" and includes arenas such as the school, the workplace, and the marketplace. The private sphere, by contrast, is built on personal preferences and values, and includes the home, places of worship, and personal relationships. In light of this sharp division between the public and private spheres, many Christians live as divided people, expressing their Christian

---

1. See Gustaf Wingren, *Luther on Vocation*, trans. Carl C. Rasmussen (Eugene, OR: Wipf and Stock, 2004).

2. Lesslie Newbigin, *The Gospel in a Pluralist Society* (Grand Rapids: Eerdmans, 1989), 19.

faith within the private sphere among close friends, family, and fellow Christians, but separate their Christian identity from their occupational identity, creating a divided self. Thus, while Christian worship is fervent on Sunday, it might go dormant from 8:00 a.m. to 5:00 p.m. Monday through Friday because, according to cultural pressures, it belongs to the private sphere.

The challenge, then, for Christians is to understand their work to be holistically connected to their membership in the kingdom of God, as the "very thing through which I could be the salt and light Jesus called me to be."[3] Dorothy Sayers explains,

> In nothing has the Church so lost Her hold on reality as in Her failure to understand and respect the secular vocation. She has allowed work and religion to become separate departments, and is astonished to find that, as a result, the secular works is turned to purely selfish and destructive ends, and that the greater part of the world's intelligent workers have become irreligious, or at least, uninterested in religion. But is it astonishing? How can anyone remain interested in a religion that seems to have no concern with nine-tenths of his life? The Church's approach to an intelligent carpenter is usually confined to exhorting him not to be drunk and disorderly on Sundays. What the Church should be telling him is this: that the very first demand that his religion makes upon him is that he should make good tables.[4]

The work of the Christian is holy because God has made the Christian holy. Thus, when the Christian works in her vocation, she is reflecting the glory of God to the onlooking world through her work. *How* the Christian does her work reflects as much on her Christian faith as does her worship on Sunday, perhaps even more so.

In the first essay related to work, Alex Chediak applies a gospel-centered lens to examine how Christians should engage in the secular workplace, arguing that *how* Christians work is as important for displaying the power of the gospel as *what* they work at. Placing a different—though not contrary—emphasis on the topic, Jeremy Treat reframes the way Christians ought to think about work by examining three foundational shifts Christians need to make to develop a biblical theology of work. Ultimately, Treat encourages Christians to think about work vocationally, communally, and holistically.

---

3. Hugh Whelchel, *How Then Should We Work?: Rediscovering the Biblical Doctrine of Work* (McLean, VA: Institute for Faith, Work, and Economics, 2012), xxiii.

4. Dorothy Sayers, *Creed or Chaos?* (Manchester, NH: Sophia Institute, 1974), 89.

Darrell Bock's essay provides a short biblical theology of wealth and then reflects on the moral wisdom this should bring on today's complex and diverse economic situations, calling Christians to pursue justice through intangible ways. Building from the premise that money itself is neutral but the way we manage it is not, Matthew Loftus approaches the issue of global economics by encouraging personal responsibility and stewardship while also exhorting Christians of all economic backgrounds to strive for humility, generosity, justice, and compassion in the way we manage our personal finances and structure our economic systems.

In closing, Kayla Snow sets our understanding of work within the framework of the creation narrative, arguing that the rhythm of work and rest is an essential element of the created order that God has designed for humankind so that we may worship and enjoy him.

WORK IS ALSO A PLATFORM FOR EVANGELISM

◯◯ *Alex Chediak*

The 1999 film *The Big Kahuna*, starring Kevin Spacey and Danny DeVito, features a fascinating juxtaposition between work and evangelism. The movie is about a team of three salesmen for an industrial lubricant company who are dispatched to a manufacturers' convention in Wichita, Kansas. The salesmen host a cocktail party to interact with potential clients. The men are particularly hoping to land a deal with Indiana's largest manufacturer—"The big kahuna." They fail because one of the salesmen, Bob, is so busy sharing his faith with the big kahuna that he fails to promote his company's product. The movie features a lengthy dialogue in which Bob's colleagues reprimand him for his misplaced priorities.

For Christians, the movie teases out a question that nags many of us who work primarily with non-Christians (as I did before entering Christian higher education): Were Bob's priorities misplaced? After all, isn't the big kahuna's soul more important than which industrial lubricant he purchases? To put it crassly, shouldn't we pursue soul-winning to justify the necessary evil of "non-Christian" employment? After all, aside from our need for money, why else has God given us our jobs?

◯◯ A False Dichotomy

The questions I've just raised play upon a common but false dichotomy. It's not either-or but both-and. Both work and evangelism matter. But how should Christians respond when doing one seems to come at the expense of doing the other?

Mercifully, the Bible frees us from the anxiety of having to evangelize 24-7. It does so by teaching us that our work—providing any lawful (nonsinful) product or service useful to others—has intrinsic value quite apart from whether we win souls. Our work has value because it's assigned to us ultimately by God, flow-ing from the cultural mandate—the task God gave our first parents to exercise responsible dominion over the created order. It's an important part of our spiri-tual worship (see Rom. 12:1; Heb. 13:15–16). It's an important part of how we love our neighbors as ourselves, because in doing our jobs with excellence and integrity—as bakers, mechanics, lawyers, doctors, professors, and so on—we're serving others in specific ways, using the unique talents that God has entrusted to us. Our work is to be done heartily, unto the Lord (Col. 3:23–24), because in serving others, we're ultimately serving God. As Gustav Wingren said, "God does not need our good works, but our neighbor does."[1] In fact, our work-related activities not only help others, but they also help us in the sense that work (gen-erally) allows us to put food on our table, a roof over our head, and clothes on our back—lest we become a burden to others (see 2 Thess. 3:6–12). Far from being a necessary evil, work is a necessary good.[2]

Okay, but how does our work relate to the advance of the gospel? If I work hard as a teacher, banker, plumber, or whatever, at the end of the day my col-leagues and customers still need Jesus, right? Yes. But our work advances the rule and reign of Christ in at least three ways: It provides evidence for the gospel, wins an audience for the gospel, and adorns the gospel. Let's take these in order.

Our Work Provides Evidence for the Gospel

Ephesians 2:8–9 is a well-known passage, reminding us that our salvation is by grace through faith apart from our works. Less well-known is the following verse: "For we are [God's] workmanship, created in Christ Jesus for good works, which God prepared beforehand, that we should walk in them" (v. 10 NKJV). While we aren't saved by our good works, we are saved for good works. Our employment is to be a theater in which we give ourselves to good works. The way we do our jobs should give evidence to the world that the gospel is transforming us from being self-centered to being God- and others-centered.

We have to be careful here: It's possible to be an excellent employee and be pervasively self-centered. That's obviously not what we're after. We come at it the other way: Because the Holy Spirit is transforming us into being increas-ingly God- and others-centered, we will invariably (as a by-product) become better employees in whatever our vocation may be. Why? Because the grace of God teaches us to work heartily unto the Lord (Col. 3:23), to be industrious (Eph. 4:28), and "eager to do what is good" (Titus 2:14).

---

1. Wingren, *Luther on Vocation*, trans. Carl C. Rasmussen (Eugene, OR: Wipf and Stock, 1991), 10.
2. D. G. Hart, "Work as (Spiritual) Discipline," *Modern Reformation* (July/August 2002): 33–35.

Others may exceed us in skill or commitment. After all, the gospel doesn't just make us better workers, but also better spouses, parents, and citizens. So our professional commitments will be tempered by our personal commitments. We don't idolize our jobs, even if our boss or coworkers do. Still, our good works—on and off the job—will give evidence that we've experienced God's grace.

I'm reminded of a scene in the great World War II film *To End All Wars*. Japanese guards catch a group of Allied POWs with Bibles. The guards are furious and threaten to confiscate the Bibles. An allied POW pleads with the Japanese to let the POWs keep them. His line of reasoning is that "this book makes us better slaves to your emperor." That's exactly right: Christianity makes us better slaves, and (by extension) better employees. And being better employees wins an audience for the gospel.

Our Work Wins an Audience for the Gospel

There's truth in the oft-quoted phrase, "Nobody cares what you know until they know that you care." We learn best, and are influenced more, in the context of a personal relationship. That's probably more applicable today than in previous times for two reasons. One, ours is a day of information overload. We get our information from sources that have earned our trust. We block out the millions of other voices. Two, the default belief on the part of most non-Christians is that whatever you believe, at best, is true for you but nonbinding for them. So how do we win an audience for the gospel in this crowded, postmodern milieu?

We spend a large portion of our waking hours in the workplace. The way we do our jobs, and the attitude and demeanor we display to colleagues in the workplace, will either win us the right to be heard on matters of faith—or lose it. The quality of Esther's and Mordecai's lives gave them extraordinary influence with King Ahasuerus. In 1 Peter 3:1–2 wives are told that their unbelieving husbands can be "won over without words by the behavior of their wives, when they see the purity and reverence of your lives." Similarly, if our coworkers and customers see that our lives are characterized by integrity, compassion, and genuine tolerance toward the irreligious and nonreligious, it buys us the moral voice to give a reason for the hope that is in us (1 Peter 3:15)—and be heard.

Our Work Adorns the Gospel

When others do not yet know we're Christians, our work can win an audience—or prepare the way—for the gospel. When people do know we're Christians, our work, done well, adorns the gospel (see Titus 2:10). Adornments beautify.

We adorn Christmas trees because that makes them nicer to look at. If our work is done well, and heartily—with a cheerful attitude—it makes the gospel look more beautiful.

To be clear: Our work cannot make the gospel more beautiful. It doesn't add to the gospel. The gospel is the good news that God has accomplished salvation for sinners by sending his Son Jesus to live a perfect life and to be a perfect sin-bearing substitute, dying to accomplish salvation for everyone who believes and calls upon his name (see John 3:16; Rom. 6:23; 10:13). This is the best news on planet Earth, and our works cannot possibly make it any better.

Our work can, however, make this good news seem sweeter to other people. If we do our work with diligence, punctuality, professionalism, and integrity, and others know we're Christians, it makes it easier for them to believe in Jesus. If we're sloppy and inattentive to our work, it makes it harder for them to believe in Jesus. The quality of the gospel is not at stake. Its attractiveness is.

Dr. Alex Chediak (PhD, UC Berkeley) is a professor at California Baptist University. He's the author of *Thriving at College*, a roadmap for how students can best navigate their college years. He's also written *Beating the College Debt Trap*.

WORK AS FULFILLMENT OF THE CREATION MANDATE

Jeremy Treat

I f a person went to church every Sunday from the age of twenty-five to sixty-five, he or she would spend around 3,000 hours gathered with the body of Christ. If the same person worked full time during that span, they would put in around 80,000 work hours. The point is simple: the workplace, not the sanctuary, is the primary place where most Christians will live out their faith.

How, then, does faith inform work? For many, Christ's influence is relegated to the pew and doesn't extend into other compartments of life, such as work. For others, the way to apply faith to work is simply to share the gospel in the office or make loads of money that can be given to ministry and missions. According to this view, God cares about someone's work only if it is used for explicitly evangelistic purposes.

The Scriptures, however, paint a different portrait of work and its place in the life of God's people. Learning and embodying the biblical vision for work will require three key shifts from the typical view of work.

Shift 1: From Occupation to Vocation

An occupation takes up time. A career is a way to build a personal kingdom. A job can make money. A vocation, however, is a calling from God (the word "vocation" comes from the Latin *vocare*, which means "to call"). That's what work is, a calling from God to use your gifts and talents to serve others and glorify God. Many assume that a "calling" to work is reserved for only pastors and missionaries—those called to "the Lord's work." In Scripture, however, God calls people to a variety of types of work, including what are often considered secular jobs. When God wanted to bring Jerusalem from ruin to restoration, he called not only Ezra the priest but also Nehemiah the urban planner and Zerubbabel the politician.

Humanity is called to work because we were created to work. In Genesis 1, God tells Adam and Eve to "be fruitful and increase in number; fill the earth and subdue it. Rule over . . ." (Gen. 1:28). This creation mandate is about more than making babies—it's a command to make a culture. The earth was created good, but it was not complete; it had potential built into it. The commands to "subdue" and "rule over" are not calls to coercive oppression but rather to responsible stewardship. God has entrusted his image-bearers with the responsibility of cultivating and caring for his good creation.

In Genesis 2 the creation mandate is further clarified through a practical example: gardening. God places Adam in the garden, and rather than giving him a hammock, he gives him a job description: "work it and take care of" the garden (Gen. 2:15). Take note: work is a part of God's good design for creation; it is not a result of the fall. God is asking Adam to take the raw materials of the earth (dirt, seed, and water) and cultivate them for the good of creation. Gardening in this case is a prototype for all work. Electricians take the raw material of electricity and work it in such a way that it is a blessing to others. Musicians take the raw material of sound and bring order from chaos to offer something that is pleasing to God and beneficial to others. Writers take the raw materials of words and craft them in a way that brings more sense and beauty to life.[1]

Unfortunately, many Christians today think work has only instrumental value, meaning that work matters to God if it is used as an instrument for spiritual purposes such as evangelism or mission. But if work is a calling from God to cultivate and care for his creation, then all forms of work have intrinsic value (unless, of course, they violate God's moral commands). A woodworker who makes kitchen tables can trust that his work is glorifying to God because it offers a service that helps society flourish. He doesn't have to share the gospel with coworkers or customers (although evangelism is great too), nor does he have to inscribe Bible verses on the side of the table. In making tables, he is fulfilling his calling to use his gifts to develop God's creation for the good of others. The same could be said of teachers, business people, nurses, artists, and so on. The value of nonchurch work can be seen clearly throughout Scripture. Joseph worked in government. Boaz was a businessman. Lydia sold fine linens. God cares about it all.

⚙ Shift 2: From Personal Gain to the Common Good

Humanity is created to work and called to work, but because of sin, there are thorns in our vocational gardens that make it difficult to bear fruit (Gen. 3:17–18).

---

1. I am drawing here from the excellent work of Timothy Keller, *Every Good Endeavor: Connecting Your Work to God's Work* (New York: Penguin, 2012), 47.

In a fallen world, work is often used not to honor God and serve others but as a way to use others and make a name for ourselves.

There is good news! God's grace in Christ not only removes sin; it also restores God's design for creation, including the role of work. This gives a gospel perspective on work, which is different from just talking about the gospel at work. The good news of Jesus shapes our work not by momentarily looking *at* the gospel, but by always looking *through* the gospel.

The gospel frees us from trying to prove or define ourselves through work. If we are justified by grace alone through faith alone in Christ alone, then we work not for the approval of others but from the approval of God. This is difficult in an accomplishment-driven society, where we are defined by our achievements and constantly asked the question: "What do you do?" For those who are "in Christ," our identity is not based on our performance, but on God's grace. When work no longer bears the burden of the way I build my identity or prove my worth, then work can be received as the gift it was intended to be. The gospel frees work from the shackles of selfish ambition and sets it on the path of seeking the flourishing of our cities.

"The essential modern heresy," said Dorothy Sayers, "is that work is not the expression of man's creative energy in the service of Society, but only something one does in order to obtain money and leisure."[2] In fact, work is one of the primary ways one will love one's neighbor, both personally (in interaction with coworkers) and societally (in the way a company contributes to society). The goal of work is not merely profit, fame, or satisfaction. Work is not meant for your own personal advancement, but for the good of others and the flourishing of society.

⊗ Shift 3: From a Narrow to a Holistic View of God's Work

Many people think of God's work in the world only in terms of spiritual salvation. The story of Scripture, however, is not one of God plucking souls from a fallen creation, but God saving people as a part of his renewal of creation. God is constantly at work in sustaining and renewing the world. He does most of his work through us, and often he works through our work.

Psalm 136:25, for example, says God "gives food to every creature." But how does he feed them? God doesn't usually just snap his fingers and make food appear on a plate. Rather, he feeds people through the farmer, the truck driver, the grocer, the cook, and the server. As Martin Luther says, "God could easily give you grain

---

2. Dorothy Sayers, "Creed or Chaos?," in *Creed or Chaos?* (New York: Harcourt Brace, 1949), 43.

and fruit without your plowing and planting, but he does not want to do so."[3]
God is milking the cow through the vocation of the milkmaid, as Luther argued.

According to Amy Sherman, there are a variety of ways that God is at work
in the world, and the myriad of human vocations give expression to the different
aspects of God's work.[4]

Redemptive Work: God's Saving and Reconciling Actions

Pastors

Counselors

Peacemakers

Creative Work: God's Fashioning of the Physical and Human World

Musicians

Poets

Painters

Architects

Interior designers

Providential Work: God's Provision for and Sustaining of Humans and the Creation

Mechanics

Plumbers

Firefighters

Justice Work: God's Maintenance of Justice

Judges

Lawyers

Law enforcement

Compassionate Work: God's Involvement in Comforting, Healing, Guiding, and Shepherding

Doctors

Nurses

Paramedics

Psychologists

Social workers

---

3. Martin Luther, *LW*, 14:114.

4. Amy L. Sherman, *Kingdom Calling: Vocational Stewardship for the Common Good* (Downers Grove, IL: IVP, 2011), 103–4.

Revelatory Work: God's Work to Enlighten with Truth
    Educators
    Scientists
    Journalists

How might one discover their specific calling within God's holistic work? A good place to start is by pondering the words of Frederick Buechner: "The place God calls you to is the place where your deep gladness and the world's deep hunger meet."[5] Whatever you do, whether a bishop or barista, do it for the glory of God (Col. 3:23).

As a practical tip, remember: "Christian" is a better noun than it is adjective. There is no such thing as "Christian coffee," even if it's served in a café called "Grounded in Christ" or "Bean Redeemed." There are Christians, and some of them make good coffee and some make terrible coffee. The same is true for filmmakers, musicians, nurses, dentists, and so on. If you have put your faith in Christ, you are a Christian, and you are called to be a good steward of whatever the Lord has entrusted to you vocationally, whether a coffee bean or an electric guitar.

God cares about it all. He is sustaining and saving his creation. When work is understood within this story, people will want to be lawyers because they care about justice (not social status), doctors because they care about health (not wealth), business men and women because they care about people (not profit), and artists because they value beauty (not celebrity). The biblical view of vocation will not only bring meaning to our jobs in this lifetime, but it will shape our eternity as we use our gifts and talents to glorify God and serve others in the New Jerusalem forever.

Jeremy Treat (PhD, Wheaton College) is pastor for preaching and vision at Reality LA in Los Angeles and adjunct professor of theology at Biola University. He is the author of *The Crucified King: Atonement and Kingdom in Biblical and Systematic Theology* and *Seek First: How the Kingdom of God Changes Everything.*

---

5. Frederick Buechner, *Wishful Thinking: A Theological ABC* (New York: Harper & Row, 1973), 95.

THE CALL TO STEWARDSHIP

The Bible and Economics

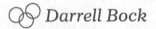 *Darrell Bock*

Money as a resource is an important part of human life. The famous song in *Cabaret* says it rather baldly with its lyric that "money makes the world go around." The use and abuse of money is a major topic of Scripture, and it is all too easy to discuss the topic by making money all good or bad. In fact, like any resource, money can be used well or poorly. It is something to steward. Scripture sees one with resources as possessing a blessed potential source of strength (Prov. 10:15). It also decries the love of money as the root of all sorts of evil (1 Tim. 6:10). So balance is needed in thinking through how money and stewardship go together. As the text suggests, the issue is not the resource, but how we handle and view it.

The Individual and Money

The personal freedom to accumulate wealth is an important concern. Biblical values address both our freedom to accumulate wealth and our obligation to help others.

Wealth properly used is seen as a blessing. Ecclesiastes 5:19 says, "When God gives someone wealth and possessions, and the ability to enjoy them, to accept their lot and be happy in their toil—this is a gift of God."

Proper use of wealth includes the need to provide for one's family—food, shelter, clothing. Other issues tied to human well-being and respect for people made in God's image include health care and other core needs of life—which in the modern world might include education to further equip oneself to contribute to society. This is part and parcel of stewarding the earth well (Gen. 1:26–28). The goal is that we not be a drain on society, but that we do our part in serving our community (2 Thess. 3:8). Society has a responsibility to help people become so equipped.

Wealth and wisdom combined serve society and contribute to its well-being—often through creatively providing services that help others function more efficiently in their lives.

Biblical passages like the ones cited above led many to define the Protestant work ethic as a hard day's work for a solid wage.[1] As we see from these biblical texts, the pursuit of riches is not a bad thing, but is tied to the pursuit of labor that serves others and manages creation well. Resources are a blessing when they are used well and when they are used to benefit our families and others in our society.

Yet Scripture also warns about the risks of wealth and its need to be managed. First, riches can all too easily produce a false sense of confidence and security. Proverbs 11:28 says, "Those who trust in their riches will fall, but the righteous will thrive like a green leaf." Another danger of wealth is that it can produce a dangerous kind of self-indulgence. Proverbs 21:17 notes, "Whoever loves pleasure will become poor; whoever loves wine and olive oil will never be rich." Further, wealth is sometimes gained by taking advantage of others. Proverbs 22:16 observes, "One who oppresses the poor to increase his wealth and one who gives gifts to the rich—both come to poverty." This passage condemns not wealth itself but wealth gained by evil means. Both oppressing the poor and cowering to the rich lead to poverty.

The prophets too warn against gaining wealth at the expense of others. One such text is Jeremiah 5:27: "Like cages full of birds, their houses are full of deceit; they have become rich and powerful."

Jesus also discussed the topic. In Luke 12:15–21, Jesus tells a parable about a rich farmer who, when his crops increased even more, did not consider, and deliberately avoided, giving to others—even building bigger barns to contain all his crops. But because he kept all for himself, God took away his life. The man's riches led to a sense of self-sufficiency that drove him away from God. Jesus was calling that sin an affront to God.

♾ Corporate Economics

Reflection on wealth and poverty has a rich legacy, extending back to before the Reformation.[2] Yet there is little in Scripture or writing from the premodern church that directly addresses corporate economics. This is because most ancient monetary life was built around agriculture, fishing, or skilled labor. Capital

---

1. This phrase "Protestant work ethic" was first discussed by Max Weber, *The Protestant Ethic and the Spirit of Capitalism*, trans. Talcott Parsons (Germany, 1905; repr., London: Unwin Hyman, 1930).
2. James Halteman and Edd Noell, *Reckoning with Markets: Moral Reflections in Economics* (Oxford: Oxford University Press, 2012), especially chs. 2 and 3.

development was minimal, as technological innovation was sporadic at best. Service industries were mostly subsumed under forms of slavery and did not contribute to a developing economy. An economy based on expansion and sharing of resources was nearly impossible in this structure. Such an economy depended on significant technological advances which didn't emerge until the medieval period and then intensified with the Industrial Revolution. These advances and their impact continue today and make for many economic possibilities.

The most important discussion about large businesses concerns how we relate to each other as people.[3] On the one hand, large businesses often depersonalize individuals in the pursuit of profit. And those who are the most responsible for personal injustice can hide behind managerial layers or the size of the operation, not to mention how sheer logistics can complicate effective, humane service. Yet, on the other hand, an effective economic system or business can provide society with several benefits.[4]

Christian Values and Economic Reflection

In moral reflection, we are not called to embrace a single macro principle such as one that says business is good or business is bad. This is an oversimplification that serves no one well. We must instead consider the kind of society that businesses build. Character matters and so does motive. Seeking profit and managing resources well are the responsibility of all who manage a business, just as allowing for a healthy, growing economy is a concern for all who govern a nation.

These discussions are complex because they involve answers at a large national or international macro level as well as in localized forms with cities or families. When we discuss capitalism, it is important to note that there are many kinds of capitalism, from highly state guided to highly entrepreneurial mostly free of regulation, plus other variations. We must be careful not to generalize when speaking about capitalism, or socialism, or a "mixed economy" such as a welfare state. What type of economy are we considering? What country provides the model economy? Is it the United States, the United Kingdom, Germany, Sweden, Japan, China, Russia, or another country? There is a spectrum, not just one model or one "pure" model. As in many of the areas we are discussing, buzzwords and sound bites alone do not help us much. Much of our political discourse

---

3. Edd Noell, Stephen Smith, and Bruce Webb, *Economic Growth: Unleashing the Potential of Human Flourishing* (Washington, DC; AEI, 2013).

4. Kenman L. Wong and Scott B. Rae, *Business for the Common Good: A Christian Vision of the Marketplace* (Downers Grove, IL: InterVarsity Press Academic, 2011), 117–22; Jeff Van Duzer, *Why Business Matters to God (And What Still Needs to Be Fixed)* (Downers Grove, IL: InterVarsity Press, 2010).

bypasses such nuances and helps no one. Reasoned discussion is what we need, not class warfare.[5]

Scriptural values about the poor, human flourishing, and concerns of justice for all humanity should guide us in our corporate economics. There needs to be a balance between upholding individual rights, generating an economy that works for the most, and taking responsibility to care well for our neighbor for those who can.

Political discussions about welfare and government aid of all kinds can be well informed by Scripture, even if the language is different. The themes of justice and love undeniably tell us to care about the poor. That care operates in two ways: meeting core needs for food, shelter, and clothing, as well as building responsibility in people so they are better able to care for themselves. This is just another tension of life in a fallen world that must be kept in balance.

In sensitively dealing with the poor, we need to exercise wisdom regarding the level of help needed to truly help. In a fascinating book, *When Helping Hurts: How to Alleviate Poverty without Hurting the Poor*, Steve Corbett and Brian Fikkert discuss engaging poverty in ways that provide real opportunity for the poor to move beyond their need.[6] In it they observe three levels of help for the poor.

The first is called *relief*. This is simply responding to disaster or giving aid that meets the short-term, immediate need. It is what they call an effort "to stop the bleeding."

The second level is *rehabilitation*, which seeks to restore people to a functional level. It teaches the person being aided how to help with their own recovery. Those being helped begin to exercise more agency in their own recovery. It is here where education or skill training comes in, as well as providing support so that those efforts can be pursued.

The final and more encompassing level is *development*. Here the goal is empowering people to care for themselves, so the distinction between "helpers" and "helped" is minimized because everyone is contributing to the full. This means enabling individuals to carry out the creation mandate of Genesis 1:26–28 to subdue the earth and be a responsible, disciplined, and caring steward of its resources. It is here that education and affordable care fit, for unless people are equipped to contribute to the world and are healthy enough to do so, their ability to help in the operation and management of our world becomes more difficult.

5. Kathryn Blanchard, *The Protestant Ethic or the Spirit of Capitalism: Christians, Freedom, and Free Markets* (Eugene, OR: Cascade, 2010), 218.
6. Steve Corbett and Brian Fikkert, *When Helping Hurts: How to Alleviate Poverty without Hurting the Poor* (Chicago: Moody Press, 2009).

As Corbett and Fikkert develop these levels of involvement, they go on to say, "One of the biggest mistakes that North American churches make—by far—is in applying relief in situations in which rehabilitation or development is the appropriate intervention."[7] People are denied agency in their own lives because an exclusive focus on relief-oriented methods of "helping" them keeps them helpless.

It does not take much to see that the two levels of help most needed for long-term help—rehabilitation and development—cannot be the responsibility of any single social entity.

But justice in regards to the poor cuts two ways: Those who have riches are called to be generous and compassionate in being a good neighbor. But those who are poor should not steal or be envious of what others have legitimately gained. We are all responsible to do what we can to change our situation. The danger of a society that cultivates a sense of entitlement is that it can lead to an unhealthy dependence on others for what one should and can provide for oneself. Rather than being merely passive recipients, we all should step up and take advantage of the opportunities that rehabilitation and development provide.

As on all difficult issues, we are in serious need of meaningful, balanced discussions about how society should help and how those in need should contribute to that help. We need to be especially sensitive to how opportunity to contribute can be blocked by how our society functions. If we'll try to take stands that reflect the heart of Jesus, we'll avoid cherry-picking arguments that bolster our own side, and consider what conforms to biblical principles. We can work to achieve a better balance and steward our world more effectively. Justice, mercy, giving, compassion, and responsibility can coexist.

Darrell Bock (PhD, University of Aberdeen) is the executive director for cultural engagement at the Hendricks Center and senior research professor of New Testament Studies at Dallas Theological Seminary. He is the author or editor of more than forty books, host of the Table podcast, and former president of the Evangelical Theological Society.

7. Ibid., 100.

CHRISTIANITY NEEDS A GLOBAL ECONOMIC PERSPECTIVE

✇ Matthew Loftus

The question of Christian cultural engagement and global economics is, quite frankly, overwhelming. There are so many different forces shaping our world and many of them are so large that most people feel more comfortable not thinking about the subject at all. Yet many Christians in developed nations are influencing the economies of other nations by what they buy, who they vote for, and how they give to various organizations. Christians in the West who have been blessed with much must learn how to steward the money that God has given us so that we don't harm others, especially our brothers and sisters around the world.

There has been trade between different nations as long as there have been different nations in contact with each other, but recent history has seen rapid developments in communications and transportation that allow information and goods to spread rapidly all over the world. This process is known as *globalization*. A farmer in rural Kenya can use his cell phone (made in China out of materials extracted from the Democratic Republic of the Congo) to video chat with his nephew studying in Canada. The nephew can then electronically send his uncle money that pays for the fuel extracted from Saudi Arabia that powers the truck made in Japan that takes the farmer's flowers to the capital city of Nairobi. The flowers are flown to a market in France, where a Brazilian tourist takes a selfie with the flowers that they send to their friends back home in South America.

Globalization has both positive and negative effects. Trucks, trains, and planes moving goods freely have given many more people opportunities to work for more than just sustenance, but it also allows wealth to be concentrated in the hands of a few people while putting other people out of work. This is particularly challenging in more developed economies, where low-skilled labor is either outsourced to other countries where wages are lower or taken over by robots. Developed countries, in turn, can subsidize their own products and then dump them on the international market, undercutting countries trying to compete. Communications technology now allows the gospel to reach nations hostile to missionaries via satellite, but it also permits false teaching and pornography to spread to anywhere there is a cell phone. The first step in stewarding our resources well in a globalized world is learning about how the global economy shapes the lives and vocations of others.

The process of development itself is a matter of stewardship. Different nations choose different priorities in developing their economies based on their resources and interests, but the sinful inclinations of human beings often make "development" an uneven and unseemly process. Many people who are rich try to hoard as much wealth as possible and consume luxuries rather than ensuring all have the necessities of life, sometimes through abject corruption. When it comes to cultural development, people hungry for that which is popular in the West will feel pressured to abandon what is good in their own culture for the graphic obscenity, the Prosperity Gospel, or atheism-soaked education being peddled by neocolonial overlords.

This immediately leads to a set of dilemmas about how we choose to spend our money. The goods we want are almost always cheaper when they've been produced by people who don't have the power to demand better wages or safe working conditions. In some cases, outright slavery and violence are used to extract particular resources or produce certain products, while the profits go to terrorist organizations or brutal militias. In some cases, it is very difficult to know how a particular material or product has been sourced.

Even when we know how a product got to us and there was no outright violence involved in its production, there is still debate about whether it is ethical to spend our money on it. Is it right to buy a shirt made by a laborer who works long hours in brutal conditions, but is still able to use their very small wage to send their children to school? Is it worth it to buy blueberries in December that have been flown in from another country? Is it good to support a company that tries to skirt requirements to pay benefits for its workers by reducing their hours?

There aren't easy answers to these questions. It is clear from the Bible, though, that God hears the cries of laborers who have been denied a fair wage (James 5:1–6) and does not accept the worship of those who oppress their workers (Isa. 58:1–4). Christian teaching throughout the ages has reinforced and expounded upon these ideas, such as in the great papal encyclical *Rerum Novarum*, published in 1891 as many of these questions were coming to the forefront of religious and social thought. In that encyclical, Pope Leo XIII says:

Let the working man and the employer make free agreements, and in particular let them agree freely as to the wages; nevertheless, there underlies
a dictate of natural justice more imperious and ancient than any bargain
between man and man, namely, that wages ought not to be insufficient
to support a frugal and well-behaved wage-earner. If through necessity
or fear of a worse evil the workman accept harder conditions because an
employer or contractor will afford him no better, he is made the victim of
force and injustice.[1]

God's commandment to obey the Sabbath also enjoins us to allow the people
who labor on our behalf to rest as well, so we ought to consider whether the
money we are spending is going to unjust employers who compel their employees
to violate this commandment. Consumers also have the power to advocate for
workers anywhere in the world in addition to refusing to buy products that they
feel are unethically produced. Just as we would not want to invest our money in
studios making hardcore pornography or have our taxes pay for a new abortion
clinic, we should strive (however imperfectly) to use our money in ways that help
other people labor in just vocations.

A different set of questions attends to our charitable giving. Many people in
developed countries, recognizing the need to help the poor in other places, give
generously to various organizations providing food, health care, or education.
Christians also spend billions of dollars every year to support missionaries and
indigenous workers spreading the gospel. This generosity has helped to communicate the gospel of Jesus Christ in word and deed around the world, fueling
incredible decreases in deaths from preventable disease around the world and
giving millions of people the opportunity to hear about Jesus.

However, good intentions are never enough to truly help. Donating clothes,
for example, often undercuts nascent textile markets in developing countries.[2]
An idea that may seem appealing to Western donors may in fact be an unwanted
"white elephant" in the community on the receiving end of that idea. Giving
money without ever inquiring into how it is spent can encourage fraud or perpetuate harmful practices.

One common example is the problem of orphanages. Most developed countries have eliminated orphanages because we recognize the inherent harms that
children may experience as a result of growing up in an orphanage, yet we are

---

1. Pope Leo XIII, "On Capital and Labor: *Rerum Novarum*" (Vatican: the Holy See. Rome, May 15, 1891).
2. Natalie L. Hoang, "Clothes Minded: An Analysis of the Effects of Donating Secondhand Clothing to Sub-Saharan Africa" (2015), Scripps Senior Theses, Paper 671, http://scholarship.claremont.edu/scripps_theses/671.

happy to give generously to international ministries that focus their attention on a handful of children. Many of these so-called "orphans" still have living parents, who may have abandoned their children at the orphanage in the hopes that they would get an education. In some cases, children may even have been kidnapped and sold to these orphanages.

In many places where Western-sponsored orphanages thrive, traditionally children who have lost one or both parents will be taken in by other relatives. It's unfair to extract these children from these support networks and their local communities, leaving behind other children who are often just as poor. That's why child sponsorship—which usually distributes benefits throughout a community and has been shown to increase the likelihood that the children sponsored will be employed[3]—is often a much better model, as are programs that try to support families in a community who have taken in orphans.

Our contemporary global economy is both complex and pervasive, giving us more power than ever before to bless others but also many ways to unsuspectingly cause harm. If we are going to enjoy the benefits of instant communication and accessible-everywhere goods, it is incumbent upon us to steward our power and wealth well. We can do this by researching supply chains, asking hard questions of the ministries we support, and advocating for a just and good economy that reflects the Bible's concern for vulnerable people and their labor.

Matthew Loftus serves as a family physician in Litein, Kenya, and is a faculty member for the Kabarak University Family Medicine Residency based in Nakuru, Kenya. He sees patients and helps to teach and supervise students and interns participating in medical training programs.

3. Bruce Wydick, et. al, "Does International Child Sponsorship Work? A Six-Country Study of Impacts on Adult Life Outcomes," *Journal of Political Economy* 121, no. 2 (2013): 393–436.

RHYTHMS OF WORK AND REST

∞ *Kayla Snow*

Genesis 2 begins with the picture of the almighty, unchanging Creator of the universe resting. From this moment in Scripture, God reveals a significant part of his plan for humankind: he shows us that life given and ordered in and through him follows the eternal rhythm of work and rest, or Sabbath. The Jewish people have, throughout history, understood and observed the rhythm of work and Sabbath with great reverence and fear. Christians, by contrast, have applied great effort to our work, but, by and large, have lost sight of the meaning, purpose, and practice of Sabbath rest. Thus, we have grown weary in our work and weary in our rest. We often work seven days a week, and, even when we rest, we do not fully enter into the rest that God shows us in Genesis 2. Yet, when we order our lives according to the rhythm of work and rest that God displays for us and gives to us, we enjoy more fully the abundance of the Christian life in the kingdom of God.

No small part of the Christian struggle with Sabbath rest arises from a misunderstanding of what Sabbath actually means for the believer. Sabbath, as we often understand it, finds its roots in Jewish teaching and tradition, and, more pointedly, Jewish law. Christians, though, have been released from the law through Christ, who fulfilled the law perfectly. When the law is removed from the Sabbath, what remains? To answer this question, we must look to the creation narrative because the Sabbath preceded the law as part of the created order.

Christians often miss the fact that the Sabbath itself is a created thing. Reflected in the creation narrative, we see God enjoying his work and delighting in its goodness. On the seventh day, God enters into a rest that is the culmination of his creation. He is not tired; he is delighted with the goodness of creation, and blesses the seventh day as a day for us to delight with him in the goodness of creation. According to Norman Wirzba, the Sabbath is "a celebration of, and sharing in, God's own experience of delight."[1] Jewish tradition affirms that the

---

1. Norman Wirzba, *Living the Sabbath: Discovering the Rhythms of Rest and Delight* (Grand Rapids: Brazos, 2006), 47.

seventh day was an act of creation, for it was the day that God created *menuha*, translated "rest."[2] Wirzba calls the creation of the Sabbath the "climax of creation."[3] In Wirzba's view, then, the creation of mankind is not the pinnacle of creation; rather, the rest found in our eternal fellowship with and delight in God is the pinnacle.

Rest without the law, though, becomes difficult—and even dangerous—to define. In her book *Keeping the Sabbath Wholly: Ceasing, Resting, Embracing, Fasting*, Marva Dawn often warns against prescribing a particular practice or timing for observing the Sabbath, noting that prescription quickly leads us back to legalism.[4] As a Christian raised in the American South, I often experienced a kind of Sunday legalism that, though often imposed with the best of intentions, actually reduced Sunday to a day of naps, television, and boredom. We set aside our work for the day, but I'm not so sure that we replaced our work with something worthy of the time. If the Sabbath is intrinsically good because God created it, then the rest offered through the Sabbath must reflect something about the nature of God, something that we can enjoy through Christ apart from the law.

The key to understanding Sabbath under the New Covenant is, of course, found in Christ, but we must first understand the *nature* of Sabbath rest as established in creation. As Jewish theologian Abraham Joshua Heschel explains, the *menuha* created on the seventh day is not a "negative concept but something real and intrinsically positive."[5] This distinction is important because it means that Sabbath is not simply about the things we cannot do; it's about the things we *should* do. Thus, we cannot enjoy Sabbath simply through abstinence, by giving up, by laying aside. Instead, Sabbath requires that we take up the very things that feed and nourish the soul. We partake of the Spirit on the Sabbath, who offers himself to us as the source of perfect rest.[6] Augustine famously writes, "Thou hast made us for Thee and our heart is unquiet till it finds rest in Thee."[7] Whatever forms of rest we enjoy in Sabbath should be rooted in Christ, without whom we find no true rest.

When our *rest* becomes about squandering time, mindless consumption, or sensuality, we do not actually enter into Sabbath rest, and our souls remain weary, tattered, and heavy, unready for the work that lies ahead. If the Sabbath is holy, which it is, then there is a sanctity to the purpose and practice of Sabbath that,

2. Abraham Joshua Heschel, *The Sabbath: Its Meaning for Modern Man* (Boston: Shambhala, 2003), 13.
3. Wirzba, *Living the Sabbath*, 47.
4. Marva J. Dawn, *Keeping the Sabbath Wholly: Ceasing, Resting, Embracing, Fasting* (Grand Rapids: Eerdmans, 1989).
5. Heschel, *The Sabbath*, 13.
6. Ibid., 7.
7. Augustine, *Confessions*, 4.

when lost, destroys its beauty and power. This sanctity is why the law was put into place. Abraham Joshua Heschel writes, "The Sabbath is not an occasion for diversion or frivolity [. . .] but an opportunity to mend our tattered lives; to collect rather than dissipate time."[8] The beauty of Heschel's words here should not be overlooked. Too often when we stop working, we waste time on activities that carry little to no eternal value. In fact, we often think that *rest* is equivalent to binge-watching our favorite show, trolling social media, or, my personal favorite, napping. None of these is intrinsically wrong. Yet none of them is truly satisfying to the soul either. In Heschel's view, time is holy; it's sacred. The sanctity of time that Heschel observes stems from the Jewish belief that God has, indeed, made the Sabbath—a day, a collection of time—a holy place wherein believers see eternity stretched out before them and are renewed by the Spirit as they dwell there. As Wirzba says, "Sabbath practice, on this view, is a sort of training ground for the life of eternity, a preparation for the full reception and welcome to the presence of God."[9] When we enjoy Sabbath here and now, we anticipate eternity.

This view of rest reframes the way we think about Sabbath in every aspect of our lives. Sabbath is not just about Sunday. Wirzba explains,

> That the Sabbath should assume such importance in the life of faith will likely sound strange to many of us because we have grown used to thinking of Sabbath observance as an add-on to the end of a busy week. Sabbath is the time for us to relax and let down our guard, to pause from the often anxious and competitive patterns of daily life. This is not what the Jews, those who first gave us the teaching about Sabbath, thought. In their view, Sabbath observance is what we work *toward*. As our most important and all-encompassing goal, it frames and contextualizes our planning, much as the desire to achieve a specific objective—a championship, a masterful performance, an exquisite meal or party—will require that we take the proper steps *all along the way*. Sabbath frames our entire life, helping us set priorities and determine which of our activities and aspirations bring honor to God.[10]

Sabbath rest, then, is not simply about escaping from or recharging for work. I am an athletic person—not an athlete in any professional sense, but a person who trains regularly and pushes my physical limits often. Recently, I've practiced High Intensity Interval Training, or HIIT, which—though a mild form of

---

8. Heschel, *The Sabbath*, 7.
9. Wirzba, *Living the Sabbath*, 31–32.
10. Ibid., 30.

torture—is incredibly effective for training the heart, boosting the metabolism, and building strength and stamina. HIIT programs are built on the basic principle that we work at maximum training capacity for short intervals and rest briefly in between each interval to restore ourselves so that we can push just as hard in the next training interval. In these training programs, the rest is as important as the work because the *rest* allows us to work at maximum capacity in each interval. We often think of Sabbath in this way, as a way to recharge physically and spiritually so that we can work at our optimum levels for the other days. Heschel combats this idea, saying, "To the biblical mind, however, labor is the means toward an end, and the Sabbath as a day of rest, as a day of abstaining from toil, is not for the purpose of recovering one's lost strength and becoming fit for the coming labor. The Sabbath is a day for the sake of life."[11] Thus, when we stop working on the Sabbath, we "cease not only from work itself, but also from the need to accomplish and be productive."[12] Sabbath rest is not about improving efficiency as if we are machines that simply need to be recharged for a few hours so they are ready to be used again. This is not how God sees us, and it is not why he has offered the blessing of Sabbath.

At its core, Sabbath is about enjoying a glimpse of eternity with our creator. That's the reality of Sabbath rest. It allows us to experience the rest that Christ offers when he says, "Come to me, all you who are weary and burdened, and I will give you rest. Take my yoke upon you and learn from me, for I am gentle and humble in heart, and you will find rest for your souls. For my yoke is easy and my burden is light" (Matt. 11:28–30). If our work is not about us, as Hugh Whelchel argues,[13] then our rest is, likewise, not about us; it points us to Christ and to his eternal work. Heschel writes,

> He who wants to enter the holiness of the day must first lay down the profanity of clattering commerce, of being yoked to toil [. . .] Six days a week we wrestle with the world, wringing profit from the earth; on the Sabbath we especially care for the seed of eternity planted in the soul.[14]

Thus, Heschel's claim is that the Sabbath allows us to cast off the "yoke of toil." As Christians, though, we know that we don't simply cast off a yoke of toil; we exchange it for the yoke of Christ.

11. Heschel, *The Sabbath*, 2.
12. Dawn, *Keeping the Sabbath*, 2.
13. Hugh Whelchel, *How Then Should We Work?: Rediscovering the Biblical Doctrine of Work* (McLean, VA: Institute for Faith, Work, and Economics, 2012).
14. Heschel, *The Sabbath*, 1.

Kayla Snow earned an MA in English from Liberty University. She currently teaches courses in research and writing and English literature for Liberty University. Her graduate research focuses largely on the influence of Christian thought and theology on the literary works of writers such as Jonathan Swift, G. K. Chesterton, J. R. R. Tolkien, and Flannery O'Connor. She has published the article "What Hath Hobbits to Do with Prophets: The Fantastic Reality of J. R. R. Tolkien and Flannery O'Connor," through *LOGOS: A Journal of Catholic Thought and Culture.*

DISCUSSION QUESTIONS

1. In his article, Loftus discusses the Sabbath and how we should not support employers who require their employees to work on Sundays. Treat, however, writes, "Work is not meant for your own personal advancement, but for the good of others and the flourishing of society." How might Treat or others approach supporting businesses that are open on Sundays?

2. One hidden danger of large businesses that Bock addresses in his article is that profits sometimes end up as more important than the people; however, Bock also speaks on the freedom to accrue money. How might one balance these two issues?

3. Treat discusses how work is a "primary way one will love one's neighbor." Seeking to understand this concept through the lens of Loftus's article on work, how might "loving one's neighbor through work" be affected by globalization?

4. Chediak argues that work advances the gospel as it "provides evidence for the gospel, wins an audience for the gospel, and adorns the gospel." In light of Loftus's discussion of globalization, would these mechanisms for advancing the gospel change or remain the same?"

5. In understanding the purpose of wealth, Bock states, "The goal is that we not be a drain on society, but that we do our part in serving our community." How would Bock's perspective, then, need to accommodate those who have no choice but to be a "drain" on society, such as the disabled, the ill, and young children?

6. Chediak discusses how work can adorn the gospel or make it seem "sweeter." He states that if we, as Christians, have good character and allow people to know we are Christians, then it may be easier for our coworkers and employers to believe in Christ. How would Chediak's position deal with the unfortunate truth that in many places, Christians in the workplace are known for being legalistic and judgmental, making the gospel actually much less "sweet"?

7. In understanding justice and love for the poor, Bock discusses the importance of "meeting core needs," which he defines as "food, shelter, and clothing." What about nonmaterial core needs, such as encouragement, compassion, and empowerment? How could the work of a Christian address these core needs alongside the material needs, bringing about both an audience for the gospel and the adornment of the gospel, as Chediak discusses?

8. In understanding Bock's three levels of helping the poor—relief, rehabilitation, and development—Bock clearly finds the level of development to be the most encompassing. In Treat's article, he cites Amy Sherman's varieties of vocations—redemptive, creative, providential, justice, compassionate, and revelatory work—in which some are more clearly related than others to the development level of helping the poor. How might Bock find "development" in each type of vocational work?

9. Loftus discusses the importance of stewarding power and wealth. In Chediak's article, he addresses how work advances the gospel in three main ways ("provides evidence for the gospel, wins an audience for the gospel, and adorns the gospel"). How could stewardship of power and wealth work to advance the gospel in the ways that Chediak mentions?

10. Snow stresses the importance of rest in relation to work. How has the church possibly imbibed our modern culture's work practices over the pattern of Genesis 2? How has this adversely impacted the church's witness?

chapter eleven

ARTS

The Bible, particularly the Old Testament, has much to say about the creative arts. The first human words recorded in the Bible are the poetry Eve inspired in Adam (Gen. 2:23). In the book of Exodus, we learn that God called a skilled artist to build the tabernacle that would hold the ark of the covenant. He also gave detailed instructions to Moses about the tabernacle's design and ornamentation. The detailed description of the artistic splendor of Solomon's temple in 1 Kings 6 affirms the importance of beauty and design. King David, author of many of the psalms, was a harpist and poet. Even the various literary genres represented in the various books of the Bible demonstrate that literary form is important, not just content. And, of course, we need only to consider the spectacular (and seemingly gratuitous) forms that fill the world the Creator made to see that God cares about artistry and beauty and manifests it in infinite varieties (Job 38–41).

The art of the early Christian era often celebrated tenets of the faith through symbols and types, even appropriating materials and myths from the surrounding pagan culture. In the Middle Ages, equipped with the power and resources of the Roman Empire, the medieval church created some of the most splendid and lasting art of all time in cathedrals and monasteries. This art was created from the labor of craftsmen and workers, funded and supported by the whole community, taking decades to build. Jacques Maritain explains,

> In the powerfully social structure of medieval civilization, the artist had only the rank of artisan, and every kind of anarchical development was forbidden his individualism, because a natural social discipline imposed on him from the outside certain limiting conditions. He did not work for the rich and fashionable and for the merchants, but for the faithful; it was his mission to house their prayers, to instruct their intelligences, to delight their souls and their eyes.[1]

---

1. Jacques Maritain, *Art and Scholasticism with Other Essays* (Minneapolis: Filiquarian, 2007), 24–25.

The relationship of the early Judeo-Christian tradition to the arts is surprisingly complex, even when that art is created or performed directly in service to or worship of God, what is called sacred or religious art. Think, for example, of stained glass windows in a church, the towering steeples of medieval cathedrals. Michelangelo's paintings in the Sistine Chapel, the Byzantine mosaics, Russian icons, or Leonardo daVinci's *The Last Supper*.

In ancient and medieval times, art of all kinds carried with it the sense of craft. All art was a work of skill and craftsmanship, and they all had a use. The laborer crafted tools for workers, the artisan made leather goods for clothing, and the painter or sculptor made works of beauty for the church and community.[2] But with the Renaissance and its return to the humanism of the ancient Greco-Roman world, art became increasingly separated from the community of faith and glorified the individual in both its subject matter and its creation. The question of the value of art for its own sake (what would come to be phrased toward the end of the nineteenth century as "art for art's sake") is a distinctly modern question. It was then that the division developed between "art" and "craft" and, correspondingly, high art and low art. As this division between the useful and the beautiful grew wider, Christians became increasingly suspicious of the merely beautiful.

The disregard, skepticism, and hostility found in pockets of the church today toward art for its own sake has a variety of roots, particularly within Protestantism. For example, Puritanism's iconoclasm (as well as that of Islam) is based on the second commandment's prohibition against graven images. The seventeenth-century Puritan Richard Baxter, for example, rejected reading literary works less on the merits of the activity itself than because he believed that time could be better spent reading Scripture and biblical commentary. Puritans also opposed the theater primarily on the basis of the prostitution and other illicit activities that often took place in the theater's vicinity and because the mockery of piety and religion was a staple of many dramas. This opposition to art that is based more on context and content than on form has continued throughout the centuries. Indeed, the central weakness in the engagement with art by the contemporary church is, arguably, in its tendency to emphasize content while overlooking form and the role of aesthetic experience as a crucial aspect of spiritual formation.[3]

---

2. For more on this history, see chapter 4 of Maritain's *Art and Scholasticism*.

3. Many recent works by Christians are working to overcome this failure. See, for example, James K. A. Smith's Cultural Liturgies Series; David Lyle Jeffrey, *In the Beauty of Holiness* (Grand Rapids: Eerdmans, 2017); Jeremy Begbie, ed., *Beholding the Glory* (Grand Rapids: Baker, 2000); William Dyrness, *Visual Faith* (Grand Rapids: Baker, 2001); W. David O. Taylor, *For the Beauty of the Church* (Grand Rapids: Baker, 2010); and Makoto Fujimura, *Culture Care*, 2nd ed. (Downers Grove, IL: IVP, 2017).

Some more recent Christian thinkers have examined the intrinsic value of art from a distinctly Christian worldview. One of the most notable among modern writers is Francis Schaeffer in his short treatise, *Art and the Bible*.[4] In arguing that art is good in and of itself, and that art is to be judged by both its form and its content, Schaeffer helped bring about a revival of interest and appreciation of the arts among evangelical Christians in the twentieth century and beyond.

In our opening essay in this section, Makoto Fujimura works to reframe the way contemporary Christians think about their role in culture, asking them to shift their view from *engaging* the culture to *making* culture by empowering Christian artists.

W. David O. Taylor's essay examines the nature of the triune God to illustrate the abundant nature by which artists can create in and through their faith. While the triune God forms the ultimate source and grounding for all our theologizing, the gospel of Jesus Christ is the ultimate self-revelation of God. Hence, Taylor's essay is complemented by Taylor Worley's application of the arc of the gospel narrative (Creation, Fall, Redemption, Restoration) to display what traits and virtues Christians should seek in art.

Jonathan Anderson's contribution reflects on John Cage's infamous *4'33"* to draw out a deeper understanding of art and the way that Christians should engage with them, concluding that believers have been made to offer and learn from contemporary arts.

In closing, Cap Stewart stands out in this section by offering a cautionary essay, seeking to raise our awareness of the potential dehumanizing impact of some art forms. In particular, he asks Christians to reevaluate their standards for consuming entertainment due to the rampant sexual objectification in the entertainment industry. Stewart urges Christians to love the entertainers as they love themselves and avoid consuming media that objectifies its actors and actresses.

---

4. Francis Schaeffer, *Art and the Bible* (Downers Grove, IL: InterVarsity Press, 2006).

CREATING FOR THE LOVE OF GOD

Cultural Engagement and Art?

◯ *Makoto Fujimura*

First, a thought about the word "engage."

Engage is a war word, or it is a word that may lead to nuptial vows as in "engage to be married."

So when we speak of "cultural engagement," it is often assumed that there are two parties warring, or two parties are getting "engaged" to be married. I am not sure if either definition describes the current malaise, and I am not sure that these intimations are what one desires in using this term. The church wants "cultural engagement" to mean battling against the years of neglecting to steward or care for culture. Thus "cultural engagement" sticks out like a sore thumb, perhaps as a result of trying to till a rocky, neglected soil.

The church's primary mission is to love with God's love. Love is generative, love is creative, love is imaginative, love makes.

Instead of engaging, we need to be making. Andy Crouch, in his book *Culture Making*, outlines this thesis very well. Similarly, James Davison Hunter, in his classic book *Culture Wars*, warned, before anyone else dared to, of the debilitating consequences of warring and creating polarities within cultures by this "engaging."[1]

I've noticed that in this "cultural engagement" model, churches are eager to create arts groups and "use" the arts for evangelism and discipleship. I've been asked to consult with churches excited to create such a program. The first advice I give: "Don't do it."

They are shocked. "But have you not been an advocate for artists in the church?"

Yes.

---

1. James Davison Hunter, *Culture Wars* (New York: Basic, 1991).

But segmenting artists into their own corner so they can share their woes is not the way I foresee transformation in culture taking place. We cannot "use" the arts any more than we can "use" a human being. As Lewis Hyde noted in his seminal book *The Gift*, art is a gift, not a commodity.[2] We can commoditize art, or at least make it "useful" to us, but we also need to realize that art and artist are in danger of losing their soul in doing so. As Hyde notes: "Works of art exist simultaneously in two 'economies,' a market economy and a gift economy. Only one of these is essential, however: a work of art can survive without the market, but where there is no gift there is no art."[3] Art in a transactional world loses her power; but art dwelling in the "gift economy" can liberate the culture. "Using" the arts for whatever instrumental purposes pulls art into the transactional realm of "bottom lines" and "programming." Instead, the arts speak of the mystery of existence, tell of the power of the ephemeral, describe the indescribable, and refuse to be categorized. Even a well-intended "target" of artist groups and "how to succeed" sessions can relegate artists to the "useful" segment of society.

Ironically and paradoxically, though, this ability of the artist to create something that society deems to be useless or inapplicable to industry is exactly what makes the arts so valuable, both as commodity and as social capital. The arts in this sense is gratuitous; but so is God's creation birthed out of God's love. God is self-sufficient, so God does not need us. So why did God create? God created because "God is love." Love makes, and it does so gratuitously, not out of need, but out of extravagance and passion. Therefore, that part of our lives that seems useless to our sense of utilitarian pragmatism is exactly the part that the Holy Spirit can speak through toward the new creation.

Instead, I say empower artists. Give attention to that "extra" that cannot be accounted for by either the market or the "need" of the church. Care for them as both beauty and mercy meets in the gospel. Commission them, have them be considered for an elder/vestry team—not so that they can help in pragmatic decisions, but in order to help us to envision, to "paint" the future together. Send them out as missionary/artists to various needy, desolate places that lack beauty, like Wall Street or hurricane ravaged Puerto Rico. Give your worship director a sabbatical to compose music. Encourage your musicians to compose music that everyone can sing (i.e., not worship music), even a non-Christian. Remove the instrumental, transactional part of the language and let art be a gift to the world.

What if artists are allowed to lead in the church, to ask "what if" generative questions?

2. Lewis Hyde, *The Gift: Creativity and the Artist in the Modern World* (New York: Vintage, 2009).
3. Ibid., 88.

What if artists are sent out, and what if they share what they learned by coming home and playing a concert, having an exhibit, or reading their writings?

What if artists journey together with patrons to discover together how to be a healing presence in the midst of chaos?

What if established artists journey together with emerging artists to cocreate into the future?

Philosopher Esther Meek states in *Loving to Know: Covenant Epistemology*, "If knowing is care at its core, caring leads to knowing. To know is to love; to love will be to know."[4] Care is the essence of creating community; care is at the heart of anything worth pursuing and at the heart of knowing. Care is at the heart of creativity and making; care is the source well of our "cautious engagement" with culture. Caring leads to prosperity and abundance.

The message of Jeremiah 29 took my family and me to spend fifteen years in New York City, ultimately leading to our children becoming "Ground Zero" children (we lived three blocks from the World Trade Center). This profound "cultural engagement" passage states:

> This is what the Lord Almighty, the God of Israel, says to all those I carried into exile from Jerusalem to Babylon: "Build houses and settle down; plant gardens and eat what they produce. Marry and have sons and daughters; find wives for your sons and give your daughters in marriage, so that they too may have sons and daughters. Increase in number there; do not decrease. Also, seek the peace and prosperity of the city to which I have carried you into exile. Pray to the LORD for it, because if it prospers, you too will prospe.r" (Jer. 29:4–7)

Several important facets of this prophetic counterintuitive voice led us into the city and its culture. First, it is God who brings us into exile, not our sins. Second, we are to not only "engage" the city, but we are to love the city, to settle down, and plant gardens. We are to keep our identity and calling as distinct realities of culture, but we are to pray for the city's and the culture's prosperity.

This is our map into the cultural journey. From this, I have been championing what I call "Culture Care," as opposed to fighting Culture Wars. Culture Care sees culture as an abundant ecosystem, or a garden to nurture. Rather than assume the "we versus them" mentality, we need to acknowledge that we all share the same ground to till. Even if we disagree with our fellow gardener, we can still work together to plant and pull weeds. In the occasional flare-ups of disagreements, such as what we should plant, or what we should pull, we can agree to disagree. Dandelions, after all, can either be part of a salad or a weed to be pulled. With enough understanding of why we are cultivating, or pulling, we may even change our minds.

But what haunts me the most about the Jeremiah edict is verse 7: "Pray to the LORD for it, because if it prospers, you too will prosper."

Have we been praying for our culture, or our city, to prosper? Or have we been fighting culture wars to deny the potential of that city and fight against her prosperity? Perhaps the reason our culture of Christ-followers has not been an abundant blessing is that we have not done well with this edict. We have not loved and sought the prosperity of the neighbors that we disagree with. What would happen now, if the Christ-followers became a radical center of generosity and began to bless our cities with beauty and mercy?

It's all about love. Love makes. It's also all about the soil of culture for the seeds of love to germinate. Let's start tilling, especially in the "winters" of our church communities. May our spring come. May God's prosperity bless even the "enemy" neighbors and strangers among us.

Makoto Fujimura, director of Fuller's Brehm Center, is a renowned artist, writer, and speaker. He founded the International Arts Movement in 1992 and established the Fujimura Institute in 2011. His book *Refractions: A Journey of Faith, Art, and Culture* is a collection of essays on culture, art, and humanity.

ART FOR FAITH'S SAKE

W. David O. Taylor

What does it mean to support art for faith's sake? Plenty of us might suppose that the answer is self-evident. But what exactly do we mean by "faith"? Do we mean an individual Christian's "faith" in God? Do we mean "the faith" as a euphemism for Christian doctrine? Do we mean a particular body of believers, as in "I'm part of the faith"?

I want to propose here that the meaning of "art for faith's sake" rests not chiefly in something that describes human beings. It rests instead on the object and ground of faith, the triune God. A proper support for the arts, I suggest, arises out of our knowledge of this kind of God, as Father, Son, and Holy Spirit, and out of our participation in the triune life.

What kind of God, then, is this? And how do the arts factor into the world that the Trinity has made possible? In this essay I wish to offer three (all-too-brief) observations about the God whom we confess as triune and relate them to the kind of art that we might say was done "for faith's sake."

God the Father: Maker of Heaven and Earth

The world that God has made is marked by hyperabundance. There is more in the cosmos than human beings need or could ever make good use of in multiple lifetimes. Birdsong, tuneful to the human ear, exceeds our need for aural pleasure. The flavor in our foods, from Chicken Korma to Krispy Kreme donuts, goes beyond what any individual deserves. Here there is excess: of light and texture, scent and sound. Here there is not just one kind of apple; here there are 7,500 cultivars of apple, from Aceymac to York Imperial.

In God's world there is *get to*, not just *have to*. Humans have to make clothes for protection against the elements. But they get to make cutwork lace and Panama hats. They have to build shelters. But they get to build basilicas and bivouacs. They have to do justice, love mercy, and walk humbly with God. But they get to do so in all sorts of ways, which are both useful and pleasing to the eye, as "The Aesthetics of Prosthetics" might demonstrate.[1] In God's world, humans get to play Pokémon and the grand piano. They get to put on plays. Like God, they get to imagine new things into being: sticky toffee pudding, Middle Earth, bronze thinkers, and virtual realities.

Because of the abundance that marks God's creation, as a sign of God's grace, humans are freed from an anxious need to feel only "useful." They get to wonder at things: why red is red, why appoggiaturas ("grace notes") affect us so acutely, why Gothic cathedrals evoke images of pyramidal peak mountains, and why, in humor, just the right punch line is everything. Humans get to explore toy stories and the perfect gesture for Princess Odette in Tchaikovsky's *Swan Lake*. Humans get to do so because it is God's everlasting pleasure to make such a world possible.

God the Son: The True Human

While it is only in Christ that we perceive the true image of humanity, it is also only in Christ that we see the extent of humanity's brokenness. In Christ's initiative, to become "flesh from our flesh," we discover both our acute need for redemption and the proper shape of our vocation: as the beloved of God, empowered by the Spirit, in Christ, to make things (like Narnian or Westerosi worlds) and to make sense of things in our world (as Maya Lin's Vietnam Veterans Memorial does).

As Jesus uses stories and parables to reveal the human condition, so artists use stories and parables to reveal humanity's glory (*Divine Comedy*) and its misery (*Crime and Punishment*), its quirkiness (Dr. Seuss) and its gravity (*M*A*S*H*). As Jesus makes the unknowable knowable, so artists make the unknowable in some sense knowable, as Christopher Nolan's movie *Interstellar* might do. As Jesus enables us to "sense" the goodness of God, so artists make the goodness of God sensible through sight (Tiffany glass), sound (*Looney Tunes*), taste (Paella), touch (Coppélia), and smell (Ikebana).

Eusebius of Caesarea once wrote that Jesus has three offices: prophet, priest, and king. It is through these offices, the fourth-century bishop argued, that Christ brings about the reconciliation of the world. If our human calling is "in Christ," then we too, in some fashion, will engage in prophetic, priestly, and kingly activities. Artists, under this light, will be in the business of bearing witness to that which is right and wrong, as Athol Fugard's play *"MASTER HAROLD"... and the Boys* does. Artists will offer the things of this world back

---

1. "The Aesthetics of Prosthetics: Aimee Mullins," YouTube, August 22, 2012, https://www.youtube.com/watch?v=CEdhSpaiRUI.

to God, as Frances Havergal's "Take My Life and Let It Be" might do. And they will make things, like silly limericks and surrealist comedies. They will do so for Christ's sake.

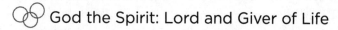 God the Spirit: Lord and Giver of Life

According to Scripture, the Holy Spirit animates the universe, breathing new life into all things. So too, in some sense, artists give life to things that seemed dead, as Andy Goldsworthy's art installations in nature might show, and breathe newness into things that have become old, as we see with The Saint John's Bible. As the Spirit illumines the things of God, so artists bring to light things that are hidden or in the darkness (Gabriel Orozco's "Sandstars" or Jeff Nichols's movie *Loving*). As the Spirit inverts, enabling the first to be last, so too artists create things that turn our worlds upside down, as Shakespeare's plays often do.

It is the Spirit who exposes the depths of the human condition. Artists also expose the depths of human grief, as the Congolese setting of the Latin Mass, Missa Luba's "Kyrie," does, while also drawing our attention to the sharpness of human joy, as we witness in Pete Docter's movie *Up*. As the Spirit improvises, so artists make the familiar strange (as with John Chamberlain's crushed car exhibits) and the strange familiar (as with Mary Doria Russell's novel *The Sparrow*). And as the Spirit unites the like and the unlike, so artists bring into relation things that might not have been expected or believed possible, such as the liturgical music of Aradhna that makes use of classical Indian musical forms.

And whatever goodness or beauty may come into the world through these works of art, it is only on account of the in-spiration of the Holy Spirit.

Conclusion

Faith in the triune God is not simply a transaction between human beings, on one side, and God, on the other. Faith is something we inhabit. More accurately, it is a Someone we inhabit—Christ himself. By the Spirit we inhabit the faithful life of the Son who presents all of creation, in love, to the Father. The Father, in turn, calls us by his Spirit to live out, here and now, in our own particular way, the life of his Son. Art for faith's sake, then, is art that has been oriented by the life of the Trinity. Such an orientation opens up an immense field of possibility, variety, style, and interest for the Christian in the arts.

With such a view of things, artists "of faith" will want to make art that, among other things, offers a foretaste of a world put to rights, marked no longer by an economy of scarcity, infected by sin, but by an economy of abundance, suffused by grace. And since no style or genre of art can exhaustively express all human interest, nor capture the mystery of God's world, it will require the whole body of Christ, over the whole course of human history, to make tangible the shalom of God through the art that it produces. Even then, of course, a whole eternity will be required to give the Godhead all the glory due its triune name.

W. David O. Taylor (ThD, Duke Divinity School) is assistant professor of theology and culture at Fuller Theological Seminary. He is the author of *The Theater of God's Glory* and *Glimpses of the New Creation*. An Anglican priest, he has lectured widely on the arts, from Thailand to South Africa. He lives in Austin with his family.

ENCOUNTERING GOD'S STORY WITH THE ARTS

◯◯ *Taylor Worley*

What makes for a truly significant encounter with art? In a lesser known and more technical work, C. S. Lewis explains the basic challenge this way: "We sit down before the picture in order to have something done to us, not that we may do things with it. The first demand any work of any art makes upon us is surrender. Look. Listen. Receive. Get yourself out of the way."[1] In other words, the place of artistic encounter must be a space of imaginative and emotional vulnerability. We must be ready to pause and wait patiently for whatever the artwork gives us and wherever the artwork takes us. Such openness and generosity of spirit is not a given. Some of us will, no doubt, find this frustrating or difficult. Many art forms require sustained and careful attention, which seems increasingly hard to come by in our media-saturated age. Christians, however, do not come to this place empty-handed. In what follows, we will explore four aspects of the biblical story (i.e., Creation, Fall, Redemption, and Restoration) and how they provide specific theological resources for engaging the arts. In particular, the Christian gospel commends to us the beautiful, prophetic, hospitable, and imaginative in art.

Before exploring these values, a crucial note must be given. Just as much as prior generations, we are consumed with the question: "What is art?" Some accounts assume or take for granted their definition of art. Here, philosophers studying the arts can lend much help. Perhaps most helpful is the Christian philosopher Nicholas Wolterstorff and his book *Art in Action*. To the question "What is art?" he responds:

---

1. C. S. Lewis, *An Experiment in Criticism* (Cambridge: Cambridge University Press, 1992), 19. He continues, "There is no good asking first whether the work before you deserves such a surrender, for until you have surrendered you cannot possibly find out."

There is no purpose which art serves, not any which it is intended to serve. Art plays and is meant to play an enormous diversity of roles in human life. Works of art are instruments by which we perform such diverse actions as praising our great men and expressing our grief, evoking emotion and communicating knowledge.[2]

This observation offers some much-needed clarity. Why do we ask the question, What is art? Do we want a tidy definition or concept that will just help us to say what is art and what is not art? Anyone who has been to an art museum with a modern or contemporary collection knows that the categories are not so simple. So instead of describing art's essence, Wolterstorff points to art's diverse functions. If we recognize that art can do many different things, we will then need to expand beyond one single value of what counts. So let's consider how these four values can complement rather than compete with one another.

Beautiful

Beauty celebrates order, harmony, symmetry, proportion, balance, and form. By far the most dominant in the history of Christianity, beauty occupies a central place in Christian engagement with the arts. Early luminaries like Augustine found much to celebrate in the Greco-Roman accounts of eternal beauty. The late-medieval and Renaissance periods—perhaps the era of the greatest artistic achievements of Christendom—bear out this reliance. In recent history, however, beauty's influence has waned considerably. Secularism has prompted the dissolution of the ancient triad of truth, beauty, and goodness, and under the influence of Romanticism the "sublime" (i.e., the overpowering, terrible, or uncanny) has replaced beauty as a dominant aesthetic value today.

As it relates to the Christian gospel, however, beauty fits with the first movement of the fourfold story of God's work in the world and corresponds most closely with the doctrine of creation (Gen. 1:31). Beauty names the aesthetic goodness, wholeness, and wonder of God's originally pristine handiwork. It connotes perfection of design and intimates completion. When everything is exactly as it should be, we are most struck by the beauty of a thing.

The beautiful, as a theological value for engaging the arts, remains primary but not solitary. While it often comes first, it should never be alone. When we attempt to let beauty tell the whole story of an artwork's worth, we are necessarily leaving out the complexity of the fall, redemption, or restoration. Such efforts

2. Nicholas Wolterstorff, *Art in Action: Toward a Christian Aesthetic* (Grand Rapids: Eerdmans, 1987), 4.

result in an unfortunately cheap account of beauty, not unlike a symphony where all the minor chords have been removed from the score. We must remember that our faith rests with a beautiful Messiah that the prophet Isaiah, perhaps paradoxically, describes this way: "He had no beauty or majesty to attract us to him, nothing in his appearance that we should desire him" (Isa. 53:2b). As in Fyodor Dostoyevsky's *The Idiot*, we are reminded that the beauty that will save the world is not the beauty we naturally expect. To our first theological value for the arts, we must have a second; the beautiful must be accompanied by the prophetic.

◯◯ Prophetic

The prophetic uncovers disorder, injustice, oppression, and evil. As a theological value, prophetic witness serves to remind us that we live amid a fallen world in rebellion to God's kingdom. If beauty operates as a stabilizing force for our experience, the prophetic serves to destabilize us. Whereas beauty provides an orientation to the ideal life in God's good world, the prophetic witness is a profound disorientation from that ideal. When beauty highlights how the world should be, the prophetic helps us to see where we have fallen short of that glory.

The biblical authors often use poignant word pictures to strengthen their prophetic witness. Many times throughout Scripture, moral failure is described as a broken or bent line:

> The way of peace they do not know;
> > there is no justice in their paths.
> They have turned them into crooked roads;
> > no one who walks along them will know peace. (Isa. 59:8)

These uses of an aesthetic evaluation like "crooked" remind us how much God values an honest description of the brokenness in the world. When Christians can value the contribution of an artist's crooked line, we will be able to encounter many of the artworks that are more focused on truth-telling and representing the way the world actually is than an ideal or detached beauty.

Like beauty, however, prophetic witness cannot be the Christian's sole value for engaging the arts. If beauty needs a prophetic witness, the prophetic depends on all the other values combined. How hard will it be to focus on meaninglessness without some eventual recourse to the meaningful? The fall is certainly not the end of God's story but rather another starting point within it. Indeed, sin, death, and evil will not win the day. Even as the art of prophetic witness allows us to see and lament the brokenness of our world and our own lives, we must hold in tension the hope that God will restore the ruins we have made and turn our mourning into exuberant praise (Isa. 61:1–3).

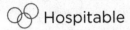 Hospitable

The hospitable promotes empathy, authenticity, inclusion, belonging, and invitation. As the next movement in this cascading flow of theological values, we want to explore hospitality in the arts. If beauty provides an orientation to the world and art's prophetic witness provides dis-orientation, then art as hospitality constitutes some reorientation. Here artworks can function as vehicles for vicariously experiencing the thoughts, feelings, or questions of an imagined other. This other may be the artist herself, the work's subject, the imagined subjectivity of the work's audience, or something else entirely. Artworks can embody the perspective of a distinct individual or community that would be necessarily unavailable to the work's viewer without it. In this way, the hospitable invokes the renewed vision of those disciples on the road to Emmaus that though they did not know with whom they were speaking, yet their hearts burned within them (Luke 24:32).

This may seem too simplistic or unheroic, but in the wake of the prophetic, the hospitable can provide the space for awaiting what's next—to anticipate some redemption. We might think about the function of the hospitable in art as making room to see a tragic story finished well. Resolution—lasting, satisfying resolution—to any story requires adequate time and space to trust that while we may have no way out, God will, in fact, make a way. The art of hospitality puts flesh and bones on this trust and anticipation. Redemption is never abstract; it's embodied and always personal. Hope is a practice, an exercise, or way of being in the world; it is not a concept. The hospitable in the arts reminds us that suffering must speak so that true hope may arise.

Imaginative

The imaginative probes the possible, the potential, even the fantastic. Now we find ourselves living in the moment of God's ongoing redemption. We only have access to the beauty of creation as a reconstructed past, and in the same way, we can only imagine the future as promised restoration, where Christ unites all things in himself (Rev. 21:5). Indeed, the resurrection glory of Christ guarantees the transformation of the world, and the imaginative in the arts helps us to picture now what is not yet. The biblical story itself invites art's creativity here because Scripture records some fascinating details about the only envoy this world has ever seen from the next. The risen Christ evidences both continuity and discontinuity with our earthly experiences. For instance, he can pass through the closed door of the disciples' room but then asks them for something to eat (John 20:19–20 and Luke 24:36–43). The Resurrection's new reality will be both familiar and strangely new at the same time, and the arts can help us imagine it even now. Indeed, much of the trajectory of modern and contemporary art refuses to settle for time-honored stylistic formulas and instead pursues the next unchartered territory for each medium. For instance, what can a painter do with paint that has never been done before?

In this way, the imaginative carries the story further—beyond resolution and toward something even better: glory beyond glory (2 Cor. 3:18). It speaks to the future state where we can truly enjoy the generative overflow of a well-resolved story. We will celebrate that the story is not only resolved but still expanding, going further, and getting better. Just as in Paul's prayer for the Ephesians, we are invited to contemplate with the arts "immeasurably more than all we ask or imagine" (Eph. 3:20).

Conclusion

Each one of these values represents a viable and vital means of engaging with the arts. Each should be given priority in turn. Unfortunately, because of the influence of fundamentalism and its disdain for secular culture, Christians have been seen as those who primarily protest, abstain from, critique, and reject cultural movements. Hopefully, this set of theological values illuminates new avenues for encountering all that is good in the arts. Of course, not everything we encounter there can or should be celebrated, but we should demonstrate in tangible ways that the faith, hope, and the love of the Christian gospel compels us to celebrate what we can. In order to do so, we must embrace these complementary values and thus encounter art from multiple perspectives. Where we do not find the beautiful, perhaps we can locate the hospitable. Where we do not find the hopeful, perhaps we can appreciate vulnerability and authenticity. Where we do not find consolation, perhaps we can accept the distance and disruption as God's own disquiet for an incomplete and imperfect world. Perhaps even the unfinished and the incomplete can create a platform for imagining a potential future resolution. In the gospel of the Lord Jesus Christ, we already have the answer to every human need, so let's be willing to allow art the chance to ask multiple and varied questions. In this way, Christians can offer much to today's world. Of all people, we should be the most patient, hospitable, and sympathetic (i.e., engaged and engaging) because our fiercely gentle Savior has certainly demonstrated that to us (Rom. 2:4).

Taylor Worley (PhD, The University of St Andrews) is associate professor of faith and culture as well as associate vice president for spiritual life and ministries at Trinity International University. He is coeditor of *Theology, Aesthetics, and Culture: Responses to the Work of David Brown.*

CONTEMPORARY ART AND THE LIFE WE'RE LIVING

✺ Jonathan A. Anderson

Many people experience modern and contemporary art as disconnected from everyday life. It often seems to be a domain of strange and difficult objects cloistered away into extravagant exhibition spaces, circulated through their own rarefied marketplace, and sustained by an academic art-speak that the general public doesn't much follow or care about. This alleged disconnection is real, but its meanings—and indeed its virtues—require further understanding. On the one hand, we might simply recognize (and forgive) the effects of specialization: art has become a robust field of study and is thus as susceptible to abstruseness and elitism as any other field—there is, after all, nothing in the art discourse any more obscure than what one finds in contemporary mathematics, medicine, theology, law, engineering, finance, etc. On the other hand, there is something about contemporary art that seems intentionally difficult and self-distancing. The artistic canon of the past two centuries celebrates artworks that poignantly jolt, withhold, surprise, and subvert expectations for what an artwork should be or do. As a general project, contemporary art intends to unsettle and to complicate that which would otherwise appear familiar, normative, and hermeneutically easy.

What is often misunderstood, however, is that this intentional strangeness and difficulty are not ends in themselves—at least not if the artwork will have enduring human significance. Rather, the entire point of artworks that unsettle expectations is to open some kind of reflective distance from which to re-view and re-cognize what has become familiar. In other words, the whole enterprise of presenting difficult art objects in spaces set aside for paying attention ultimately has less to do with detachment from everyday life than with generating renewed attentiveness to one's daily surroundings and default modes of living. Indeed, this is why contemporary art traffics in the stuff of everyday life: commonplace materials, artifacts, forms, activities, technologies, and the taken-for-granted mechanics of visual culture. Despite the common impression that contemporary art is disconnected from the everyday life of the general public, this is in fact precisely what contemporary art is most preoccupied with.

⦾ John Cage's *4'33"*

To take one influential example, consider John Cage's infamous *4'33"* (1952), a piano performance in three movements comprising four minutes and thirty-three seconds of musical rest. Cage recognized that this silent composition "would be taken as a joke and a renunciation of work," whereas he also earnestly believed that "if it was done it would be the highest form of work."[1] It was first performed in the Maverick Concert Hall in Woodstock, New York—a rustic theater that opens out into a surrounding forest. No notes were played on the piano for the duration of the performance, but the hall was in fact full of sounds: birdsongs, wind in the trees, cars traveling along a nearby road, etc. Cage's conviction was that concertgoers who had gathered expectant to hear meaningful sounds might be capable of hearing all of these background sounds—and indeed the manifold sonic textures that fill their lives—as intensely musical. Cage withheld the one instrument his audience expected to hear in hopes that their attention might turn to hear the world around them as (always) giving a surprisingly complex and elegant kind of music.[2]

Cage was influenced by Zen Buddhist mindfulness, but he also directly linked this work to Jesus' admonition to "consider the lilies of the field" (KJV)—exactly as they present themselves, without human composition—for "not even Solomon in all his splendor was dressed like one of these" (Matt. 6:25–30).[3] Cage sought the sonic equivalent: to consider the "flowers" of the sonic field, convinced that not even Beethoven in all his splendor composed sounds like those constantly surrounding us, including the subtlest of sounds produced by the most extravagant instrumentation (think, for instance, of the absolutely over-the-top "instrumentation" required to produce the sounds of wind blowing through trees or automobiles moving along a highway).

Whether or not one considers *4'33"* to be "the highest form of work," the key point is that it (alongside numerous other twentieth-century artworks that could be discussed here) profoundly clarifies art's central vocation: art is the presentation—the bringing-into-view—of any form, artifact, occurrence, and/

---

1. John Cage, in Richard Kostelanetz, *Conversing with Cage*, 2nd ed. (New York: Routledge, 2003), 69.
2. For a further description and discussion of this work, see Jonathan A. Anderson and William A. Dyrness, *Modern Art and the Life of a Culture: The Religious Impulses of Modernism* (Downers Grove, IL: InterVarsity Press Academic, 2016), 291–98.
3. See Kostelanetz, *Conversing with Cage*, 245.

or space that, in Cage's words, succeeds at "waking us up to the very life we're living."[4] Art thus has less to do with producing certain qualities of form than it does with producing a certain quality of attentiveness within a community of people. Cage's composition is obviously not impressive as a deployment of skill, formal beauty, or expressive content; rather, its primary value is as "a means of converting the mind, turning it around, so that it moves away from itself out to the rest of the world,"[5] disclosing the sheer givenness of the world and of human consciousness, attuning us to "the very life we're living" with an expanded sense of meaning, attentiveness, even gratitude.[6] Any presentation that fulfills that function is, in his estimation, an artwork of the highest order.

⚭ A Framework for Understanding

This example, and the (re)definition of art that accompanies it, provides a helpful framework through which to understand the wonderfully "strange" array that has blossomed in the arts in recent decades. First, many artists continue to take up the artifacts of everyday life—found objects, consumer products, construction materials, various forms of cultural detritus—as artistic media for exploring the lives we're living. Artists like Tara Donovan, for example, configure thousands of mass-produced disposable objects (Styrofoam cups, drinking straws, etc.) into massive forms that are simultaneously beautiful and repellent, calling into question the ethics implicit in the things we produce. Other artists, such as Jim Hodges, explore the poetic capacities of everyday things, using domestic materials like denim or silk flowers to create lyrical meditations on the fragility and dignity of human lives. Others deploy found objects as lamentations over violence and suffering: Doris Salcedo, for example, uses found chairs and concrete-filled furniture as heart-rending stand-ins for those who have "disappeared" in the violent conflict in her native Colombia.

Second, many artists physically intervene in the space of the built environment—both public and private—to explore the ways that human lives are shaped by the arrangements of our homes, neighborhoods, marketplaces, and public institutions. Theaster Gates, for example, has incorporated extensive involvement in urban revitalization into his artistic practice, restoring vacant

---

4. John Cage, "Experimental Music" (1957), in *Silence: Lectures and Writings* (Middletown, CT: Wesleyan University Press, 1961), 12.

5. Cage, in Kostelanetz, *Conversing with Cage*, 241.

6. Cage repeatedly associated *4'33"* with an experience of joy: "No day goes by without my making use of that piece in my life and in my work. I listen to it every day. . . . More than anything, it is the source of my enjoyment of life." See William Duckworth, *Talking Music: Conversations with John Cage, Philip Glass, Laurie Anderson, and Five Generations of American Experimental Composers* (New York: Schirmer, 1995), 13–14.

buildings in his hometown of Chicago to generate new forms of interaction and meaning in the community. Korean artist Do-Ho Suh speaks to issues of migration and cultural displacement by intricately reconstructing his childhood home out of translucent polyester fabrics, creating a malleable structure that is folded up and travels to exhibition spaces throughout the world. Artists like Francis Alÿs address related issues by entering directly into the flow of city life, subtly disrupting the taken-for-granted routines, patterns, and boundaries that shape lives in metropolitan public spaces.

Third, these approaches heighten the importance of the human body as both an object and a medium of artistic contemplation. For artists like Tim Hawkinson, this takes the form of lyrical sculptural improvisations on the human form, investigating the body as a site of both longing and limitation, mediacy and immediacy. Performance artists, including those influenced by Allan Kaprow, regard the body itself and its daily activities (breathing, squeezing oranges, shaking hands) as mediums and loci for exploring tacit assumptions about human embodiment, performative social norms, and daily habitus.

Fourth, many artists focus attention on mass-media technologies as domains of familiarity that need sharp scrutiny (and disruption). South African artist William Kentridge creates haunting films and installations exploring the ways that communication technologies shape and narrate collective human histories. Gillian Wearing and Lorna Simpson scrutinize the ways that everyday photographic media shape how we picture—and thus see—ourselves and each other. Wade Guyton and Raphaël Rozendaal borrow the formats and processes of digital media to derail and destabilize their effects, whereas artists like Bill Viola attempt to reclaim them for poetic contemplation of transience and transcendence.

Christianity and Contemporary Art

So how does all of this pertain to the ways Christians think about and participate in the arts? The history of modern and contemporary art is, after all, the history of art after it left the church (a history which, it should be noted, decisively begins with the Protestant Reformation, not the Enlightenment). The estrangement between modern art and the church has led many Christians to organize their "engagement" with the arts in defensive terms. These approaches have some merits, but they also have terrible deficiencies—not least of which is that they virtually ensure one's ignorance of and nonparticipation in what is actually going on in the arts today.

At least two considerations encourage another approach. First, the understanding of contemporary art sketched above clarifies the extent to which artists are actively engaged in fundamental human vocations of caring for, cultivating, and naming the earth, and heightening sensitivities to our various particular enculturated ways of living in the world. In this respect, Christians have much to affirm in contemporary art as goods in themselves, to be enjoyed and wrestled with on their own terms, without impatiently either reducing them to worldview arguments or uncritically co-opting them into the church. Second, all of the topics discussed above have deep theological questions and implications built into them, even if these tend to be underrepresented and under-interpreted in the ways that art history and criticism are generally written and taught. Scholars are increasingly recognizing that modern and contemporary art is, and has always been, engaged in questions and concerns that have deep religious roots and dimensions, though much work remains to be done to adequately explore these. Christians have much to contribute to and much to learn from engaging the arts as domains already dense with theological meaning, particularly as we become better attuned to the ways the generative strangeness of contemporary art might help awaken us to the life we're living.

Jonathan A. Anderson is an artist, art critic, and associate professor of art at Biola University. He is the coauthor of *Modern Art and the Life of a Culture: The Religious Impulses of Modernism* (with William Dyrness).

WHEN ART BECOMES SINFUL

Cap Stewart

With the rampant pornification of pop culture in the West, an overriding concern Christians express when engaging with the arts is about content. "Could this album/video game/movie be a stumbling block to me?"

Concerns like this are legitimate, but they don't go far enough. When we engage with most types of entertainment, we are interacting, in some form or fashion, with other human beings. And if objectification can negatively affect us as an audience, what is it doing to those on the other end of the equation?

"We Are Not Things"

Consider Jennifer Lawrence's experience filming the 2017 movie *Passengers*. This project provided Lawrence with her first on-screen sex scene, which she describes in her own words:

> I got really, really drunk. But then that led to more anxiety when I got home because I was like, "What have I done? I don't know." And he [Chris Pratt] was married. And it was going to be my first time kissing a married man, and guilt is the worst feeling in your stomach. And I knew it was my job, but I couldn't tell my stomach that. So I called my mom, and I was like, "Will you just tell me it's OK?"[1]

This is not simply the response of an actor pushing beyond her comfort zone. This is the response of an actor violating her conscience. The coping mechanism she chose—getting drunk—only exacerbated her anxiety and guilt.[2]

---

1. Stephen Galloway, "Jennifer Lawrence, Cate Blanchett and Six More Top Actresses on Pay Gap, Sex Scenes and the Price of Speaking Frankly: 'There Is Always a Backlash,'" *Hollywood Reporter*, https://www .hollywoodreporter.com/features/jennifer-lawrence-cate-blanchett-six-841113.
2. For a more in-depth analysis of this incident, see the following: Cap Stewart, "A Tale of Two Sexual

Tragically, Lawrence's experience is only one of many. For example, Ruta Gedmintas describes her first sex scene in the HBO series *The Tudors* like this: "I was absolutely terrified and had no idea what was going on. . . . I cried afterwards because I was thinking, 'This isn't acting, what am I doing?'"[3]

In fact, if you pay attention to the way entertainers routinely describe performing nude and sex scenes, their word choices are revealing: "awkward"[4] (Zoe Saldana), "awful"[5] (Eva Mendes), "nerve-wracking"[6] (Margot Robbie), "terrified"[7] (Reese Witherspoon), "mortifying"[8] (Jemima Kirke), "toxic"[9] (Michelle Williams), "humiliating"[10] (Claire Foy), "traumatic"[11] (Natalie Dormer), "sort of unethical"[12] (Kate Winslet), and "shell-shocked"[13] (Dakota Johnson).

There are even cases where women feel coerced in a way resembling outright sexual assault, as evidenced by the testimonies of women like Sarah Silverman,[14] Salma Hayek,[15] Kate Beckinsale,[16] Sarah Tither-Kaplan,[17] and Maria Schneider.[18] Suffice it to say, a great number of women are traumatized by these experiences

---

Assaults on Jennifer Lawrence," *Happier Far*, http://www.capstewart.com/2016/12/a-tale-of-two-sexual-assaults-on.html.

3. Gerard Gilbert, "'My Mum's Going to See This': Actors and Actresses Reveal Secrets of the Sex Scenes," *The Independent*, http://www.independent.co.uk/arts-entertainment/tv/features/my-mums-going-to-see-this-actors-and-actresses-reveal-secrets-of-the-sex-scenes-7658255.html.

4. Frankie Taggart, "Zoe Saldana: Hollywood bullied Trump," Yahoo!, https://www.yahoo.com/news/zoe-saldana-hollywood-bullied-trump-035518571.html.

5. Bang Showbiz, "Eva Mendes hates sex scenes," Azcentral, http://archive.azcentral.com/thingstodo/celebrities/free/20130325eva-mendes-hates-sex-scenes.html.

6. Cap Stewart, "What About Actors Who Willingly Undress for the Camera?" *Happier Far*, http://www.capstewart.com/2014/05/what-about-actors-who-willingly-undress.html.

7. Antoinette Bueno, "Reese Witherspoon 'Panicked' When Filming Wild's Graphic Drug & Sex Scenes," *Entertainment Tonight*, http://www.etonline.com/news/154587_reese_witherspoon_panicked_when_filming_wild_graphic_drug_and_sex_scenes.

8. Christopher Rosen, "Jemima Kirke, 'Girls' Star, On Periods, Collaborations And Sex Scenes." *Huffington Post*, https://www.huffingtonpost.com/2012/04/23/jemima-kirke-girls_n_1444001.html.

9. Lynn Hirschberg, "Michelle Williams & Ryan Gosling: Heart to Heart," W Magazine, https://www.wmagazine.com/story/michelle-williams-ryan-gosling.

10. Gilbert, "'My Mum's Going to See This".

11. Ibid.

12. Ellie Krupnick, "Kate Winslet Channels Elizabeth Taylor On V's September Cover," *Huffington Post*, https://www.huffingtonpost.com/2011/09/08/kate-winslet-v-september-cover_n_953560.html.

13. Cap Stewart, "Why Don't More Christians Like 'Fifty Shades of Grey'?" *Happier Far*, http://www.capstewart.com/2015/05/why-dont-more-christians-like-fifty.html.

14. Alistair McGeorge, "Sarah Silverman reveals she was violated while filming a sex scene for a comedy," *The Mirror*, https://www.mirror.co.uk/3am/celebrity-news/sarah-silverman-sex-scene-reveals-2816174.

15. Stephanie Merry, "Hayek's accusations about the making of Frida make us question nudity in movies." *Sydney Morning Herald*, http://www.smh.com.au/comment/hayeks-accusations-about-the-making-of-frida-make-us-question-nudity-in-movies-20171214-h04hhs.html.

16. Cap Stewart, "Hollywood's Secret Rape Culture," *Happier Far*, http://www.capstewart.com/2014/05/hollywoods-secret-rape-culture.html.

17. Daniel Miller and Amy Kaufman, "Five women accuse actor James Franco of inappropriate or sexually exploitative behavior," *Los Angeles Times*, http://www.latimes.com/business/hollywood/la-fi-ct-james-franco-allegations-20180111-htmlstory.html.

18. Lina Das, "I felt raped by Brando," *The Daily Mail*, http://www.dailymail.co.uk/tvshowbiz/article-469646/I-felt-raped-Brando.html.

because of how their privacy, dignity, and sexuality are trivialized, all in the name of entertainment.

Do the examples above represent how all performing artists feel? Certainly not. Plenty of them show few reservations about nude and sexual content. The experiences I have described may not be universal, but they are prevalent—prevalent enough to be a major concern, especially since it is nearly impossible for audience members to discern when a piece of sexualized entertainment involves serious coercion, some coercion, or no coercion at all. The end product often looks the same.

In the entertainment industry, there is a longstanding "tradition of objectifying female characters."[19] Indeed, the societal pressure placed on women to publicly perform as sexual objects is tangible and pervasive, infiltrating virtually every art form. In the realm of filmmaking, for instance, women publicly undress almost three times as often as men do.[20] Film critic James Berardinelli explains why: "For the most part, only high-profile actresses have been able to dictate no-nudity terms. Lesser-known actresses or those with lower profiles are given a 'take it or leave it' option in which they either strip or are passed over. As in any kind of commerce, it's a matter of who has the power."[21]

Women are objectified, dehumanized, and even abused because of "who has the power." And who exactly has this power? Producers, directors, and other executive heads. But even much of their influence can be traced back to another source: consumers like you and me.

There would not be so much hypersexualized material in our entertainment if there were not such a high demand for it. We may not consider ourselves as "demanding" it. We may reluctantly tolerate it only to enjoy a good story or performance. We might even do so while publicly objecting to the pornographic content. But when our pocketbook is involved, our toleration communicates only support. In the words of author Anna Lappé, "Every time you spend money, you're casting a vote for the kind of world you want."[22]

⚭ Love Your Entertainer as You Love Yourself

When debating the appropriateness of various forms of entertainment, we have largely (and, I believe, inadvertently) constructed flimsy soapboxes on the

19. Lily Rothman, "Harvey Weinstein and Hollywood's Ugly Casting Couch History," *TIME*, http://time.com/4981520/harvey-weinstein-hollywood-gender-history.

20. Ben Child, "Female nudity almost three times as likely as male in Hollywood films." *The Guardian*, https://www.theguardian.com/film/2016/apr/05/female-nudity-three-times-likely-male-hollywood-films.

21. James Berardinelli, "Barenaked Actresses." Reelviews. http://www.reelviews.net/reelthoughts/barenaked-actresses.

22. Anna Lappé, Goodreads, https://www.goodreads.com/quotes/587323-every-time-you-spend-money-you-re-casting-a-vote-for.

shifting sands of selfishness. Our personal freedom, as important as it is, becomes moot when it intrudes on the spiritual, emotional, and psychological health of others. As the apostle Paul wrote, "You, my brothers and sisters, were called to be free. But do not use your freedom to indulge the flesh; rather, serve one another humbly in love. For the entire law is fulfilled in keeping this one command: 'Love your neighbor as yourself'" (Gal. 5:13–14).

When it comes to pursuing and enjoying the arts, the freedom Christians enjoy is indeed greater than many legalists would have us believe. But that great truth is only half the truth, for it ignores a greater element to our freedom— namely, our ability in Christ to restrict our own practices so we can love our neighbor.

It is this love which we have neglected.[23] Our consumeristic mindset has largely eclipsed our ability to consider the spiritual well-being of those we pay to entertain us. Sadly, we are more concerned with staying relevant, or enjoying a cathartic experience, or keeping up with what everyone else is doing.

Instead, let us cultivate a willingness to deny ourselves any indulgence that would contribute to a performer's sexual degradation. Yes, our options will be limited—sometimes significantly. But think of all that we have to gain: valuing the inherent worth and dignity of others regardless of their ability to amuse us; severing the root of secret lusts that might be hiding beneath the surface; enjoying more freedom from self-centeredness; gaining greater mastery over the temptations of pornography (in all its forms); developing a healthier sexuality, which focuses more on the needs of others than it does on itself; growing in pure, holy, and erotic love for one's spouse; and experiencing a cleaner conscience through several small acts of selfless love. The rewards of loving our neighbor are rich and deep, and we will soon wonder at how small and petty those things were that we once feared to lose.

Cap Stewart has developed his love of stories through drama, radio, videography, independent filmmaking, and collecting and reviewing film scores. His cultural commentary has appeared, among other places, on *Reformed Perspective*, *The Gospel Coalition*, and *Speculative Faith*. Cap has been writing about theology and the arts at capstewart.com since 2006.

---

23. I am deeply indebted to pastor and author Wayne A. Wilson, whose chapter "The Law of Love" in his book *Worldly Amusements* has been the catalyst for my writings on loving our entertainers as we love ourselves.

DISCUSSION QUESTIONS

1. In Taylor's essay, he declares that the artists of faith should make art that points to God's grace and intended shalom. How do you think that someone who holds to this tradition would deal with art that portrays depravity, or the darker side of existence? Is there a place for this kind of art in Taylor's position, and if so, what place does it have?

2. Worley declares to Christians that in engaging the arts, "Where we do not find the beautiful, perhaps we can locate the hospitable." How might Stewart interact with this call to affirm the "good" in art that simultaneously portrays or utilizes the "bad"?

3. Fujimura warns against "culture warring," saying that we should be able to "work together to plant and pull weeds together" with "gardeners" in the culture with whom we disagree in order to love and seek prosperity for our neighbors. However, Stewart declares that in supporting certain art, we are actually condoning the mistreatment of actors and actresses—directly violating their prosperity, in a sense. How might someone from Fujimura's tradition suggest we work alongside "gardeners" that propagate harm in arts (such as Stewart's example) without condoning through passivity their actions?

4. In his article, Stewart is fairly clear that for the sake of the entertainer's dignity and protection, Christians should refuse to indulge in art forms (film, specifically) that could potentially exploit sexuality in any way. How might Worley respond to this total elimination of a large percentage of film in specific relation to sexuality?

5. In Worley's essay, he makes it clear that certain virtues in the arts such as the "beautiful" and the "prophetic," do not stand alone in the Christian tradition, but need the other virtues to tell the full story of the cross. How does this reconcile with his concluding statement that Christians should seek to celebrate art for the virtues that they do see in it, even if all the other virtues are not present? Is there a danger here?

6. In his essay, Anderson discusses a definition of art that identifies "the highest order" of art as any presentation (whether an immense fresco or a silent piano

piece) that succeeds in "attuning us to 'the very life we're living' with an expanded sense of meaning, attentiveness, even gratitude." Are there any other authors that you read in this section that might disagree with what makes a piece of art "the highest order," and if so, who and why?

7. Anderson begins his article by admitting that art, both as a complex discipline and by its very nature, is often difficult to understand. Then, at the end of this article, he declares that art has deep theological truths and questions at its root that Christians should engage with and not ignore. In light of his introductory admissions, however, could it be dangerous for the Christian to engage art if they do not have adequate training and tools to understand the depths of its complexity?

8. While Taylor and Fujimura tend to stress the Christian engaging in art as a "maker" or creator, Worley and Anderson emphasize the Christian's role in art as "engagers" or experiencers. Are these two opinions contradictory or complementary?

9. Taylor uses attributes of God to justify the Christian's engagement in the arts. Worley, however, uses Christian values. How do you think that these two views would interact? Do you think that they are essentially saying the same thing, or would they distinctly disagree?

10. In Fujimura's essay, he says that rather than engaging, Christians should be making art. However, with so much art already being produced, where does this leave the Christian in regards to understanding the art that surrounds them constantly?

chapter twelve

WAR, WEAPONS, AND CAPITAL PUNISHMENT

There is no singular Christian position on the role Christians should take in war and how Christians should think about weapons and capital punishment. Throughout history, thoughtful Christians have understood the Bible's teaching on these topics quite differently based on their interpretations of Scripture—with Genesis 9 and Romans 13 functioning as pivotal texts in the debate—and their understanding of church history as well as the pressures of their own historical context. At least part of the challenge Christians face when determining how and what we ought to think about going to war—and, more broadly, violence—stems from the seeming discontinuity between the Old Testament's record of and teaching on war and Christ's attitude and teachings on the subject. Positions on war, weapons, and capital punishment depend, at least in part, on the hermeneutical relationship one holds between the Old and the New Testaments. The God of the Old Testament at times leads his people—the Israelites—into war to free them from their oppressors, to deliver them from their enemies, and secure for them the Promised Land. Christ, on the other hand, teaches his followers to love their enemies, to pray for them, and, following his example, even to die for them. It is widely recognized that the early church fathers maintained pacifist positions, drawing hard lines between the government and military of the age and membership within the kingdom of God. This duality meant that they generally acknowledged the empire's right to administer capital punishment while also admonishing Christians against being involved in the administration of executions.[1]

One of the earliest pacifists recorded in church history is Justin Martyr (c. 150 CE).[2] Second-century Christians identified themselves as "warriors but

---

1. See James J. Megivern: *The Death Penalty: An Historical and Theological Survey* (New York: Paulist Press, 1997), 9–50.

2. Kirk MacGregor, "Nonviolence in the Ancient Church and Christian Obedience," *Themelios* 33, no. 1 (May 2008): 17.

of a special kind, namely, peaceful warriors" because they "refused to practice violence and, on the warrior side, they excelled . . . in showing fidelity to their cause and courage in the face of imminent death."[3] The record shows that for some early Christians, nonviolence was viewed "as an essential attribute of discipleship" required even of new converts who had held military or other positions requiring violence.[4] In fact, during the reign of Marcus Aurelius (161–180 CE), "the church perceived military service and following Jesus as mutually exclusive, a choice which Roman soldiers attracted to the gospel were forced to make."[5] Tertullian maintained that the very nature of the gospel required those who believed it to "accept death when under attack" rather than act violently against their aggressors.[6] He even went so far as to prohibit Christians from holding governmental offices wherein their decisions would naturally affect matters of life or death for others.[7] The church's stance on nonviolence relaxed, however, as Rome experienced an extended period of peace under the *pax Romana*, and Tertullian did eventually allow converts to continue to hold posts in those professions so long as peace prevailed.[8] And so it did, for a time.

The first major shift in the view of the Christian's relationship to violence occurred because the church found itself in the position to offer ethical guidance on governmental and geopolitical issues. Augustine is famously credited with developing the foundations for Just War theory, the guiding principles by which Christians traditionally have condoned and participated in war with other nations. Augustine writes,

> What is the moral evil in war? Is it the death of some who will soon die in any case, that others may be subdued to a peaceful state in which life may flourish? This is mere cowardly dislike, not any religious feeling. The real evils in war are love of violence, revengeful cruelty, fierce and implacable enmity, wild resistance, and the lust of power, and such like; and it is generally to impose just punishment on them that, in obedience to God or some lawful authority, good men undertake wars against violent resistance, when they find themselves set in positions of responsibility which require them to command or execute actions of this kind.[9]

---

3. Ibid., 18.
4. Ibid., 18.
5. Ibid., 19.
6. Ibid., 19.
7. Ibid., 20.
8. Ibid., 21.
9. Augustine. "Against Faustus, Book 22" in *From Irenaeus to Grotius: A Sourcebook on Christian Political Thought*, ed. Oliver and Joan O'Donovan (Grand Rapids: Eerdmans, 1999), 117.

In other words, Augustine, affirming what the Old Testament reveals about the nature of the Lord through his interactions with Israel while simultaneously upholding what Christ teaches about the kingdom of God in the New Testament, suggests that violence is not wrong in and of itself. Rather, Augustine argued, it is the unrestrained *love of violence* that is evil and ought to be resisted and restrained through holy violence if necessary. In *The City of God* he argues against the objection that the first commandment forbids all killing:

> The divine authority itself, however, did make certain exceptions to the rule that it is against the law to kill a human being. But these exceptions include only those whom God orders to be killed, either by a law he provided or by an express command applying to a particular person at a particular time. In addition the one who owes this service to his commander does not himself kill; rather he is, like a sword, an instrument in the user's hand. Consequently, those who, by God's authority, have waged wars have in no way acted against the commandment which says, *you shall not kill*; nor have those who, bearing the public power in their own person, have punished the wicked with death according to his laws, that is, according to the authority of the supremely just reason.[10]

These statements, among others, not only laid the groundwork for Just War theory[11] and promoted the ongoing Christian defense of capital punishment, but also, when misapplied, opened the door for the justification of the Crusades, a period of church history in which violence against the church's enemies was aggressively pursued. By the modern period, the church had turned much of its warring and violence inward, in the form of the various forms of violence the church of Rome and its Protestant Reformers wreaked upon one another across Europe.

The founding of America, prompted by the religious wars that impinged on the religious liberties of emerging Christian sects, itself depended on violence and weaponry at the personal and community level as European settlers came and, in the name of religious freedom, wrested land from Native Americans. At the root of the nation's formation in the early colonies and later in its westward expansion, and eventually in its own Civil War, was a rationale for the use of weapons and violence to seize and settle the land. This long history continues to influence national debates on gun control and gun violence.

---

10. Augustine, *The City of God*, books I–X, in *The Works of Saint Augustine: A Translation for the 21st Century*, ed. Boniface Ramsey, trans. William Babcock (Hyde Park, NY: New City, 2012), 24 (1.21).

11. John Langan, "The Elements of Augustine's Just War Theory," *Journal of Religious Ethics* 12, no. 1 (Spring 1984): 19–38.

By the early twentieth century, when the world itself was at war, Christians who conscientiously objected were the exception rather than the rule. The church, along with the rest of the world, faced unprecedented violence from weapons far more powerful than anything seen before. "Everywhere by overwhelming majorities Christian people pronounced in word and act the same decision, viz. that to fight, to shed blood, to kill—provided it be done in the defense of one's country or of the weak, for the sanctity of treaties or for the maintenance of international righteousness—is at once the Christian's duty and his privilege."[12] In other words, Christians by and large returned to a more philosophically and theologically sound understanding of the Just War theory instituted by Augustine and largely supported the great World Wars as necessary to curb the evil that was oppressing and killing innocent people.

Of course, the wars of the twentieth century were not limited to those two great wars of the first half of the century. In fact, the century saw wars and heard rumors of wars in every corner of the world. And the Christian response to these wars has continued to vary, with the two most prominent scholarly views being a responsible application of the Just War theory and passivism. Famous contemporary pacifist Stanley Hauerwas explains the distinctions even within pacifism, saying, "My pacifism, which is based upon Christological presuppositions, does not look on our disavowal of war as a strategy to make the world less violent. Indeed, my own view is that Christians are called to nonviolence not because our nonviolence promises to make the world free of war, but because in a world of war we, as faithful followers of Jesus, cannot imagine being other than nonviolent."[13]

The specter of terrorism and weapons of mass destruction in the twenty-first century has shifted the debate in ways that could not have been foreseen even in the world wars. Today Just War theory and pacifism must take into account the possibility of entire nations of innocent people being maimed or destroyed by the press of a button or the release of noxious substance. Moreover, with the aid of modern news reporting and technology, our acute awareness of the horrific evil and mass violence that continues to be perpetrated around the world raises the question for some whether capital punishment is, at least in extreme cases of reprehensible brutality, the proper punishment. Yet even for some who in theory see merit in the case for the death penalty, the apparent systemic racial and socio-economic injustices have caused them to oppose capital punishment in practice. Much of the American church, seemingly, has faced these issues more fervently at the ballot box than at the altar.

---

12. C. John Cadoux, *The Early Christian Attitude to War*, rep. ed. (New York: Gordon, 1975), 127–28.

13. Stanley Hauerwas, "Pacifism, Just War & the Gulf: An Exchange," *First Things*, May 2, 1991, https://www.firstthings.com/article/1991/05/pacifism-just-war-the-gulf-an-exchange.

This section includes three sets of articles that clearly take opposing positions. First, Matthew Arbo presents a theological and philosophical argument against capital punishment, while Joe Carter presents an argument in favor of capital punishment founded in a study of the Noahic covenant.

In the second set of positions, Bruce Ashford lends his support for biblical Just War theory, arguing that it is the most logically and theologically coherent approach to understanding the function of war and violence in light of Scripture. In contrast, Ben Witherington III presents an argument in favor of Christian personal pacifism, rejecting violence at the personal level based on Christian moral and ethical standards while recognizing that God has given authority to secular governments to enact violence when necessary.

Third, Rob Schenck argues that Christians should, in following Christ's example, avoid gun ownership and lethal violence, while Karen Swallow Prior, drawing from her personal experiences and pro-life principles, presents her argument for gun ownership, urging Christians—and particularly Christian women—to use wisdom and conscientious stewardship to develop their views on gun ownership and violence.

THE CASE AGAINST THE DEATH PENALTY

Matthew Arbo

Christians are not obligated to support capital punishment and indeed should not support it. That is the claim I intend to argue for here. My reasons for opposing the death penalty are both philosophical and theological. Let me begin with philosophical objections, which I divide into practical and theological objections to capital punishment. The justice in capital punishment does not consist in feelings of satisfaction achieved through retaliation or vengeance, but in setting to right what really can be set to right.

Practical Objections

Evidence also suggests that capital punishment does not serve as an effective deterrent to capital offenses. First, if a crime is unpremeditated, or committed in the heat of passion, then clearly the threat of execution never entered the wrongdoer's mind before committing the crime. In addition, many who have committed capital offenses admit to ignoring the possibility of being executed for their crime. Moreover, in fourteen states without the death penalty, homicide rates are at or below the national average. Positive evidence of the death penalty's effectiveness at dissuading violent crime is not compelling.

Consider the following US statistics:

- More than half of death row inmates are people of color.
- Since 1977, the overwhelming majority of death row inmates (77 percent) have been executed for killing white victims, even though African-Americans were victims in half of all homicides.
- Since 1973, 140 individuals on death row have been exonerated.
- Almost all death row inmates could not afford their own trial attorney.

- Since 1976, 82 percent of all executions have taken place in the South.
- Of the 344 exonerees represented by the Innocence Project, 20 served time on death row. Of those 344 exonerations, 71 percent involved eyewitness misidentification, 46 percent involved misapplication of forensic evidence, and 28 percent involved false or coerced confessions.
- Of those 344, a full two-thirds were people of color.[1]

These represent but a small sample of the practical problems endemic to the criminal justice system.[2] I wish to highlight the problems of attorney representation and racial bias, in particular. Given the current strain placed on public defenders, both because of case load and prolonged underfunding, it is difficult to see how every violent offender who cannot afford their own counsel is comparably represented by state-appointed counsel, no matter how well-meaning or talented that counsel might be. Mounting evidence also suggests people of color receive a disproportionate percentage of the capital sentences. Together these findings constitute reason enough to place a temporary national stay on capital punishment.

℘ Theological Objections

I transition now to theological objections to the death penalty. First, if one wishes to base one's justification for capital punishment on *lex talionis* of the Old Testament, then one must demonstrate how death as a punitive measure is morally right, not merely permissible. Jesus' instruction in Matthew 5:38–41 makes clear that retaliatory interpretations of the law are incorrect. If one is subject to wrongdoing or injustice, Jesus implores forbearance and charity, dismissing any reading that justifies vengeance. It is especially difficult in practice to disentangle vengeance from retribution in capital punishment. Governing authorities are sometimes required to use force in upholding the law and securing peace, of course, but nothing requires them to kill offenders to do so (cf. Rom. 13). In pleading for measured clemency, the Christian is not being insubordinate or disrespectful.

A second theological point is one offered long ago by Augustine: once the condemned is put to death, that person is no longer eligible for evangelization and conversion. Clemency extends the possibility of rebirth in Christ. It doesn't

---

1. These statistics come from the innocence project and the exoneration database from the University of Michigan. See https://www.innocenceproject.org/dna-exonerations-in-the-united-states/ and https://www.law.umich.edu/special/exoneration/Pages/about.aspx.

2. For more on the state of the criminal justice system, including some policy reform proposals, see William Stuntz's superb book *The Collapse of American Criminal Justice* (Cambridge: Belknap, 2011).

guarantee conversion, obviously, but execution certainly ends the opportunity. Historically the church has taken this particular opportunity very much to heart.

Third, the Christian faith is fully and entirely pro-life, beginning to end. This commitment has broad enough scope to include even the condemned. Every human being has dignity and no one, not even the monstrous, can lose their dignity altogether. If Christians take human dignity seriously, we should criticize any penalty that fosters attitudes of contempt toward the condemned. The Deuteronomic code, for example, limits the number of times the guilty can be flogged, for otherwise "your fellow Israelite will be degraded in your eyes" (Deut. 25:1–3). Degradation is here distinguishable from shame, which may rightly attend punishment; but execution is degradation by definition. As Oliver O'Donovan puts it, "When the suffering of punishment becomes an object of vulgar curiosity and fascination, even experiment, the condemned person ceases to count among us as a human being deserving of neighbor-love, and ordinary human respect seems to vanish."[3]

Let me address two possible objections. First, some may wish to take issue with the appeal to Matthew 5:38–41 as a criticism of *lex talionis*. They will say Jesus' instruction is directed to disciples, to the church, and does not apply to civil authorities. This objection is valid in part, for Jesus is indeed addressing followers. But the text does not specify that it is only followers he speaks to, nor does it preclude the possibility of a civil authority also being Christian. Thus, if I am right, then the Christian apologist for capital punishment must give distinctly Christian reasons that respect the force of Jesus' teaching: does it avoid vengeance, and what distinctly Christian good does it establish that no other punishment can?

The second objection has to do with my dismissal of Genesis 9:6 as constituting a sufficient Christian principle for capital punishment. The text itself seems straightforward: whoever sheds the blood of man, so shall his blood be shed; for God made man in his image. Destroying the image of God carries grave consequences. This is a powerful theological claim, and because Genesis 9:6 figures so centrally in defenses of capital punishment, I wish here to offer a more detailed response to the objection.

A tremendous amount could be said about what is happening in Genesis 9, from its unique postflood context to the repeated use of "blood" language. In its application to capital punishment, however, it is the principle in verse 6 that has been enshrined in legal history. Taken literally, the verse does not speak to

3.   Oliver O'Donovan, *Ways of Judgment* (Grand Rapids: Eerdmans, 2007), 124.

capital punishment. In spirit, however, it serves as an important legal rationale for retribution, a retribution based on the intrinsic value of the image of God.

The covenant in Genesis 9 has two distinct but integrated parts—verses 1–7 and 8–17. In the first part, God tells Noah and his sons what they are to do and explains to them the relation they now share with other creatures. God gives them "everything," but with a couple of stipulations: They may not eat meat with blood in it, nor may another man's blood be shed. That's the immediate context for verse 9, which then pronounces the penalty for shedding another's blood. Humanity is distinctive among creatures because of the image of God. Then the command to be fruitful is repeated, and only after this, in the second part, is the covenant broadened to include every living creature. It just doesn't make any sense to read verses 1–7 as including all creatures when all the provisions of the covenant are about distinctly human activities.

I see something distinctive in verse 6 and believe it should be interpreted in light of Christ's saving work and the New Covenant he has established with this church. I do so because other provisions of the covenant in Genesis 9:1–7 have only loose application to the church today, and in some instances are also fulfilled in Christ himself. Is "everything that moves" really meant to be food for us? It is possible, if not probable, that in context this is precisely what is being commanded. Are we obliged to follow it? All humanity? Or only the church? If so, what are we supposed to make of Paul's instruction in 1 Corinthians 8 and 10 about eating and abstaining? God also tells Noah and his sons that he gives them "everything." If that is true, how are we to interpret John 3:34–36 in which Jesus explains that the Father loves the Son and "has given all things into his hand"? The Noahic covenant is still meaningful and relevant for the church, of course, but for these reasons I do not interpret verses 1–7 as a self-standing moral prescription.

Interpreting verse 6 as is, apart from Christ's work and covenant, carries rather odd implications. As mentioned, verse 6 presumes the logic of *lex talionis*, but at almost no place in history has the principle been upheld in literal terms—i.e., that punishment should identically match the wrong. Not even in odd Islamic codes does this happen. When someone steals from another's produce stand, for example, the penalty is to remove the offender's hand, not to steal produce from the offender, when the latter would more accurately reflect *lex talionis*. When politically institutionalized, as after many generations it inevitably would be, penal codes do not specify total replication of the wrong upon the wrongdoer, but of proportionate justice upon the wrongdoer, particularly in form and severity.

The pivotal question is how the Noahic covenant is reinterpreted in light of Christ's finished work. The church cannot draw a straight line from Genesis 9:6

to formal justification of capital punishment. It has to be interpreted and applied in light of the New Covenant and the mission it confers upon the church. The church is a people reconstituted in the grace and love of Christ. It is his command to love God and love neighbor. Could the condemned be a neighbor, I wonder? Are we loving family and friends of the slain, for example, when we affirm their longing to see the killer executed? If all human beings are bearers of the image of God, who are we supposed to love: the killed or the killer? If we cannot love the killed, then would it be possible to love some idealized Killed, a victim representing all who are lost? Genesis 9:6 doesn't settle these sorts of questions and wasn't meant to. This also begins to get at my claim that killing a person as punishment for killing is a paradoxical thing to "support." How do we love bearers of the image and support the killing of them at the same time?

Those are my objections and explanations. I put them frankly, knowing many readers will vehemently reject my arguments. I ask only that readers consider whether capital punishment in fact gives the condemned what they deserve or whether it simply assuages the anger, however justifiable, of those with a relation to the slain, who equate "justice is served" with "the one who killed my loved one has been killed."

A legitimate Christian defense of capital punishment must demonstrate the good it serves without recourse to satisfying vengeance. Christians are aware of at least one example of an innocent man being unjustly executed. How many more are we willing to accept for the sole purpose of maintaining a penalty we could just as well do without? Many so-called Christian defenses of capital punishment are, I fear, more emotive and utilitarian than theological.

Matthew Arbo (PhD, University of Edinburgh) serves as assistant professor of theological studies and director of the Center for Faith and Public Life at Oklahoma Baptist University. He is the author of *Walking Through Infertility* and *Political Vanity*. Arbo serves as an elder at Frontline Church in Oklahoma City.

THE DEATH PENALTY IS BIBLICAL AND JUST

∞ Joe Carter

When considering the morality of an issue like capital punishment, the first question Christians must ask is, "Has God spoken about the topic?"

In attempting to answer this question, many Christians look to the Mosaic law. Denying the legitimacy of the death penalty is made more difficult when we recognize that the law God gave the Israelites included twenty-one different offenses that would warrant the death penalty.

The problem with this approach, of course, is that the law of Moses applied only to Israel. Since this particular covenant was made between God and the Hebrew people, it was never universally applicable. But while the Mosaic law doesn't provide a sound basis for a defense of modern capital punishment, there is a covenant that does: the Noahic covenant.

After God destroyed mankind with a flood, he established a covenant with Noah, his family, and with his descendants. Along with the promise that he would never destroy the earth by water again, God included this moral command: "Whoever sheds human blood, by humans shall their blood be shed; for in the image of God has God made mankind" (Gen. 9:6).

This verse not only provides a moral norm for capital punishment but also delegates the responsibility to mankind—to a legitimate, though undefined, human authority—and limits it to a particular crime: murder. Since this covenant is "everlasting" (9:16) and "for all generations to come" (9:12), it's as applicable today as it was in the age of Noah.

But who is the legitimate authority to carry out this duty? In Israelite society, the family of the victim carried out God's mandate. When more advanced forms of governing authorities were created, this duty was transferred to magistrates.

Some Christians argue that since modern liberal governments do not recognize the authority of God, the modern state is free from having to carry out his mandates. The result is that the question of capital punishment must be considered a matter of social, and sometimes individual, justice. Since capital punishment does not serve a legitimate societal interest, they contend, its only purpose is to slake a victim's quest for vengeance.

This argument turns on the assumption that outlawing private revenge frees governments from the responsibility to implement God-mandated capital punishment. But what basis do we have for believing that claim?

In the ancient Near East, a person claiming wrongdoing was expected to seek personal justice by retaliating in kind. This seeking of justice would often escalate into a private vendetta, and eventually into a blood feud between families or tribes. The resulting suffering would often far outweigh the original injustice.

The Mosaic law, however, placed a limit on personal vengeance, allowing only what was directly proportional to the injury done. This is known as the *lex talionis*, the law of retaliation (Ex. 21:23–24; Deut. 19:21; Lev. 24:20–21). The phrase "eye for an eye" doesn't literally mean you could poke someone's eyes out (as Ex. 21:26–27 makes clear) but only that the compensation had to be in exact proportion to the damages. (We should also note that the judges—Israel's version of the civil magistrate—used the verses to adjudicate on the matter. A third party mediated the vengeance.)

In the Sermon on the Mount, Jesus places an even greater restriction on the *lex talionis*: "You have heard that it was said, 'Eye for eye, and tooth for tooth.' But I tell you, do not resist an evil person. If anyone slaps you on the right cheek, turn to them the other cheek also" (Matt. 5:38–39).

This is a radical limitation on what was once considered an individual right to justice. But we should carefully note what Jesus didn't say in this passage. What he left out of the verse he quoted is as important as what he included. Exodus 21:23–24 states: "If there is serious injury, you are to take life for life, eye for eye, tooth for tooth, hand for hand, foot for foot."

Notice Jesus starts quoting at "eye for eye" instead of "life for life." Murder was not, nor had it ever been, a matter of individual vengeance. When a person commits murder, they are committing an offense against God himself and not against a mere individual, his family, or even society. Jesus' command only applies to individual vengeance; it does not abrogate God's command in the Noahic covenant.

Different orderings of the social contract may shift the burden of carrying out capital punishment from one societal sphere (the family) to another (the civil magistrate). But the duty must be carried out. If Christians believe their governing authorities are legitimate, then we must expect them to take on the role instituted by God himself.

The apostle Paul makes clear that governing authorities are tasked with implementing the wrath of God on the evildoer. In Romans 13:1–6 Paul makes a logical argument with multiple, interrelated premises.

1. All authorities have been established by God.
2. All Christians are subject to these governing authorities.
3. All such authorities have been instituted by God for the good of the people.
4. Governing authorities are God's servants.
5. Resisting these authorities is resisting what God has appointed and will result in divine judgment upon the individual.
6. Governing authorities that "bear the sword" are carrying out God's wrath on the wrongdoer.

The passage by Paul is unambiguous: Governing authorities are instituted by God to carry out God's wrath on the evildoer. Whether citizens of the state recognize his lordship over civil government is inconsequential; the Bible makes it clear that nations and rulers are servants of God (see Isa. 45:1; Jer. 25:9; Dan. 4:32).

We may choose to reject the legitimacy of this arrangement, but in doing so we are choosing to reject God's wisdom. If Christians believe governing authorities are legitimate, then we must expect them to carry out this mandate against murderers. For officials of the church to slander the officials of the state by claiming they are "not in keeping with the gospel of Jesus Christ" while they are carrying out God's command is scandalous.

This is not the only scandal, however. There are serious concerns with how the death penalty is applied and carried out in the United States. While the Bible establishes a justification and requirement for capital punishment, it does not address the problems with its application. We have a moral responsibility to redress these wrongs through the political process. What we must not do, though, is allow our apprehension about the means, method, and scope of capital punishment to override our obedience in carrying out the Creator's command.

Long ago, God made a promise to never again destroy the human race with a flood. When we see the rainbow in the sky, we are to "remember the everlasting covenant between God and all living creatures of every kind on the earth" (Gen. 9:16). As Christians, we should remember more than just the covenant. When we see a rainbow, we should remember that we are made in the image of God. And when we see the electric chair, we should remember too the price to be paid when we destroy the image-bearer.

Joe Carter is an editor for the Gospel Coalition, the editor of the *NIV Lifehacks Bible*, and author of *The Life and Faith Field Guide for Parents*. He serves as an elder at Grace Hill Church in Herndon, Virginia.

WHEN WAR IS JUST

Bruce Riley Ashford

At the age of fifty-three, after having served as commander-in-chief of the Continental Army, George Washington stated, "My first wish is to see this plague of mankind, war, banished from the earth."[1] No doubt many of us also wish that war would be banished from the earth. But, like Washington, we must recognize that war is sometimes inevitable in a world populated by sinners.

A Biblical "Just War" View of War and Peace

The Bible reveals to us an overarching story about the world. This story stretches all the way back to God's creation of heaven and earth and leans forward to Jesus Christ's return to defeat his enemies and renew the heavens and earth. This divine narrative is the true story of the whole world, and it is the context within which we can begin to make sense of war and peace.

At the time of creation, God's world was characterized by a comprehensive peace and harmony (Gen. 1–2). In fact, the Hebrew word that is translated as "peace" is shalom. This term means more than mere absence of war. It signifies something more comprehensive: universal flourishing, delight, peace, order, and justice.

When Adam and Eve sinned, they broke this shalom and left the world in the condition we now know and inhabit (Gen. 3). Because of sin, our world is no longer characterized by universal flourishing, delight, or peace. Instead, it is riddled with the effects of sin, including the horrifying realities of war. But God, in his love, sent his Son to save us from sin and sin's consequences (John 3:16–18); in fact, he promises that he will send his Son again in the future to defeat his enemies and institute a peaceful kingdom (Rev. 21–22).

---

1. Letter from George Washington to David Humphreys on July 25, 1785.

In the meantime, before the Son returns to consummate his peaceful king-dom, the Bible gives some specific principles that are applicable to war and peace. First, it makes clear that we cannot force the world to be a war-free utopia. Until Jesus returns, there will continue to be "wars and rumors of wars" because "the end is not yet" (Matt. 24:6 NKJV). Second, God has ordained governments to use force as an appropriate tool to defend their citizens (Ps. 144:1; Rom. 13:1–7). Third, Christians should always hope and pray for peace, but should accept the fact that war will sometimes be necessary. And because war is necessary, they should view the military as an honorable vocation (Luke 3:14).

Two Flawed Approaches to War

The view that has just been outlined is known as the "Just War" view. It draws upon biblical teaching to argue that deadly force is sometimes necessary because we live in a fallen world. However, not all Christians hold the "Just War" view.

Pacifism (Be Peaceful by Laying Down Your Sword)

Some Christians are pacifists. Pacifists refuse to use deadly force because they believe it is evil to do so. Some pacifists will approve of the military using deadly force as long as the pacifist himself doesn't participate, but consistent pacifists refuse to support any type of violence at all. They draw upon passages such as the Sermon on the Mount, in which we are told that we should love our enemies and be peacemakers (Matt. 5:9, 38–46).

Although well-intentioned, pacifism is idealistic and does not make sense of a fuller biblical teaching. It overlooks the Bible's teaching that God instructs the government to bear the sword (Rom. 13:3–5), Jesus used violence to cleanse the temple (John 2:15–16), and told his disciples to carry swords in case they needed them (Luke 22:36). Pacifists are right to want peace but are wrong to think that government should not wield the sword in a fallen world.

Crusade (Seek Universal Peace by Means of the Sword)

Other Christians reject "Just War" criteria and support wars of crusade. A war of crusade is religious and/or ideological. It is led by a religious (e.g., imam) or ideological (e.g., Lenin) authority who wishes to defeat evil and impose their vision of the "good."[2] Crusaders see themselves as waging war on behalf of ulti-mate good by imposing an ideal social order. Instead of showing restraint in war by, for example, distinguishing between combatants and noncombatants,

---

2. Roland H. Bainton, *Christian Attitudes toward War and Peace: A Historical Survey and Critical Re-evaluation* (Nashville: Abingdon, 1960), 14.

they tend to want to annihilate the old social order by converting, punishing, or destroying the enemy.

Crusaderism's own idealistic picture does not make sense of biblical teaching. Although there are instances in which the Bible views a crusade mentality approvingly, those instances are ones in which God himself instructed Israel to go to war (e.g., Num. 31:1–54) or in which God will lead a final crusade to defeat his enemies and institute a one-world government (Rev. 19:11–21).

Criteria for Waging a Just War

Over the millennia, Greek philosophers, Roman lawyers, Christian theologians, and others have developed specific criteria that must be met if a nation-state is to be justified in becoming engaged in a just war. Those criteria are:[3]

Just Cause: A nation must go to war only if it is defending against an unjust aggression. In other words, a nation should not go to war merely to topple another nation's leader, install a preferred political or economic system, or expand its own power.[4]

Competent Authority: The decision to go to war must be made by the ruler or ruling body that is responsible for maintaining that nation's order and security.

Comparative Justice: A nation should go to war only if this war leads to greater justice than refraining from war and tolerating the other nation's injustice.

Right Intention: A nation may go to war only if the intention is to restore the peace. It may not go to war for the purpose of glorifying itself, enlarging its territory, or humiliating its opponent.

Last Resort: A nation must exhaust all realistic nonviolent options (e.g., diplomacy, economic sanctions) before going to war.

Probability of Success: A nation must determine that it has a realistic hope of achieving victory.

---

3. For a fuller exploration of these criteria as they apply to a recent war, the Persian Gulf War, see Daniel R. Heimbach, "The Bush Just War Doctrine: Genesis and Application of the President's Moral Leadership in the Persian Gulf War," ch. 17 in *From Cold War to New World Order: The Foreign Policy of George H. W. Bush*, ed. Meena Bose and Rosanna Perotti (Westport, CT: Greenwood, 2002), 441–64.

4. The question of what counts as "just cause" has been hotly contested in recent years. In particular, just war theorists have debated whether "preemptive" or "preventive" rationales can count as just. The author of this chapter considers the former a just cause and the latter unjust. For a comparison and contrast of these two views, see Michael Walzer, *Just and Unjust Wars: A Moral Argument with Historical Illustrations*, 4th ed. (New York: Basic, 2006), 74–85.

Proportionality of Projected Results: A nation must determine that the anticipated results of the war are worth more than the anticipated costs.

Right Spirit: A nation must never go to war with anything other than regret. It should never wage war with a lust for power or delight in humiliating the enemy.

Just as there are criteria for becoming engaged in war, so there are also criteria for a nation's conduct during the war. The nation must not use more force or do more killing than is necessary to achieve its legitimate military goals. It must distinguish between combatants and noncombatants, avoid using evil means such as rape or the desecration of holy places, treat POWs with humane decency, and cease fighting once it becomes clear there is no chance of winning.

Conclusion

Augustine, the fifth-century church father, once wrote,

> But perhaps it is displeasing to good men to . . . provoke with voluntary war neighbors who are peaceable and do no wrong, in order to enlarge a kingdom? If they feel thus, I entirely approve and praise them.[5]

Pacifists, Crusaders, and Just War proponents agree that the world clashes with conflict, and also that God's full shalom will not be restored until Jesus returns. Inevitably in our broken world, nations and kingdoms will "provoke . . . neighboring kingdoms . . . as a way to enlarge [their] own kingdom." Thus, not only should Christians themselves seek peace with neighbors, domestic and foreign, but they must encourage nations' leaders to seek peace and to exercise force only after having met specific criteria that ensure the ensuing conflict is justified.

Bruce Riley Ashford (PhD, Southeastern Baptist Theological Seminary) is provost and professor of theology and culture at Southeastern Baptist Theological Seminary. He has written a number of books, including *Letters to an American Christian* and *The Gospel of Our King*. He is a frequent writer for *Fox News Opinion* and other national media outlets.

---

5. Augustine, *City of God* 4.14, in *A Select Library of the Nicene and Post-Nicene Fathers of the Christian Church*, series 1, vol. 2, *St. Augustin's City of God and Christian Doctrine* (repr., Grand Rapids: Eerdmans, 1993), 72.

BLESSED ARE THE PEACEMAKERS

◎ *Ben Witherington III*

Perhaps some of you saw the highly acclaimed film *Hacksaw Ridge*, which came out in the fall of 2016. It tells the true story of a Christian, Desmond Doss, who served in World War II on Okinawa and rescued seventy-five soldiers during that battle, all while carrying no weapon at all, indeed refusing to do so. He is the only pacifist to have received the Congressional Medal of Honor. What his story makes perfectly clear is that Christian pacifism has nothing to do with cowardice or being passive. Indeed, Doss's witness suggests that it takes far more courage to crawl across a battlefield and rescue the wounded without a weapon than with one.

At its core, and for me personally, the commitment to pacifism comes from the desire to fully obey the teachings of Jesus and Paul on this subject, teachings found in Matthew 5–7 and the second half of Romans 12 and 13. The gist of the matter is, as Wendell Berry makes clear, when Jesus called us to love our enemies, he did not mean love them to death at the point of a gun.[1] He really meant "thou shalt not kill" or, if you prefer, "you shall not murder" (Ex. 20:13). This is not an optional added extra commandment of Jesus; it is something that reflects the necessary corollary to the call of the great commandment—"Love your neighbor as yourself." It means that one treats every human life as of sacred worth, whether unborn human life, or born human life. For me, this means being totally pro-life. I cannot be party to abortions, capital punishment, or war in any combat capacity. I am amazed at the lack of consistency in some Christians' so-called pro-life ethic. Being pro-life means more than being pro-birth.

Let me be clear: this does not mean that I expect my government or any government to run on the principles of the Sermon on the Mount. I'm quite familiar with Romans 13 and what it says. I do not agree with the Amish reading of that text, which suggests that God merely ordered but did not authorize

---

1. Wendell Berry, *Blessed Are the Peacemakers: Christ's Teachings about Love, Compassion, and Forgiveness* (Berkeley: Shoemaker Hoard, 2005).

human authorities and governments. No, it was Jesus himself who told us that all legitimate human authority comes from God, and that even Pilate had such authority given him by God.

The issue here is not what is legitimate for a non-Christian government to do, or not do. One cannot impose a specifically Christian ethic on a secular government, or at least one ought not to do so. People have to be convinced in their own hearts of the Christian faith and its ethics—convinced, not coerced by government. The ethics of the kingdom are ethics for disciples of Jesus, and not until you are a disciple do they have authority over you.

What Jesus specifically calls for is not merely to resist retaliation to someone's attack; he calls for forgiveness of those who offend against us in any way. You will remember the story in Matthew 18 where Peter asks Jesus how many times must he forgive someone who sins against him. Jesus replies that infinite forgiveness is called for. Indeed, Jesus is depicted in the Lukan crucifixion narrative as even forgiving those who nailed him to the cross! This is not natural; it is the gospel of grace—it is supernatural. Forgiveness is the one thing that can break the cycle of violence. From Cain and Abel until now, violence has generated only more violence.

Paul puts it this way in Romans 12:17–21, "Do not repay anyone evil for evil.... Do not take revenge, ... but leave room for God's wrath, for it is written: 'It is mine to avenge; I will repay,' says the Lord." (this is also the message of the bloodiest book in the NT—Revelation). "Do not be overcome by evil, but overcome evil with good" (such as providing one's enemies with the necessities of life). Here's a truth we should have suspected all along. Doing violence to others does violence to yourself, not least to your God-given conscience. When you meet persons who have come back from Iraq or Afghanistan and discover they have PTSD, as a Christian, you should hardly be surprised. Killing someone is the opposite of affirming that they are of sacred worth—the opposite of loving them as you love yourself. God hears the blood of the innocents crying from the ground, and believe me, there are always innocents and noncombatants caught in the crossfire.

I find it more than a little ironic that so many people who insist on taking the Bible not merely seriously, but literally, skirt lightly over the teachings of Jesus and Paul on this subject. They ignore the plea, "Why not rather be wronged? ... you yourselves cheat and do wrong" (1 Cor. 6:7–8). They dismiss whole denominations like the Mennonites and the Amish who affirm Christian pacifism. They ignore the witness of the earliest Christians in the first four centuries of Christian history who were prepared to give their lives for others, but were not willing to take other people's lives away from them. I am old enough to remember and to have supported the civil rights movement of the 1960s, and even today, we should not ignore the witness of people like Rev. Martin Luther King Jr., through whom great social change came about with nonviolent witness and protest against racism. He held to "active pacifism" and was inspired by E. Stanley Jones's discussions of the life of Gandhi, who in turn was inspired by Jesus. Jones was a graduate of Asbury College and the person for whom our mission school at Asbury Seminary was named.

What Christian personal pacifism means for me is that I could not serve in the military in a combat capacity, but I could serve as a chaplain or medic—someone trying to rescue and put people back together, even in a war zone. I could serve in a police department as an EMT dispatcher or the like. What I cannot and will not do is have or carry around the instruments of death—guns. There is a powerful scene in the older movie *The Witness*, starring Harrison Ford as a policeman, where the Amish grandfather tells his grandson when he sees Ford's weapon on the kitchen table one morning, "Touch not the unclean thing, for murder is a grave sin."

I happen to believe that in a society that involves both Christians and others, there is a place for a loyal minority witness to a better way than violence, namely the way of the cross and of Christ. I love my country as much as anyone, but my job is not to do any and every task possible in our society; my job is to bear witness to the better kingdom way of loving even one's enemies, praying for those who persecute you, and forgiving those who harm you.

Am I being naïve about the wicked ways of a fallen world? No, not at all. I will serve my country in ways that do not lead to the harming of others and as such provide a preview of coming attractions, because as Isaiah told us, the day is coming when we will train for war no more and beat our weapons into implements of farming (Isa. 2:4). While empires may rise and fall, the kingdom of God is forever. Because I know this, I choose to make my first priority always the serving of that peaceable kingdom that will one day come fully on earth as it is in heaven.

When there is a conflict between my kingdom values and our American values, then the American values have to be set aside. Christ and his gospel must always be first, and the example of Christ's life, who helped, healed, delivered, loved one and all, and even forgave his enemies, must be followed. Again, this is not optional. It is obligatory for a Christian.

Inevitably, the question of "lesser of two evils" situations arise. What if the life of the mother is almost certainly going to be lost if the pregnancy goes to full term? What then? Some pacifists would say, pray hard and trust God. Others have said, though murder is always a serious sin, it would be an even more serious sin to deprive the other children of this, and so an abortion is seen as a sin, but not an unforgivable one. Nevertheless, one must repent of the sin of terminating the unborn's life.

The same logic would apply if someone attacks a pacifist's family. Personally, what I hope I would do in such a situation is the following: (1) try to get in the way of the assailant and convince him to not harm others but direct his attention to me; (2) if necessary use nonlethal force to subdue him and his efforts (again remember pacifists are opposed to the use of violence, particularly lethal violence, not the use of all force); (3) if even this doesn't work, then I might try to do nonlethal harm to the assailant.

For the Christian pacifist, the most important thing is salvation, whether of one's own family or of the assailant. When you kill someone, you deprive them of the opportunity to (1) know Christ, or (2) repent if they have lapsed from their faith. It is precisely because the pacifist believes only God has enough knowledge to pass final judgment on people and will take care of the matter at the final judgment, that it is not necessary for his children to try to be judge, jury, and executioner of other human beings.

For those looking for detailed exegesis of some of the key passages, I would refer them to my Matthew and Romans commentaries (Smyth and Helwys Commentary, Eerdmans). For those wanting thoughtful discussion about the ethics and theology of Christian pacifism, I commend Ron Sider's *Christ and Violence*, John Howard Yoder's classic study *The Politics of Jesus*, and S. Hauerwas and W. Willimon, *Resident Aliens*.

Ben Witherington (PhD, University of Durham) is Amos Professor of New Testament for Doctoral Studies at Asbury Theological Seminary and on the doctoral faculty at St. Andrews University in Scotland. Witherington has written more than fifty books, including *The Jesus Quest* and *The Paul Quest*, and is considered a top evangelical scholar.

THE NEED TO RESTRICT GUNS

 *Rob Schenck*

f I'm going to train you in how to use a firearm, you must assure me you can use the weapon to kill in an instant, without hesitating. Understand? If you can't do that, you're more dangerous with the gun than without it, because, in a violent confrontation, it will be taken from you and used to kill you and go on to kill others."

The admonition from my volunteer firearms instructor, a US Marine reservist, was a tough challenge; firearms were not a part of my world. As a minister, I never imagined using lethal force in any situation. My job was to preach, teach, and work toward harmony between man and God and between one person and another. Killing did not fit in my toolkit, but, as part of a research project on evangelicals and American gun culture, I wanted to know my subject matter firsthand.

The unusual exercise began when Abigail Disney, an award-winning documentary filmmaker, sought me out as a nationally known evangelical pro-life advocate. She was a nonreligious progressive, and she wondered about the ardent stance my community took on unfettered gun rights, as compared to our adamant opposition to abortion rights. "How can you be pro-life and pro-gun?" she asked.

What mystified Abby was how people who believed in the Sermon on the Mount, with its beatification of peacemakers, would so jealously guard the right to use lethal weapons. After all, didn't Jesus command his followers to "love your enemy"?

For most Christians, the topic of lethal weapons and Jesus doesn't usually come up in the same sentence, but they must. American evangelicals in particular constitute a demographic sector most likely to embrace unfettered gun rights and access to firearms. Other Christians enthusiastically defend the Second Amendment to the US Constitution, which indicates that owning and using a gun for self-defense is a right protected by the highest law in the land. Still other

Christians, among them Mennonites and Brethren groups, take a diametrically opposite position, objecting to the use of lethal weapons of any kind based on moral grounds.

Concerned about a growing threat of terrorism, more and more congregants and pastors have armed up. Churches have recruited armed volunteer security details, while some pastors and Christian leaders even conceal-carry their weapon in the pulpit.

The embrace of deadly force by Christians raises several moral, ethical, and even theological questions that must be addressed. Quite simply, under what circumstances may a follower of Christ kill another human being? When is one's own life more important than that of another, even an enemy? How is readiness to kill a perceived "enemy" consistent with Jesus' command to "Love your enemies and pray for those who persecute you" (Matt. 5:44)?

Different answers to these questions divide Christians. A quick search of phrases like, "God and guns," "biblical self-defense," and "Christians and killing," will result in a plethora of websites, Bible studies, and books often presenting very different conclusions based on the same biblical material. How might we approach such an unsettled matter? We could begin by agreeing on authority. Who—or what—has the last word on such an inquiry?

Most evangelicals subscribe to a tenet that defines the Bible as "the inspired, the only infallible, authoritative Word of God." Other Christians balance the Bible with creeds, councils, traditions, or teaching bodies, such as the Catholic Magisterium, or, in Orthodoxy, "the conscience of the Church." It would seem, then, that the question of when and how a Christian may use lethal force in self-defense must rely on what the Bible says and what church authorities say. But evangelicals—and all Christians—are, in the end, focused most on the person and work of Jesus Christ. We are "Christo-centric." This includes how we read Scripture and interpret it. In other words, the model and teaching of Jesus is the ultimate key to unlocking the will of God—in the pages of Scripture and in his dealings with humankind.

In John 14:8–10, Philip asked Jesus to "show us the Father." In response, Jesus said to him, "Anyone who has seen me has seen the Father." And, "The words I say to you I do not speak on my own authority. Rather, it is the Father, living in me, who is doing his work." Based on this instruction, we must ask, "What does Christ say about God's will in the defensive use of a deadly weapon?"

Luke 22:36–38 is often cited when the subject of guns and lethal force are raised. In that passage, Jesus directed his disciples, "If you don't have a sword, sell your cloak and buy one," to which they responded, "See, Lord, here are two swords." This brief exchange is used to justify a Christian's purchase and use of deadly weapons for self-defense. Besides the problem of relying on one unique and isolated passage as an authority for faith and practice, there is also historical context to consider. First, the only protective law enforcement available to the disciples in that time was the Roman guard and by the time of Luke's writing the Empire had become hostile toward Christians. It would be centuries before there was a civilian police force anywhere in the world. In New Testament times, protecting oneself meant you were entirely on your own. With these elements in mind, it is easy to see that Jesus was simply preparing his disciples for what may await them in the days ahead, including physical threats. However, he still had more to teach them, and it would come by way of his arrest, torture, and ultimate execution. In each phase of these physical assaults against Jesus, not only did he not retaliate, but he forbid his disciples from using any type of force to protect him.

Some say it was only because Jesus was on a messianic mission to surrender his physical life to accomplish God's plan of salvation that the disciples were prohibited from using force to protect him. Yet, this does not explain why, when Stephen was later martyred, the same disciples who proudly displayed their arms to Jesus did not use them to protect one of their own. Nor did Stephen offer resistance to his persecutors. If Christ permitted reasonable self-protection, why then did the disciples not employ it?

The answer is found in what is required to orient oneself to kill and the consequences of killing. Killing is central in this discussion. Using a gun to "scare off" a threat is never a good idea. First, guns can escalate a confrontation. Second, using a gun is itself a very uncertain response to a threat. It is difficult to hit a moving target, and bullets are indiscriminate in where they land, putting bystanders at great risk. In addition to all of this, a shooter cannot know who may be on the other side of a door or wall. This positions the shooter to err toward defending his own life at the expense of others, a position of power that, I would argue, is also a position of pride. It is, in fact, in direct conflict with the admonition to "Do nothing out of selfish ambition or vain conceit. Rather, in humility value others above yourselves" (Phil. 2:3). In my own experience with firearms, I have felt the rush of self-confidence and even domination that often goes with having lethal firepower at your immediate disposal. There is an element of pride to the process that puts the shooter at odds with what Paul is calling Christians to choose.

For evangelicals, there is one particular theological problem when it comes to easy access to deadly force. We believe all human beings are lost in sin, "For all have sinned and fall short of the glory of God," (Rom. 3:23) and, "The heart is deceitful above all things, and desperately wicked" (Jer. 17:9 KJV). Jesus said of this sinful human condition, "For out of the heart come evil thoughts—murder, adultery, sexual immorality, theft, false testimony, slander" (Matt. 15:19). So, by definition, whoever may be handling a deadly weapon is, by biblical definition, "desperately wicked."

As my firearms instructor told me, anyone that bears arms must be ready to use them to take human life in an instant. If this impulse to kill is affected by our sinful nature, as the Bible makes clear it is, then any shooter is vulnerable to killing unjustifiably. Of course, even in the most justifiable of circumstances, the taking of a human life is regrettable, and the shooter must be prepared in the aftermath to experience a full spectrum of emotions from unhealthy triumphalism or gloating to doubt, guilt, shame, and remorse. Military chaplains speak of debilitating "moral injury" suffered by soldiers who have killed under the most justifiable circumstances. This indicates killing is not natural to humans; it is always an anomaly. For Christians, the act of killing, whether offensive or defensive, is a product of sin and spiritual rebellion.

For all these reasons and more, civilized peoples have largely delegated the onerous task of killing for protection to a select few who are highly trained, highly regulated, and held highly accountable. These include members of the armed forces, police officers, government agents of various kinds, and specially certified private security personnel. In this way, society limits the danger of wrongful shootings.

American evangelicals have made concerted efforts to preserve the constitutional right to "bear arms," but we must ask why we haven't matched our enthusiasm for killing to finding nonlethal forms of protection. Bible believers celebrate human life as a gift from God. We dedicate ourselves to the Lord Jesus, who said, "The thief comes only to steal and kill and destroy; I have come that they may have life, and have it to the full" (John 10:10). As Christians, we decry murder and abortion because they violate the sanctity of God-given life. Surely, as prayerfully motivated Christ-followers, we can find solutions to danger that do not include a constant disposition toward killing.

In a fallen world there will be killing, both as an act of murder and as an act of self-preservation. However, this reality does not resolve the serious ethical, moral, and spiritual questions about a Christian's use of deadly force. Owning and using a gun may be legal, but that doesn't make it moral. Killing another human being may be a reality, but that doesn't mean we should condone it. I suggest we follow the model of Jesus and eschew defensive guns and the violence that goes with them whenever and wherever we can.

Rob Schenck is the president of the Dietrich Bonhoeffer Institute and is an ordained evangelical minister with degrees in Bible, theology, religion, and Christian ministry. He is author of *Costly Grace: An Evangelical Minister's Rediscovery of Faith, Hope, and Love* and the subject of Abigail Disney's Emmy-award-winning documentary *The Armor of Light*, exploring evangelical gun culture.

CAN GUNS BE PRO-LIFE?

❀ *Karen Swallow Prior*

It's not every Christmas morning you wake up with a Bersa .380 in your Christmas stocking.

The story started on an isolated stretch of road, escalated into flagging down a police car, and resolved with more calls to the police and their surprise visit at the home of a very dirty old man. The handgun was the epilogue.

But this isn't about guns as much as it is about how Christian women should think and act in matters of self-defense, given the realities of today. For the record, I'm for gun control, but that term includes greatly divergent types of control that are not the purpose of this essay.

I run 35 to 40 miles a week. Living as I do in a rural area, those miles are on roads of varying degrees of inhabitation. I live in a low-crime area—all the more reason to resist the lull of a false sense of security, especially when being a woman alone is enough to make one vulnerable. So I spend a fair amount of time during those miles being wary, vigilant, and proactive with self-defense strategies.

The first trouble I had, years ago when I lived in another state with more crime, was a flasher who parked on my road in the early mornings, awaiting my daily runs. He would keep far away, face me to, um, service himself, then get in his car and speed off before I was close enough to read his license plate. Teamwork with a neighbor, however, resulted in identification, a house call by the police, and an end to his shenanigans.

The incident that birthed the Bersa started with a truck pulling up beside me and the driver asking me if I "wanted a ride." It's surprising how many such offers one encounters when one is out running. (Note: if you see me running along the road in running shoes and running shorts, rest assured, I do not want a ride. Besides, I'm dying to know: has anyone ever really gotten lucky with such an offer?) When the truck turned around and passed me again, I successfully used what was then the first strategy of my self-defense plan (which I can't disclose publicly without rendering it useless). This was before I was in the habit of taking a cell phone with me (the purpose of such runs being, after all, the sense of lightness and disconnectedness), but miraculously, when I got out on the main road, a police car drove by and I flagged it down. Even so, it took one more encounter with the man before the police were able to put an end to it.

That's when my husband bought me the handgun.

So I wasn't surprised to read in my local newspaper that a new shooting range in my area is attracting a significant portion of female clients. Locations around the country reflect similar patterns. A poll conducted by Gallup in 2014 reported that 38 percent of women surveyed and 58 percent of women polled said they believed having a gun in the house makes it safer.[1]

I know that Christians in favor of tighter gun control laws argue that as Christians, particularly ones like me who strongly identify as pro-life, we, of all people, should "love our enemies" and "turn the other cheek." But while as a Christian I try to cultivate my willingness to lay down my life for the sake of the gospel or for the life of another, I don't believe I'm supposed to risk my life for a would-be rapist. To me, being pro-life means protecting my own life too.

No one seriously contests the right to defend oneself. Self-defense is a natural right, and a self-evident one at that. The disagreement is merely over how much lethal force one must be prepared to use in fighting back against an attack on the innocent. Rescuing the innocent is commanded by Scripture, as in Psalm 82:4, which says, "Rescue the weak and the needy; deliver them from the hand of the wicked" (ESV). And Proverbs 25:26 states, "Like a muddied spring or a polluted fountain is a righteous man who gives way before the wicked" (ESV).

Some might say I should simply give up my love of the outdoors and running (which I've enjoyed since I began running cross-country in junior high), join a gym, maybe, or drive twenty miles one way into the city to run in a more populous area. But surrendering my freedom and giving in to evil so willingly doesn't seem like the call of the Christian either. Matters of stewardship play into the equation too: stewardship of my time, talents, and my physical and mental health. More than anything else, running meets these needs in my life.

Besides, the handgun is a self-defense strategy of last resort. I now run with a phone. I pay attention to my surroundings at all times. I text the plate numbers of any suspicious vehicles (or those whose drivers offer me a ride) to my husband's phone and call immediately if I am alone on a long stretch and encounter an unfamiliar, parked, or slow-moving vehicle. And I gave up running on the beautifully forested road where the man in the truck accosted me the first and second time (the final time was on my own road).

1. Justin McCarthy, *Gallup*, "More Than Six in 10 Americans Say Guns Make Homes Safer," November 7, 2014, https://news.gallup.com/poll/179213/six-americans-say-guns-homes-safer.aspx.

Ultimately, in my running, as in all things, I must put my trust in the Lord, yet without testing him.

I was reminded of God's sovereign protection in yet another incident. I was running uphill on a two-mile stretch of a private, uninhabited dirt road when I saw an older model car with an out-of-state plate parked up ahead. A man was leaning against the car smoking a cigarette. Quickly, I pulled my phone from the pack that holds all my necessaries and called my mother, whom I knew to be home. I stayed on the phone with her as I ran a wide berth around the man and his car. As I crested the hill, I saw a police car sitting at the top. Unbeknownst to me, the officer, from his elevated position at the crossroads, had been able to see us the entire time and waited for me to arrive safely.

Yes, God is watching over me. Yet, I am still called to wisdom and good stewardship of all the gifts he's given me, including my life and health.

This piece has been adapted from an article that first appeared on ChristianityToday .com on July 26, 2012. Used by permission of Christianity Today, Carol Stream, IL 60188. The original title was "Packing Heat and Trusting in Providence: Why I Own a Handgun."

Karen Swallow Prior is an award-winning professor of English at Liberty University. She earned her PhD in English at SUNY Buffalo. Her writing has appeared at *The Atlantic, Christianity Today, Washington Post, Vox, First Things, Sojourners, Think Christian*, and other places. She is a senior fellow at the Trinity Forum, a research fellow with the Ethics and Religious Liberty Commission of the Southern Baptist Convention, a senior fellow at Liberty University's Center for Apologetics and Cultural Engagement, and a member of the Faith Advisory Council of the Humane Society of the United States.

DISCUSSION QUESTIONS

1. Schenck discusses in his article against Christians carrying guns that using weapons involves an element of pride. Explain his logic and then explain why you agree or disagree.

2. Carter, in his pro–capital punishment article, uses verse 6 of the Noahic covenant in Genesis 9 as the foundation for his argument that capital punishment is a biblical mandate. Explain how someone might see Genesis 9:6 as a commandment that is not to be universally applied.

3. Witherington uses the specific argument that to be pro-life requires a Christian to be a pacifist. Can a person be pro-life and pro–Just War? Explain why or why not.

4. Both Schenck and Witherington use the life of Jesus, his character, and his teachings to espouse a selfless, weaponless, pacifistic Christian life. How would someone from Ashford's tradition respond to this use of Jesus' life and teachings?

5. How might someone from Schenck's tradition respond to Prior's claim that "No one seriously contests the right to defend oneself"?

6. Arbo presents statistics in his anti-capital punishment article that indicate possible but extremely serious corruption in the capital punishment arena. Can someone who supports capital punishment address these concerns, or must they require a change of position? Explain your answer.

7. Schenck poses the question: "How is readiness to kill a perceived 'enemy' consistent with Jesus' command to 'Love your enemies'?" How might someone from Prior's or Ashford's tradition respond to this question?

8. Ashford gives a list of criteria that must be met before a war can be supported in good conscience by Christians. How do you think that someone from Witherington's position would respond to their criteria?

9. A few different terms have been used by all of these authors, but each seems to have a different set of presupposed definitions. How is each author defining "murder," "enemy," "pro-life," "protect," and "selfish/selfless"?

10. Carter claims in strong language that verse 6 of the Noahic covenant, in regards to capital punishment, "delegates the responsibility to mankind." How might Schenck respond to this claim, especially in his discussion of pride and selfishness?

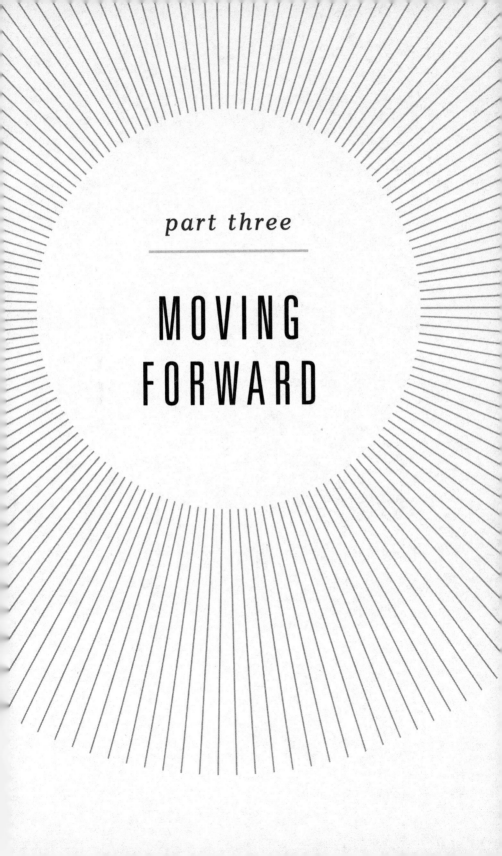

part three

MOVING
FORWARD

chapter thirteen

GOSPEL-SHAPED CULTURAL ENGAGEMENT

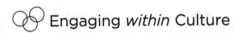 Engaging *within* Culture

Christians aren't somehow immune from culture. As we reflect on culture, it is not something "out there" that we jump in and out of; we are all swimming in culture. As we discussed in chapter 1, culture provides a prereflective grid that we live in and see the world through. This means that our Christian lives can't help but be impacted by our cultural location. There is no such thing as a culture-free human, no less a culture-free Christian. The question is not *if* we will be in or out of culture, but *how* will we live in our particular cultural space and time as Christians. Or to put this question differently, how might the gospel itself, the very core proclamation of Christianity, serve as our guide to living faithfully in our present context?

1. Cultural Engagement in Light of the Gospel Balances an Embrace of Culture with a Critique of Culture.

Historian Andrew Walls argues that the gospel itself implies two opposing tendencies that should serve as guide rails as we interact with the world around us. In the person of Jesus Christ, God comes to us as we are. God became human. He entered into space and time. He took on flesh and lived within a particular culture. God thus affirms the physicality of the world and the particularities that make up human life, implicit from the opening scenes of the biblical story and stretching through the vision of the New Testament church and the coming new heavens and new earth. By affirming the particularities of humanity—in what Walls refers to as the indigenizing principle—the gospel story reminds us of "the impossibility of separating an individual from his social relationships"[1] and the

---

1. Andrew F. Walls, *The Missionary Movement in Christian History* (Maryknoll, NY: Orbis; Edinburgh: T&T Clark; Oxford: Oxford University Press, 1996), 7.

future redemption of the whole person. We are each born into a particular time, culture, and family. And God accepts us as social and cultural beings.[2] Yes, God redeems us—a salvation that profoundly shapes all of our lives, including our values, priorities, ideas, families, and work. But the result is not uniformity. The marriage supper of the Lamb will include the splendor of diversity. And as we await the kingdom's final consummation, the church grows within culture, not apart from it. "The fact, then, that 'if anyone is in Christ, the new creation has come' [2 Cor. 5:17] does not mean that he starts or continues his life in a vacuum, or that his mind is a blank table."[3] Instead, the believer "has been formed by his own culture and history, and since God has accepted him as he is, his Christian mind will continue to be influenced by what was in it before. And this is as true for groups as for persons. All churches are culture churches—including our own."[4] And yet, the indigenizing principle should be balanced with a second principle, what Walls calls the pilgrim principle.

The pilgrim principle affirms that God transforms *sinful* people. As pilgrims, we are looking forward to the eternal city. This is not our home. The Christian's life will at times be foreign, even offensive, to the norms of any given society. The gospel positions us at a critical distance from our particular cultures. So while the indigenizing principle emphasizes that God does not simply obliterate the social, familial, or vocational dimensions of an individual who becomes a Christian, the pilgrim principle reminds us that the cultural strands that are built into the fabric of an individual need to be transformed by Christ. Walls explains, "The Christian has all the relationships in which he was brought up, and has them sanctified by Christ who is living in them. But he has also an entirely new set of relationships, with other members of the family of faith into which he has come, and whom he must accept, with all their group relations (and 'disrelations') on them, just as God has accepted him with his."[5]

Similar to Walls, theologian Miroslav Volf emphasizes the importance of recognizing that being critically distant from culture does not mean that we should or even could be completely separated from it. "The proper distance from a culture does not take Christians out of that culture. Christians are not the insiders who have taken flight to a new 'Christian culture' and become outsiders to their own culture; rather when they have responded to the call of the Gospel they have stepped, as it were, with one foot outside their own culture while with the other remaining firmly planted in it. They are distant; and yet belong."[6]

---

2. Ibid., 7–8.
3. Ibid.
4. Ibid.
5. Ibid., 9.
6. Miroslav Volf, *Exclusion & Embrace* (Nashville: Abingdon, 1996), 49.

The indigenizing and pilgrim principles serve as guard rails as we engage culture. The pilgrim principle steers us away from the error of cultural captivity, whereby we naïvely assume our culture's priorities and consume its artifacts without discernment. The particular world we inhabit is not just "common sense" or "the way things are done." All human cultures are distorted by sin, and the pilgrim principle reminds us that we are prone to blindly overlook the maladies of our own culture, taking part in them and even promoting its vices as virtues. This is because, as we discussed in chapter 1, these disorders are part of what we largely assume is normal. But as Christians, we now inhabit the true story (Creation, Fall, Redemption, Re-Creation) with knowledge of the ultimate aim (Christ and his kingdom), so we are better situated to see reality and critically engage our own culture and its various false mythologies and disordered aspirations.

The indigenizing principle reminds us that "distance from a culture must never degenerate into flight from that culture but must be a way of living in a culture."[7] "Distance without belonging isolates" us from the world around us and runs the risk of neglecting the good of the created order. Moreover, failure to maintain the indigenizing principle can ironically also result in a fall back into an insidious "belonging without distance," driving us into a counterdependence and leading us to find identity in a subgroup that demonizes those who are unlike *us*.[8] The gospel points us forward to unity found in Christ, and diversity found in an array of beautiful artistry and ingenuity within different cultures. As Christians, our unique ethnic and cultural features are not removed. Our identity in Christ and our membership in his kingdom transcends, but does not erase, our cultural particularities. Thus, our culture particularities are appreciated, but not idolized. Because we aren't bound to the ultimacy of any culture, we are open to what other cultures can contribute and freed to challenge the sins of particular cultures, starting with our own. This relieves us from the false nostalgia that blithely insists on returning to some "golden age" within our native culture while simultaneously keeping us from demonizing everything in a particular culture or time period.

2. Cultural Engagement in Light of the Gospel Is Informed and Wise.

Wisdom and humility are closely linked in the Scriptures. Humility leads us to learn from experts, even those who we might ultimately disagree with. Listening and learning are prerequisites for faithful engagement.

We live in a world exploding with information. The worldwide web has made

---

7. Ibid, 50.
8. Ibid.

it much easier to research topics and learn from the leading "experts" around the world. And to the publication of books, there is no end. One might assume that the massive pools of information at our fingertips would make the potential for informed engagement easier, and in one sense, it obviously can.

Yet the vast proliferation of research on a given topic can also be overwhelming. The web creates a sometimes confusing egalitarian world—a PhD in economics can be challenged online by a college freshman. Their opinions are placed side by side. Everyone gets to chime in and be heard. And weeding out the reliable from the facile is not always so straightforward. When everyone claims to be an "expert," and you can find someone with an advanced degree who supports just about any theory, being rightly informed is not always as easy as a Google search. Knowledge—the possession of data—is easily obtainable. But to make sense of the data, the need of the day is the recovery of wisdom—knowing the most important truths and being able to practically live them out in particular contexts.

Engagement that is "informed" and "wise" is not code for "leave it to us experts with PhDs." The unfortunate habit of some Christians triumphantly posturing as experts should not cause those with more humble and nuanced messages to become squeamish about engagement and remain on the sidelines. Quite the opposite—we *need* those Christians who will do it differently.

Engagement shouldn't be left to an elite few because, for one, the "experts" often tend toward an overly narrow focus, without an eye for bigger questions or integration between disciplines. University research programs are designed to train up specialists in a specific topic in a particular field. The result can be a person who is a genius when it comes to, say, mapping the human genome or the historical events that led to the Thirty Years' War, but is reticent and often averse to connect this expertise to the larger and most important questions—the questions of the good, the true, and beautiful. The point here is not to denigrate experts—we should be thankful for experts and should consult their work. But "expertise" does not equal "wisdom."

Yet part of informed engagement means researching what the experts in a particular field are saying; neglect to do this means you will often be wrong and you will almost certainly lose credibility. We need generalists working together with the experts. We need people who will look at the world through a telescope and those who will look at it through a microscope. This will lead to a community that is both informed and wise.

Growing into communities of wisdom will also require renewed imaginations—"The faculty of perceiving the whole."[9] As theologian Kevin

---

9. Kevin Vanhoozer, *First Theology: God, Scripture and Hermeneutics* (Downers Grove, IL: InterVarsity, 2002), 350.

Vanhoozer explains, "The wise person relates herself to God, the world and others in a way that is fitting, and hence in a manner that leads to human flourishing (and to the glory of God): 'In all that he does, he prospers' (Ps 1:3)."[10] How might we gain this godly wisdom?

We must learn to live and breathe the biblical narrative. The gospel story gives us a wide-angle lens that allows us to understand the world and opens up our imagination for how things might be different—even how they should be different. Through a gospel lens we live, learn, and interact with others. The story of the cross and the resurrection gives us, yes, knowledge of reality, but also calls us into a lived experience—a story—that is the syllabus for wisdom. This is what C. S. Lewis meant when he famously said, "I believe in Christianity as I believe that the sun has risen: not only because I see it, but because by it I see everything else."[11] Christianity provides a way of looking at the world that illuminates everything around us. We believe in order to understand. Rather than insulating us into our own parochial worlds, the gospel beckons us to open our eyes to everything—to take in knowledge wherever we find it and to understand what we find through the prism of the gospel, the true story that shines a light on every aspect of life. But more than just seeing life through this story, wisdom comes from stepping into this story—learning to reason, live, and interact from within the story. This happens when our lives are imbedded in the church—God's community of wisdom bearers and the training ground for the gospel narrative. Through our communal worship, prayers, sacraments, confessions, listening, and teaching, we situate ourselves in God's story and the Spirit teaches us to experience the world and imagine what could be in light of the coming kingdom.

3. Cultural Engagement in Light of the Gospel Displays a Humble Confidence.

The gospel creates a people possessing two qualities that at first glance can seem to oppose one another: humility and confidence. Central to the good news is that we are sinners saved by grace. The more understanding we have of ourselves in light of God, the more we have an overwhelming sense of our own deficiencies—and even more so, our own evil. "Woe to me! . . . I am ruined! For I am a man of unclean lips, and I live among a people of unclean lips, and my eyes have seen the King, the LORD Almighty" (Isa. 6:5). Humility is a result of understanding our personal bankruptcy before God. What do we have to boast about? Paul answers: "May I never boast except in the cross of our Lord Jesus

---

10. Ibid.
11. C. S. Lewis, "Is Theology Poetry?" in *The Weight of Glory and Other Addresses* (New York: HarperCollins, 1980), 140.

Christ" (Gal. 6:14). The cross is a constant reminder that we have nothing to boast about other than the work of God (Eph. 2:8–9). What good things do we possess that are not gifts from God (James 1:17)? Our talents, abilities, and work ethic are gifts from the Lord's providential hands. This posture of humility and gratitude before God should impact *how* we engage. "Gentleness and respect" (1 Peter 3:15) is not something that can be simply conjured up; true humility comes from resting in his grace. And it is in resting in this grace that we also find true confidence: "If God is for us, who can be against us?" (Rom. 8:31). We engage with boldness, but without the glow of superiority.

The cross not only impacts the tone of our interactions and our posture but it also changes our expectations for engagement. The road to glory, after all, traveled through Golgotha. If they persecuted our Savior, as his followers we need to realign our expectations for our reception. The crucified Messiah sets us on the path of a cruciform life, with chastened expectations of what cultural engagement will achieve before he returns. Our lives can point to the kingdom, but they can't usher it in.

Hence the gospel does not lend itself to naïve optimism. We live in a sinful world, and salvation came by way of a shameful cross. But neither does the gospel leave us in despair. *Death is not the final scene.* Resurrection and Pentecost followed closely behind, and along with them, hope. The Spirit casts our eyes on what is still yet to come: the promises that will be answered "yes" in Christ, propelling the church joyfully on mission. The vision of the ultimate realities of the coming kingdom—which feature such qualities as justice, love, and beauty—are "the norm for what good culture-making looks like in a fallen-but redeemed creation."[12] The church, by the work of the Spirit, is set apart to offer glimpses of this future kingdom.

So as we await Christ's return with a humble confidence, the gospel frees us from naïveté and despair about cultural change. Instead, in hope and joy we set out upon our mission to make disciples, love our neighbors, and pray as Jesus taught us: "[May] your kingdom come, [may] your will be done, on earth as it is in heaven" (Matt. 6:10).

12. James K. A. Smith, *Awaiting the King: Reforming Public Theology* (Grand Rapids: Baker Academic, 2017), 31.

chapter fourteen

CREATING CULTURE

Andy Crouch

Our *posture* is our learned but unconscious default position, our natural stance. It is the position our body assumes when we aren't paying attention, the basic attitude we carry through life. Often it's difficult for us to discern our own posture—as an awkward, gangly teenager I subconsciously slumped to minimize my height, something I would never have noticed if my mother hadn't pointed it out. Only by a fair amount of conscious effort did my posture become less self-effacing and more confident.

Now, in the course of a day, I may need any number of body *gestures*. I will stoop down to pick up the envelopes that came through the mail slot. I will curl up in our oversized chair with my daughter to read a story. I will reach up to the top of my shelves to grab a book. If I am fortunate, I will embrace my wife; if I am unfortunate, I will have to throw up my hands to ward off an attack by an assailant. All these gestures can be part of the repertoire of daily living.

Over time, certain gestures may become habit—that is, become part of our posture. I've met former Navy SEALS who walk through life in a half-articulated crouch, ready to pounce or defend. I've met models who carry themselves, even in their own home, as if they are on a stage. I've met soccer players who bounce on the balls of their feet wherever they go, agile and swift. And I've met teenage video-game addicts whose thumbs are always restless and whose shoulders betray a perpetual hunch toward an invisible screen. What began as an occasional gesture, appropriate for particular opportunities and challenges, has become a basic approach to the world.

Gestures Toward Culture

Something similar, it seems to me, has happened at each stage of American Christians' engagement with culture. Appropriate gestures toward particular

345

cultural goods have become, over time, part of the posture Christians unconsciously adopt toward every cultural situation and setting. Indeed, the appeal of the various postures of condemning, critiquing, copying, and consuming is that each of these responses to culture is, at certain times and with specific cultural goods, a necessary gesture.

Condemning Culture

Some cultural artifacts can only be condemned. The international web of violence and lawlessness that sustains the global sex trade is culture, but there is nothing to do with it but eradicate it as quickly and effectively as we can. The only Christian thing to do is to reject it. Likewise, Nazism, a self-conscious attempt to enthrone a particular culture and destroy others, was another wide-ranging cultural phenomenon that demanded Christian condemnation, as Karl Barth, Dietrich Bonhoeffer, and other courageous Christians saw in the 1930s. It would not have been enough to form a "Nazi Christian Fellowship" designed to serve the spiritual needs of up-and-comers within the Nazi party. Instead, Barth and Bonhoeffer authored the Barmen Declaration, an unequivocal rejection of the entire cultural apparatus that was Nazi Germany.

Among cultural artifacts around us right now, there are no doubt some that merit condemnation. Pornography is an astonishingly large and powerful industry that creates nothing good and destroys many lives. Our economy has become dangerously dependent on factories in far-off countries where workers are exploited and all but enslaved. Our nation permits the murder of vulnerable unborn children and often turns a blind eye as industrial plants near our poorest citizens pollute the environment of born children. The proper gesture toward such egregious destruction of the good human life is an emphatic *Stop!* backed with all the legitimate force we can muster.

Critiquing Culture

Some cultural artifacts deserve to be critiqued. Perhaps the clearest example is the fine arts, which exist almost entirely to spark conversation about ideas and ideals, to raise questions about our cultural moment, and to prompt new ways of seeing the natural and cultural world. At least since the Renaissance, artists in the Western tradition want the rest of us to critique their work, to make something of what they have made. Indeed, the better the art, the more it drives us to critique. We may watch a formulaic blockbuster for pure escapism, laugh ourselves silly, and never say a word about it after we leave the theater. But the more careful and honest the filmmaking, the more we will want to ask one another, "What did you make of that?"

By the same token, other "gestures" toward art are almost always beside the point. Serious works of art are not made to be consumed—slotted unthinkingly into our daily lives—nor, by law in fact, may they be simply copied and appropriated for Christian use. Of all the possible gestures toward culture, condemnation, in particular, almost always ends up sounding shrill and silly when applied to art. It is difficult to think of a single instance where condemnation of a work of art has produced any result other than heightened notoriety for the work and the artist.

Consuming Culture

There are many cultural goods for which by far the most appropriate response is to consume. When I make a pot of tea or bake a loaf of bread, I do not condemn it as a worldly distraction from spiritual things, nor do I examine it for its worldview and assumptions about reality. I drink the tea and eat the bread, enjoying them in their ephemeral goodness, knowing that tomorrow the tea will be bitter and the bread will be stale. The only appropriate thing to do with these cultural goods is to consume them.

Copying Culture

Even the practice of copying cultural goods, borrowing their form from the mainstream culture and infusing them with Christian content, has its place. When we set out to communicate or live the gospel, we never start from scratch. Even before church buildings became completely indistinguishable from warehouse stores, church architects were borrowing from "secular" architects. Long before the contemporary Christian Music industry developed its uncanny ability to echo any mainstream music trend, Martin Luther and the Wesleys were borrowing tunes from bars and dance halls and providing them with Christian lyrics. Why shouldn't the church borrow from any and every cultural form for the purposes of worship and discipleship? The church, after all, is a culture-making enterprise itself, concerned with making something of the world in the light of the story that has taken us by surprise and upended our assumptions about that world. Copying culture can even be, at its best, a way of honoring culture, demonstrating the lesson of Pentecost that every human language, every human cultural form, is capable of bearing the good news.

When Gestures Become Postures

The problem is not with any of these gestures. All of them can be appropriate responses to particular cultural goods. Indeed, each of them may be the only appropriate response to a particular cultural good. But the problem comes when these gestures become too familiar, become the only way we know how to respond to culture, become etched into our unconscious stance toward the world, and become postures.

Because while there is much to be condemned in human culture, the posture of condemnation leaves us closed off from the beauty and possibility as well as the grace and mercy in many forms of culture. It also makes us into hypocrites, since we are hardly free of culture ourselves. The culture of our churches and Christian communities is often just as lamentable as the "secular" culture we complain about, something our neighbors can see perfectly well. The posture of condemnation leaves us with nothing to offer even when we manage to persuade our neighbors that a particular cultural good should be discarded. And most fundamentally, having condemnation as our posture makes it almost impossible for us to reflect the image of a God who called the creation "very good" and, even in the wake of the profound cultural breakdown that led to the flood, promised never to utterly destroy humankind and human culture again. If we are known mostly for our ability to poke holes in every human project, we will probably not be known as people who bear the hope and mercy of God.

There is much to be said for critiquing particular cultural goods. But when critique becomes a posture, we end up strangely passive, waiting for culture to deliver us some new item to talk about. Critique as a posture, while an improvement over condemnation, can leave us strangely unable to simply enjoy cultural goods, preoccupied with our interrogation of their "worldview" and "presuppositions." The posture of critique also tempts us toward the academic fallacy of believing that once we have analyzed something, we have understood it. Often true understanding requires participation—throwing ourselves fully into the enjoyment and experience of someone or something without reserving an intellectual, analytical part of ourselves outside of the experience, like a suspicious and watchful librarian.

Cultural copying too is a good gesture and a poor posture. It is good to honor the many excellences of our cultures by bringing them into the life of the Christian community, whether that is a group of Korean-American chefs serving up a sumptuous church supper of *bulgogi* and *ssamjang*, or a dreadlocked electric guitarist articulating lament and hope through a vintage tube amp.

But when copying becomes our posture, a whole host of unwanted consequences follow. Like the critics, we become passive, waiting to see what interesting cultural good will be served up next for our imitation and appropriation. In fast-changing cultural domains, those whose posture is imitation will find themselves constantly slightly behind the times. Church worship music tends to be dominated by styles that disappeared from the scene several years before. Any embarrassment about being cultural laggards is mitigated by the fact that our copy-culture by definition will never be seen by the vast majority of the mainstream culture. And in this way, when *all* we do is copy culture for our own Christian ends, cultural copying fails to love or serve our neighbors.

The greatest danger of copying culture, as a posture, is that it may well become all too successful. We end up creating an entire subcultural world within which Christians comfortably move and have their being without ever encountering the broader cultural world they are imitating. We breed a generation that prefers facsimile to reality, simplicity to complexity (for cultural copying, almost by definition, ends up sanding off the rough and surprising edges of any cultural good it appropriates), and familiarity to novelty. Not only is this a generation incapable of genuine creative participation in the ongoing drama of human culture making; it is dangerously detached from a God who is anything but predictable and safe.

Finally, consumption is the posture of cultural denizens who simply take advantage of all that is offered up by the ever-busy purveyors of novelty, risk-free excitement, and pain avoidance. It would not be entirely true to say that consumers are undiscerning in their attitude toward culture, because discernment of a kind is at the very heart of consumer culture. Consumer culture teaches us to pay exquisite attention to our own preferences and desires. Someone whose posture is consumption can spend hours researching the most fashionable and feature-laden cell phone; can know exactly what combination of espresso shots, regular and decaf, whole and skim, amaretto and chocolate, makes for their perfect latte; can take on extraordinary commitments of debt and commuting time in order to live in the right community. But while all of this involves care and work—we might even say "cultural engagement"—it never deviates from the core premise of consumer culture: We are most human when we are purchasing something someone else has made.

Of all the possible postures toward culture, consumption is the one that lives most unthinkingly within a culture's preexisting horizons of possibility and impossibility. The person who condemns culture does so in the name of some other set of values and possibilities. The whole point of critique is becoming aware of the horizons that a given culture creates, for better or worse. Even copying culture and bringing it into the life of the Christian community puts culture to work in the service of something believed to be more true and lasting. But consumption, as a posture, is capitulation: letting the culture set the terms, assuming that the culture knows best and that even our deepest longings (for beauty, truth, love) and fears (of loneliness, loss, death) have some solution that fits comfortably within our culture's horizons, if only we can afford to purchase it.

🕮 Artists and Gardeners

What is missing from our repertoire, I've come to believe, are the two postures that are most characteristically biblical but have been least explored by Christians in the last century. They are found at the very beginning of the human story, according to Genesis: like our first parents, we are to be creators and cultivators. Or to put it more poetically, we are artists and gardeners.

The postures of the artist and the gardener have a lot in common. Both begin with contemplation, paying close attention to what is already there. The gardener looks carefully at the landscape; the existing plants, both flowers and weeds; the way the sun falls on the land. The artist regards her subject, her canvas, her paints with care to discern what she can make with them.

And then, after contemplation, the artist and the gardener both adopt a posture of purposeful work. They bring their creativity and effort to their calling. The gardener tends what has gone before, making the most of what is beautiful and weeding out what is distracting or useless. The artist can be more daring: she starts with a blank canvas or a solid piece of stone and gradually brings something out of it that was never there before. They are acting in the image of the One who spoke a world into being and stooped down to form creatures from the dust. They are creaturely creators, tending and shaping the world that the original creator made.

I wonder what we Christians are known for in the world outside our churches. Are we known as critics, consumers, copiers, condemners of culture? I'm afraid so. Why aren't we known as cultivators—people who tend and nourish what is best in human culture, who do the hard and painstaking work to preserve the best of what people before us have done? Why aren't we known as creators—people who dare to think and do something that has never been thought or done before, something that makes the world more welcoming and thrilling and beautiful?

The simple truth is that in the mainstream of culture, cultivation and creativity are the postures that confer legitimacy for the other gestures. People who consider themselves stewards of culture, guardians of what is best in a neighborhood, an institution, or a field of cultural practice gain the respect of their peers. Even more so, those who go beyond being mere custodians to creating new cultural goods are the ones who have the world's attention. Indeed, those who have cultivated and created are precisely the ones who have the legitimacy to condemn—whose denunciations, rare and carefully chosen, carry outsize weight. Cultivators and creators are the ones who are invited to critique and whose critiques are often the most telling and fruitful.

Cultivators and creators can even copy without becoming mere imitators, drawing on the work of others, yet extending it in new and exciting ways—think of the best of hip-hop's culture of sampling, which does not settle for merely reproducing the legends of jazz and R&B but places their work in new sonic contexts. And when they consume, cultivators and creators do so without becoming mere consumers. They do not derive their identity from what they consume but from what they create.

If there is a constructive way forward for Christians in the midst of our broken but also beautiful cultures, it will require us to recover these two biblical postures of cultivation and creation. And that recovery will involve revisiting the biblical story itself, where we discover that God is more intimately and eternally concerned with culture than we have yet come to believe.

This article first appeared in the September 2008 issue of Christianity Today. *Used by permission of Christianity Today, Carol Stream, IL 60188.*

Andy Crouch (MDiv, Boston University School of Theology) is partner for theology and culture at Praxis, an organization working as a creative engine for redemptive entrepreneurship. His most recent books include *The Tech-Wise Family: Everyday Steps for Putting Technology in Its Proper Place* and *Strong and Weak: Embracing a Life of Love, Risk, and True Flourishing.*

INDEX

holiness, 15, 79, 273
Holy Spirit
  as animator, 286,
  person of the Trinity. *See* Trinity, Holy
    Spirit
  in the life of the believer, 101, 167
  restored by, 236
  transformed by, 253
hope in the future, 107–9, 128, 244, 291
hope, 105, 134, 194–95, 254, 291–92, 320,
  344, 348
hospitality, 177–78, 183, 186, 291
House, Wayne, 101
Hoyt, John A., 211
Hulme, Mike, 191
Humane Society, 152, 201, 209, 211, 215,
  334
humility, 16, 53, 57–59, 118, 166, 195–96,
  237–38, 251, 329, 341, 343–44
Hunter, James Davison, 26, 30, 38, 51, 219,
  280
Hyde, Lewis, 281
idol, idolatry, 37, 40, 64, 69, 173, 233, 254
immigration, 159, 161–62, 176–187,
  243–44
in vitro fertilization, 128–29, 131, 137–40,
  144
Industrial Revolution, 103, 120–21, 123,
  193, 208, 263
Irwin, Paul G., 211
Israelites, 125, 169, 176, 182, 270, 305, 315
Jacobs, Alan, 59
Jewish culture, 77, 87, 270
Jones, E. Stanley, 325
Kaprow, Allan, 297
Keller, Timothy, 36, 44
Kentridge, William, 297
King, Martin Luther, Jr., 161, 172, 325
Kinsley, Michael, 155
Kinzer, Lance, 226
Köstenberger, Andreas, 56–58, 101
Koyzis, David, 235
Kroeger, Catherine, 112
Ku Klux Klan, 164
Kuyper, Abraham, 221, 230, 235–38

language
  of engaging culture, 21, 43
  misuse, 149, 151, 186
  purpose of, 150–51
Lahl, Jessica, 129–30, 139, 157
Lappé, Anna, 301
Larsen, Timothy, 167–68
Latino history in the US, 161
Lawrence, Jennifer, 299–300
leadership
  domestic, 100–2, 114
  political, 185, 211, 234
  church, 71
Lee-Barnewall, Michelle, 102
Lee, Robert E., 171
Legend, John, 133
Leithart, Peter, 47–48
Levin, Yural, 226
Levitical law, 64
Lewis, C. S., 68, 138, 288, 343
liberal theology, 45, 68, 74, 162
liberalism, 48, 162, 181, 223, 227, 315
Lincoln, Abraham, 171–72
localism, 225–6
Loftus, Matthew, 251, 269, 275–76
Looney Tunes, 285
Lowe, Ben, 162, 180, 186–87
love
  and obedience, 53, 116, 174, 179, 185,
    200, 280, 323, 327–28
  communal, 79–80, 147, 173, 178, 195,
    200, 213, 249, 253, 258, 276, 279,
    282, 305, 320, 333, 349
  God's, 15, 60, 162, 166, 212, 264,
    280–82, 313–14, 325
  in action, 118, 122, 125, 130, 148, 286,
    302
  marital and familial, 110, 125, 136, 144,
    151, 173, 302
  of sin, 261, 262, 306–7, 324
  speaking in love, 16, 150, 153–54
Luther, Martin, 126, 213, 249, 258–59, 347
MacIntyre, Alasdair, 38–39, 54
Macy, Gary, 112
Madigan, Kevin, 112

Apologetics at the Cross

An Introduction for Christian Witness

Joshua D. Chatraw and Mark D. Allen

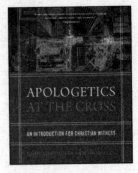

Amid the pluralism and secularism of Western culture, Christian apologetics has experienced a renewal of interest. In *Apologetics at the Cross*, Joshua D. Chatraw and Mark D. Allen provide an introduction to the field, acquainting students and lay learners with the rich history, biblical foundation, and ongoing relevance of apologetics.

Unique in its approach, *Apologetics at the Cross* presents the biblical and historical foundations for apologetics, explores various contemporary methods for approaching apologetics, and gives practical guidance in "how to" chapters that feature many real-life illustrations. With their respectful approach, which pays special attention to the attitude and posture of the apologist, Chatraw and Allen equip Christians to engage skeptics with the heart as well as the mind.

Conversational in tone and balanced in approach, *Apologetics at the Cross* provides a readable introduction to the field of apologetics. Readers will be informed and equipped for engaging a wide range of contemporary challenges with the best in Christian thought.

Available in stores and online!

ZONDERVAN ACADEMIC